QUEENSHIP AN]
DISCOURSE
ELIZABETHA]

This book re-evaluates the nature of Elizabethan politics and
Elizabeth's queenship in late sixteenth-century England, Wales and
Ireland. Natalie Mears shows that Elizabeth took an active role in
policy-making and suggests that Elizabethan politics has to be perceived in terms of personal relations between the queen and her
advisers rather than of the hegemony of the privy council. She challenges current perceptions of political debate at court as restricted and
integrates recent research on court drama and religious ritual into the
wider context of political debate. Finally, providing the first survey of
the nature of political debate outside the court, Dr Mears challenges
seminal work by Jürgen Habermas, as well as of seventeenth- and
eighteenth-century historians, by showing that a 'public sphere'
existed in late sixteenth-century England, Wales and Ireland. In doing
so, she re-evaluates how sociologists and historians have, and should,
conceptualise the 'public sphere'.

NATALIE MEARS is Lecturer in Early Modern History at the University of Durham. She has published in *Historical Journal* and *History*
and a number of collections of essays.

CAMBRIDGE STUDIES IN EARLY MODERN
BRITISH HISTORY

Series Editors

ANTHONY FLETCHER
Emeritus Professor of English Social History, University of London

JOHN GUY
Fellow, Clare College, Cambridge

JOHN MORRILL
*Professor of British and Irish History, University of Cambridge,
and Vice-Master of Selwyn College*

This is a series of monographs and studies covering many aspects of the history of the British Isles between the late fifteenth century and the early eighteenth century. It includes the work of established scholars and pioneers work by a new generation of scholars. It includes both reviews and revisions of major topics and books, which open up new historical terrain or which reveal startling new perspectives on familiar subjects. All the volumes set detailed research into our broader perspectives and the books are intended for the use of students as well as of their teachers.

For a list of titles in the series, see end of book.

QUEENSHIP AND POLITICAL DISCOURSE IN THE ELIZABETHAN REALMS

NATALIE MEARS

University of Durham

CAMBRIDGE
UNIVERSITY PRESS

CAMBRIDGE UNIVERSITY PRESS
Cambridge, New York, Melbourne, Madrid, Cape Town, Singapore, São Paulo, Delhi

Cambridge University Press
The Edinburgh Building, Cambridge CB2 8RU, UK

Published in the United States of America by Cambridge University Press, New York

www.cambridge.org
Information on this title: www.cambridge.org/9780521819220

First published 2005
This digitally printed version 2008

A catalogue record for this publication is available from the British Library

ISBN 978-0-521-81922-0 hardback
ISBN 978-0-521-09313-2 paperback

Contents

Plates

Acknowledgements

For a project that has spanned both a little over three years of a Ph.D. and a further four since, I have a worrying amount of debts to acknowledge, some of which I feel sure I will forget to honour. Despite being an avid and extremely nosy reader of other people's acknowledgements, I would like to break with tradition and begin with thanking those to whom I owe a personal, rather than academic or professional debt: my Mum and Dad. They haven't given me access to obscure archives or granted me permission to cite from manuscripts, but without their unstinting support, financially and emotionally, over the past several years you wouldn't be reading this today. To them, and my sister, Melanie, this book is dedicated.

Second, I would like to thank the three people to whom I feel I owe the most academically. Robin Harcourt Williams, librarian and archivist to the marquess of Salisbury at Hatfield House, let me do voluntary work in the archives before going to university. Little did either of us know that it would convert me into an early modernist but I enjoyed working with him and the papers so much that I could neither leave the archives when my year was up nor the Cecils as a subject of study. I have come a long way since then, and regrettably further away from the Cecils than I sometimes wish, but whatever I was studying, he (and his secretaries, especially Janet and Pauline, and Gem Goscomb) has been unfailingly helpful with access to the library, interested in my progress and a great friend. Thank you for all the great times I've had in the archives and on our jaunts out. John Guy, my former supervisor, was everything one could ask of a supervisor and a lot more: ever supportive, encouraging and enthusiastic, however busy he was. I owe a tremendous debt to him and I hope that he will think this book is a suitable, if small, first down-payment. Similarly, I would like to thank John Morrill, one of my undergraduate dissertation supervisors, for talking about me to John

Guy in a pub one day (allegedly): it was my introduction to John Guy, St Andrews and the start of my academic career.

My other academic debts are legion. John Guy, John Morrill, Anthony Milton, Liz Evenden and Jessica Winston have all been kind enough to read through all, or parts, of the book. I am extremely grateful for their comments though, as usual, all errors and infelicities remain my own work. For reading or discussing work on which this book is based I would like to thank Keith Brown, David Crankshaw, Tom Freeman, Steve Gunn, Roger Mason, Brett Usher, Alex Walsham, Jenny Wormald and the members of the early modern seminars at the IHR (particularly Pauline Croft and Conrad Russell) and Oxford (particularly Steve Gunn and Jenny Wormald). For references and pointers, I would like to thank Stephen Alford, James Daybell, Michael Ferber, Tom Freeman and Ian Gadd. I would particularly like to thank Simon Adams who, during my Ph.D., was more helpful (and tolerant) than some dumb questions on my part have perhaps deserved. Not only did he share his knowledge of Leicester with me but he also pointed me towards BN Fonds français 15973 and very kindly lent me his microfilm when I was having difficulties getting hold of a copy. His support is greatly appreciated and valued. For general support and friendship, I would like to thank Stephen Alford, Alan Bryson, John Cramsie, Liz Evenden, Lisa Ford, Jamie Hampson, Simon Healey, Andrew Johnson, Iona McCleery, Matthew McCormack, Mark Taviner, Jessica Winston as well as Lindsey Adam and the staff at her shop 'Bonkers' in St Andrews, where I worked during my Ph.D. They have been variously wonderful office-mates, colleagues and friends who have offered advice, friendship and gingerbread men all of which were (and are) greatly valued. I hope I have listened to their counsel more graciously than Elizabeth sometimes did with Burghley and Walsingham. I would also like to thank my editors at Cambridge University Press: Bill Davies, and more recently, Michael Watson and Isabelle Dambricourt. I foolishly used to think that acknowledgements to editors were mere politeness, but, as Michael and Isabelle have done nothing but answer politely so many stupid questions and queries from me, especially in the final few weeks before submission, I am thankfully now much the wiser. Thank you both. Similarly, I would like to thank Mary Leighton, for her help with the index, and Jo North, a most helpful and patient copy-editor, who has saved me from some awful gaffes.

For their help during visits to archives and enquiries about collections, I would like to thank Robin Harcourt Williams at Hatfield House; David Park at the National Survey of Wall Paintings at the Courtauld Institute of

Art, who has been generous with his time and knowledge; Chris Smith and her colleagues at Northamptonshire Record Office; Mary Robertson at the Huntington Library; Theresa Helein and Richard Kuhta at the Folger Shakespeare Library; Kirsty Scorer at the National Monuments Record Centre (English Heritage); Patricia Moore at the Royal Commission for Ancient and Historical Monuments of Wales, as well as the staff in the Manuscripts and Rare Books rooms at the British Library and Cambridge University Library; the National Archives; Lambeth Palace Library; the Guildhall Library; Dr Williams' Library, London; Caernarfonshire Record Office and, last but by no means least, those of the university libraries where I have studied/worked: St Andrews, Swansea, Manchester and Durham. For permission to cite and quote from manuscripts I would like to thank the marquess of Salisbury; the Bibliothèque Nationale, Paris; the British Library; Caernarfonshire Record Office; the Corporation of London; Dr William's Library, London; the Fitzwilliam (Milton) Estates; the Folger Shakespeare Library, Washington DC; the Huntington Library, San Marino, California; the Trustees of Lambeth Palace Library and the National Archives. Illustrations appear courtesy of the British Library (front cover: ['To the reader, Beholde here (gentle reader)'], printed by Gyles Godet (1560), G.6456); English Heritage ('Hezekiah opening the Temple', Hill Hall, Essex) and Her Majesty the Queen (mural of Princess Elizabeth, Ashridge Manor, Hertfordshire). For financial support I would like to thank the School of Modern History, University of St Andrews; the Royal Historical Society; the Russell Trust; the Edinburgh Association of University Women; the departments of history at the Universities of Wales (Swansea), Manchester and Durham, and, particularly, the British Federation of Women Graduates who awarded me a Jane Finley Award in 1998–9.

Conventions and notes on spelling and foliation

In an attempt to minimise confusion when referring to individuals whose names/titles changed over the course of the first thirty years of Elizabeth's reign, I have referred to those who were raised to the peerage by their title throughout the main text. So, Sir William Cecil, Lord Burghley, is referred to as Burghley even prior to his elevation to the peerage in February 1571; Robert Dudley is referred to as the earl of Leicester etc. In the interests of uniformity – and, no doubt, habit, seeing my thesis was on Francis, duke of Anjou – I have also referred to both Henry (later Henry III of France) and his younger brother, Francis, as the duke of Anjou, aware that this may cause some confusion. Henry was duke of Anjou until his election as king of Poland in 1573 and, on the death of his brother, Charles IX, his accession as king of France in 1574. His younger brother, Francis, initially duke of Alençon, was made duke of Anjou in 1576 as part of a deal for him to withdraw his support from the Huguenots. In order to distinguish clearly which duke I am referring to, I have cited their first name as well as their title. In the footnotes, however, I have retained chronologically correct names so that my references match those on the documents and in catalogues. Also, I have chosen to cite the year of publication in all second and subsequent citations of contemporary news pamphlets. A number of them do have similar titles, especially when they are shortened, and I hope that this may make it a little clearer as to which one is being referred; the reader may also find it useful to be reminded of their date of publication.

All quotations are in the original spelling; 'u', 'v', 'i' and 'j' have been transcribed as individual writers or printers used them and contractions have been expanded silently. Words crossed out in editing are shown using <brackets> and contemporary additions are in *italics*. Conjectured reconstructions, where the manuscripts has been damaged or where the words are not fully legible, are shown in [square brackets].

Manuscripts in both the National Archives and British Library have been refoliated a number of times, though not consistently: where some manuscripts have an abundance of folio numbers, other volumes have none at all. For SP12 and SP63 I have followed the bold printed numbers in the top right-hand corner. For other SP classes I have followed the small pencil numbers at the bottom centre or centre-right of the page. Citations of documents in unfoliated volumes (such as SP78/4 and SP83/13) have no folio reference except in two cases. First, where I have wished to specify the location of information in longer documents I have (mentally) foliated the documents on an individual basis, i.e. fo.1r, fo.1v etc. Second, where a copy-book of letters has been incorporated into a larger volume (e.g. SP83/9) I have used its foliation/pagination which is clearly marked in the top right (recto side) and left (verso) corners. In all cases, the item number of the document is also cited. For the Cotton manuscripts in the British Library I have followed the pencil numbers at the top and bottom right-hand of the page (recto). BN, Fonds français 15973 is, in Simon Adams's words, 'eccentrically foliated': there are two sets of folio numbers but readers are warned that the most consistent series (and the one that I have followed) is written on the *verso* side. References to other manuscripts should be fairly clear.

Abbreviations

Additional	British Library, Additional Manuscripts
APC	*Acts of the Privy Council of England*, ed. John Roche Dasent *et al.*, new series (46 vols., London, 1890–1964)
ASSI 35	National Archives, Assizes: Norfolk, Home and South-Eastern Circuits: Indictment files
BL	British Library, London
BN	Bibliothèque Nationale, Paris
C3	National Archives, Court of Chancery: Six Clerks Office: Pleadings, Series II, Elizabeth I to the Interregnum
CRO	Caernarfonshire Record Office, Caernarfon, Wales
'Carnsew's diary'	'William Carnsew of Bokelly and his diary, 1576–7', ed. N. J. G. Pounds, *Journal of the Royal Institution of Cornwall*, new series, 8 (1978), pp. 14–60
Collected Works	*Elizabeth I: collected works*, ed. Leah Marcus, Janel Mueller and Mary Beth Rose (Chicago and London, 2000)
Cotton	British Library, Cotton Manuscripts
CP	Hatfield House, Hertfordshire, Cecil Papers
CSP Foreign	*Calendar of State Papers, Foreign. Elizabeth I*, ed. J. Stevenson *et al.* (23 vols., London, 1863–1950)
CSP Rome	*State Papers, relating to English affairs, in the Vatican Archives and Library*, ed. J. M. Rigg (2 vols., London, 1916–26)
CSP Spanish	*Letters and State Papers relating to English affairs, preserved principally in the archives of Simancas*, ed. M. A. S. Hume (4 vols., London, 1892–99)

CSP Venice	*State Papers and manuscripts relating to English affairs, existing in the archives and collections of Venice, and in other libraries of Northern Italy*, ed. R. Brown *et al.* (37 vols., London, 1864–1947)
CUL	Cambridge University Library, Cambridge
DWL	Dr Williams' Library, London
E190	National Archives, Exchequer, Port Books
E351	National Archives, Exchequer, Pipe Office, Declared Accounts
Egerton	British Library, Egerton Manuscripts (references to the Egerton MSS at the Huntington Library are prefixed with 'Huntington')
Folger	Folger Shakespeare Library, Washington DC
Guildhall MS	Guildhall Manuscripts, Guildhall Library, London
Harleian	British Library, Harleian Manuscripts
Hasler	*The history of parliament. The House of Commons, 1558–1603*, ed. P. W. Hasler (3 vols., London, 1981)
HMC Finch	*Historical Manuscripts Commission. Report on the manuscripts of Allan George Finch, of Burley-on-the-Hill, Rutland* (4 vols., London, 1913–65)
HMC Gawdy	*Historical Manuscripts Commission. Report on the manuscripts of the family of Gawdy, formerly of Norfolk (1509–1675)* (London, 1885)
HMC Rutland	*Historical Manuscripts Commission. The manuscripts of his grace the duke of Rutland, GCB, preserved at Belvoir Castle* (4 vols., London, 1888–1905)
HMC Salisbury	*Historical Manuscripts Commission. Calendar of the manuscripts of the most honourable the marquis of Salisbury, K. G. etc*... (24 vols., London, 1883–1976)
Huntington	Huntington Library, San Marino, California
KB27	National Archives, Court of King's Bench, Plea and Crown sides: Coram Rege Rolls
Lansdowne	British Library, Lansdowne Manuscripts
LPL	Lambeth Palace Library, London
Machyn's diary	*The diary of Henry Machyn, citizen and merchant of London, from AD 1550 to AD 1563*, ed. J. G. Nichols (Camden Society, original series, 42; London, 1848)
m. (pl. mm.)	membrane

MS (pl. MSS)	Manuscript
NA	National Archives, London (formerly the Public Record Office)
NRO	Northamptonshire Record Office, Northamptonshire
PRO31	National Archives, Collection of Transcripts: Paris Archives, Baschet's transcripts
Royal	British Library, Royal Manuscripts
Sadler state papers	*The state papers and letters of Sir Ralph Sadler*, ed. Arthur Collins (2 vols., Edinburgh, 1809)
SP12	National Archives, State Papers Domestic, Elizabeth
SP15	National Archives, State Papers Domestic, Edward VI to James I, Addenda
SP52	National Archives, State Papers Scotland, Elizabeth
SP59	National Archives, State Papers Scotland, Border Papers
SP63	National Archives, State Papers Ireland, Elizabeth
SP70	National Archives, State Papers Foreign, Elizabeth
SP78	National Archives, State Papers France
SP83	National Archives, State Papers Holland and Flanders
SP94	National Archives, State Papers Spain
SP104	National Archives, State Papers Entry Books
STAC4	National Archives, Court of Star Chamber: Proceedings, Philip and Mary
STAC5	National Archives, Court of Star Chamber: Proceedings, Elizabeth I
STC	*A short-title catalogue of books printed in England, Scotland, and Ireland and of English books printed abroad, 1475–1640*, compiled by A. W. Pollard and G. R. Redgrave, revised and enlarged by W. A. Jackson, F. S. Ferguson and K. F. Pantzer (3 vols., London, 1986–91)

Introduction

The quatercentenary of Elizabeth's death has provided a focus for historians and other commentators to reappraise, as much as celebrate, Elizabeth's queenship. Specialised monographs and essay collections, biographies by leading academic historians as well as popular writers, reissues of popular biographies, David Starkey's three-part television documentary and the exhibition at the National Maritime Museum, London, have attested both to the continuing debate Elizabeth excites and her popular appeal.[1] She came seventh in the BBC's 'Great Britons' contest in 2002, one of only two women in the top ten.[2]

Yet, in contrast to works that were issued in 1958 to mark the quatercentenary of her accession, the picture recent works have painted of Elizabeth, particularly in academic circles, has been darker than that portrayed by Sir John Neale, Sir Roy Strong and others.[3] Whereas, for Neale and Strong, Elizabeth was a genuine champion of Protestantism, who ruled effectively over an increasingly prosperous and politically and culturally significant realm, adored and celebrated by her subjects, for more recent historians Elizabeth's reign was troubled and its legacy more so. Though Geoffrey Elton attacked Neale's interpretation of Elizabethan

---

1 Michael Dobson and Nicola J. Watson, *England's Elizabeth* (Oxford, 2002); Susan Doran and Thomas S. Freeman (eds.), *The myth of Elizabeth* (Basingstoke, 2003); David Starkey, *Elizabeth: apprenticeship* (London, 2000); Susan Doran, *Queen Elizabeth I* (London, 2003); Carol Levin, *The reign of Elizabeth I* (Basingstoke, 2003); Levin (ed.), *Elizabeth I: always her own free woman* (Aldershot and Burlington, VT, 2003); Jane Dunn, *Elizabeth and Mary: cousins, rivals, queens* (London, 2004); Alison Plowden, *Elizabeth I* (Stroud, 2004); Anne Somerset, *Elizabeth I* (London, 1992); Alison Weir, *Elizabeth the queen* (London, 1999). A second volume, following his *Elizabeth I: apprenticeship*, is due from David Starkey in 2005.
2 The other was Diana, Princess of Wales, who came third. BBC Press Release, 25 Nov. 2002, http://www.bbc.co.uk/pressoffice/pressreleases/stories/2002/11_november/25/greatbritons_final. shtml.
3 J. E. Neale, 'November 17th', in Neale, *Elizabethan Essays* (London, 1958), pp. 9–20; Roy Strong, 'The popular celebration of the Accession Day of Queen Elizabeth I', *Journal of the Warburg and Courtauld Institutes*, 21 (1958), pp. 86–103.

parliaments,[4] the first significant assault on Elizabeth's queenship was Chris Haigh's *Elizabeth I*, which argued that Elizabeth was, if an astute politician able to manipulate council, court and subjects through courtly love, emotional blackmail and propaganda, also an indecisive and vain monarch. She was both a bully and weak, who created many of her own problems, whether this was by conciliating conservative religious opinion too much at the beginning of her reign or allowing both council and court to become a dangerously narrow clique in her final years.[5] This negative picture has been developed further, increasingly highlighting the political and religious fissures between Elizabeth and her leading subjects. John Guy has pointed to the significant differences in political beliefs between Elizabeth and many of her councillors, like Burghley, Leicester and Walsingham.[6] Patrick Collinson and Stephen Alford have demonstrated that, in conjunction with conflicts over political issues, these differences created tensions over the issues of marriage and succession, with councillors willing to invoke quasi-republican ideas to provide remedies and to force Elizabeth into action.[7] Collinson, Peter Lake, Brett Usher, Thomas Freeman and others have highlighted the continuing conflict between Elizabeth and moderate puritans over the perceived failure of the religious settlement of 1559 to reform the church fully.[8]

4 G. R. Elton, 'Tudor government: the points of contact. I. Parliament', *Transactions of the Royal Historical Society*, fifth series, 24 (1974), pp. 183–200; Elton, 'Tudor government: the points of contact. II. The council', *Transactions of the Royal Historical Society*, fifth series, 25 (1975), pp. 195–211; Elton, 'Tudor government: the points of contact. III. The court', *Transactions of the Royal Historical Society*, fifth series, 26 (1976), pp. 211–28 and all reprinted in Elton, *Studies in Tudor and Stuart politics and government* (4 vols., Cambridge, 1974–92), III, pp. 3–57; Elton, *The parliaments of England, 1559–1581* (Cambridge, 1986); Elton, 'Queen Elizabeth', *Studies*, I, pp. 238–46; Elton, 'Arthur Hall, Lord Burghley and the antiquity of parliament', *Studies*, III, pp. 254–73; Elton, 'Piscatorial politics in the early parliaments of Elizabeth I', *Studies*, IV, pp. 109–30.

5 Christopher Haigh, *Elizabeth I* (Harlow and London, 1988; revised edn, 2001).

6 John Guy, 'The rhetoric of counsel in early modern England', in Dale Hoak (ed.), *Tudor political culture* (Cambridge, 1995), pp. 292–310; Guy, 'The 1590s: the second reign of Elizabeth I?', in Guy (ed.), *The reign of Elizabeth I: court and culture in the last decade* (Cambridge, 1995), pp. 1–19; Guy, 'Tudor monarchy and its critiques', in Guy (ed.), *The Tudor monarchy* (London and New York, 1997), pp. 78–109.

7 Patrick Collinson, 'The monarchical republic of Queen Elizabeth I', *Bulletin of the John Rylands University Library of Manchester*, 69 (1987), pp. 394–424; Collinson, 'The Elizabethan exclusion crisis and the Elizabethan polity', *Proceedings of the British Academy*, 84 (1993), pp. 51–92; Stephen Alford, *The early Elizabethan polity: William Cecil and the British succession crisis, 1558–1569* (Cambridge, 1998).

8 Patrick Collinson, *The Elizabethan puritan movement* (Oxford, 1967) and countless subsequent works including 'The downfall of Archbishop Grindal and its place in Elizabethan political and ecclesiastical history', in Peter Clark, A. G. R. Smith and Nicholas Tyacke (eds.), *The English Commonwealth, 1547–1640* (Leicester, 1979), pp. 39–57; Peter Lake, *Moderate puritans in the Elizabethan Church* (Cambridge, 1982); Lake, *Anglicans and puritans? Presbyterianism and English conformist thought from Whitgift to Hooker* (London and Boston, Mass., 1988); Brett Usher, 'The

Despite this plethora of publications, there remains room for further studies of Elizabeth and her reign. Much academic research around the recent anniversary has focused on Elizabeth's posthumous reputation and image rather than the nature of her queenship. Michael Dobson and Nicola Watson have explored different depictions of Elizabeth in printed histories, fiction, drama, film, opera, television and art from 1603 to the present.[9] A collection edited by Susan Doran and Thomas Freeman has reassessed contemporary and posthumous perceptions of the queen in texts like John Foxe's *Acts and monuments* (commonly known as the 'Book of martyrs') and William Camden's *Annals* as well as popular perceptions (that her opposition to clerical marriage was a bar to ecclesiastical preferment).[10]

Conversely, crucial questions about Elizabeth's queenship, the nature of court politics and policy-making, the extent to which political issues were discussed outside the court and how Elizabethans perceived their queen and her governance, remain disputed or unanswered. John Neale's and Conyers Read's influential readings of Elizabethan governance – that it was based on social connections and was divided by factionalism – have been challenged. Simon Adams demonstrated that the near-contemporary sources on which Neale and Read based their arguments – Camden's *Annals* (Books 1–3, 1615; Book 4, 1629) and Sir Robert Naunton's *Fragmenta regalia* (1641) – were infused with personal agendas and modelled on classical styles. He has also shown that factionalism was absent from the court until the disruptive influence of Robert Devereux, second earl of Essex, was felt in the 1590s – a position with which many historians agree.[11] Yet, revisionist history largely failed to deal with the wider questions raised by Neale and Read: the role of social connections and

deanery of Bocking and the demise of the Vestiarian Controversy', *Journal of Ecclesiastical History*, 52 (2001), pp. 434–55; Thomas S. Freeman, '"The reformation of the church in this parliament": Thomas Norton, John Foxe and the parliament of 1571', *Parliamentary History*, 16 (1997), pp. 131–47; Freeman, 'Providence and prescription: the account of Elizabeth in Foxe's "Book of martyrs"', in Doran and Freeman (eds.), *Myth of Elizabeth*, pp. 27–54; Caroline Litzenberger, 'Defining the Church of England: religious change in the 1570s', in Susan Wabuda and Caroline Litzenberger (eds.), *Belief and practice in Reformation England* (Aldershot, 1998), pp. 137–53.

9 Dobson and Watson, *England's Elizabeth*, passim.

10 Doran and Freeman (eds.), *Myth of Elizabeth*, passim. The specific essays mentioned are those by Thomas S. Freeman, Patrick Collinson and Brett Usher.

11 Simon Adams, 'Favourites and factions at the Elizabethan court', reprinted, with postscript, in Guy (ed.), *Tudor monarchy*, pp. 253–74; Natalie Mears, '*Regnum Cecilianum*?: a Cecilian perspective of the court', in Guy (ed.), *Reign of Elizabeth*, pp. 46–64; Paul E. J. Hammer, 'Patronage at court, faction and the earl of Essex', in Guy (ed.), *Reign of Elizabeth*, pp. 65–86; Hammer, *The polarisation of Elizabethan politics: the political career of Robert Devereux, second earl of Essex, 1585–1597* (Cambridge, 1999). The main exception is Susan Doran in her *Monarchy and matrimony: the courtships of Elizabeth I* (London, 1996).

ideology in politics. With the exception of Haigh's *Elizabeth I* – which outlined instances where Elizabeth took counsel from individuals, including those who were not privy councillors[12] – Elizabethan politics was increasingly seen in Eltonian, institutional terms. The privy council was identified as the central advisory and policy-making body, even when research by David Starkey, George Bernard, Eric Ives, Cliff Davies, Steve Gunn and Penry Williams re-emphasised the importance of social connections in early Tudor governance *vis-à-vis* Elton's 'Tudor revolution in government'.[13] Instances of informal counselling, highlighted by Haigh and others, were conceived in terms of exceptions to the rule, often means by which Elizabeth consciously isolated herself from the council whose opinions conflicted with hers.[14]

Similarly, though the work of Paula Scalingi and Constance Jordan has shown that contemporary debate on royal power was dominated by the issue of female monarchy in the second half of the sixteenth century, there is little consensus about the role gender played in Elizabeth's queenship.[15] Feminist historians, such as Allison Heisch, Mary Thomas Crane, Mary Hill Cole and Anne McLaren, have argued that gender was the defining force in Elizabeth's reign. According to Crane, Elizabeth played with gender conventions to wrong-foot her counsellors; Heisch, Cole and McLaren have seen Elizabeth more as a prisoner of her gender.[16] In her

---

12 Haigh, *Elizabeth I*, ch. 4.
13 Michael Barraclough Pulman, *The Elizabethan privy council in the fifteen-seventies* (Berkeley and Los Angeles, CA, 1971); Alford, *Early Elizabethan polity*, passim. Compare with David Starkey, 'Court and government', in C. Coleman and David Starkey (eds.), *Revolution reassessed: revisions in the history of Tudor government and administration* (Oxford, 1986), pp. 29–58; Starkey, 'Representation through intimacy: a study in the symbolism of monarchy and court office in early-modern England', in I. Lewis (ed.), *Symbols and sentiments: cross cultural studies in symbolism* (London, 1977), pp. 187–224 (both reprinted in Guy (ed.), *Tudor monarchy*, pp. 189–213 and pp. 42–78 respectively); Starkey, 'Intimacy and innovation: the rise of the privy chamber, 1485–1547', in Starkey *et al.* (eds.), *The English court: from the Wars of the Roses to the Civil War* (London and New York, 1987), pp. 71–118; G. W. Bernard, *The power of the early Tudor nobility: a study of the fourth and fifth earls of Shrewsbury* (Brighton, 1985); Eric Ives, *Anne Boleyn* (Oxford, 1986); C. S. L. Davies, *Peace, print and Protestantism, 1450–1558* (London, 1976); S. J. Gunn, *Early Tudor government, 1485–1558* (Basingstoke and London, 1995); Penry Williams, *The Tudor regime* (Oxford, 1979).
14 Haigh, *Elizabeth I*, ch. 4; Pulman, *Elizabethan privy council*, passim though especially pp. 52–3.
15 Paula L. Scalingi, 'The scepter or the distaff: the question of female monarchy', *The Historian* (USA), 41 (1978–9), pp. 59–75; Constance Jordan, 'Woman's rule in sixteenth-century British political thought', *Renaissance Quarterly*, 40 (1987), pp. 421–51; Patricia-Ann Lee, 'A bodye politique to governe: Aylmer, Knox and the debate on queenship', *The Historian* (USA), 52 (1990), pp. 242–61.
16 Allison Heisch, 'Queen Elizabeth I and the persistence of patriarchy', *Feminist Review*, 4 (1980), pp. 45–56; Mary Thomas Crane, 'Video and taceo: Elizabeth I and the rhetoric of counsel', *Studies in English Literature 1500–1900*, 28 (1988), pp. 1–15; Mary Hill Cole, *The portable Queen:*

increasingly influential work, McLaren has suggested that Elizabeth's gender forced her to redefine her queenship in 'extraordinary' and providential terms: as a corporate activity, executed jointly by her and her male counsellors.[17] In contrast, while acknowledging that gender formed part of the politico-cultural milieu of the age, Patrick Collinson, John Guy, Stephen Alford and others have all identified religion as the key factor. Elizabeth consistently refused to resolve the central problems the regime faced: reforming the church fully and securing a Protestant succession, to prevent the accession of Mary Stuart and the reconciliation of England to Rome. Simply, Elizabeth remained under constant pressure to live up to Protestant expectations that her accession had inspired.[18]

Gender has also influenced more recent studies of public discourse on or during Elizabeth's reign. Carole Levin's *'The heart and stomach of a king'* has analysed popular public debate of Elizabeth's queenship, concluding that ordinary Elizabethans shared the concerns of her most eminent privy councillors: Elizabeth's failure to follow gender expectations by marrying and having a child to succeed her. The strengths of Levin's study are that she has sought to examine popular knowledge and discussion of major political issues and has implied that such debate was independent of elite discourse in the court and council. It contrasts with earlier work which has defined public debate as directed by the council to 'bounce' Elizabeth into action, whether this involved planting speeches in parliament or commissioning pamphlets, such as John Stubbe's *The discouerie of a gaping gulf* (1579) against the Anjou match.[19] However, Levin's study is also problematic because she assumes a consciousness and deliberate manipulation of gendered imagery by Elizabeth and her

Elizabeth I and the politics of ceremony (Amherst, 1999); A. N. McLaren, *Political culture in the reign of Elizabeth I: queen and commonwealth, 1558–1585* (Cambridge, 1999).

17 McLaren, *Political culture*, esp. pp. 6–8, 23–35, 43–5.

18 Collinson, 'Monarchical republic', pp. 402, 407; Guy, 'The 1590s', pp. 1–19; Guy, 'Tudor monarchy and its critiques', pp. 93–100; Alford, *Early Elizabethan polity*, passim. For a detailed discussion of Elizabethan historiography since Neale and Read, see John Guy, 'Elizabeth I: the queen and politics', in W. R. Elton and John M. Mucciolo (eds.), *The Shakespearean international yearbook. 2: where are we now in Shakespearean studies?* (Aldershot, 2002), pp. 183–202.

19 M. A. R. Graves, 'The management of the Elizabethan House of Commons: the council's "men-of-business"', *Parliamentary History*, 2 (1983), pp. 11–38; Graves, 'The common lawyers and the privy council's parliamentary men-of-business, 1584–1601', *Parliamentary History*, 8 (1989), pp. 189–215; Graves, 'Elizabethan men of business reconsidered', *Parergon*, 14 (1996), pp. 111–27; Graves, 'Thomas Norton, the parliament man: an Elizabethan MP, 1559–1581', *Historical Journal*, 23 (1980), pp. 17–35; Graves, *Thomas Norton: the parliament man* (Oxford, 1994); Patrick Collinson, 'Puritans, men of business and Elizabethan parliaments', *Parliamentary History*, 7 (1988), pp. 187–211 (reprinted in Collinson, *Elizabethan Essays*, pp. 59–86); Collinson, 'Exclusion crisis', pp. 76–8.

subjects that is disconcertingly and anachronistically modern. It also fails to distinguish between different types of participants in debate – ambassadors, Catholic polemicists, puritan clergymen, yeomen and labourers – and denies that other issues, like religion, had equal or greater importance.[20]

Levin's work, therefore, leaves important questions about the nature of Elizabethan public debate unanswered: who participated in debate, why and what did they say? Moreover, the significance of these questions has grown since the publication of an English translation of Jürgen Habermas's highly influential work on the public sphere, *Strukturwandel der Öffentlichkeit* (*The structural transformation of the public sphere*).[21] Though Habermas's definition of the public sphere, and his identification of the late seventeenth century as its birth date, have been widely challenged, there remains a reluctance to date the emergence of a public sphere in England earlier than the early or mid-seventeenth century.[22] Preliminary research on the existence of public debate in Elizabethan England points to the need to reconsider these issues fully and in detail.

This study attempts to answer these questions. It grew out of my doctoral work on Elizabeth's final marriage negotiations, with Francis, duke of Anjou, brother of Henry III of France, between 1578 and 1582.[23] In the course of reconstructing the negotiations and exploring how they could help us define the nature of politics and political culture in the much-neglected mid-Elizabethan period, two things struck me. First, an examination of the process of the negotiations in 1579 drawn from memoranda principally in Burghley's archive, suggested that Elizabeth not only took a more active role in policy-making than some recent studies had suggested, but that the privy council did not take the leading advisory role. Rather, Elizabeth appeared to select individual councillors whom she trusted to discuss the marriage separately from formal conciliar meetings. Moreover, related issues and incidents, such as attempts to secure the release of the former Scottish Regent, the earl of Morton, in 1580–1, suggested that Elizabeth took counsel from those who were not

---

20 Carole Levin, '*The heart and stomach of a King': Elizabeth I and the politics of sex and power* (Philadelphia, PA, 1993).

21 Jürgen Habermas, *The structural transformation of the public sphere: an inquiry into a category of bourgeois society*, trans. Thomas Burger with Patrick Lawrence (Cambridge, Mass., 1989).

22 The most important collection of essays is Craig Calhoun (ed.), *Habermas and the public sphere* (Cambridge, Mass., 1992); see also pp. 24–5, nn. 53–6 for further references.

23 Natalie Mears, 'The "personal rule" of Elizabeth I: marriage, succession and catholic conspiracy, c.1578–1582' (Ph.D. thesis, St Andrews, 1999).

privy councillors, such as her Scottish agent, Thomas Randolph, often privileging their advice over that given by councillors.[24]

Second, my re-evaluation of the circumstances surrounding the publication of John Stubbe's controversial pamphlet against the marriage, *The discouerie of a gaping gulf* (1579), raised questions about the extent to which public political debate was organised by the regime. It proved difficult to ascertain close connections between Stubbe and Leicester and Walsingham, often regarded as the commissioners of the pamphlet. Closer connections existed between Stubbe and Burghley, through Burghley's secretaries, Vincent Skinner and Michael Hickes, who were Stubbe's friends and contemporaries at Cambridge and Lincoln's Inn. These connections appeared to be confirmed not only by the possibility of an earlier collaboration between Stubbe, Skinner and Hickes on *The life off the 70. Archbishopp off Canterbury presentlye sitting Englished* (1574), but by apparent references in *A gaping gulf* to memoranda by Burghley and Sussex now extant in Burghley's archive. Equally, however, a reconstruction of Stubbe's political assumptions, his education, religious commitment and his earlier forays in print – including his collaborative work with Skinner and Hickes – made the likelihood that Stubbe was commissioned to parrot the words of others less convincing. Rather, it appeared that Stubbe wrote the pamphlet because of his own concerns about the marriage and his belief that he could counsel the queen or comment on political issues. It raised the possibility that a forum for public debate existed in Elizabethan England.[25]

These two themes form the basis of this study. On the one hand, therefore, I have sought to explore the nature of Elizabethan court politics – both policy-making and wider political debate – and of Elizabeth's queenship, to test the extent to which the methods I found characteristic of the late 1570s and early 1580s were evident earlier in the reign. On the other, I have attempted to expand the model of public debate I identified with Stubbe across a broader social and geographic canvas. Therefore, chapter 2 seeks to answer the questions posed by Neale and Read about the nature of Elizabethan court politics; chapter 3 discusses the specific question of whether Elizabeth's queenship, and court politics, were shaped by her gender or by other factors. In what often felt like a 'book of two halves', chapter 4 attempts, in part, to connect the discussion of

---

24 Ibid., chs. 3 and 5.
25 Ibid., ch. 4; Natalie Mears, 'Counsel, public debate, and queenship: John Stubbs's *The discoverie of gaping gulf*, 1579', *Historical Journal*, 44 (2001), pp. 629–50.

court politics to the examination of public debate. Having established in the previous two chapters that the court was the main forum for policy-making, chapter 4 explores ways in which political issues were discussed at court aside from direct counselling by Elizabeth's trusted advisers. Chapter 5 lays the foundation for examining the nature of public debate by surveying how news circulated in England, Wales and Ireland; the nature of public debate itself is explored in chapter 6. Though both the issues of debate, and the factors which may have encouraged participation, are highlighted in chapters 5 and 6, chapter 7 focuses on how a variety of Elizabethans understood and perceived Elizabeth's queenship.

In what appeared to be an increasingly ambitious project, especially concerning the nature of public debate, a number of points have under-pinned my approach. First, my methodological approach to Elizabethan politics has been to combine study of real politics with political culture, part of what has been termed 'New Tudor Political History'.[26] Influenced by political theorists and historians, like Quentin Skinner, John Guy, Patrick Collinson and others, I have increasingly understood Tudor politics as the interplay between people, institutions and ideas. Therefore, I have found it necessary to explore the social, educational and ideological background of political actors in order to understand how they perceived the Elizabethan regime, the issues facing it and their own responses. Second, though this study was initially conceived to concentrate on the mid-Elizabethan period, which has been rather neglected, it grew to consume the first decade of the reign too. Indeed, it covers what John Guy has identified as the first of two coherent periods into which Elizabeth's reign can be divided, 1558–1585/7.[27] This was partly born out of the availability of sources: a number of crucial pieces of evidence on political discourse at court and in the country dated from the 1560s, while corresponding material for the 1570s could be rare. My desire to explore the origins of what I perceived to be a more active style of leadership by Elizabeth was also important. However, whilst not the primary focus of this study, the result has been to enable me to reconsider Guy's arguments about the coherence of the so-called 'first reign' and pursue reservations about these arguments which I had experienced during my doctoral research.

Third, I have found it more useful to define the court in terms that lie between David Starkey's very narrow definition and the much wider ones

26 John Guy, 'General introduction', in Guy (ed.), *Tudor monarchy*, pp. 1–10.
27 Guy, 'The 1590s', pp. 1–19.

of Perez Zagorin and Malcolm Smuts.[28] Whilst Starkey's emphasis on the royal household, and in particular on the monarch's personal body servants in the privy chamber, ignores the nobility and gentry who were physically attendant at court but lacked official positions, Zagorin's inclusion of all county officials, and Smuts's of courtiers' London houses and the Inns of Court, seems too liberal. Though there were close connections between the court and the counties, on which Tudor governance relied, a blanket inclusion of all officials conceals the differing levels of contact individuals had with the queen and her immediate regime. In turn, this blurs differences in access to, and involvement in, political debate at court which, as will be shown in later chapters, could be practically and ideologically distinct from that in the counties. Rather, when I talk of the court, I refer to the royal household and those aristocrats and gentry, male and female, who were resident or attendant at the royal palaces for at least part of the year. This has been estimated to be approximately two-thirds of the nobility and as many as fifty to sixty gentry families in the early and middle years of the reign.[29] I see the court as a collection of individuals – some with official positions, others without – rather than as an institution or a physical space, circumscribed by the palace walls or dictated by proximity to Elizabeth. Hence, individuals became courtiers because they were attendant, in one way or another, on the monarch but did not cease to be courtiers when they returned to their estates or went abroad on official business. One of the most important, and interesting, aspects of the court and its relationship with public debate is the permeable barrier between the two, a permeability created by courtiers who were able to traverse or occupy the different physical spaces of the royal palaces and the counties. To explore this more accurately, however, we need to think of the court as a collection of individuals and to use the term 'courtiers' more readily than 'the court'.

Fourth, perhaps unsurprisingly for a former student of St Andrews, I have also attempted to take a 'British' approach. It has become increasingly clear, thanks to the work of Jane Dawson and Roger Mason, that leading Elizabethans, like Burghley, perceived politics in 'British' terms, looking at the strategic and ideological problems and benefits posed by

---

28 Starkey, 'Representation through intimacy', pp. 187–224; Starkey, 'Court and government', pp. 29–58; Starkey, 'Intimacy and innovation', pp. 71–118; Perez Zagorin, *The court and the country* (New York, 1969); Malcolm Smuts, 'Cultural diversity and cultural change at the court of James I', in Linda Levy Peck (ed.), *The mental world of the Jacobean court* (Cambridge, 1991), pp. 99–112.
29 Haigh, *Elizabeth I*, pp. 65, 107.

constituent parts of the British Isles.[30] If their work has informed my understanding of Elizabethan court politics, then I have also attempted to translate this to my exploration of public debate. I have consciously tried to explore public debate in England, Wales and Ireland, even if, because of the imbalance of evidence, England has assumed the lion's share. Irish debate in particular seems to make important correctives to our current understanding of early modern discourse and point to some important avenues of research.

Fifth, though Peter Lake's and Michael Questier's recent study of the public sphere, *The anti-christ's lewd hat*, has demonstrated how much information on the dissemination and reception of printed texts can be gained from the texts themselves – something that I had recognised in reading countless pamphlets in the British Library – I have chosen to try and reconstruct the nature of the public sphere by identifying real readers and real participants, through book inventories, booksellers' accounts, cases of seditious and slanderous words etc.[31] Sixth, having outlined how I use the term 'court', it seems equally imperative to delineate how I have used a number of different labels for the public sphere and public debate in the course of the following exploration – though I discuss explicitly what we should call the Elizabethan public sphere at the end of chapter 6. I use 'public sphere' to denote the concept of the public sphere and as an initial term to refer to the Elizabethan public sphere prior to defining exactly what we should call it, or (with the adjective 'Elizabethan') as a short-hand to signify that I am referring to the concept of the public sphere in relation to the Elizabethan period. I use 'public discourse' to denote an unsituated discourse, a common theme debated by a variety of people who were not always aware of each other's existence. Conversely, I use 'public debate' as an umbrella term to refer very generally to the act of discussing political issues by those who were not members of the court.

Finally, this study is not concerned with conceiving the public sphere, as Habermas and others have done so, in terms of an essential prerequisite of liberal-democracy and one of its major causes. Thus, it does not seek

---

30 Jane E. Dawson, 'William Cecil and the British dimension of early Elizabethan foreign policy', *History*, 74 (1989), pp. 196–216; Roger A. Mason, 'Scotching the Brut: politics, history and national myth in sixteenth century Britain', in Mason (ed.) *Scotland and England, 1286–1815* (Edinburgh, 1987), pp. 60–84; Mason, 'The Scottish Reformation and the origins of Anglo-British imperialism', in Mason (ed.), *Scots and Britons: Scottish political thought and the union of 1603* (Cambridge, 1994), pp. 161–86.
31 Peter Lake with Michael Questier, *The anti-christ's lewd hat: protestants, papists and players in post-Reformation England* (New Haven and London, 2002).

primarily to respond to some of the most recent research, notably by David Zaret, that traces the origins of public opinion and the development of conscious appeals to it to legitimate political action.[32] Rather, it is born out of the debate on the nature of Tudor political history as articulated by Patrick Collinson in his inaugural lecture as Regius Professor of Modern History at Cambridge in 1989 and uses the notion of the public sphere as a new, and necessary, conceptual framework to examine Elizabethan political discourse.[33] Chapter 1, therefore, details the historiography of Elizabethan court politics and political debate and discusses the conceptual frameworks needed to resolve some of the unanswered questions it poses. It also lays down some of the problems posed by extant sources and how these shape our pursuit of a better understanding of political awareness and debate under Elizabeth.

32 David Zaret, *The origins of democratic culture: printing, petitions and the public sphere in early-modern England* (Princeton, NJ, 2000), passim but esp. pp. 3–4, 7–8.
33 Patrick Collinson, '*De republica Anglorum*: or, history with the politics put back', in Collinson (ed.), *Elizabethan essays* (London, 1994), pp. 1–29.

CHAPTER I

Elizabethan court politics and the public sphere

In his inaugural address as Regius Professor of Modern History at Cambridge in November 1989, Patrick Collinson called for a 'new political history': 'social history with the politics put back in, or an account of political processes which is also social'.[1] A veiled critique of revisionist history, and specifically Geoffrey Elton's *Political history: principles and practice* (1970), Collinson took issue with Elton's belief that sovereign and separate states were the only political units worthy of study.[2] He argued it was essential 'to explore the social depths of politics', 'to find signs of political life at levels where it was not previously thought to have existed' and to explore not only horizontal connections at these levels, but also vertical connections between local communities, lordship and monarchy.[3]

Collinson's lecture tapped into an existing vein of dissatisfaction with the perceived failure of revisionist history to deal effectively with questions first raised by Sir John Neale and Conyers Read about the roles of ideology and social connections in early modern politics. Simon Adams, George Bernard, Cliff Davies, Steve Gunn, Eric Ives, Wallace MacCaffrey, David Starkey and Penry Williams had all begun to reconstruct a more socially derived understanding of Tudor politics prior to Collinson's lecture. They emphasised the centrality of social connections and clienteles to the process of governance and, as a result, identified the court, rather than the privy council, as the main political forum.[4]

---

1 Collinson, '*De republica Anglorum*', pp. 11, 8–9. See Collinson's contribution to this approach, notably his articles, 'Monarchical republic' and 'Elizabethan exclusion crisis'.
2 Collinson, '*De republica Anglorum*', pp. 8–9.
3 Ibid., p. 11.
4 A highly selective list of these scholars' contributions includes Simon Adams, 'Favourites and factions at the Elizabethan court', reprinted, with postscript, in Guy (ed.), *Tudor monarchy*, pp. 253–74; G. W. Bernard, *The power of the early Tudor nobility: a study of the fourth and fifth earls of Shrewsbury* (Brighton, 1985); C. S. L. Davies, *Peace, print and Protestantism, 1450–1558* (London, 1976); S. J. Gunn, *Early Tudor government, 1485–1558* (Basingstoke and London, 1995); Eric Ives, *Anne Boleyn* (Oxford, 1986); Wallace T. MacCaffrey, 'Place and patronage in Elizabethan politics', in S. T. Bindoff, J. Hurstfield and C. H. Williams (eds.), *Elizabethan government and*

Similarly, studies of counties, towns, villages and manors had begun to show that such communities were largely self-governing, utilising social networks amongst the local elite, and that, as a result, opportunities for debate on local issues could be frequent.[5] This was acutely manifested in the parish of Swallowfield. Geographically straddling Berkshire and Wiltshire, but administratively under the jurisdiction of Wiltshire, in 1596 the local elite drew up a constitution to provide rules that 'we may the better and more quyetlye lyve together in good love and amytie' without constant recourse to the justices of Wiltshire, who could be up to twenty miles distant.[6] Indeed, Collinson went so far as to suggest that the 'Swallowfield articles' demonstrated the penetration of republican ideas inherent in autonomous and self-governing communities.[7]

For Collinson, this apparent dichotomy between, on the one hand, the claims to absoluteness by Tudor monarchs and, on the other, the self-autonomy of the counties, towns and villages they ruled, was no dichotomy at all. Rather, it exemplified contemporary perceptions of English government, articulated by leading humanists, theorists and courtiers, Sir Thomas Elyot and Sir Thomas Smith, as a 'mixed polity', in which the monarch governed with the assistance of the political community.[8] Instead, it raised questions about contemporary notions of the 'public', as represented in terms such as the 'public weal' that Elyot and others used to define the political community. In Collinson's words, 'Did "the public", in the sense of "the great British public", already exist?'[9]

society: essays presented to Sir John Neale (London, 1961), pp. 95–126; MacCaffrey, *The shaping of the Elizabethan regime: Elizabethan politics, 1558–1572* (Princeton, NJ, 1968); MacCaffrey, *Queen Elizabeth and the making of policy, 1572–1588* (Princeton, NJ, 1981); MacCaffrey, *Elizabeth I: war and politics, 1588–1603* (Princeton, NJ, 1992); C. Coleman and David Starkey (eds.), *Revolution reassessed: revisions in the history of Tudor government and administration* (Oxford, 1986); David Starkey *et al.* (eds.), *The English court: from the Wars of the Roses to the Civil War* (London and New York, 1987), pp. 71–118; Penry Williams, *The Tudor regime* (Oxford, 1979).

5 The literature on these fields is extensive, but see, for instance, A. Hassall Smith, *Country and court: government and politics in Norfolk, 1558–1603* (Oxford, 1974); Diarmaid MacCulloch, *Suffolk under the Tudors: politics and religion in an English county, 1500–1600* (Oxford, 1986); Peter Clark, *English provincial society from the Reformation to the Revolution: religion, politics and society in Kent, 1500–1640* (Hassocks, 1977); Steve Rappaport, *Worlds within worlds: structures of life in sixteenth-century London* (Cambridge, 1989); Ian Archer, *The pursuit of stability: social relations in Elizabethan London* (Cambridge, 1991); Margaret Spufford, *Contrasting communities: English villagers in the sixteenth and seventeenth centuries* (Cambridge, 1974); Margaret McIntosh, *A community transformed: the manor and liberty of Havering, 1500–1620* (Cambridge, 1991).

6 Collinson, 'Monarchical republic', pp. 395–6; Collinson, '*De Republica Anglorum*', pp. 23–4; Steve Hindle, 'Hierarchy and community in the Elizabethan parish: the Swallowfield articles of 1596', *Historical Journal*, 42 (1999), pp. 835–51.

7 Collinson, '*De Republica Anglorum*', pp. 23–4.

8 Ibid., pp. 16–20.   9 Ibid., p. 17.

Collinson rejected some contemporary opinion that identified the political community with parliament. Though MPs did seek to influence major policies – such as in the debates on Elizabeth's marriage and the succession in 1563 and 1566 – parliament did not meet regularly enough to constitute a major political forum. Rather, he emphasised the role of humanist-trained statesmen, particularly those at a secondary or tertiary level. They were regularly employed by the council as 'one man think-tanks', writers of position papers and givers of verbal advice on a range of specialist issues including law, finance, engineering and navigation. Not only did such men claim to represent the public interest but, Collinson suggests, as writers of printed pamphlets, they actually did represent and speak to a wider politically aware citizenry.[10]

In the short space of a lecture, it was impossible to trace the connections, if any, between the political community of humanist intellectuals and of self-governing elites in counties, towns and parishes. Yet, it was these questions that were some of the most interesting that Collinson's lecture, and the direction of recent research on Tudor politics generally, raised. Did these communities comprise the same individuals, were they connected through familial connections, social networks or ideology, or were they distinct entities? Though their sphere of action appeared different – policy-making and local governance respectively – were they part of the same 'public'? Indeed, these questions seemed increasingly apposite as re-examinations of the notion of the public sphere began to suggest that a wide social spectrum of men and women participated in political debate and that the origins of the public sphere could be found in the early seventeenth century. The nature of Tudor, and specifically Elizabethan, politics and political debate could inform the wider debate on the nature and origins of the early modern public sphere.

If we are to explore the 'vertical connections' between monarchy, lordship and subjects – those between policy-making and the centre and provincial or local politics – we have to begin by addressing the constituent parts separately. The legacy of Elton's redefinition of Tudor politics, in opposition to Neale's and Read's conceptualisation, remains strong for Elizabeth's reign. Equally, there has been little research on the nature of political debate outside the court, other than that conducted by moderate puritan elites and in printed pamphlets. How has our understanding of these two dimensions been shaped, what tools can we use to explore these further and what problems still lie ahead?

10 Ibid., pp. 19–21.

THE DEBATE ON THE NATURE OF ELIZABETHAN POLITICS

In three influential articles published between 1977 and 1987, David Starkey argued that the main political forum under Henry VIII was the king's privy chamber. Its male staff, as intimate body servants and boon companions of the king, became important agents of royal policy, acting as diplomats, military commanders and special messengers, as well as assuming crucial financial responsibilities in the chamber and representative and legal ones in the localities. In addition, the Chief Gentlemen of the privy chamber undertook important secretarial duties by obtaining the king's signature and operating the dry stamp, as well as acting as key points of access to him.[11] Informal in style, founded on personal intimacy with the king and centred on key body servants in the privy chamber, Starkey's model of Henrician politics was the antithesis of Geoffrey Elton's 'national, bureaucratic' government outlined in his seminal *The Tudor revolution in government*.[12] Though it became evident in his debate with Elton in the *Historical Journal* in 1988 that Starkey had exaggerated certain aspects of his argument, notably the privy chamber's role in policy-making,[13] it was his wider points about the personal nature of Tudor monarchy that were the most difficult to dispute.[14] As a result, Starkey's arguments perpetuated the debate, over which Elton had disputed with Neale, about whether the court or the council was the main locus of politics under the Tudors.

Starkey's conception of Henrician politics chimed broadly with growing research on Elizabeth. Chris Haigh's study of the queen, Wallace MacCaffrey's political trilogy and work on court patronage and Simon Adams's on factionalism and the earl of Leicester all re-emphasised the importance of personalities and social dynamics in Elizabethan politics.[15]

11 Starkey, 'Representation through intimacy', pp. 187–224; Starkey, 'Court and government', pp. 29–58 (both reprinted in Guy (ed.), *Tudor monarchy*, pp. 42–78 and 189–213 respectively); Starkey, 'Intimacy and innovation: the rise of the privy chamber, 1485–1547', in Starkey *et al.* (eds.), *The English court*, pp. 71–118.

12 G. R. Elton, *The Tudor revolution in government* (Cambridge, 1953). See also Elton, *Policy and police: the enforcement of the Reformation in the age of Thomas Cromwell* (Cambridge, 1972); Elton, *Reform and renewal: Thomas Cromwell and the common weal* (Cambridge, 1973).

13 The documents for which the two leading gentlemen of the privy chamber, Sir Anthony Denny and Sir Thomas Heneage the elder, obtained Henry's signature were bills and petitions and hence were unrelated to major political decisions.

14 G. R. Elton, 'Tudor government', *Historical Journal*, 31 (1988), pp. 425–34; David Starkey, 'A reply: Tudor government: the facts?', *Historical Journal*, 31 (1988), pp. 921–31.

15 Haigh, *Elizabeth I*; MacCaffrey, *Shaping of the Elizabethan regime*; MacCaffrey, *Making of policy*; MacCaffrey, *War and politics*; MacCaffrey, 'Place and patronage'; Adams, 'Favourites and factions'; Adams, 'Faction, clientage and party: English politics, 1550–1603', *History Today*, 32

They demonstrated that Elizabethan politics was less about institutions (as defined by Elton) than the interaction between those institutions, people and ideas. All placed a particular emphasis on individuals: Chris Haigh highlighting instances when Elizabeth sought advice from those who were not councillors (usually to circumvent the council) and Simon Adams arguing that policy-making was dominated less by the privy council than by an inner ring of its members who had an established personal intimacy with the queen.[16]

Redefining Elizabethan politics as informal and personal facilitated, and stimulated, the development of other crucial strands. First, feminist historians, like Paula Scalingi and Constance Jordan, drew attention to the importance of Elizabeth's gender. They showed how, from 1553, contemporary attitudes to female monarchy dominated the debate on royal power, defining expectations of how Elizabeth would govern (through her male councillors) and acting both as motivation for her to subvert conventions in order to assert her independence in policy-making and as the tools to achieve this.[17] Second, beginning with John Guy's survey in his *Tudor England*, and then receiving specialist treatment in both collections of essays, like *Tudor political culture*, and monographs, like *The early Elizabethan polity* and *Political culture in the reign of Elizabeth I*, historians have sought to explore the ideas and assumptions held by individual actors and gauge how these shaped their political actions.[18] John Guy has explored the different 'languages' of counsel.[19] Quentin Skinner has demonstrated the importance of classical-humanist education for sixteenth-century governors.[20] The interaction between ideas and political action have been explored by, for instance, Stephen Alford. He has rescued Burghley from his reputation as an uninspiring politique and pen-pusher, first established by Thomas Babington

(1982), pp. 33–9; Adams, 'Eliza enthroned?: the court and its politics', in Christopher Haigh (ed.), *The reign of Elizabeth I* (Basingstoke and London, 1984), pp. 55–77; Adams, 'The Dudley clientele and the House of Commons, 1559–1586', *Parliamentary History*, 8 (1989), pp. 216–39; Adams, 'The Dudley clientele, 1553–1563', in G. W. Bernard (ed.), *The Tudor nobility* (Manchester and New York, 1992), pp. 241–65; Adams, '"Because I am of that contreye and mynde to plant myself there": Robert Dudley, earl of Leicester and the West Midlands', *Midland History*, 20 (1995), pp. 21–74; Adams, 'The patronage of the crown in Elizabethan politics: the 1590s in perspective', in Guy (ed.), *Reign of Elizabeth I*, pp. 20–45.

16 Haigh, *Elizabeth I*, ch. 4; Adams, 'Eliza enthroned?', pp. 62–3.
17 Scalingi, 'The scepter or the distaff', pp. 59–75; Jordan, 'Woman's rule', pp. 421–51. See also Lee, 'A bodye politique to governe', pp. 242–61.
18 John Guy, *Tudor England* (Oxford, 1988), ch. 15; Hoak (ed.), *Tudor political culture*; McLaren, *Political culture*.
19 Guy, 'Rhetoric of counsel'.
20 Skinner, *Reason and rhetoric*, chs. 1 and 2.

Macauley in the early nineteenth century, and demonstrated that Burghley's actions were shaped by his Protestant beliefs, ideals of Ciceronian citizenship and his 'British' perspectives.[21] Patrick Collinson has pointed to the prevalence of quasi-republican ideas and how these influenced proposals to remedy the Elizabethan succession question.[22]

Classical-humanism and republican ideas also pervaded local politics and political debate. Markku Peltonen has shown that Ciceronian ideas of citizenship were also assumed by provincial citizens, such as George Pettie (a member of the Leathersellers Company) and John Barston (town clerk of Tewkesbury).[23] He has also shown that quasi-republican ideas, articulated in conciliar and parliamentary debates on the succession and Mary Stuart, underpinned some provincial responses to local government, including vagrancy, as well as proposals for the reform of Ireland. They include John Hooker's *Orders enacted for orphans* ([1575]), prepared for Exeter; John Barston's *Safegarde of societie*, drawn up after the incorporation of Tewkesbury in 1576; and Thomas Beacon's *Solon his follie* (1594).[24] Patrick Collinson and Steve Hindle have explored the republican ideas evident in the 'Swallowfield articles' of 1596.[25]

Far from leading to a greater consensus, these developments have led to a growing tension over the nature of Elizabeth's queenship and what shaped it. On the one hand, feminist historians have asserted that the defining factor was Elizabeth's gender. Mary Thomas Crane has argued that Elizabeth appropriated humanist ideas of counsel (that monarchs sought counsel from wise, old men) and conventions of feminine behaviour (silence) to give the appearance that she was ruled through counsel while, in practice, ignoring advice.[26] Mary Hill Cole has suggested that Elizabeth disrupted the 'normal' functioning of government by going on progress, exploiting the resultant 'chaos' to wrong-foot her councillors, justify her slowness in decision-making and impose her policies directly on her realm.[27] Allison Heisch and Carole Levin have propounded that Elizabeth deliberately cultivated images of virginity and maternity, both to allay contemporary fears of female monarchy and as strategies to retain

---

21 Alford, *Early Elizabethan polity*, passim.
22 Collinson, 'Monarchical republic'; Collinson, 'Elizabethan exclusion crisis'.
23 Markku Peltonen, *Classical humanism and republicanism in English political thought, 1570–1640* (Cambridge, 1995), pp. 57–9.
24 Ibid., pp. 57–68, 74–96.
25 Collinson, 'Monarchical republic', pp. 395–6; Collinson, '*De Republica Anglorum*', pp. 23–4; Hindle, 'Hierarchy and community'.
26 Crane, 'Video and taceo', pp. 1–15.
27 Cole, *Portable queen*.

her autonomy.[28] More negatively, Anne McLaren has argued that continuing debate over the royal supremacy, reinforced by the lack of an adult male king and biblical arguments disqualifying women from holding office, forced Elizabeth to redefine her queenship in 'extraordinary' and providential terms: it was a corporate activity, executed jointly by her and her male counsellors.[29]

On the other hand, John Guy, Patrick Collinson and Stephen Alford, while agreeing that attitudes to female monarchy formed the politico-cultural milieu of relationships between Elizabeth and councillors, have argued that Elizabeth's queenship was shaped more by a fundamental dissonance over political issues and creeds ('mixed polity' versus 'imperial monarchy'). Elizabeth refused to deal with (or even take counsel on) issues that were most important to her councillors: marriage, the succession, Mary Stuart and intervention in Scotland and the Netherlands. Believing her authority was 'imperial' – that it was ordained by God, that the royal prerogative could not be limited by counsel and that specific issues (the succession and religion) could only be discussed with her consent – she also refused to defer to councillors' views that she should seek and accept their advice. Politics was thus characterised by constant tension. Elizabeth restricted debate within and outwith the court, ignored the advice of the privy council and refused to deal with issues they thought were central. Equally, councillors sought to 'bounce' her into action by transferring debate into parliament, and, in 1587, dispatching the signed warrant for Mary's execution when Elizabeth had instructed William Davison, one of the Secretaries, to retain it.[30]

These debates suggest that our understanding of Elizabethan politics is distant from Elton's emphasis on institutions and bureaucracy, but this is an illusion. It actually remains rooted in the same ideas. Michael Pulman's study of the mid-Elizabethan polity is strongly Eltonian. He argued that policy was made by the privy council who presented consensus advice for Elizabeth to accept or reject. Attempts by non-councillors to offer advice provoked hostility and Elizabeth exercised a self-imposed restraint on seeking counsel outside the privy council.[31] More recent, socially or culturally derived studies have painted a similar picture. Wallace MacCaffrey has suggested that those excluded from the council

---

28 Levin, *'Heart and stomach of a king'*; Heisch, 'Queen Elizabeth I', pp. 45–56.
29 McLaren, *Political culture.*
30 Collinson, 'Monarchical republic', pp. 402, 407; Guy, 'The 1590s', pp. 1–19; Guy, 'Tudor monarchy and its critiques', pp. 93–100; Alford, *Early Elizabethan polity.*
31 Pulman, *Elizabethan privy council,* passim, though especially pp. 52–3.

'were denied any major role in power-brokering or decision-making.'[32] Though Simon Adams argued that policy-making was made by an inner ring of privy councillors, conciliar membership appears to have been as, if not more, significant than personal intimacy with the queen.[33] Stephen Alford has argued that the debate on intervention in Scotland on 27 December 1559 'established a pattern of action by Council throughout the decade.'[34]

Moreover, Starkey's attempt to assert the political importance of the privy chamber has not met with universal support. Pam Wright argued that the privy chamber ceased to play an important role on Elizabeth's accession because it was dominated by women and because of Elizabeth's own preferences: she wanted the privy chamber to act as a 'cocoon' not a 'cockpit'. As a result, it lost many of its administrative and financial functions: the sign manual reverted to the principal secretary, who also assumed control of chamber finance; the privy purse ceased to be a major spending department, while gentlemen of the privy chamber, though they continued to act as envoys, mediators and representatives in the localities, lacked both the standing and the weighty administrative duties of their Henrician predecessors.[35] In conjunction with MacCaffrey's, Adams's, and Alford's work, Wright's arguments suggested that the court, as defined by Adams, played little role in Elizabethan politics.

The limited impact of new, socially and culturally derived interpretations of Elizabethan politics and political discourse has been shaped by a number of factors. While the explorations of the interaction between political culture and practical politics has proved fruitful, differences between the political perspectives of monarch and subject have been defined in monochromatic terms. There is a broad consensus among historians that Elizabeth adopted 'descending' theories of participation: the theory of 'imperial monarchy' (that she was divinely appointed by God, that she should seek the advice of her counsellors but was not bound to accept such advice). Equally, that her subjects tended to adopt 'ascending' theories – the concept of the 'mixed polity' – which privileged the role of counsel and councils in policy-making. However, while it has been argued that 'ascending' theories were pervasive, penetrating beyond a court elite into civic political culture, there has been little attention paid

32 MacCaffrey, *Making of policy*, pp. 425–6.
33 Adams, 'Eliza enthroned', pp. 62–3.
34 Alford, *Early Elizabethan polity*, pp. 69–70, 208 and passim.
35 Pam Wright, 'A change in direction: the ramifications of a female household, 1558–1603', in Starkey et al. (eds.), *The English court*, pp. 147–72, quotation from p. 159.

to the fact that 'descending' theories were also adopted by subjects, such as
Charles Merbury in *A briefe discourse of royall monarchie* (1581).[36]

Gender has also had a negative impact. Feminist readings of Elizabeth's
reign have highlighted the importance of gender, and have stimulated a
lively debate about the extent to which it defined Elizabeth's queenship.
However, some recent works seem to be methodologically flawed. Anne
McLaren's increasingly influential study is based on only a small number
of canonical treatises and, with the exception of exploring 'speech acts' in
the parliaments of 1566 and 1572, is not mapped onto actual political
practice. Moreover, by suggesting that it was *because* the Elizabethan privy
chamber was dominated by women that its political and administrative
importance declined, Pam Wright indicated that Elizabeth's reign was not
fertile soil for Starkey's paradigm.[37] Reappraisals of Wright's arguments
have been cosmetic: there has been little attempt to assess the importance
of patronage in the Elizabethan polity (and hence the significance of
women's roles therein) or challenge her fundamental points about the
political participation of privy chamber men and women.[38]

Starkey's narrow definition of the court may also have been unhelpful.
By identifying the court with the privy chamber, there has been less scope
to explore the role of the wider royal household and its members as well
as of other courtiers, especially while Wright's arguments about female
privy chamber servants remains dominant. Oddly, Perez Zagorin's and
Malcolm Smuts's wider definitions of the court – encompassing the royal
household, office holders in major crown departments like the Exchequer, county officials, the London homes of courtiers and the Inns
of Court[39] – have done little to break the antithesis between 'court' and
'council', evident in the debates between Neale, Read, Elton and Starkey.
Historians have focused on the boundaries of the court, exploring its
relationship with its immediate physical environs rather than areas or

36 Guy, 'Rhetoric of counsel', pp. 292–310; Guy, 'The king's council and political participation', in
John Guy and A. Fox (eds.), *The Henrician age: humanism, politics and reform, 1500–1550* (Oxford,
1986), pp. 121–9, 138–42; Peltonen, *Classical humanism*, pp. 8–19, 57–71; Charles Merbury, *A
briefe discourse of royall monarchie, as of the best common weale* (London, 1581; *STC* 17823). See also
McLaren, *Political culture*, passim.
37 Wright, 'A change in direction', pp. 147–72.
38 J. B. Greenbaum Goldsmith, 'All the queen's women: the changing place and perception
of aristocratic women in Elizabethan England, 1558–1620' (Ph.D. thesis, Northwestern, 1987);
C. Merton, 'The women who served Queen Mary and Queen Elizabeth: ladies, gentlewomen and
maids to the Privy Chamber, 1553–1603' (Ph.D. thesis, Cambridge, 1993), esp. ch. 6
39 Zagorin, *Court and the country*, passim; Smuts, 'Cultural diversity and cultural change',
pp. 99–112.

individuals involved in policy-making.[40] The very real differences between different institutions have also been blurred, especially between
the royal court and the Inns of Court which, despite close social and
cultural ties (and the fact that some students looked to the royal court for
advancement), were distinct entities with stark differences in ideology,
political perspectives and spheres of activity. In addition, since the revival
of interest in court studies in the early twentieth century, most attention
has focused on the role of courtly ritual, behaviour and etiquette particularly in response to Norbert Elias's seminal works, *The court society*
(written in the 1920s; published in 1969) and *The civilising process*
(1969).[41] Jeroen Duindam has effectively undermined Elias's arguments
about the 'civilising' of aristocratic behaviour by monarchs in the two
most important European courts, Versailles and Vienna.[42] In his *The
illusion of power*, Stephen Orgel demonstrated that Jacobean masques
embodied, demonstrated and upheld the status quo of Stuart power,
stimulating reappraisals (positive and negative) of drama and masques
by New Historicists.[43]

Practical issues regarding sources have also been important. By focusing
on major archival collections such as the State Papers, the British Library
collections and the Cecil Papers at Hatfield House, historians have
privileged the role of key individuals, like Burghley, Leicester and
Walsingham, and ignored those of others either, like Sir Walter Mildmay,
whose papers are housed in local archives, or secondary figures where
evidence is more fragmentary. Paradoxically, where substantial archive
resources are extant for secondary figures – notably the diplomat and
clerk of the privy council, Robert Beale – the absence of a reliable
catalogue until recently has prevented the archive from being exploited to the full. A detailed catalogue of Beale's manuscripts was not

40 For example, Smuts, 'Cultural diversity and cultural change', Pauline Croft, 'Robert Cecil and
the early Jacobean court', and Linda Levy Peck, 'The mentality of a Jacobean grandee', in Linda
Levy Peck (ed.), *The mental world of the Jacobean court* (Cambridge, 1991), pp. 99–112, 134–47 and
148–68 respectively.
41 Norbert Elias, *Die höfische Gesellschaft* (Darmstadt and Neuwied, 1969); Elias, *The court society*,
trans. Edmund Jephcott (Oxford, 1983); Elias, *Über den prozeß der Zivilisation* (2 vols., Bern,
1969); Elias, *The civilizing process*, trans. Edmund Jephcott (2 vols., Oxford, 1978, 1982). Elias's
arguments are effectively summarized in Jereon Duindam, *Myths of power: Norbert Elias and the
early modern court*, trans. Lorri S. Granger and Gerard T. Moran (Amsterdam, [1994?]).
42 Duindam, *Myths of power*, esp. chs. 3 and 4.
43 Stephen Orgel, *The illusion of power: political theatre in the English Renaissance* (Berkeley, LA and
London, 1975); John Adamson, 'The making of the *ancien-régime* court, 1500–1700', in Adamson
(ed.), *The princely courts of Europe: ritual, politics and culture under the Ancien-Régime, 1500–1700*
(London, 1999), pp. 7–41; David Bevington and Peter Holbrook, 'Introduction', in Bevington
and Holbrook (eds.), *The politics of the Stuart court masque* (Cambridge, 1998), pp. 3–5.

available until Patricia Basing's invaluable two-volume work was published in 1994.[44]

It is unclear for how much longer some of our assumptions about Elizabethan politics can be sustained. Despite the flaws in Starkey's arguments, the tide of socially and culturally derived conceptions of early Tudor governance seems so strong that it is increasingly imperative to address fully their implications for Elizabeth's reign. There is evidence that 'descending' theories of counsel were held by members of the elite and that counsellors were ineffective in pressing their policies on to the queen: after all, it took Burghley nearly thirty years to get rid of Mary Stuart! Moreover, if the debate on the importance of gender to Elizabeth's queenship remains heated and dynamic, reappraisals of the political role of early modern women have fundamentally undermined Wright's assertions that the Elizabethan privy chamber was disabled by the gender of most of its members. Beginning with Barbara Harris's seminal article, 'Women and politics in early Tudor England' in 1990, it has become increasingly clear that aristocratic and gentle women were able to play important, informal political roles in Tudor governance aside from being the patronage brokers that Wright suggested.[45]

ELIZABETHAN PUBLIC DEBATE AND THE HABERMASIAN PUBLIC SPHERE

If the debate on the nature of Elizabethan politics remains heated, then our understanding of public political debate, though more virgin soil, is even more riven by conceptual and practical problems. Despite the evidence of autonomy in local government and of humanist and republican ideas in provincial treatises, public political debate continues to be seen as an offshoot of conciliar debate. The humanist intellectuals, whom

---

44 *The British Library Catalogue of Additions to the Manuscripts: the Yelverton Manuscripts, Additional Manuscripts 48000–48196* (2 vols., London, 1994). For further details of Beale's archive, see Mark Taviner, 'Robert Beale and the Elizabethan polity' (Ph.D. thesis, St Andrews, 2000), pp. 1–2, 20–45.

45 The list of relevant works is extensive. Barbara Harris's most important works include 'Women and politics in early Tudor England', *Historical Journal*, 33 (1990), pp. 259–81; 'The view from my Lady's chamber: new perspectives on the early Tudor monarchy', *Huntingdon Library Quarterly*, 63 (1999), pp. 215–47 and *English aristocratic women, 1450–1550: marriage and family, property and careers* (Oxford, 2002). A recent, wide-ranging exploration of different aspects of women's involvement in early modern politics is James Daybell (ed.), *Women and politics in early modern England, 1450–1700* (Basingstoke, 2004) which includes my own reassessment of Wright's important article: Mears, 'Politics in the Elizabethan privy chamber: Lady Mary Sidney and Kat Ashley', pp. 67–82.

Collinson identified as central to the political community, included men like Thomas Norton, Robert Beale, Thomas Digges and John Stubbe. Though their political activity was not confined to supporting the privy council, the activities which Collinson and Michael Graves identified as of greatest significance were those which were directly related to it. They were active in providing position papers and advice for the regime or, in the case of Stubbe, publishing pamphlets to 'bounce' Elizabeth into action. Those who were MPs also managed conciliar business in the Commons, acting as 'men of business' by preparing legislation, sitting on committees and speaking in favour of bills. Conversely, occasions when they made outspoken comments on political issues – Norton on the Anjou match in 1581, James Morrice on the *ex officio* oath in 1593, for example – occurred when they became 'froward': guided by zeal, rather than policy; acting independently, rather than speaking from a prepared script. It was aberrant behaviour both in terms of the punishment it earned – imprisonment – and because it was contrary to their role as 'men of business', and hence members of the political community.[46]

A central problem with current conceptions of Tudor public debate is the failure to connect them to the broader conceptual framework of the 'public sphere', established by sociologists and historians working on the seventeenth and eighteenth centuries. Jürgen Habermas's classic definition of the public sphere, and the debate that has succeeded it, has dominated our understanding of public political debate in the later early modern period, especially since the publication of the English translation in 1989.[47] Despite significant challenges, his definition provides a range of ways to explore the origins, nature and characteristics of public debate and its participants, as well as remaining the standard by which all pretenders to a public sphere are measured. Moreover, not only does it provide a potentially useful framework in which to conceptualise Elizabethan public debate but it may help to illuminate some of the connections raised by Collinson in his seminal lecture in 1989. By emphasising the act of discussing major political issues, the notion of the public sphere provides one dimension in which we may both 'find signs of political life at levels

46 Graves, 'Management of the Elizabethan House of Commons', pp. 11–38; Graves, 'Common lawyers and the privy council's parliamentary men-of-business', pp. 189–215; Graves, 'Elizabethan men of business reconsidered', pp. 111–27; Graves, 'Thomas Norton, the parliament man', pp. 17–35; Graves, *Thomas Norton*; Collinson, 'Puritans, men of business and Elizabethan parliaments', pp. 187–211; Collinson, 'Exclusion crisis', pp. 76–8.

47 Habermas, *Structural transformation*.

where it was not previously thought to have existed' and explore political connections across Elizabethan society.[48]

Habermas's definition of the public sphere was rooted in his two concepts of the public articulation of political authority or opinion. First, the 'publicness of representation' or 'representative publicness' (*repräsentative Öffentlichkeit*). Characteristic of the middle ages, this was the visible manifestation of power through individuals, symbols and actions. It occurred not only in representative assemblies, where members represented their lordship 'before' rather than 'for' the people, but in insignia, dress, demeanour, oratory and court displays, such as jousts and tournaments.[49] Second, the bourgeois public sphere (*bürgerliche Öffentlichkeit*). Changes in bourgeois culture, courtly display, religion and trade in the early modern period prompted the development of greater bureaucracy, more efficient tax collection and larger standing armies which combined to make political authority more visible, palpable and public than previously. Born out of this, by the late seventeenth century, was the bourgeois public sphere itself: a community of educated, professional, wealthy, bourgeois men engaged in critical public debate against the government.[50]

'Representative publicness' was not a public sphere but an attribute of status. First, because it was dependent on one's position as a feudal landlord: the authority to control the social organisation of labour and to impose law and order. Second, because there were no clear distinctions between 'private' and 'public' as lordship was often exercised through the noble household which fused 'private' and 'public'.[51] Conversely, the bourgeois public sphere was a public sphere: political authority was made public, the state was identified with public interests and, crucially, an educated and wealthy elite defined themselves as the 'public' and constantly appraised the regime's performance in public debate.[52]

Habermas's definition of the public sphere has been the subject of much debate. Work by Aytoun Ellis, Lois Schwoerer and Stephen Dobranski has reinforced arguments that the public sphere was dominated by men,[53]

---

48 Collinson, '*De republica Anglorum*', p. 11.
49 Habermas, *Structural transformation*, pp. 7–8.
50 Ibid., pp. 9–25.
51 Ibid., pp. 5–6.
52 Ibid., pp. 18–28.
53 Aytoun Ellis, *The penny universities: a history of the coffee houses* (London, 1956); Lois G. Schwoerer, 'Liberty of the press and public opinion: 1660–1695', in J. R. Jones (ed.), *Liberty secured? Britain before and after 1688* (Stanford, CA, 1992), pp. 199–230; Stephen B. Dobranski, '"Where men of differing judgements croud": Milton and the culture of coffee houses', *The Seventeenth Century*, 9 (1994), pp. 35–56.

while David Zaret and John E. Willis have continued to emphasise that it was socially, economically and intellectually elitist.[54] Yet equally, Habermas's model has been criticised.[55] Both Steve Pincus and Brian Cowan have challenged its gender exclusivity, pointing to the participation of women in public debate.[56] Pincus has also undermined its social exclusivity by demonstrating that coffee houses – which Habermas identified as the key meeting place for participants – were open to a variety of social classes, as well as religious and political opinions. Neither was the public sphere solely a metropolitan phenomenon: coffee houses were quickly established in Oxford, Cambridge, York, Exeter, Tunbridge Wells, Dorchester and Amersham.[57] Zaret and Dobranski have underlined how Habermas's public sphere was biased towards Puritanism and Whiggery.[58] Moreover, Zaret has highlighted the significance of religion and science, rather than commercial interests, in the development of the public sphere. The Reformation encouraged widespread participation in public debates and stimulated appeals to popular opinion in the seventeenth century, particularly during the Civil War, Regicide and Restoration.[59] As a result of these debates, the nature of the public sphere has been redefined and its origins pushed back to the early seventeenth century: Zaret, for instance, has located its roots primarily in the growing emphasis on representation and the increasing numbers of contested elections under James VI and I.[60]

The Habermasian public sphere provides one way to conceptualise Elizabethan public debate. Certainly the sixteenth century experienced some of the factors which Habermas identified as crucial to the formation of the bourgeois public sphere: humanism, the development of print, long-distance trade, changing concepts of 'private' and 'public' and the growth in the state's ability to impose its will on its subjects.[61] However, it

54 David Zaret, 'Religion, science, and printing in the public spheres in seventeenth-century England', in Calhoun (ed.), *Habermas and the public sphere*, p. 224; John E. Willis, 'European consumption and Asian production in the seventeenth and eighteenth centuries', in John Brewer and Roy Porter (eds.), *Consumption and the world of goods* (London, 1993), p. 141.
55 Calhoun, 'Introduction', in Calhoun (ed.), *Habermas and the public sphere*, p. 35.
56 Steve Pincus, '"Coffee politicians does create": coffeehouses and Restoration political culture', *Journal of Modern History*, 67 (1995), pp. 807–34; Brian Cowan, 'What was masculine about the public sphere? Gender and the coffeehouse milieu in post-Restoration England', *History Workshop Journal*, 51 (2001), pp. 127–57.
57 Pincus, '"Coffee politicians does create"', pp. 811–14 and passim.
58 Zaret, 'Religion, science, and printing', p. 226; Dobranski, '"Men of differing judgements"', p. 39.
59 Zaret, 'Religion, science, and printing', pp. 216–19, 220–4.
60 Ibid., pp. 219–20.
61 Habermas, *Structural transformation*, pp. 9–22.

is also problematic; we cannot just push back the chronological boundaries of the public sphere to 1558. Fundamental characteristics of Habermas's model appear absent from our current understanding of Elizabethan England, Wales and Ireland. Both Habermas and subsequent historians emphasised the role of print, and specifically newsletters, pamphlets and newspapers, as essential for the circulation of news and debate; yet, printed newsletters and *corantos* did not exist or circulate widely until the early seventeenth century while, as both Fritz Levy and Richard Cust have indicated, printed pamphlets were not produced in large numbers until after 1585.[62] Coffee houses, the principal forum for the public sphere, did not exist in the Elizabethan realms. Though Peter Clark has suggested that political issues were discussed in inns and taverns, these institutions have been seen as inimical to the public sphere because they encouraged constant drinking, did not allow customers to read or discuss issues over one sobering drink, and did not provide customers with access to newspapers and newsletters. Habermas's emphasis on the critical-rational nature of public discourse is also problematic as some evidence of political debate in Elizabethan England was rooted in fantastical stories of the queen's illegitimate pregnancies and individuals' claims to be Edward VI.[63] Indeed, Zaret has suggested that the concept of 'political opposition', which was inherent in Habermas's definition of the public sphere, was anachronistic in the sixteenth century because concepts of political service were dominated by ideas of loyalty to the crown and service itself was dependent on crown patronage.[64]

There are also wider issues. Though Habermas understood the public sphere as physically located – primarily in metropolitan coffee houses – this has been increasingly challenged. Alexandra Halasz, for instance, has conceived the public sphere as an 'unsituated' discourse: public debate occurred in the pages of printed news pamphlets and its participants were authors, printers, sellers and readers.[65] Equally, the growing diversity in which the public sphere in the seventeenth and eighteenth centuries

---

62 The earliest *corantos* in England were imported from Antwerp and the United Provinces; they were not printed in England until 1621. F. J. Levy, 'How information spread among the gentry, 1550–1640', *Journal of British Studies*, 112 (1982), pp. 20–3; Levy, 'The decorum of news', *Prose Studies*, 21 (1998), pp. 17–21; Richard Cust, 'News and politics in early seventeenth-century England', *Past & Present*, 112 (1986), pp. 60–90.

63 See the examples cited by Levin in *'Heart and stomach of a king'* and below in chapters 6 and 7.

64 Recent research on the existence of quasi-republican ideas and resistance theory would appear to question these assumptions. Zaret, *Origins of democratic culture*, p. 36.

65 Alexandra Halasz, *The marketplace of print: pamphlets and the public sphere in early modern England* (Cambridge, 1997), pp. 15–16, 23–7, 28–34, 162–4, 166–78.

has been characterised by historians has raised questions as to whether the public sphere can be defined as a singular entity, or existed as multiple, and overlapping, spheres.[66] Crucial in itself for helping to define the nature of the public sphere, both the extent to which it was situated and a single entity has an important impact on the way we should define the public sphere in terms of language, i.e. not merely whether we should use the singular or plural, but whether we should speak specifically of a public sphere or a public discourse.

Problematic though the notion of the public sphere and its application to the Elizabethan period may be, it remains a valid and useful perspective from which to explore the nature of political debate outside the court. It sets questions about the identity of participants in public debate (in terms of social status and gender) and their geographical location, as well as about the subjects and means of debate. In turn, these questions enable us to explore some of the crucial questions raised by recent research in Tudor politics: the extent to which political issues penetrated the lives of ordinary Elizabethans and the vertical connections through cross-sections of the population. Moreover, by looking at the discussion of major political issues, domestic and foreign, it provides a new dimension to our understanding of provincial politics: potentially as concerned with issues of 'national' importance as of the local community.

THE SOURCES FOR EXPLORING ELIZABETHAN PUBLIC DEBATE: PROBLEMS

There are practical problems to reassessing the nature of Elizabethan court politics and public discourse, relating to extant sources and the methodology of analysing them. As was apparent in Starkey's study of the Henrician privy chamber, informal political connections, influence and conversations can be difficult to trace in the written records simply because they were informal and unlikely to be recorded. The explosion of correspondence between members of the regime during the sixteenth century lessens the acuteness of this problem for Elizabeth's reign, but it remains a fact that we are sometimes only able to perceive an individual's actions through chance and indirect recording: in correspondence between privy councillors or courtiers when one was on embassy, for instance. As a result, evidence has to be used qualitatively rather than

66 Calhoun, 'Introduction', pp. 37–8.

quantitatively; as a window on what may have been, rather than a comprehensive picture.

Evidence of public debate is even more scattered and fragmentary, seeming to privilege or neglect people of different social and economic backgrounds, genders and geographical location. Perhaps influenced as much by modern emphasis on newspapers as Habermas's privileging of print, studies of news and public debate increasingly focus on printed pamphlets, newsletters and *corantos*, as demonstrated by the works of Alexandra Halasz, Joad Raymond, Peter Lake and Michael Questier.[67]

Though, as Lake's and Questier's exploration of crime pamphlets has shown, much can be gleaned from pamphlets – as artefacts and texts – about the circulation of news and political debate, equally, textual analysis has its limitations. It gives little sense of the dissemination of pamphlets or how they were read. The former can be accessed through booksellers' inventories and accounts, library inventories and probate records. Even here, though, problems remain. Booksellers' inventories or accounts remain extant only in small numbers, while inventories tend to favour aristocratic and gentry readers. Though probate inventories are extant for many individuals below these social levels, they rarely record such transient items as broadsides and small pamphlets. How pamphlets were read is much more difficult to gauge because we lack the kind of evidence – details of ownership and marginalia – which has been used so productively to explore learned responses to academic texts.[68] We also need to consider other questions: not merely the cost of pamphlets and the levels of literacy – which may point to the market for political pamphlets – but more fundamental issues about language. Not only were Gaelic and Welsh the predominant languages in Ireland and Wales respectively, but English was characterised by different dialects and some regions of England, like Cornwall, had their own languages. These issues are important: if we are to explore both the penetration of political debate in the provinces and definitions of the public sphere, then we must be able to locate actual participants, even if we ultimately conclude that any Elizabethan public sphere was unsituated.

Research on oral culture, as well as on the survival of manuscript publication, has pointed to alternative forms of communication which

---

67 Joad Raymond, *Pamphlets and pamphleteering in early modern Britain* (Cambridge, 2003); Lake with Questier, *Anti-christ's lewd hat.*
68 Lisa Jardine and Antony Grafton, '"Studied for action": how Gabriel Harvey read his Livy', *Past & Present*, 128 (1990), pp. 30–78.

worked alongside print and may have reached parts of the population that print did not. Yet, even here, our sources can favour some groups of Elizabethans more than others. Private letters, for example, stand as evidence for the circulation of news via correspondence in their own right; they can also reveal oral communication through reportage. A small number of diaries and notebooks exist which can be illuminating: those of Henry Machyn, William Carnsew, the Italian, Alessandro Magno, and the 'Journall of matters of state'. Yet, with the exception of Carnsew – who was a relatively poor gentleman farmer in Cornwall – they reinforce the social and geographic bias towards the gentry and to the south-east of England of other sources.

One means by which it seems possible to fill this social gap is by using cases of seditious and slanderous words, recorded in assize indictments, letters to the privy council and other sources. The majority of individuals cited at the assizes or to the council were of yeoman status or below; they also include some cases brought against women. Yet, these too are problematic. The indictments are extant only for the home counties and are incomplete: the series for Hertfordshire does not start until 1576. Moreover, James Cockburn has suggested that the formula by which indictments had to be recorded has undermined, rather than under-pinned, the accuracy of their information. Particularly when compared to extant recognizances, it is apparent that names, occupations and places of residence were often wrong. Similarly, samples of files from the early seventeenth century have shown that between a third and a half of indictments recorded the date of the offence incorrectly – by as much as seventy-two days.[69] Whilst these problems have their greatest impact on statistical crime surveys and arguments on the seasonal incidence of crime and on the gender and social status of criminals, they are not without their effects for this study. The precise date of an offence may be insignificant, but the gender and social standing of individuals accused of seditious and slanderous words are important because they will help demonstrate the kinds of people who were involved in political debate.

There are also problems with how the offence – of seditious or slanderous words – was recorded. Inaccuracy in recording information on other types of offences – dates, value of goods stolen, whether the accused was an instigator or accessory – raises questions about how accurately seditious statements were recorded. Indictments do not record

---

69 J. S. Cockburn, 'Early modern assize records as historical evidence', *Journal of the Society of Archivists*, 5 (1974–7), pp. 220–7.

the entirety of the conversation, only those statements which were deemed seditious or slanderous. If this obliterates the context of the speech – what prompted it, who else took part, what others said – then there is also little sense of what the speaker deemed most important or representative of his views. Indeed, at best, indictments represent only what the justices saw as admissible in a court of law. And, of course, cases of seditious and slanderous words only record negative comments; more positive appraisals of the regime or of particular issues are harder to come by.

Equally, these problems are not insurmountable, especially if the evidence is used in a qualitative rather than quantitative way. Assize records may favour the south-east, booksellers' inventories may be few and far between, diaries may be even more scarce, but they provide windows into the political life of a range of people. Moreover, when collected together, they can often seem greater than the sum of their parts. There may be no extant assize indictments or book inventories for Cornwall, but William Carnsew's diary does point not only to the circulation of printed texts in his circle, but to verbal communication between gentry, tenants and servants. Equally, though inventories are rare, we are lucky to have ones for provincial markets in Cambridge, Norwich, Shrewsbury and Dublin. Roger Ward's inventory for Shrewsbury is particularly important because it may point to the circulation of texts in Wales, where otherwise information is limited. Moreover, what appear to be problems – such as the variety of languages in Elizabeth's dominions – can help us refine our understanding of the public sphere, which is particularly important in respect of new arguments that the public sphere existed in multiple, overlapping forms. If multiple public spheres existed, were they divided on regional lines? Did language create distinct spheres? Were different issues of interest to different groups of people, whether defined by geography, social status, gender, political or religious affiliation?

THE SOURCES FOR EXPLORING ELIZABETHAN PUBLIC DEBATE: BENEFITS

When perceived in a more positive light, the diverse aspects of the public sphere on which problematic sources can touch are as fundamental to our understanding both of the notion of the public sphere and of early modern politics as to Elizabethan public debate itself. While Habermas's concept of the public sphere was socially exclusive and political debate has, hence, been assumed to be the preserve of the elite, conversely, the 'public' in 'public sphere' is synonymous with the 'people'. By charting participants in Elizabethan public discourse we can begin to resolve this contradiction. It also enables us to trace more precisely how and why 'politics', and specifically political issues, penetrated Tudor society, socially and geographically. We should be able to indicate, if not comprehensively, what issues concerned different social groups or subjects in different parts of Elizabeth's realms. Thus we may be able, in Collinson's words, 'to find signs of political life at levels where it was not previously thought to have existed'.[70] Second, backed by an empirical approach that seeks to explore public debate in terms of real people in real places, they enable us to chart vertical political connections across society and explore the relationship between the centre and localities, monarchy and subject, which Collinson also highlighted as essential.

More broadly, they enable us to refine our understanding of contemporary culture, and specifically political culture. Peter Burke's seminal work on the polarisation of early modern culture has been widely challenged. Burke argued that, between 1500 and 1800, the 'little tradition' of unlearned, popular beliefs and attitudes became the sole preserve of yeomen, artisans and labourers rather than shared between them, the nobles and gentry, while the 'great tradition' of learned culture remained elitist.[71] It was a process stimulated as much by elite attacks on the 'little tradition' to establish moral and religious improvement, as by social polarisation caused by social and economic change, the growth of literacy, commercialisation and the impact of the Scientific Revolution. More recent research, however, has suggested that greater divisions were created by gender and by geographic location.[72] Similarly, reappraisals of the ownership and readership of cheap print – broadsides, chapbooks and small pamphlets – suggests that such texts were not confined to the poor and less literate audience for which they were designed but had a socially wide appeal.[73] Charting empirically the reaches of public political debate

---

70 Collinson, '*De republica Anglorum*', p. 11.
71 Peter Burke, *Popular culture in early modern Europe* (London, 1978). See also Keith Wrightson and David Levine, *Poverty and piety in an English village: Terling, 1525–1700* (London, 1979); Anthony Fletcher and John Stevenson (eds.), *Order and disorder in early modern England* (Cambridge, 1985); Peter Borsay, *The English urban Renaissance: culture and society in the provincial town, 1660–1770* (Oxford, 1989); Tim Harris, 'Problematising popular culture', in Harris (ed.), *Popular culture in England, c.1500–1800* (Basingstoke and London, 1995), pp. 1–27.
72 Susan Dwyer Amussen, 'The gendering of popular culture in early modern England' and David Underdown, 'Regional cultures? Local variations in popular culture during the early modern period', both in Harris (ed.), *Popular culture in England*, pp. 48–68 and 28–47 respectively.
73 Tessa Watt, *Cheap print and popular piety, 1550–1640* (Cambridge, 1991).

contributes both to our understanding of popular political culture, which has been largely neglected, and to the contemporary (popular) culture of which it was part. To what extent does public debate, and the attitudes and motives behind it, reinforce or undermine how we perceive contemporary culture and the social, gender and geographical divisions that characterised it? Was there a social polarisation, or distinction, in the issues that dominated public debate and the means by which they were articulated?

Thus, if this study is less concerned with one of the major elements in the historiographical and sociological debate on the public sphere – its role as a cause, and essential prerequisite, of the establishment of liberal-democracy[74] – then it is hoped that it can make a contribution to the smaller, but no less important fields of early modern politics and political debate.

74 See Introduction, pp. 10–11.

CHAPTER 2

Elizabeth I and the politics of intimacy

A series of meetings in 1579 provides a lens for reconstructing not only the process of Elizabethan counselling but also for understanding the wider structure of policy-making. At the end of March 1579, Lord Burghley, the earls of Leicester and Sussex, Sir Francis Walsingham, Dr Thomas Wilson (the two principal secretaries) and Lord Hunsdon (one of Elizabeth's cousins, governor of Berwick and warden of the East March) were appointed by Elizabeth to discuss Francis, duke of Anjou's offer of marriage. Their meetings began on 27 March and continued to around 3 April.[1] According to Gilbert Talbot, writing to his father, the earl of Shrewsbury, the meetings began at eight o'clock in the morning and continued until dinner, after which the councillors conferred with Elizabeth and then reconvened for further deliberation.[2] Councillors presented their individual opinions to Elizabeth on 13 April.[3] On 3 and 4 May, Elizabeth ordered the privy council to discuss three articles for the marriage treaty which had previously been referred or denied but were now resubmitted by Jean de Simier, Anjou's agent.[4] A long lull in organised discussions followed until 4 October, when selected councillors reconvened for further debate.[5] A larger group met two days later on the 6th, deciding 'to require hir Majesty, to shew hir own mynd . . . that the

---

1 Digest of Marriage proceedings 1570 – Nov. 1579, CP148, fo. 74v.
2 Gilbert Talbot to the earl of Shrewsbury, 4 Apr. 1579, LPL, Talbot Papers 3197, fo. 307r.
3 The remedyes sought for to preserve hir Maty and the state in peace, if she shall not marry, 13 Apr. 1579, CP148, fos. 39r–41v.
4 The councillors were Lord Burghley, Lord Chancellor Bromley, the earls of Lincoln, Sussex, Leicester and Warwick, Lord Hunsdon, Sir Francis Knollys, Sir James Croft, Sir Christopher Hatton, Thomas Wilson and Sir Walter Mildmay. The articles were that Anjou be crowned king, have joint authority with Elizabeth in patronage and have an annual income of £40,000 during his lifetime. CP148, fo. 75v.
5 An ordre how to procede to the discussion of the Questions moved concerning the Queens Mariadg with Monsieur Aniou, 2 Oct. 1579, CP148, fos. 47r–54v ; Notes on the marriage and succession, 4 Oct. 1579, CP148, fo. 58r.

resolutions might not be to the Contrary.'[6] Elizabeth's reaction – bursting into tears and then railing at them for not making a 'universall request' for her marriage – prompted a further meeting after which councillors 'offred to hir Majesty all our services in furderance of this Marriadg, if so it should lyk hir' on the 8th.[7]

Talbot perceived the meetings between 27 March and c.3 April as conducted by the privy council acting at less than its full strength but, though all attendees were councillors, the meetings can not be mapped onto those of the privy council as recorded in the council's registers.[8] According to both the first council register (1540) and Sir Julius Caesar, Chancellor of the Exchequer (1606–14), writing in 1625, the purpose of the registers was to act as a point of reference, recording the council's actions and copies of its letters, rather than the substance of debates.[9] Crucially, however, no privy council meetings are recorded at all between 26 and 30 March. Letters from the council were subscribed by a group of councillors on the 29th but this does not match the attendance of the conferences on the marriage: for instance, Leicester did not subscribe but Sir Francis Knollys did. A meeting occurred on 31 March but attendance was not recorded and so it cannot be mapped onto the marriage debates.[10] On 4 October, councillors selected to discuss the marriage – Burghley, Sussex, Leicester, Hunsdon, Walsingham, Wilson and Sir Christopher Hatton (vice-chamberlain) – met at Westminster while the privy council met at Greenwich. Attendance was also different: Sussex and Leicester did not attend the privy council meeting, while Knollys (treasurer of the Chamber), Sir Thomas Bromley (the Lord Chancellor), and the earls of Lincoln and Arundel did.[11] Likewise, Wilson's absence from the privy council meeting on 6 October suggests that the meeting to debate the marriage operated separately from the privy council's proceedings.[12]

6 The Anjou marriage, 6 Oct. 1579, Hatfield, CP140, fos. 6r–7v; At the counsell board at Greenwich, 6 Oct. 1579, NRO, Fitzwilliam (Milton) Political III, fos. 14r–16v; The summe & principall heades of a Conference at westminster touching Queene Elizabethes mariag, 4 Oct. 1579, Additional 4149, fos. 104r–105v; Minute by Lord Burghley on the marriage, 6 Oct. 1579, CP148, fo. 59r.
7 Messadg accorded to be delyvered to hir *Majesty*, 7–8 Oct. 1579, CP148, fos. 64r–65v.
8 LPL, Talbot Papers 3197, fo. 307r.
9 *Proceedings and ordinances of the privy council of England, 10 Richard II–33 Henry VIII*, ed. H. Nicolas (7 vols., London, 1834–7), VII, p. 4; Notes *concerning* the Priuate Counsell, 31 Oct. 1625, Additional 34324, fos. 238r–239v.
10 *APC*, XI, pp. 87–92.
11 Poin[t]s of state considered vpon by the Counselle at Grenwiche, 6 Oct. 1579, Additional 4149, fos. 104r–105v; *APC*, IX, p. 276.
12 *APC*, IX, p. 276.

Two other points are also suggestive. First, the council's clerks were not used as secretaries; this role was assumed by Burghley. Clerks could be asked to leave the council chamber: in 1541, William Paget was asked to leave when the council, meeting with the Chief Justices and 'other of the King's learned counsel', discussed Lord Dacre's case (though they talked so loudly he could hear them between two closed doors).[13] Stephen Alford has also shown how, in the 1560s, there was a close working relationship between Burghley and one of the clerks, Bernard Hampton, which blurred the lines between council business and Burghley's own.[14] However, the absence of the council's clerks could also suggest the meetings in March, April and October operated separately from those of the privy council. This is rendered more likely by the clear distinction Elizabeth made between the roles of the two groups on 3 May: the select group were to examine the marriage as a resolution to the problems raised by the succession and Catholic conspiracy, the privy council only specific articles in the marriage treaty. Though Burghley attempted to open up the debate on the marriage as a whole in the privy council, Elizabeth's message was clear: she did not want the privy council to debate policy, only elements for its realisation.[15]

This distinction in roles suggests a conscious organisation of counselling in which the privy council did not take the leading advisory role. The group of selected councillors acted as a probouleutic group, conducting the primary examination and discussion of policy. If Talbot's broad description can be believed, they did not initially present Elizabeth with one piece of advice (as per Michael Pulman's model[16]) but consulted with her on a daily basis.[17] Individual opinions were offered on 13 April and, more controversially, 7 October: Elizabeth's anger in October may have been a delaying tactic because, unresolved on the marriage, she could not 'shew to us [the councillors] any inclination of hir mynd'.[18] In contrast, the privy council was used to examine issues at a secondary stage: specific (albeit important) elements for the implementation of policy. Even when

---

13 William Paget to Sir Thomas Wriothesley, 27 June 1541, *Letters and Papers, Foreign and Domestic, Henry VIII*, ed. J. S. Brewer *et al.* (22 vols., London, 1864–1932), XVI, p. 450.

14 Pulman, *Elizabethan privy council*, p. 52; Alford, *Early Elizabethan polity*, pp. 11, 32, 57, 66, 125–6, 168, 173, 178, 207, 213–14.

15 Reports as to the conferences with Simier, 3–4 May 1579, CP148 fos. 42r–43v.

16 Pulman has argued that, in the 1570s, the privy council discussed policy, came to a conclusion and then offered this conclusion as advice to Elizabeth, for her to accept or reject. Pulman, *Elizabethan privy council*, ch. 4.

17 LPL, Talbot Papers 3197, fo. 307.

18 Message from the Council on the marriage, 7–8 Oct. 1579, CP148, fo. 64v. I have examined this episode in more detail in Mears, '"Personal rule" of Elizabeth I', ch. 3.

probouleutic discussion was opened up to a larger number of individuals – as on 6 October – meetings continued to operate independently of the privy council.

Restricting probouleutic debate to a small group of personally selected councillors was particularly appropriate for an issue – Elizabeth's marriage – which she defined as one of the *arcana imperii* ('mysteries of state') reserved for her own judgement and on which she had sought to restrict debate in council, parliament and public debate since her accession. Indeed, the circumscription of counsel in the spring of 1579 ran alongside orders Elizabeth issued to limit uninformed debate, rumour, gossip and opinion within and beyond the court.[19] Similar examples of probouleutic groups can also be found for negotiations with the Archduke Charles of Austria in 1567, Henry, duke of Anjou in 1571 and in the later stages of negotiations with Francis, duke of Anjou, in April 1581.[20] But to what extent was this organisation of counsel – using groups of specially selected individuals to explore issues first and then either opening up questions to the privy council as a whole or deputing them to work out the details of a policy – characteristic of Elizabethan policy-making as a whole?

PROBOULEUTIC GROUPS

Probouleutic groups were used throughout the first thirty years of Elizabeth's reign for a variety of important issues: meetings appear to have occurred on 27 December 1559;[21] 20 June 1562 (to discuss the proposed interview between Elizabeth and Mary Stuart);[22] 1 May, 4 June and 24 and 26 September 1565 (to discuss the Darnley marriage);[23] at

19 LPL, Talbot Papers 3197, fo. 307r.
20 Elizabeth to the earl of Sussex [draft], 12 Dec. 1567, SP70/95, fos. 131r–133v; Burghley to Sir Francis Walsingham, 3 May 1571, DWL, Morrice D, p. 275; same to same, 5 June 1571, DWL, Morrice D, p. 285; Elizabeth to same, 8 June 1571, DWL, Morrice D, pp. 288–9; same to same, 9 July 1571, DWL, Morrice D, pp. 298–9; the earl of Leicester to same, [15 Aug. 1571], DWL, Morrice D, p. 339; [Journal des Négotiations des commissaires et Ambassadeurs français du 24 avril au 1ᵉʳ mai 1581], Discours envoyé au Roy et a Monseigneur son frere avec la depesche de Messᵉ le Prince Dauphine et aultres Commissaires, du XXVᵉ d'avril 1581, PRO31/3/28, fos. 285r–287v.
21 Cecil to Sir Ralph Sadler and Sir James Croft, 31 Oct. 1559, Additional 33591, fo. 250v (endorsement). I would like to thank Stephen Alford for this reference.
22 Reasons pro contra, 20 June 1562, Cotton Caligula B. 10, fos. 211r–212v; Arguments pro contra the progr[ess to] Northumberland, 20/30 June 1562, Cotton Caligula B. 10, fos. 209r–210v.
23 Determination of the privy council [endorsed by Cecil], 1 May 1565, SP52/10/40, fo. 91r (another copy: A determination of the privy counsell, 1 May 1565, Harleian 6990, fo. 68); A summary of the consultacion and advise [edited by Cecil], 4 June 1565, Cotton Caligula B. 10, fos. 301r–308v; A consultation at westminster begon the 24. and renewed the 26. of September [Cecil's hand], 26 Sept. 1565, Cotton Caligula B. 10, fos. 358r–359v; *APC*, VII, pp. 105, 217–19, 260–4.

Hampton Court on 30 and 31 October 1568 (on Scotland);[24] 29 April 1570 (to examine whether Mary Stuart should be released and restored to her crown);[25] 18 July 1571 (to respond to answers given by both Regent Lennox and Mary Stuart's supporters to English proposals for a cessation of arms in Scotland);[26] on or before 15 January 1576 (whether to supply financial aid to William of Orange and the Dutch rebels);[27] and on 22 March 1578 (to investigate the possibility for a mediated peace between Philip II and the Dutch).[28]

Further meetings took place on 10 July 1580 at Nonsuch (on the Low Countries);[29] on 18 September 1580 at Richmond (to discuss instructions for Robert Bowes, whose mission to Scotland to force Esmé Stuart, duke of Lennox, to surrender custody of the strategically important castle of Dumbarton had reached an impasse);[30] and in March 1581, when Walsingham reported to Thomas Randolph, English envoy to Scotland, that only certain councillors had 'been made acquainted with the cause [the earl of Morton's arrest]'.[31] In March 1583, Burghley, Walsingham, Bromley and Sir Walter Mildmay (Chancellor and under-treasurer of the Exchequer and a privy councillor since 1566) met at Burghley's London house to discuss the building of an Anglophile party after the forced departure of Lennox after the Ruthven Raid the previous August,[32] and on 9 July 1586, Burghley, Hatton and Walsingham were appointed to discuss the proceedings of Leicester's expedition to the Netherlands, including

---

24 Hampton Court, matters of Scotland [Cecil's hand], 30 Oct. 1568, CP155, fo. 128r.
25 Hampton Court in the presence of the Queens Majesty, 29 Apr. 1570, Cotton Caligula C. 2, fos. 63r–65v; MacCaffrey, *Shaping of the regime*, pp. 376–7.
26 A consultation on the affairs of Scotland, 18 July 1571, Cotton Caligula C. 3, fo. 188r–188v.
27 The meeting may have taken place on or before 9 January, as de Guaras reported 'a committee of them [councillors] has been appointed to debate and reply to the pretensions of the envoys; the committee consisting of Lord Chancellor Bacon, Lord Treasurer Burghley, the earl of Leicester, and Secretary Walsingham'. Yet, as attendance does not match that noted in Burghley's memoranda, there may have been two meetings or de Guaras may have been mistaken in his identification of which individuals were selected. De Guaras to [Zayas?], 9 Jan. 1576, *CSP Spanish*, II, pp. 518–19; To be answered to them of Holland [Burghley's hand], 15 Jan. 1576, SP70/137, fos. 25r–26v; MacCaffrey, *Making of policy*, pp. 200–4.
28 Notes on the Low Countries, 22 Mar. 1578, SP83/5/93; 'Journal of Sir Francis Walsingham from December 1570 to April 1583', *Camden Miscellany VI* (Camden Society, os, 106; London 1871), p. 35.
29 Memorial on the Low Countries [Burghley's hand], 10 July 1580, SP83/13/37; The heades of certaine speaches delivered by her Majestie vnto the Ambassador of Spayne, 10 July 1580, SP94/1/52, fos. 146r–148v.
30 A purpose of Councell at Richmond for directinge of Robt Bowes, 18 Sept. 1580, Cotton Caligula C. 6, fo. 82r–82v; Walsingham to Bowes, 18 Sept. 1580, SP52/28/85.
31 Walsingham to Thomas Randolph, 18 Mar. 1581, SP52/29/46.
32 Walsingham to Robert Bowes, 2 Mar. 1583, SP52/31/48.

the issue of financial cost.[33] Walsingham told Leicester that Elizabeth 'can by no meanes (as I have heretofore wrytten vnto your Lord) indvce that the cavses of that contrye shood be svbiect to any *debate in* counsell . . . otherwyse then as she her self shall dyrect'.[34]

Walsingham's reports make clear that the conferences in March 1581, March 1583 and July 1586 operated separately from the privy council; the other meetings cannot be mapped onto those of the privy council, suggesting they also functioned as probouleutic groups. The privy council did not meet on 20 June 1562, 1 May, 4 June, 24 and 26 September 1565, 18 July 1571 or 22 March 1578.[35] Where privy council and probouleutic group meetings occurred on the same day (10 July 1580) attendance does not match: Hatton did not attend the privy council meeting while Sir James Croft (Controller of the Household and privy councillor since 1570) and Wilson (both excluded from the probouleutic meeting) did.[36] Moreover, memoranda arising from meetings in 1570, 1576 and 1578 are in Burghley's hand, not one of the council's clerks'.

The loss of the privy council registers for the early months of the reign make it impossible to establish definitively if the meeting on 27 December 1559 – which Alford has seen as a landmark in establishing the conciliar workings of the early Elizabethan polity – was that of the privy council or a probouleutic group. Similar lacunas in the registers between 3 May 1567 and 24 May 1570, and between June 1582 and February 1586, make the remaining meetings less easy to pin down, but there are some suggestive hints. Memoranda by Burghley for the meetings on 29 April 1570 and 15 January 1576 report that the discussions took place in Elizabeth's presence and with her active involvement. This was a situation unprecedented for a formal privy council meeting as far as the registers attest and suggests the meetings functioned separately from the council.[37] The privy council met on the same day – 18 September 1580 – when Robert Bowes's instructions were discussed and it is difficult to ascertain whether the meetings were conducted separately.[38] Burghley's report of the debate, 'A purpose of

---

33 Walsingham to Leicester, 9 July 1586, Cotton Galba C. 9, fos. 290v–291r.
34 Walsingham to Leicester, 25 Apr. 1586, Cotton Galba C. 9, fo. 193v. For Elizabeth's own reference to how counsel had been limited see, Instructions of Sir Thomas Heneage sent by the queen to the earl of Leicester, 10 Feb. 1586, Cotton Galba, C. 8, fo. 22r.
35 *APC*, VII, pp. 105, 214–15, 217–19, 260–1; VIII, pp. i, 36–7; XI, pp. 78–9, 86–7. There are no entries recorded between 27 April 1565 and 10 May 1565, 29 May 1565 and 9 June, and 16 July 1571 and 2 August 1571, so it is possible that the registers for these periods are missing.
36 *APC*, XII, pp. 91–2.
37 Cotton Caligula C. 2, fos. 63r–65v; SP70/137, fos. 25r–26v.
38 *APC*, XII, pp. 202–3.

Councell at Richmond', does not list attendance and is ambiguously phrased: does 'Councell' mean the privy council or a less defined body or action?[39] Walsingham's letter to Bowes of the same date does not clarify the issue; nor is it clear from his comments whether Elizabeth was present during discussion.[40] However, as a probouleutic group was clearly used to explore the continuing response to the duke of Lennox's hegemony in Scotland in March 1581, it is possible that this was also the format for discussion of the same issues the previous September.

Probouleutic debate was dominated by an inner ring of individuals: Burghley, Leicester, Sussex and (after his appointment as secretary in 1573) Walsingham were the central figures, selected to attend most (or, in Burghley's case, all) of the meetings identified above for which we have evidence of attendance. Walsingham's fellow principal secretary between 1577 and his death in 1581, Dr Thomas Wilson, was also important. All combining household office with their conciliar status, their roles as probouleutic counsellors derived from their personal relationships with the queen rather than conciliar office. In Burghley's, Walsingham's and Wilson's case this was reinforced by the specific duties conferred on them as principal secretaries which meant they acted as the main channel of communication to and from Elizabeth.[41] Burghley's pre-eminence continued after his appointment to the Lord Treasurership primarily because of his close relationship with Elizabeth but also because the new principal secretary, Sir Thomas Smith, found it difficult to obtain Elizabeth's signature or draw her to a resolution and because Burghley maintained a close working relationship with Wilson and Walsingham.[42] The relative insignificance of conciliar status in determining the composition of the inner ring was further highlighted by the inclusion of Lord Hunsdon in the marriage debates in spring 1579. Never politically prominent, he was Elizabeth's cousin and had been able to assume unofficially an *ad hoc* role as counsellor prior to his formal appointment.[43] It underlined the extent to which these meetings functioned separately from the privy council.

39 Cotton Caligula C. 6, fo. 82r–82v.
40 SP52/28/85.
41 Taviner, 'Robert Beale', pp. 111–13.
42 Smith to Burghley, 15 Oct. 1572, Harleian 6991, fo. 15; same to same, 18 Dec. 1572, Harleian 6991, fo. 71r; same to same, 7 Jan. 1573, Harleian 6991, fo. 19r–19v; same to same, 8 Jan. 1573, Harleian 6991, fo. 21r–21v; same to same, 10 Jan. 1573, Harleian 6991, fo. 23r–23v; Mary Dewar, *Sir Thomas Smith: a Tudor intellectual in office* (London, 1964), pp. 172–4; Wilson to Burghley, 1 Oct. 1578, SP12/126/1; Walsingham to same, 7 Apr. 1585, Harleian 6993, fos. 76r–77v.
43 Lord Hunsdon to Burghley, 24 Aug. 1577, Cotton Caligula C. 5, fo. 42r–42v. Hunsdon was the son of William Carey (c.1500–28) and Henry VIII's mistress, Mary Boleyn, sister of Anne.

It is also important to note that Elizabeth's use of probouleutic groups was not a method of counselling imposed unwillingly on councillors: Burghley has been described as 'an instinctive conciliarist' but he and his colleagues' actions were actually less monochromatic.[44] The groups formed to discuss the treaty articles for Elizabeth's proposed marriage with Henry, duke of Anjou, in 1571 and Anglo-Scottish relations in 1583 appear to have been initiatives suggested by Burghley and Walsingham respectively.[45] Moreover, there is also evidence to indicate that councillors took initiatives to counsel Elizabeth informally and *ad hoc*. In July 1571, Burghley told Walsingham, 'I have done my uttermost, and so hath other Counsellors here my Lord Keeper [i.e. Sir Nicholas Bacon] hath earnestly dealt in it, and so hath my Lord of Sussex, my Lord of Leicester hath also in my dealing ioyned earnestly with me'.[46] Similar examples stretch across the period: learning Elizabeth had reversed her previous day's decision not to demand that Leicester resign the governor-generalship of the Netherlands, Burghley and Walsingham 'this morning [1 April 1586] at sermon tyme . . . cam to hir Majesty' to persuade her to return to her original decision.[47]

'AD HOC' AND EXTRA-CONCILIAR COUNSEL

As these examples testify, probouleutic debate operated alongside informal, *ad hoc* counselling by individuals or small groups for both the formulation of policy and oversight. In June 1565, Elizabeth sought advice informally from Leicester on the marriage proposals of Charles IX and, in 1569, of Archduke Charles of Austria. In 1569, she sought advice from Sir Francis Knollys (on Mary Stuart) as well as Burghley (on the duke of Norfolk) and Sir Ralph Sadler – a privy councillor since November 1558

---

44 Alford, *Early Elizabethan polity*, passim, but especially pp. 210, 168, 176–9; Collinson, 'Monarchical republic', pp. 418–20.
45 DWL, Morrice D, p. 285; SP52/31/48.
46 Cecil to Walsingham, 9 July 1571, DWL, Morrice D, pp. 308–9.
47 Burghley to Leicester, 6 Dec. 1585, Cotton Galba C. 8, fo. 197r; same to same, 27 Dec. 1585, Cotton Galba C. 8, fo. 215r–215v; Thomas Dudley to same, 11 Feb. 1586, Cotton Galba, C. 9, fo. 79r–79v; William Davison to same, 17 Feb. 1586, Cotton Galba, C. 9, fo. 83v; same to same, 28 Feb. 1586, Cotton Galba C. 8, fo. 43r; Burghley to same, 6 Mar. 1586, Cotton Galba C. 9, fo. 116r; Sir Thomas Sherley to same, 7 Mar. 1586, Cotton Galba C. 9, fo. 122r–122v; Burghley to same, 31 Mar. 1586, Cotton Galba C. 9, fo. 153r–153v; same to same, 1 Apr. 1586, Cotton Galba C. 9, fo. 167r; Walsingham to same, 11 July 1586, Cotton Galba C. 9, fo. 300r. See also: DWL, Morrice D, p. 285; Burghley to Walsingham, 9 July 1571, DWL, Morrice D, pp. 308–9; Smith to Burghley, 18 Dec. 1572, Harleian 6991, fo. 17r; Harleian 6991, fo. 21r–21v; Leicester to Walsingham, 20 July 1578, SP83/7/73, fos. 1r–2v; Burghley to same, 10 Aug. 1581, Harleian 6265, fo. 52r–53v.

and a former warden of both the East and Middle Marches – on the Northern rebels.⁴⁸ On hearing the news of the death of the earl of Mar, Regent of Scotland, in November 1572, Elizabeth talked 'to and fro' with Leicester about the need to support the Anglophile Scots. Convinced by his arguments that a speedy response was imperative, she immediately sought Burghley's opinion on what support would be most effective.⁴⁹ Indeed, as Principal Secretary, Sir Thomas Smith found that Elizabeth would sign nothing without consulting with Burghley first – a habit he felt she sometimes used as a delaying tactic.⁵⁰ The Vice-Chamberlain, Sir Christopher Hatton, though a peripheral member of the probouleutic group (he can only be definitely identified as attending the meeting on 10 July 1580), was a central figure in *ad hoc* counselling from 1577. He was a recognised source to tap, in the earl of Morton's words, for 'the better knallege of heir hienes mynd': in 1578 Morton recommended the commendator of Dunfermline seek his advice as to how best to frame offers of Anglo-Scottish amity so they would be accepted.⁵¹ Hatton was active in advising Elizabeth to accept Dunfermline's offers and worked with Burghley, Wilson and Leicester in the following months to persuade her to deliver the promised financial bonds to the Dutch States-General.⁵² With Burghley and Walsingham in 1586, he not only tried to persuade Elizabeth not to recall Leicester from the Netherlands but also dealt with a wide range of problems, from the supply of men and money to allaying Elizabeth's irritation provoked by rumours that Leicester's wife was making sumptuous preparations to join her husband.⁵³

---

48 Cecil to Smith, 3 June 1565, Lansdowne 102, fo. 110v; Knollys to Elizabeth, 1 Jan. 1569, CP155, fo. 74r; Cecil to same, 6 Oct. 1569, Cotton Caligula C. 1, fo. 456r–456v; Sir Ralph Sadler to Cecil, 9 Jan. 1569, Additional 33593, fos. 107r–108v; Cecil to Sadler, 14 Jan. 1569, Additional 33593, fo. 129r; same to same, 18 Jan. 1569, Additional 33593, fo. 141r–141v.

49 Leicester to Burghley, 4 Nov. 1572, CP7, fo. 57r. See also, Harleian 6991, fo. 21r; Sussex to Burghley, [1576?], CP9, fo. 49r; Wilson to same, 15 Sept. 1578, SP83/9/23; Walsingham to same, 14 Oct. 1578, SP12/126/9, fo. 19r. Examples of Sussex's and Walsingham's role can be seen in Sussex to Walsingham, 29 Aug. 1578, SP83/8/59 and Walsingham to the Lord Deputy of Ireland, 1 Jan. 1582, CP11, fo. 76r.

50 Smith to Burghley, 12 Mar. 1574, Lansdowne 19/86, fo. 187r; Dewar, *Sir Thomas Smith*, pp. 173–4.

51 The earl of Morton to Walsingham, 9 July 1578, SP52/27/47, fo. 98r.

52 Walsingham to Sir Christopher Hatton, 16 June 1578, Additional 15891, fo. 46v; same to same, 27 June [1578], Additional 15891, fos. 47v–48r; Morton to Walsingham, 9 July 1578, SP52/27/47, fo. 98r; Edmund Tremayne to same, 29 July 1578, SP83/7/91; Dr Thomas Wilson to the ambassadors, 9 Sept. 1578, SP83/9/16; same to same, 15 Sept. 1578, PRO, SP83/9/23.

53 Cotton Galba C. 9, fo. 79r–79v; Cotton Galba C. 9, fo. 116r; Cotton Galba C. 9, fos. 122r–123v; Sherley to Leicester, 21 Mar. 1586, Cotton Galba C. 9, fos. 139v–140r; Walsingham to same, 9 July 1586, Cotton Galba C. 9, fo. 290v.

Though this *ad hoc* counselling was dominated by the inner ring of counsellors used for probouleutic discussions, it also involved other household officials, agents and ambassadors. Extant evidence is far less abundant than for figures like Burghley, Walsingham and Leicester, but a qualitative assessment suggests that three key figures were Sir Nicholas Throckmorton, ambassador to France and to Mary Stuart, Sir Thomas Heneage, Treasurer of the Chamber, and Thomas Randolph, frequently agent or ambassador to Scotland. Throckmorton was a central figure in the first decade of the reign: the Spanish ambassador, Guzman de Silva, actually mistook him for a privy councillor in 1565.[54] He advised Elizabeth on the proposed interview with Mary in 1562; on appointing a resident agent with Admiral Coligny, the Huguenot leader in France, in 1563; and on the marriage negotiations with the Archduke Charles in 1564.[55]

Heneage's position as one of Elizabeth's intimates is suggested by a number of episodes. He seems to have first caught Elizabeth's eye in 1565, but was an established point of access to her by the following year: Hugh Fitzwilliam, chargé d'affaires in France, petitioned him to persuade Elizabeth to grant him a sufficient allowance or recall him.[56] In 1570, he had assumed roles of an *ad hoc* secretary and a counsellor, defending himself from accusations about the latter by arguing he only gave advice when it 'pleased her [Elizabeth] to aske myne opinyon'.[57] He also worked with Burghley to convey information to Elizabeth and Smith.[58] With Burghley and Leicester, he was both one of Walsingham's main correspondents in 1571 and one of Lord Buckhurst's during the latter's embassy to France in February and March 1571 to discuss the Anjou marriage.[59] Buckhurst and Heneage were close friends but their correspondence had a definite purpose: Buckhurst was keen to use Heneage as a point of contact

54 Guzman de Silva to Philip II, 9 July 1565, *CSP Spanish*, I, p. 447.
55 Sir Nicholas Throckmorton to Elizabeth, 17 Apr. 1562, SP70/36, fos. 38r–46v, much of which is in cipher and not fully deciphered. For a draft, with parts marked to be put in cipher, see SP70/36, fos. 58r–67v; Cecil to Smith, 4 Oct. 1564, Lansdowne 102, fo. 102r; Throckmorton to Elizabeth, 6 Jan. 1563, SP70/48/31, fo. 75r–75v; same to same, 13 Jan. 1563, SP70/48/77, fo. 193r. Throckmorton's role is examined in more detail in Sebastian Walsh, '"Most trusty and beloved": friendship, trust and experience in the exercise of informal power within the early Elizabethan polity – the case of Sir Nicholas Throckmorton' (BA dissertation, Durham, 2004).
56 De Silva to Philip II, 23 July 1565, *CSP Spanish*, I, p. 454; Taviner, 'Robert Beale', pp. 111–14.
57 Sir Thomas Heneage to Cecil, 12 Aug. 1570, CP157, fo. 55r.
58 Cecil to Heneage, 29 July and 30 July 1570, both in *HMC Finch*, I, p. 10.
59 Taviner, 'Robert Beale', pp. 99–100; Heneage to Burghley, 16 July 1571, SP70/119, fo. 34r–34v. Buckhurst's letters to Heneage are calendared in *HMC Finch*, I, pp. 13–18 and are now in the Beinecke Rare Books and MSS Library, Yale University but are available as photocopies in the British Library (RP36). See in particular the letters dated 8, 11, 15, 21, 24 Feb. and 8 Mar. 1571, RP36, pp. 5–26.

with Elizabeth, 'from whos mouthe your majesty might understand their particular discours with much better speche then my pen coulde geue them.'[60] In 1586, Heneage was appointed by Elizabeth as a special messenger to convey her opposition to Leicester's assumption of the governor-generalship of the Netherlands in 1586.[61] He was also part of an intelligence network among Elizabeth's other intimates.[62]

Thomas Randolph's importance as an extra-conciliar counsellor was most clearly demonstrated during his embassy to Scotland to secure Morton's release and impeach Lennox's hegemony in 1581. His advice overrode contrary counsel from inner ring counsellors in London, Hunsdon at Berwick and the earl of Huntingdon (president of the Council of the North) at York to stimulate Elizabeth into reversing her decision to use military force.[63] Already harbouring reservations about the success of a military enterprise, Randolph's direct observation of the Scottish court only confirmed his opinion.[64] Though sceptical of how far Lennox could be trusted to maintain the amity, he saw no option but to investigate a mediated settlement.[65] Elizabeth specifically asked him to outline his views at further length; her orders for the suspension of military preparations and then dismissal of troops followed shortly afterwards.[66] However, Randolph's position as an intimate was established as early as 1565: Throckmorton, another of Elizabeth's extra-conciliar intimates, was instructed to work closely with him in 1565 to try and prevent the Darnley

---

60 For their friendship, see BL, RP36; Taviner, 'Robert Beale', pp. 113–14.
61 Instructions for sir Thomas Heneadge, 10 Feb. 1586, Cotton Galba, C. 8, fos. 22r–26v; Wilson to Burghley, 18 Oct. 1578, SP12/126/11.
62 Cecil to Heneage, 16 Aug. 1570, *HMC Finch*, I, pp. 10–11; SP70/119, fo. 34r–34v.
63 Bowes to Burghley and Walsingham, 1 Jan. 1581, SP52/29/1; same to same, 3 Jan. 1581, SP52/29/2; same to [?], 16 Jan. 1581, Harleian 6999, fo. 24r–24v; Walsingham to Randolph, 25 Jan. 1581, SP52/29/14; [Walsingham] to [Huntingdon], 15 Mar. 1581, Harleian 6999, fo. 84r–84v; Lord Hunsdon to Walsingham, 30 Mar. 1581, Harleian 6999, fo. 138r–138v; [Walsingham] to the earl of Huntingdon and Hunsdon, 31 Mar. 1578, Harleian 6999, fo. 140r. Elizabeth was also unnerved by the French ambassador's repeated warnings that Henry III would not tolerate any infringement of Franco-Scottish relations and worried about the financial cost and political aims of military intervention. Harleian MS 6999, fo. 84r–84v; Walsingham to Randolph, 15 Mar. 1581, SP52/29/47; Mauvissière to Henry III, 10 Feb. 1581, BN, Fonds français 15973, fos. 398r–399r, 400v–402r; same to Catherine de Médici, 28 Feb. 1581, BN, Fonds français 15973, fo. 409r; same to Henry III, 10 Mar. 1581, BN, Fonds français 15973, fos. 414v–415r; same to same, 24 Apr. 1581, BN, Fonds français 15973, fo. 434v; Privy council to Hunsdon, 10 Apr. 1581, Harleian MS 6999, fo. 165r.
64 Randolph to [Walsingham], 8 Feb. 1581, Harleian 6999, fos. 39r–40v.
65 Harleian 6999, fo. 39r; Walsingham to Randolph, 7 Mar. 1581, SP52/29/44; SP52/29/47.
66 Walsingham to Randolph, [18 Mar.] 1581, SP52/29/46; same to Hunsdon, 5 Apr. 1581, Harleian 6999, fo. 162r (draft); privy council to same, 10 Apr. 1581, Harleian 6999, fo. 165r; Walsingham to same, 10 Apr. 1581, Harleian 6999, fo. 166r.

marriage. He was privy to the plot to murder David Riccio, Mary Stuart's secretary, in March 1566, and was part of a network circulating this information among Burghley, Leicester and Elizabeth. He was left to distribute pensions among the Scots at his discretion and, when Elizabeth discovered that Hunsdon was withholding payment in 1572, Hunsdon was overruled.[67] Though his advice was sometimes accepted only slowly, or ignored, he was perceived by some Scots as influential: Lord William Maitland of Lethington, Mary Stuart's secretary from 1561 and a regular ambassador to England for both Mary and Regent Moray, believed he had been instrumental in persuading Elizabeth to back the king's party in 1570.[68]

Henry Killigrew (agent and ambassador), John Somers (clerk of the signet) and Edward Stafford (gentleman pensioner) provide further lenses through which we can understand Elizabeth's use of household officials, agents and ambassadors. All three were employed on sensitive missions: part of Killigrew's mission to Scotland in 1572 was to realise plans to deliver Mary Stuart to the Scots for her trial and execution without indicating it was an English initiative.[69] They were distinct from other ambassadors and agents, however, in that Elizabeth consulted with them directly before making decisions (though she did not necessarily accept their advice). Despite receiving reports in July 1578 from Walsingham and Lord Cobham (ambassadors to the Netherlands) and William Davison (resident agent in Antwerp), that there was 'noo hoppe' of a negotiated settlement between the States and Don John of Austria (Philip II's half-brother and governor-general of the Netherlands) and that she should deliver to the States the bonds for £100,000 she had promised in March, Elizabeth refused to make a decision until she had consulted with Somers, who had accompanied Walsingham and Cobham.[70] On 16 July 1578 she

---

67 Katharine Pitman Frescoln, 'Thomas Randolph: an Elizabethan in Scotland' (Ph.D. thesis, West Virginia, 1971), pp. 211, 253–61, 346–8.

68 Ibid., pp. 285–7.

69 Secret instructions for Henry Killigrew, [10] Sept. 1572, CP7, fo. 47r; Amos C. Miller, *Sir Henry Killigrew: Elizabethan soldier and diplomat* (Leicester, 1963), pp. 132–6. See also pp. 30–45, 74–82, 93–5, 101–16. Stafford was regularly sent to Henry III, Catherine de Médici and Anjou between 1578 and 1580, initially to stop Anjou's negotiations with the States-General and subsequently over the marriage. All missions are listed in Gary M. Bell, *A handlist of British diplomatic representatives, 1509–1688* (Royal Historical Society, 16, London, 1990). Some details are erroneous, for instance, the names of Norris's and Walsingham's secretaries 1566–1571 and 1570–73 respectively (see, Taviner, 'Robert Beale, pp. 74–83). For Somers, see also Conyers Read, *Mr Secretary Walsingham and the policy of Queen Elizabeth* (3 vols., Oxford, 1925), III, p. 75.

70 Lord Cobham to Burghley, 12 July 1578, SP83/7/52, fo. 1r; Walsingham to Leicester, 14 July 1578, Cotton Galba C. 6 (part 2), fo. 75r; Walsingham to Burghley, 18 July 1578, SP83/7/57

conferred with him and Burghley, continuing the discussion 'privately' with Somers the following day, before summoning Burghley.[71] She continued to consult with Somers on the marriage in 1581 when he served Cobham, now resident ambassador in France, and acted as a special envoy to Francis, duke of Anjou.[72] In January 1580, Stafford was in direct correspondence with Elizabeth during his special embassy to France, referring Burghley to his letters to the queen to learn of the 'great deale of circumstance' he had reported.[73] Elizabeth specifically delayed conveying to Cobham her answer to proposals for a non-dynastic Anglo-French alliance until 'she shall haue had some conference with mr stafforde *touching* Monsieurs [i.e. Anjou's] disposition that waye.'[74]

They also assumed *ad hoc* counselling and secretarial roles, like other inner ring counsellors, if less regularly. In 1572, Killigrew advised Elizabeth to 'assure herself and her estate against the malicious enemies and underminers thereof' by dealing with Mary Stuart.[75] In the winter of 1584–5, supporting Sir Ralph Sadler as custodian of Mary Stuart, Somers offered advice, via Burghley and Walsingham, on local men able to assist Lord St John (proposed as Mary's new custodian) and possible candidates for the post of superintendent of the household.[76] He had already sounded out one man for the latter (William Agarde) and recommended, if he was appointed, that he should be made a gentleman usher extraordinary to enhance his standing.[77] The lengthy memorandum on the Anjou match dating from March 1579, attributed in *HMC, Salisbury* to Stafford was actually written by Sussex: it is in his hand and there is a close similarity of arguments, phrases and spelling with his letter to Elizabeth of 28 August 1578.[78] Though this indicates that Stafford was

(calendared as 14 July, Walsingham has written 'xviiith of July' at the close of the letter); same to Davison, 22 June 1578, SP83/7/27; same to Burghley, 2 Sept. 1578, SP83/9/3x, fos. 61r–62v.

71 Privy council to Cobham and Walsingham [minute edited by Burghley], 18 July 1578, SP83/7/64; Burghley to same, 18 July 1578, SP83/7/65.

72 SP83/7/65; Walsingham to John Somers, 19 July 1581, SP78/5/121, fo. 237r; same to same, 11 July 1581, SP78/5/110, fo. 212r.

73 Sir Edward Stafford to Burghley, 28 Jan. 1580, SP78/4a/11.

74 Memorandum to Cobham [draft], 24 Dec. 1580, CP11, fo. 65r.

75 Henry Killigrew to Elizabeth, 8 Feb. 1572, SP70/122, fo. 67r.

76 Somers to Walsingham, 6 Nov. 1584, *Sadler state papers*, II, p. 444; same to same, 13 Jan. 1585, ibid., II, p. 483; same to Burghley, 25 Jan. 1585, ibid., II, pp. 497–9; Sadler to Burghley, 25 Jan. 1585, ibid., II, p. 495; same to same, 5 Feb. 1585, ibid., II, p. 501; Somers to Burghley, 1 Mar. 1585, ibid., II, pp. 528–9.

77 *Sadler state papers*, II, pp. 497–9; Somers to Burghley, 21 Jan. 1585, ibid., II, p. 492.

78 Obyectyons to be made against the marryage, Mar. 1579, CP148, fos. 12r–16v; *HMC Salisbury*, II, p. 245 but cf. Conyers Read, *Lord Burghley and Queen Elizabeth* (London, 1960), pp. 210, 562 (fns. 18, 21); Sussex to Elizabeth, 28 Aug. 1578, CP10, fos. 30r–33v. Comparing CP148, fos. 12r–16v with CP10, fos. 30r–33v show the hand and spelling is the same, e.g. 'wordell' for 'world'.

neither contributing to the probouleutic examination of the match nor evaluating the issue independently, he was still involved in informal counselling. In October 1578 he persuaded Elizabeth to seek further advice from one of the Principal Secretaries before he completed a letter she had instructed him to write to Francis, duke of Anjou, to halt the departure of his envoy, Jean de Simier, dispatched to pursue the marriage negotiations. This may not have been the sum of his involvement: reporting his actions to Burghley, Stafford stated he had 'by her Commandement delte in yt [the marriage]' though there is no extant evidence to reveal what this may have been.[79] Both Stafford and Somers assumed *ad hoc* secretarial roles: Stafford was close enough to be called upon before Walsingham, Wilson or Burghley to write the projected letter to Anjou and trusted enough to be made privy with Elizabeth's dealings when consultation was otherwise 'both sildome & slender'.[80] Somers was recommended to be Walsingham's temporary replacement as Principal Secretary in 1583 during his embassy to Scotland, though he 'fyndethe hym selfe unapt for the seruyce.'[81]

A final key extra-conciliar counsellor was the merchant and financier, Sir Thomas Gresham.[82] Like Throckmorton, he appears to have submitted written advice, on debasement and foreign exchanges, shortly after Elizabeth's accession and may have been attendant on the new queen within days of her elevation.[83] But his real significance lay in acting as a major clearing house of continental news and information. This included not only news from Antwerp, where he was primarily based (his deputy or manager, Richard Clough, assuming these duties when Gresham returned to England) but also from Scotland, France, Denmark, Sweden,

---

Two of the three sections of the memorandum cover the same areas as the letter. The objections, answers and benefits are similar in order and content; for the benefits, those of the memorandum follow the letter's order, for the discommodities two of the points were brought forward in the memorandum, which also contains a fuller passage on the queen's fertility. The phrasing of the objections is often exactly the same and large parts of the answers appear copied or closely paraphrase the letter.

79 Stafford to Burghley, 27 Oct. 1578, William Murdin (ed.), *Collection of state papers, relating to affairs in the reign of Queen Elizabeth from the year 1571 to 1596 . . .* (London, 1759), p. 318. It is unclear from Stafford's comment – 'Mr secretarye' – whether he meant Walsingham or Wilson. The privy council registers suggest both were regularly at court at this time.

80 Leicester to Walsingham, 7 Aug. 1578, SP83/8/14, fo. 3r.

81 Walsingham to Burghley, 6 Aug. 1583, Harleian 6993, fo. 54v.

82 For a brief biography of Gresham, see Ian Blanchard, 'Sir Thomas Gresham, c. 1518–1579', in Ann Saunders (ed.), *The Royal Exchange* (London, 1997), pp. 11–19.

83 'Information of Sir Thomas Gresham, mercer, towching the fall of the exchaunge, MDLVIII', in J. W. Burgon, *The life and times of Sir Thomas Gresham* (2 vols., London, 1839), I, pp. 483–6. For Gresham's attendance on Elizabeth see ibid., I, pp. 216–18.

Germany, Spain, Rome, Naples, Venice, Constantinople and Tripoli.[84] Residence in Antwerp and a temporary position as English ambassador to Margaret, duchess of Parma (Regent of the Netherlands), on Thomas Chaloner's appointment to Spain, were important but it was his extensive network of servants and contacts with other merchants that facilitated his unrivalled access to news. In addition to Clough in Antwerp, Gresham's network extended from Richard Payne in Middleburg and Harry Gerbrande in Dunkirk – two ports from which, he argued, it was necessary for Elizabeth to have daily intelligence – to John Gerbridge in Toledo as well as Robert Hogan and Jaspar Schetz (two of Philip II's servants).[85] Indeed, such was his monopoly over news and access to good communications that the earl of Sussex, when on embassy at the Imperial court, directed all his letters from Vienna via Gresham at Antwerp.[86]

As with probouleutic and *ad hoc* counselling, counsellors took initiatives in extra-conciliar counsel too. In June 1578, recognising that a negotiated settlement to the Dutch revolt was unlikely and aware that Elizabeth was reluctant to accept Sluys as a gage for further loans to the States, Walsingham used William Davison to persuade Elizabeth to deliver the promised bonds for £100,000. He told Davison to set down in a letter to Wilson 'such reasons as may induce her majestie to forbeare the repayment of the twenty thousande poundes due uppon the first receipt made by the bondes of the hundreth thousande' and proceeded to detail those reasons, reflecting closely arguments he would later expound to Burghley.[87] His use of Wilson was deliberate: as his fellow secretary, Wilson was a recognised channel of communication to Elizabeth; it would also make Davison's advice more likely to appear independent than if Walsingham conveyed the letter.

THE NATURE OF ELIZABETHAN COUNSEL AND ELIZABETH'S ROLE IN POLICY-MAKING

Elizabethan counselling was therefore neither institutionalised nor conciliar, as Pulman argued, but informal and dynamic. Elizabeth took an active role in organising, managing and seeking counsel, constructing probouleutic groups or consulting with individuals on an *ad hoc* basis.

84 Ibid., I, pp. 298–300, 361, 235–7 and see the various letters from Gresham in the early 1560s, pp. 268–74, 292–3, 296–300, 308–10, 332–4.
85 Ibid., I, 278–9, 290, 362–7, 389–97; II, pp. 7, 19–22, 131–42, 181.
86 Ibid., II, pp. 181–2.
87 SP83/7/27; SP83/9/3x, fos. 61r–62v.

She also appointed small groups of individuals to consult with foreign ambassadors and agents, in a similar format to probouleutic debates, and report back to her:[88] for example, on 13 August 1562 with Marshall de Vielleville, Catherine de Médici's envoy.[89] As a result, the privy council did not act as the principal advisory body, though it continued to play an important role both in the examination of secondary issues (e.g. the treaty articles in 1579) and in administration. Collective, probouleutic debate functioned separately from council meetings, in terms of personnel, time and, occasionally, location. *Ad hoc* counselling was also both frequent and significant. Moreover, though all members of the probouleutic groups were privy councillors, their selection derived from their personal relationship with Elizabeth rather than their conciliar status. Neither was Elizabeth's role in the act of counselling passive: she consulted actively with both probouleutic groups (March–April 1579) and individuals, talking 'to and fro' with Leicester about the impact of Mar's death on Anglo-Scottish relations.

The active role played by Elizabeth and the use of informal and non-institutionalised methods were also characteristic of other stages of policy-making: information gathering and decision-making. Elizabeth received information directly and indirectly through letters that she read herself or asked others to summarise; she also asked counsellors to summarise the contents of letters they received from agents and ambassadors.[90] On 9 August 1581, Burghley delivered Walsingham's letters from France to the queen, 'shewinge her also that I had others directed to my self. but she said she would firste reade her owne'. Having done so, Elizabeth demanded that Burghley report the contents of his letters, provoking a dispute because he argued it was too long and detailed for him to condense. Elizabeth eventually conceded to hear the entire letter.[91] She also received information informally, through court gossip.[92] The receipt

88 Burghley to Walsingham [copy], 3 May 1571, DWL, Morrice D, pp. 275–7; Elizabeth to Smith [draft], 8 June 1571, Cotton Caligula C. 3, fos. 183r–185v (calendared as written to Smith but a copy – DWL, Morrice D, pp. 288–9 – has Walsingham as the recipient which seems more likely). The conference had with the Bishop of Rosse, 8 Aug. 1571, Cotton Caligula C. 3, fos, 92r–93v; Questions to be moved to Mendoza, 17 Mar. 1578, SP94/1/14; Copy of the same with answers, [n.d.], SP94/1/14a; Questions to Mendoza [20 Mar. 1578], SP104/163, fo. 98r; 'Journal of Sir Francis Walsingham', p. 35; Mendoza to Philip II, 19 Mar. 1578, *CSP Spanish*, II, pp. 564–6; [Walsingham] to Bowes, 9 May 1583, SP52/31/17.
89 Cecil to Throckmorton, 17 Aug. 1562, SP70/40, fo. 158r; *APC*, VII, pp. 125–6; Wallace T. MacCaffrey, 'The Newhaven expedition, 1562–1563', *Historical Journal*, 40 (1997), pp. 5–9.
90 Harleian 6991, fo. 23r; Harleian 6265, fo. 52r–52v; CP7, fo. 57; Walsingham to Bowes, [27 Feb.] 1583, SP52/31/45; Cotton Galba C.9, fo. 83r.
91 Harleian 6265, fo. 52r–52v.
92 Cotton Galba C. 9, fo. 79v.

of information, and ensuing debate, was subject to Elizabeth's schedule and health: on 6 February 1568, she read only two of Sussex's letters from the Imperial court about the negotiations for the marriage with the Archduke Charles because they arrived just as she was going out hunting and she did not want 'to lose the day's pleasure.'[93] In November 1572, Leicester had to wait before discussing Mar's death with her because, at six o'clock, she 'was at her wonted repose'.[94] In 1578, a 'payne . . . in her face' prevented consultation on the Netherlands.[95]

Elizabeth also took the lead role in decision-making. In April 1571 she decided that Walsingham should only deliver to Charles IX and Catherine de Médici her answers to the French articles for the marriage treaty with Henry, duke of Anjou, and not additional articles proposed by the English. Upon 'some late intelligence brought thence', she believed that if she stuck fast to her answers on Anjou's free exercise of religion, they would be accepted.[96] On hearing that Lennox had seized possession of Dumbarton castle in August 1580, she immediately dispatched Robert Bowes to James VI's court to seek Lennox's surrender of the castle and ordered Hunsdon to prepare troops along the border to force surrender militarily if Bowes's mission failed.[97] Decision-making could be painfully slow and subject to Elizabeth's vacillation: characteristically, having slept on her bellicose instructions to Bowes in 1580, she revoked the final clause the following day.[98] The reasons behind this will be explored more fully in chapter 3 but it can be noted here that it was not always because she was pathologically indecisive or financially stingy.[99] She did find it difficult to resolve personal questions, like marriage, but issues central to the agenda also raised practical and politically sensitive problems. In 1580, Elizabeth considered that any hasty offer of military assistance would bring the Scots more quickly into a civil war and that Lennox would seize the king, take him to Dumbarton whence he would either remove him to France or

---

93 De Silva to Philip II, 7 Feb. 1568, *CSP Spanish*, II, p. 6.
94 CP7, fo. 57r.
95 Walsingham to Hatton, 9 Oct. 1578, Additional 15891, fo. 49v. See also Cecil to Throckmorton, 20 Aug. 1567, SP59/14, fo. 49r.
96 Burghley to Walsingham, 19 Apr. 1571, DWL, Morrice D, pp. 250–1.
97 Bowes to Walsingham, 22 Aug. 1580, SP52/28/70, fo. 135r–135v; same to Burghley and Walsingham, 27 Aug. 1580, SP52/28/72, fo. 139r–139v; Walsingham to Leicester, 31 Aug. 1580, Cotton Caligula C. 3, fos. 614r–615; same to Bowes, 31 Aug. 1580, SP52/28/76, fos. 147r–148v. See also Burghley to Leicester, 12 Jan. 1586, Cotton Galba C.9, fo. 16v.
98 Walsingham to Bowes, 1 Sept. 1580, SP52/28/77, fo. 149r. See also Burghley to Walsingham, 5 June 1571, DWL, Morrice D, p. 284.
99 Keith M. Brown, 'The price of friendship: the "well-affected" and English economic clientage in Scotland before 1603', in Mason (ed.), *Scotland and England*, pp. 139–62.

call in foreign aid.[100] Proposals to resolve the succession politically that included Mary's exclusion from the English succession and a tripartite agreement (with France and Scotland) condoning her deposition and preventing her restoration to the Scottish crown were also problematic: to condone Mary's deposition was to sanction precisely the behaviour that Spain, France and the Papacy were perceived to be engineering against her.[101]

The active role Elizabeth played in policy-making, her use of probouleutic groups, informal and extra-conciliar counselling and the ways her actions intersected with those of other political actors raise two immediate issues central to our understanding of the structure of Elizabethan court politics. First, they demonstrate that counsel was polymorphic and policy-making interactive. Elizabeth not only managed and organised counselling on an informal and dynamic basis but counsellors adopted similar methods. Combined with pervasive humanist-classical concepts of citizenship – to argue in the law courts, debate in public assemblies and counsel a monarch – and attitudes towards female monarchy, this meant the line between Elizabeth actively seeking counsel and receiving unsolicited advice was increasingly blurred. Second, they undermine the importance of the privy council as the principal advisory and policy-making body. In effect, they demand a new paradigm for policy-making be reconstructed, conceived in terms of the networks of individuals active in policy-making, either directly through interaction with Elizabeth or with key counsellors and actors.

ELIZABETH'S NETWORK OF COUNSELLORS AND AGENTS

Burghley, Leicester, Sussex, Walsingham, Hatton, Wilson, Throckmorton, Heneage and Randolph were at the core of Elizabeth's network, followed by outer rings formed by others like Killigrew, Somers, Stafford and Gresham. Yet, the informal and dynamic nature of counselling in particular raises questions about how a new paradigm for Elizabethan court politics can be reconstructed beyond this. Counselling is a key focus because it enables us to see the interaction between individuals, but as already noted, the line between Elizabeth seeking counsel and receiving unsolicited advice was indistinct. Compounded further by the fact that counsel was an ongoing process, it questions whether the paradigm

---

100 SP52/28/77, fo. 149r.
101 Degrees, 1577, Cotton Caligula C. 3, fo. 543r–543v.

should be defined only in terms of individuals from whom Elizabeth actively sought advice. There is also a secondary question of whether her acceptance of counsel should act as a barometer of an individual's importance.

In sketching an outline of the paradigm (focusing on representative individuals, rather than providing a definitive list), I have privileged active consultation with individuals, as well as secretarial duties. These were areas of direct interaction with Elizabeth that suggest a degree of intimacy and trust. Offering unsolicited advice has been incorporated if there are signs of solicited consultation with Elizabeth too: Killigrew, Somers and Stafford provide examples. The acceptance of counsel is not used as a standard: Elizabeth's active role in policy-making, her attitudes towards monarchical power and counsel and her personal understanding of the problems she faced make this less acceptable. After all, the central characteristic of the structure of Elizabethan policy-making outlined above is precisely her active role.

Forming an extra, peripheral dimension to the inner core of probouleutic and *ad hoc* counsellors were the Lord Keeper, Sir Nicholas Bacon, Sir Francis Knollys, the earls of Lincoln and Ormond and Lord Hunsdon. Bacon, Knollys and Lincoln had all been regular members of probouleutic debate in the 1560s (as far as evidence attests) and active in *ad hoc* counselling or consultation.[102] But Bacon was not selected for probouleutic debate after 1572 (he died in 1579) and neither Knollys nor Lincoln after 1576, though Lincoln was part of the delegation (with Burghley, Sussex and Leicester) to inform Simier of the queen's and privy council's answers to the three treaty articles he had resubmitted for further consideration in May 1579.[103] Both Bacon and Knollys, however, continued to offer advice to Elizabeth informally in letters, either directly or through one of the secretaries.[104]

Hunsdon's only definite appearance in probouleutic debates occurred in 1579, though he also attended (with Randolph) the dinner organised by Burghley for Dunfermline in July 1578 and was selected, with

---

102 Cotton Caligula B. 10, fos. 301r–308r; Cotton Caligula B. 10, fos. 358r–359v; Cotton Caligula C. 2, fos. 63r–65v; Cotton Caligula C. 3, fos. 92r–93v; DWL, Morrice D, pp. 308–9, 339; Robert Tittler, *Nicholas Bacon: the making of a Tudor statesman* (Athens, OH, 1976), pp. 139–43; Alford, *Early Elizabethan polity*, pp. 78–9, 140–2, quoting SP63/18, fo. 62v; Knollys to Cecil, 2 June 1568, Cotton Caligula C. 1, fo. 119r; Harleian 6991, fo. 17r.

103 SP70/137, fos. 25r–26v; Answer made by the lordes Treasorer, Admirall . . ., 4 May 1579, CP148, fo. 44r.

104 Sir Nicholas Bacon to Elizabeth, 15 Sept. 1577, Additional 15891, fo. 4r–4v; Tittler, *Bacon*, pp. 178–80, 183–4; Sir Francis Knollys to Wilson, Harleian 6992, fo. 89r.

Walsingham, to interview the Scottish ambassador in May 1583.[105] As governor of Berwick, Anglo-Scottish relations were his particular field of expertise and he offered advice from at least 1575 (on the dispute between Sir John Forster, warden of the Middle March, and Sir John Carmichael, keeper of Liddesdale).[106] Ormond's position was distinctive. A favourite, nearly comparable to Leicester and Hatton, the earl does not appear to have been active in policy-making but he did exploit his access to Elizabeth to advance or defend his own family's and clientele's interests, particularly against the Lord Deputies, like Sir Henry Sidney and Sir John Perrot, whose attempts to establish personal authority in Ireland conflicted with Ormond's own.[107]

Orbiting at a further remove were the wider groups of agents, ambassadors as well as officials who held posts in England, Wales and Ireland. Even here, however, it seems possible to make a tentative sketch of how the lines of Elizabeth's main network extended into this wider group. For instance, Thomas Sackville, Lord Buckhurst, Sir Henry Norris and Fulke Greville seem to have been favoured by Elizabeth, while Dr Valentine Dale was not. Buckhurst was appointed a special ambassador to France to negotiate the match with Henry, duke of Anjou; Norris (resident ambassador of France, 1566–71) acknowledged he was inexperienced and relied heavily on one of his secretaries, John Barnaby, yet he and his wife were close friends of Elizabeth's.[108] Greville accompanied Duke John Casimir, son of the Elector Palatine who had led English forces in support of the Dutch the previous year, back to Germany in 1579 and Francis, duke of Anjou to Antwerp in 1581; he was also special ambassador to the Netherlands in 1582 charged with enquiring into William of Orange's recovery from a recent assassination attempt. In contrast, though Valentine Dale was appointed to replace Walsingham as resident ambassador to France in 1573, Elizabeth cavilled at her own choice: he was 'but a simple man & she liketh not that he shoulde deale in them [the marriage negotiations]'.[109]

105 Burghley to Randolph, 21 July 1578, Harleian 6992, fo. 104r; SP52/31/17.
106 Cotton Caligula C. 5, fo. 42r–42v; Hunsdon to Burghley, 19 Aug. 1578, Cotton Caligula C. 5, fo. 129r; Harleian 6999, fo. 138r–138v; Harleian MS 6999, fo. 165r; Hunsdon to Walsingham, 26 June 1581, Harleian MS 6999, fos. 211r–212r.
107 Ciaran Brady, 'Political women and reform in Tudor Ireland', in Margaret MacCurtain and Mary O'Dowd (eds.), *Women in early modern Ireland* (Edinburgh, 1991), pp. 85–6; John Dudley to Leicester, 29 Mar. 1566, SP15/13, fo. 8r.
108 Taviner, 'Robert Beale', pp. 74–8, 87; Leicester to Hatton, 11 Sept. 1582, Additional 15891, fos. 72v–73r; Elizabeth to Lady Norris, 22 Sept. 1597, Folger, Folger MS V.b.214, fo. 68r.
109 Harleian 6991, fo. 19r.

Thomas Leighton and Robert Bowes provide additional lenses for defining the network at this level. Like Killigrew and Stafford, Leighton was employed on sensitive diplomatic missions: in 1568, he carried Elizabeth's letters to Mary Stuart; in 1574, he was sent to France ostensibly to commiserate on Charles IX's poor health but really to remonstrate with Catherine de Médici for Francis, duke of Anjou's imprisonment at Vincennes.[110] He made contact with Anjou and conveyed his requests for English aid to escape, actions which were only nullified by Charles IX's death and Anjou's subsequent transferral to the Louvre.[111] Bowes had an intensive period of activity as an envoy or ambassador to Scotland between 1577 and 1583, during which he was involved in negotiations (often with Randolph) to strengthen Anglo-Scottish amity after Morton's fall in 1578 and secure his release, and Lennox's removal from power, in 1581. Yet neither had a central role in counselling: there is no evidence that Leighton offered advice, while Bowes's advice – specifically on challenging Lennox's ascendancy in 1580–1 and restoring Anglo-Scottish amity in 1582 – was made either at the request of the privy council or his own initiative.[112] Moreover, his advice on the need to use force against Lennox in 1581 was ultimately overruled by Randolph's.[113] Important in the diplomatic network, Leighton and Bowes appeared to operate on the periphery of Elizabeth's inner networks. Similar examples – those who were frequently employed as special agents and ambassadors – are Thomas Wilkes, Daniel Rogers and Thomas Bodley.[114]

110 Hasler, II, pp. 458–9; Read, *Walsingham*, I, pp. 282–3, 362–5. He was also dispatched twice to the Netherlands in December 1577–February 1578 to threaten Don John with full English intervention if he did not enter into peace negotiations and to France in 1588 to urge Henry III to proclaim Guise a traitor, to back the Huguenots and offer English aid in 1588. See Read, *Walsingham*, III, pp. 214–15.
111 Read, *Walsingham*, I, pp. 282–3, 362–5.
112 Cotton Caligula C. 5, fo. 129r; Bowes to Walsingham, 10 May 1580, SP52/28/20, fo. 43r; Privy council to Burghley and Walsingham, 13 Sept. 1580, Cotton Caligula C. 6, fos. 80r–81v; Bowes to Walsingham, 7 Sept. 1582, in *The correspondence of Robert Bowes of Aske*, ed. John Stevenson (Surtees Society, 14; London, 1842), pp. 180–1.
113 SP52/29/1; Harleian 6999, fo. 138r–138v; Huntingdon to Walsingham, 2 Apr. 1581, Harleian 6999, fo. 152r.
114 Wilkes was special agent or ambassador to Spain 1577–8, the Netherlands in 1578, 1582 and 1586, as well as to France and the Netherlands in the 1590s. Rogers was agent (1576–8, 1578–9) and special ambassador (1578) to the Low Countries and had audiences with Casimir (1576 and 1578–9), the Elector Palatine (1577, 1578–9) and the Landgrave of Hesse (1577); and was special ambassador to the Emperor in 1580 (during which time he was imprisoned) and Denmark, 1587–8. (See also J. A. van Dorsten, *Poets, patrons and professors: Sir Philip Sidney, Daniel Rogers, and the Leiden humanists* (Leiden and Oxford, 1962), pp. 9–75.) Bodley was one of Stafford's secretaries during his residency in France and then agent; he was special ambassador to Denmark and the duke of Brunswick in 1585 and Denmark again in 1588. Both Wilkes and

Elizabeth's network was male-dominated but not exclusively male. Parallel to the inner ring of counsellors was a group of female intimates often holding feed or unfeed privy chamber posts.[115] They included Frances Newton, Lady Cobham; Elizabeth Fitzgerald, countess of Lincoln; Elizabeth Brooke, marchioness of Northampton; Anne, countess of Warwick; Mary Shelton, Lady Scudamore; Lady Mary Sidney; Elizabeth, Lady Carew; Bridget Skipworth-Cave; Blanche Parry; Lady Dorothy Stafford; and her daughter, Elizabeth, Lady Drury.[116] Even more than secondary male figures, evidence of their political activity is fragmentary, but evidence points to them acting in two crucial ways: as barometers of the queen's moods or channels of communication, even for her most trusted advisers, and as negotiators in marriage diplomacy, especially in the 1560s. In a memorandum of 1559, the Spanish ambassador, the Count of Feria, identified Elizabeth Brooke, marchioness of Northampton as 'in high favour with the queen [and] has served His Majesty when opportunity has occurred'; she was cultivated by both de Quadra and Guzman de Silva, successive Spanish ambassadors.[117] Lady Cobham, the countess of Lincoln and Mary Sidney were all in contact with Feria's wife, Jane Dormer, one of Mary I's most trusted ladies-in-waiting.[118] In August 1571, Elizabeth told Lady Drury that the earl of Rutland should return from France knowing that she was in correspondence with him and would inform him.[119] Lady Cobham and Lady Stafford asked Sussex, the Lord Chamberlain, to request Lady Scudamore to return to court, though it is unclear from Sussex's letter whether they

Bodley were also English representatives on the Dutch council of state the late 1580s and early 1590s. See Bell, *Handlist of British diplomatic representatives*, passim.

115 The wages of the ladies and others of the Privie Chamber and bedchamber, 22 May 1589, Lansdowne 59/22, fo. 43r–43v which includes the dates of warrants (or letters patent) for appointments; Payments of money to the Ladies and Gentlemen of the Privy Chamber, 1579, Lansdowne 104/18, fo. 41r. See also Lansdowne 29/68, fo. 161r–161v (1580), Lansdowne 34/30, fo. 76r–76v (1582).

116 De Silva to Philip II, 8 Oct. 1565, *CSP Spanish*, I, pp. 487–8; *Russia at the close of the sixteenth century, comprising the treatise 'Of the Russe Common Wealth' by Dr Giles Fletcher, and the travels of Sir Jerome Horsey, knt*, ed. Edward A. Bond (Haklyut Society; London, 1856), pp. 233–4; Mendoza to Philip II, 27 Jan. 1582, *CSP Spanish*, III, p. 274; Merton, 'Women who served', pp. 96–7.

117 Bishop de Quadra to Philip II, 13 Sept. 1561, *CSP Spanish*, I, p. 214; Memorandum of the count of Feria, 1559, ibid., p. 36; de Silva to the duchess of Parma, 23 Sept. 1564, ibid., p. 381. The marchioness never held an official post in the privy chamber but was a long-standing intimate of Elizabeth's.

118 *CSP Spanish*, I, p. 214; bishop of Aquila to the duchess of Parma, 7 Sept. 1559, ibid., p. 96; Merton, 'Women who served', pp. 166–7; *CSP Spanish*, I, p. 454.

119 Elizabeth Stafford to the earl of Rutland, 16 Aug. 1571, *HMC Rutland*, I, pp. 95–6.

were acting on Elizabeth's command.[120] A letter appointing Sir Edward
York to a command of infantry in Ireland was delivered by the countess of
Warwick's messenger on the Signet Office's behalf.[121] Even the likes of
Leicester, Burghley and Heneage maintained contacts with privy chamber
women.[122] In April 1587, Lady Cobham made use of her intimacy with
Elizabeth to try and smooth Burghley's return to court in the aftermath of
Mary's execution: she advised him 'to hasten your commynge hether' and
promised to deliver a letter to Elizabeth.[123] Lady Scudamore was an
intermediary for Heneage.[124] Indeed, Robert Beale's 'Instructions for a
Principall Secretarie . . . for Sir Edwarde Wotton' (1592) explicitly
acknowledged the importance of privy chamber women in facilitating
the Principal Secretary's duties: 'Learne before your accesse her majesties
disposicion by some in the Privie Chamber, with whom you must keepe
credit: for that will stande yow in much steede'.[125]

In 1559, Mary Sidney acted as Elizabeth's go-between with de Quadra
in the Archduke Charles's marriage negotiations until de Quadra tried to
force Elizabeth's hand on accepting Charles's visit and to bind her to
accepting his proposal: Elizabeth retreated from the negotiations and
denied anyone had commission from her to deal with the ambassadors.
'I am obliged to complain of somebody in this matter, and have complained of Lady Sidney only, although in good truth she is no more to
blame than I am, as I have said privately.'[126] Male members of the privy
chamber also played political roles: John Tamworth (gentleman of the
privy chamber and keeper of the privy purse, 1559) was special ambassador
to Mary in 1565; Charles Howard (gentleman of the privy chamber, 1558)

120 Sussex to Lady Scudamore, n.d., Additional 11042, fo. 131r.
121 Merton, 'Women who served', pp. 183–4.
122 Taviner, 'Robert Beale', pp. 243–4; Lady Cobham to Burghley, 10 Apr. 1587, SP12/200/20, fo.
   38r; same to same, 15 June 1584, SP12/171/25, fo. 43r; Cecil to Heneage, 30 July 1570, *HMC
   Finch*, I, p. 10; SP15/13, fos. 7r, 8r–8v; John Dudley to Leicester, 29 Mar. 1566, SP15/13, fo. 111r–
   11v. Leicester's sister, Mary Sidney, and sister-in-law, the countess of Warwick, were unfeed
   members of the privy chamber and Elizabeth's intimates.
123 SP12/200/20, fo. 38r; SP12/171/25, fo. 43r. See also Merton, 'Women who served', pp. 168–9.
124 W. Poyntz to Heneage, 4 July 1583, *HMC Finch*, I, pp. 24–5; same to same, 23 July 1583, ibid.,
   p. 25.
125 'Instructions for a Principall Secretaries obserued by R. B. for Sir Edwarde Wotton A. D. 1592',
   Additional 48149, fo. 8r.
126 *CSP Spanish*, I, p. 95; de Quadra to the Emperor, 2 Oct. 1559, ibid., pp. 98–9; same to same, 16
   Oct. 1559, ibid., p. 101; same to Philip II, 13 Nov. 1559, ibid., pp. 111–13; same to same, 18 Nov.
   1559, ibid., p. 115. For a more detailed discussion of this episode see Natalie Mears, 'Politics in
   the Elizabethan privy chamber: Lady Mary Sidney and Kat Ashley', in Daybell (ed.), *Women
   and politics in early modern England*, pp. 67–82.

and George Howard (gentleman usher from c.1558) were special ambassadors to France in 1559.[127]

Indeed, there are occasional glimpses that privy chamber servants performed some of the representative functions that Starkey controversially argued were undertaken by Henry VIII's staff. Specifically, John Somers recommended that William Agarde should be appointed a gentleman usher extraordinary if he was made superintendent of Mary Stuart's household.[128] Membership of the privy chamber would enhance Agarde's standing – he would be one of Elizabeth's body servants – and his authority: he would be a representative of the crown. It was a symbolic gesture: Agarde clearly had not served in the privy chamber and was neither a body servant nor one of Elizabeth's intimates. But it played on the relationship between intimacy and representation evident under Henry VIII and of which Somers was acutely aware. He knew how sceptical Mary was of her custodians' authority as he later advised that Elizabeth should write directly to her informing her of Sir Amias Paulet's appointment and emphasising his authority derived directly from (and depended only on) Elizabeth.[129]

There was a high degree of homogeneity among key personnel at and across all levels of Elizabeth's network. Though Sussex seems to have been temporarily frozen out of full correspondence with Walsingham and Cobham during their embassy to the Netherlands in 1578 – probably because of his support for the Anjou match – generally the inner ring of counsellors worked together consistently.[130] In 1571, Burghley, Leicester, Sir Nicholas Bacon and Lord Howard of Effingham sought to persuade Elizabeth to accept the marriage proposal of Henry, duke of Anjou; in 1586, Burghley, Walsingham and Hatton worked to allay Elizabeth's anger over Leicester's assumption of the governor-generalship of the Netherlands.[131] This co-operation extended beyond the inner ring: Burghley, Hunsdon and Randolph dined with Dunfermline prior to the Scottish ambassador's first audience with Elizabeth in July 1578; strategy may have been discussed.[132] Working relationships were also established with Elizabeth's female intimates and privy chamber men. Burghley's main contacts were Lady Cobham and Lady Carew; he also had contacts

---

127 Subsidy roll (royal household), assessment, 18 Elizabeth [1575–6], NA, E179/69/93, m. 2.
128 *Sadler state papers*, II, pp. 497–9.
129 Starkey, 'Representation through intimacy', pp. 53–5; *Sadler state papers*, II, pp. 528–9.
130 Sussex to Walsingham, 6 Aug. 1579, SP83/8/13.
131 DWL, Morrice D, pp. 308–9; Cotton Galba C. 9, fo. 79r–79v; Cotton Galba C. 9, fo. 153r–156r.
132 Harleian 6992, fo. 104r.

with Heneage and some of the grooms, like Thomas Gorges and Thomas Knyvet.[133] Killigrew's brother, William, was appointed a groom of the privy chamber on 31 October 1578.[134] These were underlined by direct connections: Hatton was Captain of the Guard and Vice-Chamberlain.[135]

This cohesion was reinforced not only by familial connections – in Simon Adams's words, 'they were practically all each others' cousins in the most literal sense' – but by clienteles, shared ideological outlooks, educational experience and, for some (like Burghley, Bacon and Knollys), Edwardian political experience.[136] Burghley, Bacon and Killigrew were brothers-in-law as were Knollys and Hunsdon; two of Knollys's daughters, Lettice and Elizabeth, married, respectively, Leicester (1579) and Thomas Leighton (1578).[137] Randolph married Walsingham's cousin, Ann, in 1571 and though she died in childbirth three years later, Walsingham continued to refer to him as 'cousin'. Familial connections between male counsellors and Elizabeth's female intimates in the privy chamber were strong. Lady Mary Sidney was Leicester's sister, the countess of Warwick his sister-in-law. Lincoln's wife, Elizabeth, Edward Stafford's mother (Lady Stafford) and sister (Lady Drury) were all royal intimates.[138] Knollys's wife, Catherine, was one of Elizabeth's intimates until her death in 1569; Leighton's wife, Elizabeth, was regularly in attendance from 1583.[139] Social connections were also important. For instance, Somers, Killigrew and Randolph were friends: in his will, Somers left Randolph six spoons with 'bigge knoppes'.[140] Wilson, Killigrew and Leighton had been members of John Dudley, the duke of Northumberland's clientele in the early 1550s which Leicester, his son, subsequently inherited.[141]

There was a shared perception of key political issues – the succession, Mary Stuart and Catholic conspiracy – manifested in letters of advice (by Burghley in 1569, Bacon in 1577 and Knollys in 1578), discourses like Wilson's 'A discourse touching this kingdoms perils' (1578), *pro contra*

133 SP12/200/20, fo. 38r; SP12/171/25, fo. 43r; *HMC Finch*, I, p. 10.
134 Lansdowne 59/22, fo. 43v.
135 Cecil to Heneage, 22 May 1569, *HMC Finch*, I, p. 6; same to same, 9 Aug. 1569, ibid., p. 6; ibid., p. 10; Wright, 'Change in direction', pp. 163–5.
136 Adams, 'Eliza enthroned?', p. 69; Alford, *Early Elizabethan polity*, pp. 24–5.
137 Tittler, *Bacon*, pp. 49–52; Miller, *Killigrew*, pp. 96–100.
138 Lansdowne 59/22, fo. 43r.
139 Wright, 'Change in direction', p. 170. Knollys's daughters, Elizabeth and Lettice, were also maids of honour, though Lettice's importance was negative after her marriage to Leicester and effectual banishment from court.
140 Randolph to Killigrew, [18 November] 1562, *CSP Foreign*, V, p. 621; NA, 49 Brudenell (PROB11/68).
141 Adams, 'Dudley clientele', pp. 241–2.

memoranda for probouleutic debates (especially on the Netherlands in 1576 and the Anjou match in 1579) and correspondence between individuals on Anglo-Scottish and Anglo-Dutch relations.[142] Despite disagreements on how to challenge Lennox's ascendancy most effectively in 1581, Randolph and Hunsdon shared others' recognition of the strategic danger posed by Scotland – and a frustration that Elizabeth had failed to cultivate amity by distributing pensions to the Scots.[143] One senses that Walsingham's anger at Randolph's reports may have arisen as much from a feeling that he was breaking ranks over how Anglo-Scottish amity was to be achieved as from his stated reasons that a negotiated settlement would be dishonourable and ineffective.[144] The only area in which there appears to have been significant disagreement – and where historians have been able to sustain convincingly arguments of factionalism prior to the 1590s – was over Ireland. Yet, though clear policy differences existed, particularly between Sussex and Leicester in the 1560s, these were partly a product of the increasing competition for royal favour and the office of Lord Deputy. Despite the quagmire of Irish politics, the Lord Deputyship was seen as an important springboard to a dazzling political career and the sponsorship of a successful candidate an important barometer of one's standing as a patronage broker.[145]

142 Cotton Caligula C. 1, fo. 456r–456v; Cotton Caligula C. 3, fo. 543r; Additional 15891, fo. 4r–4v; Harleian 6992, fo. 89r; A discourse touching this kingdoms perils, 2 Apr. 1578, SP12/123/17 (see also Albert J. Schmidt, 'A treatise on England's perils', *Archiv für Reformations Geschichte*, 46 (1955), pp. 243–9); Consideration of the state of holland [Burghley], 17 Oct. 1575, SP70/135, fos. 256r–257v; To be considered in the matter of Holland and zeeland, 12 Jan. 1576, SP70/137, fos. 14r–15r; A consideration of the cause of the Low Countries [Burghley], 2 June 1578, CP9, fo. 115r–115v; Opinion on whether to send aid [Wilson], [Mar.] 1578, SP83/5/117; To be advised in the motion of mariadg, 27 Mar. 1579, CP148, fos. 23r–24v; CP10, fos. 30r–33v; W. J. Tighe, 'The counsel of Thomas Radcliffe, earl of Sussex, to Queen Elizabeth I concerning the revolt of the Netherlands, September 1578', *Sixteenth Century Journal*, 18 (1987), pp. 323–31; Answers to the obiections made agaynst the marriadg with Mons. Dallanson, 27 Mar. 1579, CP148, fos. 25r–26v; Memoranda on the marriage, 29 Mar. 1579, SP78/3/17, fos. 34r–35r; The perils that may happen to the Q. Majesty if she lyve unmarried, 31 Mar. 1579, CP148, fos. 29r–30v; A collection of the perils to be feared to ensew if hir Majesty shall not marry, 1 Apr. 1579, CP148, fos. 32r–38v; CP148, fos. 39r–41v; Hatfield, CP148, fos. 12r–16v; State of affairs, [1579?], SP12/133/23, fos. 50r–52v; A discourse towching the diseased state of the realme and the remedies [n.d.], Harleian 1582, fos. 46r–50v; Hatfield, CP140, fos. 6r–7v; Walsingham to Hatton, 23 June 1578, Additional 15891, fo. 48v–49r; SP52/29/14; Sussex to Walsingham, 6 Jan. 1581, SP52/29/4; Hatton to Burghley, 26 Sept. 1580, Additional 15891, fos. 27r–27v; *Correspondence of Robert Dudley, earl of Leycester, during his government of the Low Countries in the years 1585 and 1586*, ed. John Bruce (Camden Society, original series, 27; London, 1844), passim; Alford, *Early Elizabethan polity*, passim.

143 For example: Harleian 6999, fo. 138r–138v.

144 SP52/29/47.

145 For example, see Brady's detailed accounts of Sussex's and Sidney's fortunes in Ireland and at court, Ciaran Brady, *The chief governors: the rise and fall of reform government in Tudor Ireland, 1536–1588* (Cambridge, 1994), chs. 3 and 4.

Concern over the political agenda was underpinned by a shared commitment to the preservation of Protestantism – it was, in Walsingham's words, 'the greatest and best parte of theyr [children's] inheritaunce'[146] – and by a strong self-perception of their duties as counsellors, whether this derived from traditional ideals of noble counsel or newer, classical-humanist concepts which emerged principally from Sir John Cheke's circle in Cambridge in the 1530s and 1540s (which included Burghley, Bacon, Wilson and Smith). The latter were strengthened as members moved to London to study at the Inns of Court or work at court.[147]

COUNSELLORS' NETWORKS AND THEIR INTERACTION WITH ELIZABETH'S NETWORK

Elizabeth's network of counsellors, intimates, secretaries and favoured agents and ambassadors forms the core of this new paradigm of Elizabethan policy-making but not its entirety. Alongside it existed a range of interrelated networks, emanating from Elizabeth's trusted counsellors and intimates, that overlapped, but were not fully coterminous with, Elizabeth's. These extended beyond the queen's network to individuals who, less important to Elizabeth, were of greater significance to her intimates. Five key figures, illustrating probouleutic, extra-conciliar, secretarial and news-gathering functions of this network, are Sir Walter Mildmay, William Davison, Edmund Tremayne, Robert Beale and Sir Thomas Gresham.

Mildmay's recorded presence at probouleutic meetings was limited to two occasions: the large gathering on 6 October 1579 on the Anjou match and in March 1583, when he, Burghley, Walsingham and Sir Thomas Bromley, the Lord Chancellor, discussed the building of an Anglophile party in Scotland. It is unclear whether on that occasion he was selected by Elizabeth, called upon by Burghley or Walsingham, or was present by chance. He seems to have offered advice to Elizabeth directly on 28 March 1578 on committing herself fully to aiding the States-General though it is unclear whether this was solicited or Mildmay's own initiative.[148]

Despite his peripheral position in Elizabeth's network, Mildmay occupied a more central position among inner ring counsellors, like Burghley,

---

146 Walsingham to Randolph and Bowes, 16 Mar. 1578, Harleian 6992, fo. 100v.
147 Guy, 'Rhetoric of counsel', pp. 292–300; Skinner, *Reason and rhetoric*, pp. 66–74; Alford, *Early Elizabethan polity*, pp. 16, 21–4.
148 Sir Walter Mildmay's advice to the queen on the Low Countries, 28 Mar. 1579, NRO, Fitzwilliam (Milton) Political 186.

Sussex and Walsingham. He was part of a network that circulated news and information on important issues, receiving information directly from Walsingham and Randolph as well as from his son, Anthony, who was in Scotland during Randolph's embassy to Scotland in January 1578 and was part of Walsingham's and Cobham's train in the Netherlands later the same year.[149] More importantly, Mildmay took part in the examination and discussion of key issues among inner ring counsellors that ran alongside, and was preparatory to, their probouleutic and *ad hoc* counselling functions. This is most clearly demonstrated by three extant memoranda commenting on Sussex's letter to Elizabeth of 28 August 1578 on the Anjou match, along with further notes taken by a third party (possibly his son-in-law, Sir William Fitzwilliam) of Mildmay's comments, dated 9 May 1579.[150] A further example exists in his archive: 'A discourse Concerninge the safetie of England by adnexinge Holland zelande to that conntrie' is believed to date from 1580 though Mildmay was not selected for the probouleutic meeting on the Netherlands on 10 July.[151] Sussex's letter was either freely circulating at court or Mildmay was given access to it, either from Sussex himself or from Burghley, in whose archive Sussex's letter remains. It suggests that not only was Mildmay examining issues for himself but that this operated within a network functioning effectually independently of Elizabeth's: she had sought to restrict debate and gossip on the marriage at and beyond the court.

William Davison was used by Walsingham, as an extra-conciliar counsellor, to persuade Elizabeth to deliver the bonds for £100,000 to the States in June 1578.[152] His significance in counsellors' networks, during his time as agent in the Netherlands (1577–9), was, however, broader. He operated as much as an agent for inner ring counsellors as for Elizabeth: his reports that Bussy d'Amboise (governor of the duchy of Anjou and

---

149 Randolph to Mildmay, 9 Mar. 1578, NRO, Fitzwilliam (Milton) Political 153, fo. 1r; Anthony Mildmay to same, 9 Mar. 1578, NRO, Fitzwilliam (Milton) Political 222; same to same, 11 Mar. 1578, NRO, Fitzwilliam (Milton) Political 220, fo. 1r; Randolph to same, 20 Mar. 1578, NRO, Fitzwilliam (Milton) Political 153, fo. 1v; Anthony Mildmay to same, 20 Mar. 1578, NRO, Fitzwilliam (Milton) Political 220, fos. 1v–2r; Walsingham to same, [5 July?] 1578, SP83/9/3E.

150 Notes taken oute of a letter written from the Earle of Sussex, [after 28 Aug. 1578], NRO, Fitzwilliam (Milton) Political 111, pp. 11–18; Certaine notes drawen oute of a letter sent by the Earle of Sussex, [after 28 Aug. 1578], NRO, Fitzwilliam (Milton) Political 111, pp. 19–21; Notes taken out of a letter from the Earl of Sussex, [after 28 Aug. 1578], Huntington Library, San Marino, CA, Egerton 1189; These pointes I took in woordes from Sir walter mildmaie, 9 May 1579, NRO, Fitzwilliam (Milton) Political 111, fo. 13r.

151 A discourse Concerninge the safetie of England by adnexinge Holland zelande to that conntrie, [1580], NRO, Fitzwilliam (Milton) Political 123.

152 SP83/7/27.

commander of Francis, duke of Anjou's army) was in 'dayly communica-cion with the Spanish Ambassador the Queen mother & the duke of Guise' confirmed their suspicions that Anjou sought to annexe the Netherlands to France.[153] More importantly, he was part of discussions among inner ring counsellors leading up to the probouleutic meeting on 22 March 1578 and Elizabeth's audience with the Spanish ambassador, Bernardino de Mendoza, on the 24th. Wilson told him his opinion (laid out earlier in his memorandum, 'Opinion on whether to send aid'); Walsingham informed him of Hatton's views.[154] Davison also seems to have played an important counselling role to Leicester, supplying him with a thorough evaluation of, and justification for, Elizabeth entering into a war to support the Dutch.[155]

Davison's correspondence with Leicester seems particularly significant. It is hard to believe that it was neither unsolicited nor unengaging: he had been rebuked earlier for writing too little information and too much of his own opinion in his official letters to the Secretaries, probably as a result of a personal rivalry with Thomas Leighton.[156] With Sussex, Leicester appears to have taken a leading role in the interviews with Mendoza on 16 and 20 March. Marginalia in the memorandum for the interview on the 20th, penned by Walsingham's secretary, Laurence Tomson, suggests Leicester asked the first question while the rest of the interview was conducted by Sussex. Superficially, Leicester appeared to try to ascertain whether Philip II was prepared to allow Elizabeth to act as mediator. In the context of growing fears of Catholic conspiracy, however, his question looked more like an attempt to gauge Philip's reaction to Elizabeth's involvement in the revolt and confirm the veracity of rumours that he was planning to attack England in partial retaliation.[157] Davison's evaluation gave Leicester – already committed to the revolt (he had campaigned to lead an embassy to negotiate a peace) – the ammunition to defend and justify the more proactive line his question implied.[158]

Edmund Tremayne's role was similar. Appointed a clerk of the privy council in 1571, in the summer of 1578 he acted as an important point of contact between Walsingham in Antwerp and the English court,

---

153 Davison to Walsingham, 8 Mar. 1578, SP83/5/67 (and copy to Hatton, Additional 15891, fos. 26r–28v); Davison to the secretaries, [11 May] 1578, SP83/6/60, fos. 118r–119r.
154 Wilson to Davison, 27 Mar. 1578, SP83/5/104; SP83/5/117; Walsingham to Davison, 16 May 1578, SP83/6/65, fo. 130r.
155 [Davison] to Leicester, Mar.[?] 1578, SP83/5/12.
156 Walsingham to Davison, 2 May 1578, SP83/6/42; PRO, SP83/6/65.
157 SP94/1/14.
158 Leicester to Davison, 9 Mar. 1578, SP83/5/69.

particularly Hatton. Using information supplied by Hatton and other counsellors (Hatton also read some of his letters before they were dispatched), he discussed and then conveyed to Walsingham the substance of negotiations with Elizabeth over Dutch aid and with the Scottish ambassador, Dunfermline, for Anglo-Scottish amity.[159] His letter to Walsingham of 29 August 1578 suggests he deliberately used Hatton to investigate how Walsingham's reports were received by Elizabeth and to explore Elizabeth's attitudes to the Dutch revolt: 'After this courtlie dialogue, I was so bold to ask him how her majestie was contented now with your advertisements . . . [and] how her majestie was moved to deale in thenterprise of the States.'[160] Like Davison, he was part of an intelligence network: Burghley 'imparting vnto me the state of thinges in Ireland' in 1579.[161] Tremayne's interest in Ireland dated back to at least 1569 when he was commissioned by the privy council to report on the war that had broken out between the Butler and the Geraldines, led by James Fitzmaurice Fitzgerald; he returned to Ireland as a special agent in 1573. This may have provided the stimulus for a series of treatises or advises on Irish reform, written between 1571 and 1575.[162]

Tremayne's treatises on Irish reform form a connection with the role of Robert Beale. Another clerk of the privy council and a diplomat – unofficially accompanying Henry Killigrew to the Palatinate in 1569 and appointed, with Sir William Winter, to negotiate the release of the Merchant Adventurers ships detained at Flushing in April 1576 – Robert Beale's role was as a diplomatic adviser and secretary.[163] Early treatises, on Mary Stuart in 1571 and 1572, were both bids for advancement and derived from his own religious and political outlook; Killigrew sought to have the first ('Reasons why the French kinge should recommend the Quene of Scotts cause') translated and selectively distributed for propaganda purposes. Later treatises, on Germany in 1583 and the Dutch revolt in 1587, were signs of his acknowledged expertise. Polemical treatises for Burghley also followed in the 1580s and 1590s.[164] Beale's secretarial activity was diverse: he was employed to correct Stafford's instructions in 1583 and, on Somers's refusal, to be Walsingham's temporary replacement while he was on embassy to Scotland; he continued to assist Walsingham on his return.

---

159 Tremayne to Walsingham, 20 July 1578, SP83/7/72; same to same, 29 July 1578, SP83/7/91.
160 Tremayne to Walsingham, 29 Aug. 1578, SP83/8/56.
161 Tremayne to Burghley, 22 Aug. 1579, SP12/131/76.
162 Brady, *The chief governors*, pp. 140–6; Docquet book of privy seal warrants, 1571–80, NA, PSO5/1 (unfoliated: see June 1573).
163 Taviner, 'Robert Beale', pp. 66, 158–68.
164 Ibid., pp. 176–8, 191–6.

He was asked by Walsingham to compile a list of complaints and Elizabeth's answers from his knowledge and experience with which to charge Mary in October 1586 and he was recalled from his position as one of the English representatives on the Dutch council of state in 1587 because Elizabeth wanted to use him in drafting the treaty.[165]

Though Sir Thomas Gresham was an important source of financial advice for Elizabeth, he was also a regular correspondent with Burghley, Leciester and Sir Thomas Parry (Elizabeth's Cofferer when she was a princess and, later, the Controller of her royal household) in the 1560s. Indeed, a letter to Burghley in April 1560 suggests that Gresham ordered his factor in England to wait on the Principal Secretary every morning at six o'clock.[166] Most of his letters, conveying news from Antwerp and across the continent, were directed to this triumvirate. Some information may have been incidental and parochial – news that a preacher had spoke against Elizabeth in Antwerp in April 1560[167] – but much was more significant: rumours that the Count of Egmont (stadholder of Flanders and a leading Catholic nobleman who opposed Philip's persecution of the Dutch Protestants) and William of Orange planned to come to Antwerp in 1560; that Philip II planned to aid the French against the Scottish Lords of the Congregation the same year; and about Elizabeth's marriage and the defeat of the Spanish by the Turks at Tripoli.[168]

As with Elizabeth's network, there were also strong social, familial, education and ideological ties across these 'horizontal' networks. Mildmay was married to Walsingham's sister, Mary (died 1576), and worked closely with Burghley in the Exchequer, after Burghley's appointment to the Lord Treasurership in 1572.[169] Beale, Davison and Killigrew were friends: Davison had been Killigrew's secretary in Scotland in 1566 and Beale had accompanied him to the Palatinate in 1569.[170] Beale was not, as commonly thought, Walsingham's secretary in France, but a household familiar and friend; they became brothers-in-law, marrying the sisters, Ursula and Edith St Barbe.[171] Beale was recommended as a clerk of the

---

165 Ibid., pp. 169–72.
166 Gresham to Cecil, 18 Apr. 1560, in Burgon, *Sir Thomas Gresham*, I, p. 221.
167 Gresham to Cecil, 16 Apr. 1560, in ibid., I, pp. 268–9.
168 Gresham to Cecil, 21 Apr. 1560, in ibid., I, p. 270; same to same, 18 Apr. 1560, in ibid., I, pp. 292–3; same to Sir Thomas Parry, 4 June [or July] 1560, ibid., I, p. 312 (and fn Y, p. 340); same to same, 16 June 1560, ibid., I, pp. 315–16; same to same, 13 June 1561, ibid., I, pp. 308–10.
169 Stanford E. Lehmberg, *Sir Walter Mildmay and Tudor government* (Austin, TX, 1964), pp. 17, 48, 111–12.
170 Taviner, 'Robert Beale', pp. 44, 66.
171 Ibid., pp. 79–80.

privy council by Burghley, Leicester and Smith in 1572 and by Walsingham as his temporary replacement in 1583.[172] Social and familial ties were underpinned by a shared humanist-classical education: Mildmay as part of Sir John Cheke's wider circle at Cambridge in the late 1530s; Beale, in Zurich under John Aylmer (himself part of the 'Cambridge connection').[173] And by late Henrician and Edwardian experience: Mildmay worked in the Court of Augmentations from 1540 while Burghley was at Gray's Inn; they both served under Somerset, Mildmay still in Augmentations and Burghley as Somerset's secretary; both were at the battle of Pinkie (1547).[174] All were committed Protestants, concerned by the threats perceived to be posed by Mary Stuart and Catholic conspiracy. Beale's time in Paris earlier in the 1560s was formative: he saw England under threat of Catholic conspiracy and, influenced by leading humanist Hubert Languet, whom he met at Wittenburg, believed that the only solution was for Elizabeth to establish a Protestant network of alliances; sentiments shared by both Mildmay and Davison.[175] Tremayne identified closely with the Dutch revolt, referring to negotiations for aid as 'our matters'.[176]

The relationship between Elizabeth's networks and those of her intimates was an interactive one. Beale's career developed from his connections with Walsingham and he was a key figure in the 'horizontal' network of inner ring counsellors, but he also established a relationship with Elizabeth that enabled him to act as Walsingham's temporary replacement (and assistant) and to be called on for drafting instructions and treaties. At a more mundane level, it appears that the regime frequently used agents' and ambassadors' own servants and family members as messengers in addition to official messengers and messengers extraordinary (based in the Chamber).[177] Norris, Walsingham, Killigrew and

---

172 Ibid., pp. 106–7; Harleian 6993, fo. 54v.
173 Winthrop S. Hudson, *The Cambridge connection and the Elizabethan settlement of 1559* (Durham, NC, 1980), pp. 55, 64–5; Taviner, 'Robert Beale', pp. 50–63.
174 Lehmberg, *Sir Walter Mildmay*, pp. 7–27.
175 Taviner, 'Robert Beale', pp. 61–5; NRO, Fitzwilliam (Milton) Political III, pp. 11–18; NRO, Fitzwilliam (Milton) Political III, pp. 19–21; Huntington, Egerton 1189; NRO, Fitzwilliam (Milton) Political III, fo. 13r; SP83/5/67; SP83/6/60, fos. 118r–119r.
176 SP83/7/91.
177 Payments for messengers and messengers extraordinary are listed under 'Riding charges' in the Declared Accounts of the Exchequer, Pipe Office (accounts of the Treasurer of the Chamber), NA, E351/541–2. These include payments for other crown servants acting as messengers. Non-crown servants are listed in the earlier section 'Messengers' or 'Other expenses' of the same accounts, along with payments for plays etc. Somers was used as a messenger in the 1560s and 1570s: E351/541, fos. 16v, 17v, 38r, 58v; E351/541, fo. 212v; E351/542, fo. 11r. Some of the commissions in the 1560s may have been when he was serving as Throckmorton's secretary,

Gresham all made use of their own servants; Walsingham also used Beale as a messenger.[178] One of Sir Amias Paulet's (ambassador to France and later Mary Stuart's custodian) regular couriers was George Pawlett: unlikely to have been Amias's son – who was probably no more than twelve years old – he may have been another relative.[179] Members of others' families were also used, reinforcing the significance of familial networks as one of the backbones of Elizabethan court politics. Edmund and Robert Carey, probably Hunsdon's sons, carried (respectively) letters between Leicester at Buxton and Elizabeth in 1578 and from Cobham in Paris in 1582.[180] Mildmay's son, Humphrey, was another of Cobham's messengers in 1582.[181]

This interaction is crucial to the new paradigm of Elizabethan policymaking. Though it was born out of familial, social and ideological connections, it was central to the functioning of policy-making and Elizabeth's exercise of her queenship. Perhaps paradoxically, this is thrown into sharpest relief by those usually perceived as secondary figures: Robert Beale and Daniel Rogers. Both men had wide European contacts, established and developed by long periods on the continent prior to their service for Elizabeth. Beale knew leading humanists, like George Buchanan, Hubert Languet and Petrus Ramus as well as André Wechel, a printer whose father had printed Jacob Sturm's educational works.[182] Rogers moved in a wider humanist circle: Abraham Ortelius; the Dutch historian, Hadrianus Junius; the poet and painter, Lucas de Heere; Jan van der Does; Justus Lipsius; Jacob Sturm as well as Languet and Buchanan.[183] These contacts were significant. They acted as credentials for establishing positions as diplomats and advisers: Beale's connections seem to have acted as an entrée into Walsingham's household in the 1560s. They also provided men like Beale and Rogers with the news, directly observed or reported indirectly from themselves or from their own networks, that was the lifeblood of their ability to fulfil their roles as ambassadors, agents and advisers.[184]

---

though he is still often described as a signet clerk. Another clerk of the signet, John Cliffe, was a messenger to the Imperial court in 1559 (E351/541, fo. 16v).

178 E351/541, fo. 93r; E351/541, fo. 103r–103v; E351/541, fos. 137r–138v; Burgon, *Sir Thomas Gresham*, I, pp. 389–97; II, pp. 131, 134–5, 137–42, 181.

179 E351/541, fo. 221v (Cheke); E351/541, fos. 210r, 211r, 211v, 212r; E351/541, fos. 222v, 223r, 223v; E351/542, fo. 7r.

180 E351/541, fo. 212r; E351/542, fo. 44r.

181 E351/542, fo. 33v.

182 Taviner, 'Robert Beale', pp. 64–5, 89–91, 192, 201, 207–8.

183 van Dorsten, *Poets, patrons and professors*, pp. 19–29, 42–3; Taviner, 'Robert Beale', pp. 207–8.

184 Taviner, 'Robert Beale', pp. 170–81.

Second, and more broadly, it highlights that Elizabethan policy-making cannot be conceived solely in terms of Elizabeth's personal network but as a complex web of 'vertical' and 'horizontal' connections. In effect, Elizabethan court politics comprised a collection of circles representing different functions and degrees of intimacy with, or importance to, Elizabeth or other individuals. These were overlapping rather than simply concentric. Individuals fulfilled different functions: Lincoln was both a member of the outer ring of probouleutic counsellors and of agents and ambassadors – he was ambassador extraordinary in 1572 to ratify the treaty of Blois. Or, they established different relationships with people: Beale was a central figure in the 'horizontal' network but became increasingly part of Elizabeth's network in the 1580s. The composition of the networks was also fluid, subject as much to death as promotion. As Beale and Rogers show, this interaction was vital to the functioning of the polity, but it also grew out of the political and cultural realities of the period. Counsel and policy-making were not restricted to or monopolised by a small body; debate was polymorphic, a factor reinforced by individuals' perceptions of their roles as nobles or citizens and their commitment to the preservation of Protestantism.

COURT POLITICS AND THE COURT

Though Elizabethan court politics needs to be reconceived in terms of networks of individuals, rather than in an institutional framework, the role of institutions like the privy chamber, the Chamber and the household do need to be reassessed. The antithesis between 'court' and 'council' has dominated our perceptions of Elizabethan politics since at least the beginning of the twentieth century, with no consensus as to which, if either, was the main locus of policy-making. Whilst Elizabeth's use of probouleutic groups and *ad hoc* counsel, and the importance of personal relationships with her in obtaining position and influence, suggests that the council was not the main locus, the precise role of the court – and what we mean by 'court' – is uncertain. It certainly does not match up to Starkey's paradigm for Henrician politics. Some of the members of the inner ring of Elizabeth's network held posts in the privy chamber: Hatton, for instance, was a gentleman of the privy chamber. Privy chamber posts were also characteristic of members of the outer rings, though this was largely because all of Elizabeth's female intimates held feed or unfeed posts there. If Elizabethan court politics was neither *primarily* institutional, nor court-based as defined by Starkey, how can we characterise it?

The royal household was the main locus for policy-making and the key institution was the Chamber, not the privy chamber.[185] Most of the inner ring counsellors held posts in the Chamber, either a recognition of their personal relationship with Elizabeth or enabling one to form. Burghley was Principal Secretary until 1572, and continued to fulfil its responsibilities on an informal basis after the appointments of Smith, Walsingham and Wilson. Walsingham and Wilson were, themselves, members of the inner ring. Sussex was Lord Chamberlain; Heneage, Treasurer of the Chamber; Randolph, Master of the posts; Somers, clerk of the signet; and Stafford, a gentleman pensioner. The Chamber's dominance was less marked in the outer rings of the network, though Knollys was Vice-Chamberlain 1559–69 until his appointment as Treasurer of the household in 1570; Beale was a clerk of the privy council from 1572, a post listed in subsidy assessments as part of the Chamber. A number of individuals from the wider network of agents and ambassadors also held Chamber posts, though some had prior diplomatic experience too: Thomas Wilkes (clerk of the privy council, 1576), Thomas Bodley (gentleman usher, c.1583) as well as Edmund Tremayne (clerk of the privy council, 1571) and Robert Corbet (Master of the posts by 1575) who was special ambassador to Luis de Requesens, governor of the Netherlands, in 1575–6.[186]

Of the inner ring, Leicester and Hatton were unusual: Leicester occupied the mastership of the horse (part of the Stables) and Hatton, the Captaincy of the Guard and post of Vice-Chamberlain, both privy chamber offices (he had been appointed a gentleman pensioner by 1564). But this oddity was more apparent than real. Though the Stables were a separate

185 David Starkey argued that Henry VII's withdrawal of the privy chamber from the control of the Lord Chamberlain established a structural differentiation between the gentlemen, gentlemen ushers and chamberers (and their female counterparts under Mary and Elizabeth) in the privy chamber and the Chamber itself. The latter comprised the principal secretaries, Latin and French secretaries, treasurer, masters of requests, jewels and the great wardrobe, the signet office, chapel royal, esquires of the body, cupbearers, carvers, sewers, officers of the rolls, wardrobe of the beds and the jewelhouse, yeomen of the chamber, gentlemen pensioners, messengers and a range of others including musicians, apothecaries and masters of the posts and the revels. Subsidy assessments from this period also list the privy seal office and clerks of the privy council as members of the Chamber. However, while contemporary records do appear to support this, Starkey's characterisation of the medieval court as a 'glorifed bedsit' is difficult to sustain. See D. A. L. Morgan, 'The house of policy: the political role of the late Plantagenet household, 1422–1485', in Starkey (ed.), *English Court*, p. 33; E179/69/93, mm. 1–11 (in which privy chamber posts are listed under 'The Queens majesties Chamber'); E179/69/93, mm. 3–4; Michael Prestwich, 'The court of Edward II', in Mark Ormrod and Anthony Musson (eds.), *The age of Edward II* (forthcoming). I would like to thank Michael Prestwich for letting me read a draft of this essay and discussing the medieval and early modern court with me.
186 Bell, *Handlist of British diplomatic representatives*.

part of the royal household from the *domus providencie* (the household below-stairs) and the *domus magnificencie* (or Chamber), the Master of the horse was often a royal intimate.[187] As has been noted, the privy chamber was a secondary locus of key personnel and the wider network. All of Elizabeth's female intimates held feed or unfeed posts there; they were important channels of communication between the queen and her male advisers. A number of envoys, agents and ambassadors were drawn from the privy chamber's male ranks (feed and unfeed). Thomas Leighton was a gentleman extraordinary from 1568 and Fulke Greville (gentleman extraordinary from 1581) was special ambassador to the Netherlands in 1582. Edward Darcy was special ambassador to Francis, duke of Anjou, and William of Orange in 1583; he was an extraordinary groom by 1583 and became a feed groom in 1595, replacing his father-in-law, Thomas Asteley.[188] He, William Killigrew and Thomas Gorges (feed grooms) all acted as occasional messengers in the late 1570s and early 1580s.[189]

Moreover, there was a close working relationship between the privy chamber and the Chamber in the secretarial aspects of policy-making. As Smith's complaints to Burghley in the early 1570s illustrated, obtaining the sign manual had reverted to the Principal Secretary, as it had done temporarily between Sir Ralph Sadler's dismissal in 1543 and the establishment of the dry stamp in 1545.[190] The privy chamber remained important because its women in particular were recognised as key points of access to Elizabeth and important barometers of her moods. This was why Beale recommended in his 'Instructions for a Principall Secretarie' that Wotton should cultivate friendships with privy chamber women: they could inform him of 'her majesties disposicion . . . [which] will stande yow in much steede'.[191] Thus, while there is no evidence to suggest that members of the privy chamber either stockpiled petitions for Elizabeth to sign or submitted material directly to her like key members of the Henrician privy chamber, they did facilitate the Principal Secretaries' duties. Furthermore, while Starkey's evidence for the Henrician period is focused on petitions, the Elizabethan privy chamber and Elizabeth's intimates seem to have been involved in politics more narrowly defined. Hatton was a

187 Morgan, 'House of policy', pp. 30–3.
188 Wright, 'Change in direction', p. 156. Wright argues Darcy's initial appointment was in 1581 but Hasler states 1583 (Hasler, I, p. 16). Lansdowne 34/30, fo. 76r–76v (1582) lists only feed members of the chamber.
189 E351/542, fo. 33r; E351/541, fos. 213v, 224r. Killigrew had also been used as a messenger in the 1560s: E351/541, fo. 47r.
190 Harleian 6991, fo. 19; Starkey, 'Court and government', p. 55.
191 Additional MS 48149, fo. 8r.

central figure in *ad hoc* consultation; Lady Mary Sidney was involved in the marriage negotiations with Archduke Charles; Lady Cobham attempted to use her access to Elizabeth to facilitate Burghley's return to favour in 1587.

Two further refinements need to be made. First, it is difficult to sustain Simon Adams's argument that court politics was subsumed into conciliar politics.[192] Though this cannot be verified architecturally as we only know the precise location for one of the probouleutic meetings (March 1583 which took place at Burghley's London house), documentary evidence clearly shows that the privy council did not act as the principal advisory and policy-making body. Political debate on key issues was conducted in probouleutic groups and *ad hoc* consultations that functioned separately from the council. Moreover, though privy councillors dominated probouleutic and *ad hoc* consultation, debate extended to those without conciliar posts: Heneage, Randolph, Killigrew and Somers. Personal intimacy with the queen dictated political influence, not conciliar office.

Second, political debate was not restricted to, nor monopolised by, Elizabeth's inner ring of counsellors. Counsellors discussed issues with friends, colleagues and members of their own network – such as discussions between Walsingham, Wilson, Leicester and Davison in 1578 – and circulated material to each other, as is evident by Mildmay's comments on Sussex's letter to Elizabeth about the Anjou match. Activity was not confined to men. Women in and outwith the privy chamber met and corresponded with each other and with men and discussed political events and issues.[193] For instance, George Blyth, one of Burghley's secretaries and, from 1574, a member of the Council of the North, informed the countess of Huntingdon of Henry III's entry into France.[194] The countess of Warwick supplied troops for Leicester's Netherlands expedition and was involved in Irish affairs in the 1580s and 1590s.[195] The countess of Sussex and Lady Anne Fitzwilliam played small diplomatic roles while their husbands were Lord Deputies of Ireland: the countess developed

---

192 Adams, 'Eliza enthroned?', pp. 62–3.
193 Cotton Galba C. 9, fo. 79v; Poyntz to Heneage, 4 July 1583, *HMC Finch*, I, pp. 24–5; same to Lady Anne Heneage, 23 July 1583, ibid., pp. 25–6; same to same, 9 Apr. 1586, ibid., pp. 26–7; Elizabeth Finch to same, 27 Apr. [1589?], ibid., p. 28; SP12/171/25, fo. 43; Elizabeth Stafford to Rutland, 16 Aug. 1571, *HMC Rutland*, I, pp. 95–6; Lady Savage to same, 28 Jan. 1576, Ibid., p. 107; Eleanor Bridges to same, Jan. 1576, ibid., p. 107; Rauf Rabbards to Lady Knyvett, 19 Oct. 1599, BL, Egerton MS 2714, fo. 29r; same to same, 24 July 1600, BL, Egerton MS 2714, fo. 73r.
194 George Blythe to the countess of Huntingdon, 20 June 1574, Additional 46367, fo. 54v.
195 Sherley to Leicester, 21 Mar. 1586, Cotton MS Galba C. 9, fo. 139v; Merton, 'Women who served', pp. 183–6.

contacts with Shane O'Neill, chieftain of the O'Neills of Tyrone in Ulster, while Lady Fitzwilliam was active at court defending Fitzwilliam's position and pressing for men, money and munitions.[196] Eleanor Butler, countess of Desmond, was a major diplomatic force in Anglo-Irish politics, acting as an intermediary between her husband and Dublin to persuade him to accept 'composition'; her role was fundamental to the decision to restore Desmond in 1574.[197] Though wondering why her experience had not taught her more patience, Burghley described Heneage's wife, Anne (daughter of Sir Nicholas Poyntz) as a 'courtyar': her 'grete stomack were meter for the Court than for Essex'.[198]

In other words, Elizabethan politics was truly 'court politics'. Counselling and policy-making were conducted primarily by the queen and a group of personal intimates, either in specially selected probouleutic groups or informally and *ad hoc*. Personal relationships could be articulated by appointment to the privy council, but it was household office that was more important: it demonstrated, or facilitated, one's personal relationship with the queen. The principal institutional focus was the Chamber, extending to the rest of the royal household (the privy chamber, the Stables), but this was always less significant than the network that was formed by Elizabeth's counsellors, intimates and favoured agents and ambassadors. Elizabethan politics was also truly 'court politics' in that debate often spilled out beyond the boundaries of Elizabeth's network to members of the court. Not the narrow clique of privy chamber staff as defined by Starkey, or the wider remit defined by Zagorin, but rather something in-between: other household officials, as well as nobles and gentry (male and female) who spent some time in the environs of the palace.[199] Burghley or Sussex circulated memoranda to Mildmay; Tremayne discussed policy with Hatton; Lady Burghley talked about the Archduke Charles match with both Guzman de Silva and the French ambassador, de Foix, in 1565.[200] This slippage is hardly surprising seeing the close connections forged between colleagues: a letter from Robert Jones, one of Somers's friends, to Richard Oseley (clerk of the privy seal) in 1562 reads like a roll-call of clerks and secretaries: Bernard Hampton (clerk of the council), Nicasius Yetsweirth (French Secretary and clerk of

---

196 Brady, 'Political women', pp. 82–3.
197 Ibid., pp. 79–80. Also significant were some of the Irish women, including Agnes Campbell (Turlough Luineach O'Neill's wife) and Grace O'Malley: ibid., pp. 80–1.
198 *HMC Finch*, I, p. 6.
199 For the definition of the court I have chosen to use, and why, see the Introduction, pp. 8–9.
200 De Silva to Philip II, 22 Apr. 1565, *CSP Spanish*, I, p. 544.

the signet), John Cliffe and William Honninge (clerks of the signet), Thomas Kerry and Edward Clarke (clerks of the privy seal).[201]

CONCLUSION

Ultimately, Elizabethan court politics cannot be defined in institutional terms. Elizabeth sought and received counsel from a personally selected group of counsellors, with whom she had a close personal relationship; she also used trusted servants as messengers, diplomats, agents and, occasionally, as informal negotiators with foreign ambassadors over the issue of marriage. Conversely, these servants could be used by trusted advisers and other members of the court to facilitate access to Elizabeth. Many held official posts in the Chamber or privy chamber as well as, for the likes of Burghley, Leicester, Walsingham, Sussex and others, in the privy council. But these were primarily the fruits of their relationship with Elizabeth not the means by which they attained political pre-eminence. This network of advisers and trusted servants was underpinned by close familial and social ties. Moreover, even when Elizabeth sought advice from a group of counsellors the meetings were not institutionalised: they appear to have been conducted separately from those of the privy council and had no official trappings, such as registers, of their own. Thus, as Starkey suggested for Henry VIII, it was, ultimately, issues of trust and personal intimacy with the monarch, backed by social and familial networks, that defined Elizabethan politics, not institutions or institutional status.

Both the composition of Elizabeth's network of advisers and servants and the centrality of the familial and social connections that underpinned it also suggest that Elizabethan court politics were not subsumed into conciliar politics. Quite simply, Elizabeth's network only partly overlapped with the council and actually extended well beyond it. Moreover, it was a network that intersected with the networks of its own members: the friends, family and colleagues with which men like Burghley, Throckmorton and Heneage worked, such as Mildmay, Tremayne and Davison. Rather conciliar politics was subsumed into court politics.

The dynamic and informal structure of Elizabethan policy-making raises two broader questions about the nature of the early and mid-Elizabethan polity. First, were Elizabeth's adoption of inner rings of counsellors and informal modes of counselling in particular, as well as

---

201 Robert Jones to Richard Oseley, 7 Oct. 1562, *CSP Foreign*, V, p. 619; E179/69/93, m. 3.

the secondary significance of the privy chamber, products of her gender? Did she seek to bypass the privy council in order to prevent councillors from ganging up on her? Did she specifically select counsellors who conformed to classical-humanist stereotypes of 'good counsellors' in order to allay anxiety about female monarchy and hide the independent stance she took in accepting or rejecting advice, as some historians have argued?[202] Second, if counsel and debate were not restricted to or monopolised by the privy council, but operated through the intersection of different networks within the court, what were the boundaries of political debate at court? How was political debate and counsel conducted beyond the examination of issues in probouleutic or *ad hoc* consultations and the direct act of counselling? And by whom?

202 Crane, 'Video and taceo', passim.

CHAPTER 3

Gender and consultation

From 1553, contemporary attitudes to female monarchy dominated the debate on royal power and formed a politico-cultural milieu for relationships between Elizabeth and her counsellors. Yet, there is no modern consensus on the extent to which gender shaped Elizabeth's queenship and policy-making. On the one hand, feminist historians, such as Allison Heisch, Carole Levin and Mary Thomas Crane, have argued that Elizabeth exploited and manipulated gender conventions to her own advantage, to assert her authority and independence.[1] Mary Hill Cole and Anne McLaren have argued that Elizabeth's gender forced her to disrupt the 'normal' process of policy-making (Cole) or redefine her queenship in 'extraordinary', providential terms (McLaren).[2] On the other hand, Collinson, Guy and Alford have asserted that Elizabeth's queenship was defined by conflicts over political issues (church reform, her marriage and the succession) and creeds (the 'mixed polity' versus 'imperial monarchy') which created constant tensions and divisions.[3]

If some feminist readings appear too coloured by a modern, feminist agenda,[4] then there are also more fundamental problems with the debate as a whole. Relationships between Elizabeth and her counsellors are defined in monochromatic terms and Elizabethan politics as adversarial. The diversity and complexity of competing factors are played down in favour of identifying a principal determinant: gender or religion. Individuals are assumed to have acted consistently (for instance, to realise a tightly defined set of religious and political – principally classical-humanist – ideals) rather than

---

1 Heisch, 'Queen Elizabeth I'; Levin, *'Heart and stomach of a king'*; Crane, 'Video and taceo'.
2 Cole, *Portable Queen*; McLaren, *Political culture*.
3 Collinson, 'Monarchical republic', pp. 402, 407; Guy, 'Tudor monarchy and its critiques', pp. 91–100; Guy, 'The 1590s', pp. 1–19; Alford, *Early Elizabethan polity*.
4 Especially Heisch and Levin, the latter of whom assumes a consciousness and deliberate manipulation of gendered imagery by Elizabeth and her subjects that is disconcertingly and anachronistically modern. See chapter 7 for a fuller evaluation.

constantly renegotiated their positions, either through circumstance or the force of competing influences. Monochromaticism reinforces the adversarial framework imposed on Elizabethan politics: differences over gender, political conviction or creed are defined as stimuli for each side to struggle to assert their supremacy in the formulation and implementation of policy until at least 1587.[5]

These two aspects provide the starting point for reassessing the nature and structure of Elizabeth's queenship at elite, court level. By taking a broader perspective of social and cultural dynamics – including humanist education and European political theory and practice – I explore whether the structure of policy-making outlined in the previous chapter was a product of Elizabeth's gender and the extent to which politics was adversarial. What was the nature of relationships between Elizabeth and counsellors? What shaped them? How should we conceptualise Elizabethan policy-making?

ELIZABETH AND THE MANIPULATION OF CONCEPTS OF COUNSEL

Beliefs that women were incapable of assuming political roles were so pervasive that, a century after Elizabeth's death, both Sarah Churchill, duchess of Marlborough's and Abigail Masham's intimacy with Queen Anne and their involvement in political debate remained highly controversial.[6] Elizabeth herself was acutely aware of these attitudes, denying that her gender disabled her from exercising monarchical power both in speeches (e.g. to the Commons on 28 January 1563) and letters.[7] Modern debates on the role of gender in Elizabethan policy-making have focused on two key areas: Elizabeth's alleged manipulation of classical-humanist, gendered and providential concepts of counsel and monarchy (Heisch, Levin and Crane)[8] and her alleged restriction of counselling to key individuals. How far can these arguments be sustained?

Elizabeth had imbued humanist ideals of governance through the classical education she received under William Grindal, protégé of Roger

---

5 For a fuller discussion of how Elizabethan politics has been conceptualised see Guy, 'Elizabeth I: the queen and politics', pp. 183–202.

6 Frances Harris, *A passion for government: the life of Sarah, duchess of Marlborough* (Oxford, 1991), esp. pp. 87–93, 105–6.

7 Queen's answer to the Commons' petition, 28 Jan. 1563, SP12/27/36, fos. 143r–144v; Walsingham to Shrewsbury, 30 Jul. 1582, in Edmund Lodge, *Illustrations of British history, biography and manners* (3 vols., London, 1791), II, pp. 276–7.

8 Crane, 'Video and taceo', pp. 1–15; McLaren, *Political culture*, passim but esp. ch. 1.

Ascham (fellow and lecturer at St John's College, Cambridge and, from 1546, public orator), between 1544 and his death in January 1548, and Ascham himself, from 1548 until 1550.[9] She continued to study classical texts with Ascham when he served as both Mary's and then Elizabeth's own Latin Secretary.[10] Little is known of Elizabeth's time under Grindal, but it is likely that his methods and interests were similar to those of his mentor. Ascham had followed a conventional, though wide-ranging, curriculum at Cambridge in the 1530s, including works by Boethius, Cicero, Aristotle and Petrus Hispanus. However, we know from his correspondence and his posthumously printed treatise on education, *The scholemaster* (1570), that Elizabeth followed a programme of studies closer to that promoted by his mentor and friend, Sir John Cheke, and outlined in *The scholemaster*: the study of the best classical authors to instil virtue, and the Bible and selected works of the church fathers to instil Christian piety.[11] She also learned French with Jean Belmain and Italian with Battista Castiglione.[12]

Within this curriculum, we know specifically that, under Ascham, Elizabeth read selected orations of Demosthenes and Isocrates in Greek every morning; Cicero in Latin every afternoon (and in the evenings) as well as the Greek New Testament, Sophocles, selected church fathers like St Cyprian and more modern works like Melancthon's *Loci communes rerum theologicarum*.[13] Specific classical texts are difficult to identify but the likeliest orations she would have read by Isocrates were 'To Demonicus', 'To Nicocles' and 'Nicocles, or the Cyprians' from *Ethics* and 'Pangyricus', 'Philip', 'Plataicus', 'Peace', 'Archidamus' and 'Areopagiticus' from *Politics*. These were all works in which Isocrates discussed the exercise of political power and the relationship between rulers and subjects. 'To Nicocles' was recommended in two of the most important European educational guides: Vives's *De tradendis disciplinis* (1531) and Elyot's *The*

9 Laurence V. Ryan, *Roger Ascham* (Stanford, CA, 1963), pp. 102–3, 23–7, 82–3. I discussed Elizabeth's education and library in more detail in 'Alcibiades' alphabet: the education and political thought of Elizabeth I', given at the early modern seminar at the University of Oxford on 1 Nov. 2001 and 'Caesar's alphabet: the education and political thought of Elizabeth I' at the Tudor-Stuart seminar at the Institute of Historical Research on 29 Apr. 2002. I would like to thank the audience for their comments, particularly correcting my attribution of one of Elizabeth's references to Alcibiades to Augustus Caesar.

10 Ryan, *Ascham*, pp. 216–17, 223–4.

11 Ibid., pp. 21, 19–20, 106, 260–1; Roger Ascham, *The scholemaster: or the plaine and perfite way of teaching children* . . . (London, 1570; *STC* 832), esp. sigs. 16v–20r, 51v–66r.

12 Louis Wiesener, *The youth of Queen Elizabeth, 1533–1558*, ed. from the French by Charlotte M. Yonge (2 vols., London, 1879), I, p. 85.

13 Ascham, *The scholemaster*, sig. 35; Ryan, *Ascham*, pp. 105–6.

boke named the gouernour (1531). Elyot also recommended 'To Demonicus'.[14] Though it is unclear which of Demosthenes's orations Elizabeth read in the 1540s, we know that she read the opposing orations of Aeschines and Demosthenes, *Against Ctesiphon* and *On the crown* in August and September 1555, and *On the embassy* and *On the (false) embassy* in the 1560s.[15] She also learned a speech against Aeschines by Isocrates and translated a number of works including Seneca's *Epistles*, Cicero's letter to Curio, Euripides, two orations by Isocrates and a dialogue by Xenophon; she may have also written a commentary on Plato but this is no longer extant.[16] Extant library inventories show she had copies of Aristotle's and Plato's *Works*, Xenophon's *Cyropaedia*, Cicero, as well as works by Plutarch, Euclid, Livy, Quintilian, Sabellecus and Thucydides; in 1554, she requested her cofferer, Thomas Parry, to deliver her copy of Cicero to her at Woodstock. These were all works and authors recommended in the curricula defined by Cheke, Elyot, Vives and Ascham.[17] As queen, she also received copies and translations of works by Plato, Aristotle and Euclid as gifts, though we do not know if she read them.[18]

These texts taught both the rhetorical skills needed to examine and debate arguments as well as more substantive issues about what

---

14 Foster Watson, *Vives: On education. A translation of the 'De tradensis discplinis' of Juan Luis Vives* (Cambridge, 1913), p. 260; Sir Thomas Elyot, *The boke named the gouernour* (London, 1531; *STC* 7635), fo. 36r–36v.

15 Ryan, *Ascham*, pp. 216–17, 223; Ascham, *The scholemaster*, sig. Bii[r]; Aeschines, 'Against Ctesiphon', ed. and trans. Charles Darwin Adams, *The speeches of Aeschines* (Cambridge, Mass. and London, 1938); Demosthenes, 'On the Crown', in *Demosthenes: On the Crown (De Corona)*, trans. S. Usher (Warminster, 1993).

16 Ryan, *Ascham*, p. 20; Caroline Pemberton (ed.), *Queen Elizabeth's Englishings* (Early English Text Society, os, 113; London, 1899), p. vii; Thomas Park (ed.), *Nugae Antiquae: being a miscellaneous collection of original papers . . . by Sir John Harington . . . Selected . . . by the late Henry Harington* (2 vols., London, 1804), I, pp. 109–14, 140–3. It is not clear whether one of the orations by Isocrates Pemberton states Elizabeth translated was the same as that that Ryan states she learned by heart. The precise identity of the Xenophon work is unclear as it does not appear in *The Gentleman's Magazine*, 2 (1742) as Pemberton states; neither have I been able to locate a reference to the commentary by Plato outside Pemberton.

17 M. Omont, 'Inventory of books at the palace of Richmond, 1535', *Études Romanes dédiées à Gaston Paris* (Paris, 1891), pp. 1–13; A catalogue of the Library of King Henry the Eighth made in the 34th year of his Reign, Additional MS 4729 (and another copy, Additional MS 25469); The names of all the bookes within the newe librarye placed by Thomas Knyvett the 20th of December 1581, Royal MS 17.B.28.3, fos. 128v–145r; Maria Perry, *The word of a prince: a life from contemporary documents* (Folio Society; London, 1990), p. 101; Ryan, *Ascham*, pp. 18–21; Mears, 'Alcibiades' alphabet: the education and political thought of Elizabeth I' (early modern seminar, University of Oxford, 1 Nov. 2001); Mears, 'Caesar's alphabet: the education and political thought of Elizabeth I' (Tudor-Stuart seminar, Institute of Historical Research, London, 29 Apr. 2002). See below, n. 24.

18 For instance: Count Steracq to Elizabeth, 20 Aug. 1566, *CSP Foreign*, VIII, pp. 120; Ludovicus Regius to Cecil, 16 Mar. 1568, Ibid., p. 430; Norris to Cecil, 16 May 1567, ibid., p. 231.

constituted good governance, relevant both to princes and 'priuate persone[s]'.[19] The opposing orations of Aeschines and Demosthenes, for instance, showed strengths and weaknesses in putting forward a coherent and cogent argument. In *Against Ctesiphon*, Aeschines made his first point (that Ctesiphon's attempt to have Demosthenes crowned was illegal because Demosthenes had not submitted his accounts for audit prior to the coronation) very strongly; Demosthenes's response was evasive and unconvincing. Yet, Aeschines's second argument (about the location of the coronation) was on shakier legal foundations, argued less effectively and enabled Demosthenes to defend his position well.[20] Isocrates's self-consciously styled political guides, 'To Nicocles' and 'Nicocles, or the Cyprians', outlined the duties of good governance: of rulers to their subjects and then of subjects to their ruler. A good prince should gather around him the wisest men as counsellors and to listen to them even when their advice was unpalatable or contradicted his own ideas. He should love his subjects and rule in their interests, honour the gods, ensure the laws were fair and just, husband his revenues but not fail to make a display of royal magnificence. He was to be war-like but never too belligerent.[21] Conversely, subjects were exhorted to fulfil their appointed tasks diligently, be loyal and do all they could to preserve the order and security of the state.[22]

Mapping the humanist curriculum on to Elizabeth's political thought and action is a huge task, but it does seem clear that she absorbed both simple and more sophisticated lessons from it. For instance, in 1594, she debated James VI's use of and gloss on Virgil's lines from the *Aeneid*, 'Flectere si nequeo superos, Acheronta movebo'.[23] Earlier, in 1592, she had told James VI, 'I would Isocrates' noble lesson were not forgotten, that wills the Emperor his Sovereign to make his words of more account than other men their oaths, as meetest ensigns to show the truest badge of prince's Arms.'[24] In two parliamentary speeches – her reply to the

19 Elyot, *The gouernour*, fo. 36r–36v.
20 Demosthenes, 'On the Crown', pp. 14–16.
21 Isocrates, 'To Nicocles', in *Isocrates*, trans. George Norlin (3 vols., Cambridge, Mass., 1954), I, pp. 49–61.
22 Isocrates, 'Nicocles, or the Cyprians', in *Isocrates*, trans. Norlin, I, pp. 105–13.
23 'If I am unable to sway the gods above, I will stir up Acheron [a river of the underworld]' (*Aeneid*, VII, 312). James VI to Elizabeth, 13 Apr. 1594, *Letters of Queen Elizabeth and King James VI of Scotland*, ed. John Bruce (Camden Society, os, 44; London, 1849), p. 102; Elizabeth to James VI, May 1594, Additional 23240, fo. 132r–32v (*Collected works*, pp. 377–9); James VI to Elizabeth, 5 Jun. 1594, *Letters of Queen Elizabeth*, ed. Bruce, pp. 105–8. See also Elizabeth's Latin oration at the University of Cambridge, 7 Aug. 1564, *Collected works*, pp. 87–8.
24 Elizabeth to James VI, 11 Sept. 1592, *Letters of Queen Elizabeth*, ed. Bruce, p. 76; Isocrates, 'To Nicocles', pp. 57, 59.

Commons' petition for her marriage on 28 January 1563 and her second speech on Mary Stuart in the sixth session, on 24 November 1586 – Elizabeth justified her slowness in decision-making by referring to the story of Augustus Caesar who recited the alphabet before making a decision to prevent him making rash and ill-advised choices.[25]

However, it is difficult to sustain Crane's arguments that Elizabeth deliberately manipulated humanist conventions of counselling – particularly appointing old, male counsellors – to assert her independence as a female ruler.[26] With the exceptions of Leicester (the same age), the fourth duke of Norfolk, and Hatton (younger), early and mid-Elizabethan privy councillors were older than the queen: from Walsingham (three years older) to Sadler (twenty-six years older).[27] Key extra-conciliar counsellors – Randolph, Killigrew, Somers – were also older than Elizabeth. But these appointments were not a deliberate sleight of hand to allay fears of female rule; nor were they, as McLaren suggests, choices imposed on Elizabeth because, as a woman, she lacked the same freedom as a king to choose counsellors within the model of 'mixed monarchy' as defined by leading political theorists – Christopher St German, Thomas Starkey and Sir Thomas Elyot – in the 1530s.[28] In advice proffered to James VI in 1592, Elizabeth specifically rejected that any monarch, other than a minor, was restricted in their choice of counsellors, asking rhetorically, 'Must a king be prescribed what counsaylours he shall take, as if you were there [i.e. their] ward?'[29]

Though it had become customary to draw on experienced administrators and experts prior to 1558,[30] Elizabeth's appointments reflected the centrality of household service, familial connections and similarity of outlook to Tudor governance. Her first privy council was dominated by those who had been members of her household prior to 1558 (Cecil, Sir Thomas Parry), relations (Knollys, Howard of Effingham, Richard

25 SP12/27/36, fo. 143r; The 2 Copy of her *Majesty's* second speech 24 Nouember Before her Majestie corrected it, 24 Nov. 1586, Lansdowne 94/35 fos. 87v–88r. I would like to thank John Cramsie for these references. In the copy of her speech of 1563 in the State Papers Elizabeth did not name Caesar; she refers to him in her speech of 1586 (Lansdowne and Cambridge University Library versions). However, in other versions she refers to Alcibiades. The reference comes from Plutarch's *Moralia*, which notes Athenodorus counselled Caesar to recite the alphabet before answering difficult points (Plutarch, *Moralia*, trans. Frank Cole Babbitt (14 vols., London and New York, 1927–), III, p. 233.
26 Crane, 'Video et taceo', pp. 6–7; MacLaren, *Political culture*, pp. 69–73.
27 Pulman, *Elizabethan privy council*, pp. 44–6.
28 McLaren, *Political culture*, pp. 69–73, 144.
29 *Letters of Queen Elizabeth*, ed. Bruce, p. 76.
30 MacCaffrey, *Shaping of the regime*, p. 24.

Sackville) and those with Henrician, Edwardian or Marian experience.[31] Some, like Cecil, Howard, Knollys and Sackville, fitted into more than one category. Reappointments had not been indiscriminate. Those with Protestant convictions, like Cecil, Mildmay and Bacon, were retained or brought back into service; Marians with strong Catholic sympathies, like Lords Hastings and Montague, were dropped, as was William Paget, since 1555 the most active Marian counsellor. The high survival rate of Marian peers was partly due to the fact that many – like Derby, Pembroke and Shrewsbury – were leading magnates who could represent the crown in the localities and provide military support.

Household service, familial connections and similarity of outlook, rather than humanist concepts of 'good counsel', shaped Elizabeth's network. Heneage had been steward of Hatfield from 1560/1; Cobham served her as a princess; Hunsdon and Buckhurst were cousins, as was, more distantly, Charles Howard, second Lord Howard of Effingham. Effingham had also been a staunch supporter under Mary.[32] Sir James Croft had been involved in Wyatt's Rebellion, imprisoned in the Tower with Elizabeth and had been Lord Deputy of Ireland, 1551–2. Leicester and Hatton were favourites; Sir Henry Norris was a friend. In the outer rings, Edward Darcy and Fulke Greville rose through their personal relationships with the queen; Thomas Leighton, Henry Killigrew and Edward Stafford had familial or professional connections with existing members of her network. Aristocratic advisers were also represented – such as the Howards, Lincoln and the earl of Bedford.[33]

If Elizabeth did not manipulate classical-humanist ideas of counsel to legitimate her gender, then neither did she rely on concepts of providential monarchy to do so, as McLaren has suggested. Rather, the frequent references to made to herself as 'Godes creature, ordeyned to obey his appoyntment' – in her speeches to assembled councillors at Hatfield on her accession and to parliament on 15 March 1576, 12 and 24 November 1586 – were conceived in terms of established conventions of divine right rather than providential monarchy.[34] To legitimate her rule by recourse to

---

31 Including Mildmay, Sir Thomas Cheyney, Sir John Mason, Sir William Petre, Sir Edward Rogers and the peers, Arundel, Derby, Clinton, Northampton, Pembroke, Shrewsbury and Winchester.
32 Conyers Read, *Mr Secretary Cecil and Queen Elizabeth* (London, 1962 edn), pp. 63–5; MacCaffrey, *Shaping of the regime*, pp. 22–44.
33 Pulman, *Elizabethan privy council*, pp. 17–51; MacCaffrey, *Making of policy*, pp. 431–57.
34 Perry, *Word of a prince*, pp. 37, 39, 129–30; Oratio Elizabethae reginae, 15 Mar. 1576, Cambridge University Library (CUL), CUL MS Dd.V.75, fo. 28r; <A copy> of her Majesties most gracious answer . . ., 12 Nov. 1586, Lansdowne 94/35, fo. 84v; [Another speech of the queen's], 24 Nov. 1586, CUL, CUL MS Gg.III.34, pp. 313–14; McLaren, *Political culture*, ch. 1, esp. pp. 23–5, 31.

a 'providential' model would not only leave the hereditary claim to the crown open (for Mary to assume) but would have necessitated the corporate exercise of authority with male counsellors. This was something Elizabeth explicitly rejected.[35] Though in her speech in November 1558 she stated that she would 'direct all my accions by good aduise and counseill', she made a clear distinction between her and her counsellors' roles. They were to be 'assistant' to her so that 'I with my Rulinge and yow with your service may make a good accoumpt to Almighty God'. The emphasis on 'service' was reiterated twice again in the speech.[36]

Elizabeth also made it clear that she would not bound to accept counsellors' advice. In 1558, she stated, 'And for Counseill and advise I shall accepte yow of my Nobility and such others of yow the Rest as in consultacion I shall thinke meet'.[37] She reiterated these views in letters sent to Mary in July 1582 (in response to a petition) and James VI in 1592 and in a stinging rebuke to Heneage in 1586. She ticked Mary off angrily for thinking that she (Elizabeth) was not

so absolut as that without thassent of such whome she [Mary] termeth 'principal members of the Crowne' she [Elizabeth] cannot direct her pollicie; or els, that uppon this charge given by her of delay used in satisfying of her requests, shee wer by them to be called to an accompt.

Mary had misunderstood 'the absoluteness of her Majesties [Elizabeth's] government'. Corporate exercise of governance, Elizabeth made clear, was appropriate only to a minority; she implicitly rejected that her gender necessitated or legitimised it. Did Mary 'repute her to be in her minoritye' or did she intend 'to use her Counsell as witnesses against her'?[38] Having repeated the distinction she made between minors and adult monarchs, Elizabeth advised James heatedly in 1592, 'Shall you be obliged to tye or undoe what they [counsellors] lyst, make or revoke? . . . If you meane, therefore, to raigne, I exhorte you to shewe you worthy the please'.[39] Provoked in 1586 by Heneage's delay in giving to the States-General her letters regarding Leicester's assumption of the governor-generalship, his assurances to the States that Elizabeth would not make peace with Philip

35 Guy, 'Elizabeth I: the queen and politics', p. 193 citing Thomas Norton's account in British Library, Additional MS 32091 of Elizabeth's objections to basing her claim to the throne on 'extraordinary' and 'providential' grounds.
36 Wordes spoken by her Maiestie to Mr Cicille, [20 Nov. 1558], SP12/1/6A, fo. 12r (*Collected Works*, pp. 51–2, using a later copy, SP12/1/7).
37 Ibid.
38 Lodge, *Illustrations*, II, pp. 276–7.
39 *Letters of Queen Elizabeth*, ed. Bruce, p. 76.

without their assent and his failure to send the States' answer to this, she thundered:

do that your are bidd, & leve your considerations for your owne affayres for in some things you had clear commandement which you did not, and in other none and did. yea to the vse of those speaches from me that might oblige me to more then I was bounde or mynde ever to yelde. We Princes be wary enough of oure bargaines, thinke youe I will be bounde by your speech to make no peace for myne own matters without their consent[?]⁴⁰

Elizabeth was, in fact, more likely to dismiss gender conventions, whether humanist or providential, than to manipulate them. In her speech to the Commons on 28 January 1563, she acknowledged that her marriage was of great political import, 'The weight and greatenes of this matter'. But she denied that, 'being a woman wanting both witt and memory,' she needed to be counselled more thoroughly than a king. '[Y]et the princely seate and kingly throne wherin God, (though vnworthy) hath constituted me, maketh these two causes to seme litle in myne eyes, though grevous perhaps to your eares'.⁴¹ She was only willing to accept conventions if they ignored her gender. When, in 1558, she told Burghley she would listen silently to his advice and asked him 'without respect of my private will . . . [to] give me that counsel which you think best and if you shall know anything necessary to be declared to me of secrecy you shall show it to myself only', Elizabeth was drawing not on gender stereotypes but on conventional medieval and humanist ideas of good *king*ship as demonstrated, for instance, in Isocrates's 'To Demonicus' and 'To Nicocles' and Thomas Hoccleve's *The regement of princes*.⁴² Isocrates advised Demonicus to weigh everything before he spoke and to keep quiet until it was essential to speak; Nicocles was advised to gather around him wise men as counsellors and listen carefully and weigh up their advice, even if it was critical.⁴³

Indeed, it is Elizabeth's reference to her 'princely seate and kingly throne' that seems to represent her perceptions of her position most effectively. In a preface to a prayer-book given to Henry VIII in 1544, she described herself as both 'imitator' and 'heir' to Henry, 'a king whome

---

40 Elizabeth to Heneage [copy made by Heneage], 26 Apr. 1586, Cotton Galba C. 9, fo. 200r; same to same [copy made by Heneage], 26 Apr. 1586, Cotton MS Galba C. 9, fo. 200v.
41 Crane, 'Video et taceo', pp. 10–11; SP12/27/36, fo. 143r.
42 John Watts, *Henry VI and the politics of kingship* (Cambridge, 1996), p. 26.
43 Crane, 'Video et taceo', pp. 6–7; Isocrates, 'To Demonicus', pp. 19, 27–31; Isocrates, 'To Nicocles', pp. 49, 55–9, 63–5.

philosophers regard as god on earth'.[44] This may have been rhetoric – it may have even been the words of her tutor, Grindal – but it suggests an early belief in divinely appointed, absolute monarchy. After 1558, she would see herself in these terms. As articulated in letters to Mary, James and Heneage, she appointed counsellors and their service depended on her will. Appointment to her service conferred a particular status: she quibbled over the earl of Worcester's diet allowance to attend the baptism of Charles IX's daughter in 1573 because, though Smith argued 'an earle had never les', it equalled that given earlier to the Lord Admiral and he 'was one of the cownsell'.[45] But appointment conveyed no obligation on her to accept advice, nor authority on counsellors to press it. As she indicated when she appointed Burghley to the privy council in 1558, she would listen silently to his advice – 'assure your self I will not fayle to keepe taciturnitye therin' – but she made no commitment to *accepting* it.[46]

Elizabeth's use of probouleutic groups could be understood as further evidence that the structure of policy-making was determined principally by her gender: they placed restrictions on counselling that could prevent privy councillors from ganging up on her and pressurising her into action.[47] Such a case appears strengthened by the clear parallels between Elizabeth's use of probouleutic groups and Marian practice, as recently reconstructed by John Guy. By integrating the State Papers with the Cotton manuscripts, he has demonstrated how Marian counselling was dominated by a small 'inner ring' of individuals, who had a special personal relationship either with Mary or Philip II (the earls of Arundel and Pembroke; Stephen Gardiner, bishop of Winchester; bishop Thirlby of Ely; Sir Robert Rochester; Sir William Paget; Sir William Petre and Cardinal Pole) and which functioned as both a probouleutic and policy-making body on a wide range of issues. This 'inner ring' was not a committee of the privy council – Pole's membership precluded this – nor an institutionalised, bureaucratic body: its membership was based on personal relations with Mary and Philip and thus subsumed into the

44 Perry (ed.), *Elizabeth I*, pp. 37–8.
45 Harleian 6991, fo. 19r.
46 SP12/1/6A, fo. 12r.
47 McLaren, *Political culture*, pp. 137–43.

court. Established prior to Mary's marriage, its practices only became more structured when Philip's absence required Petre to commit its proceedings to paper as part of his correspondence with the king.[48] Differences between Marian and Elizabethan practice were largely cosmetic: Elizabeth's probouleutic group was composed solely of councillors (though, like Mary's, Elizabeth's choice of members was personal); it was neither fixed in its composition nor permanent in its existence (varying from eleven members in 1570 to as few as four in 1583) with a consequential variation in membership. Its activities were also more circumscribed, focused on the *arcana imperii* of royal marriage and the related issues of Mary Stuart, Anglo-Scottish and Anglo-Dutch relations.

However, probouleutic groups were not unique to female monarchs; they were adopted by Henry VIII and the French kings Francis I, Henry II, Charles IX, Henry III and Henry IV. Immediately after Wolsey's fall, an 'inner ring' of close counsellors developed around Henry VIII, comprising the dukes of Norfolk and Suffolk, the earls of Wiltshire and Sussex, the marquess of Exeter, Stephen Gardiner, William, Lord Sandys, Sir William Fitzwilliam and (after 1530) Thomas Cromwell. It advised Henry on the divorce and conducted negotiations with foreign ambassadors (especially Eustace Chapuys, the Imperial ambassador), eclipsing the prominence of the council in Star Chamber.[49] Reports from the Venetian ambassadors to France indicate that a *conseil des affaires* – a small group of intimate advisers who discussed political issues with the king at his *lever* – emerged under Francis I prior to 1526 and assumed a dominant position in counselling on Francis's return from captivity.[50] This practice, rooted in the reigns of Charles VII, Charles VIII and Louis XII, was continued by Henry II. Though temporarily eclipsed under Francis II, it was re-established by Catherine de Médici under Charles IX and Henry III. Henry III's *conseil* comprised Catherine, Villeroy (the senior secretary after the death of Fizes in 1579), Bellièvre (*surintendent des*

---

48 John Guy, 'The Marian court and Tudor policy-making', early modern seminar, University of Cambridge, May 1998.

49 John Guy, 'Privy council: revolution or evolution?', in Coleman and Starkey (eds.), *Revolution reassessed*, pp. 70–1.

50 'Relazione di Francia di Matteo Dandolo', 20 Aug. 1542, in *Le relazioni degli ambasciatori Veneti al Senato durante il secolo decismoseto*, ed. Eugenio Albèri (series 1, vol. IV, Florence, 1860), pp. 33–4; 'Relazione de Marin Guistiniano', 1535, *Relations des ambassadeurs Vénitiens sur les affaires de France au xvie siècle*, ed. M. N. Tommaseo (2 vols., Paris, 1838), I, p. 106; *Inventaire des arrêts du conseil d'état (règne de Henri IV)*, ed. Noël Valois (4 vols., Paris, 1886), I, pp. xxxix–xl. See also John Guy, 'The French king's council, 1483–1526', in Ralph A. Griffiths and James Sherborne (eds.), *Kings and nobles in the later Middle Ages: a tribute to Charles Ross* (Gloucester and New York, 1986), pp. 274, 277–8.

finances) and, in the 1580s, the duc d'Epernon, one of his favourites.[51] Henry IV tended to use more *ad hoc* meetings of ministers and magnates to sound out opinions, but their consultative function was the same.[52] There were differences between Elizabethan and French practice (specifically that consultations were not conducted at the *lever*) but these were not a product of gender: in December 1563, Thomas Randolph reported that Mary Stuart had 'conferr[ed] with suche of her Counsell' while lying in bed.[53]

Probouleutic groups were also rooted in English and continental political theory, as demonstrated, for instance, by Elyot and the Savoyard, Claude de Seyssel. Elyot had served as clerk of the king's council from March 1526 to March 1530 and was appointed English ambassador to Emperor Charles V's court in 1531. His first key treatise on monarchical and counsellors' duties, *The boke named the gouernour* appeared in 1531 followed by *Pasquil the playne, Of the knowledge which maketh a wise man* (both 1533) and *The image of governance* (1541).[54] Having argued, in *The gouernour*, that monarchy was the best form of government, Elyot argued that no one emperor could rule effectively on his own but required counsel. Drawing on classical sources, including Aristotle, Elyot identified the source of such counsel as the *amici principis*: the emperor's intimates who acted as representatives of his authority and, by virtue of their relationship with the emperor and their education, wisdom and manners, could offer 'good counsel' and act as his 'eyes, earis, handes and legges'.[55]

In *Pasquil the playne* and *The image of governance*, the workings of the *amici principis* were given more definition. Again drawing on classical sources (Alexander Severus) and history (from Augustus to Constantine), Elyot identified two ranks to the *amici*, with the 'primary' rank comprising those held in particular favour by the emperor and authorised to advise on his public and personal behaviour as well as judicial and military issues. These men formed a body – the *consilium amicorum* (council of

---

51 *Inventaire des arrêts du conseil d'état*, I, pp. xxxviii–xxxix; 'Relazione di Francia di Lorenzo Contarini', 1551, in *Le relazioni degli ambasciatori Veneti al Senato* (series I, vol. IV), p. 77; 'Relazione di Franca', 1561, *Relations des ambassadeurs Vénitiens*, I, p. 512; *Inventaire des arrêts du conseil d'état*, I, pp. xl–xliii; N. M. Sutherland, *The French secretaries of state in the age of Catherine de Médici* (London, 1962), p. 40.

52 *Inventaire des arrêts du conseil d'état*, I, pp. xliii–xliv; Edmund H. Dickerman, *Bellièvre and Villeroy: power in France under Henry III and Henry IV* (Providence, RI, 1971), pp. 32–3.

53 Randolph to Cecil, 31 Dec. 1563, SP52/8/79, fo. 175.

54 F. W. Conrad, 'The problem of counsel reconsidered: the case of Sir Thomas Elyot', in Paul A. Fideler and T. F. Mayer (eds.), *Political thought and the Tudor commonwealth: deep structure, discourse and disguise* (London, 1992) pp. 75–6, 78.

55 Conrad, 'Problem of counsel', pp. 76–7, 81–2; Isocrates, 'To Nicocles', pp. 53–7.

friends) – conceived not in institutional terms but as an informal body, often meeting the emperor at the *salutatio* to discuss issues. Characteristic of Severus's practice, as well as every reign from Augustus to Constantine, the *consilium amicorum* mapped on to English probouleutic groups under Henry VIII, Mary and Elizabeth.[56]

Like Elyot, Seyssel had practical experience: he had served as a counsellor to Louis d'Orleans and Filippo de Brescia, duke of Savoy, and had been a member of Louis XII's Grand Council, as well as a royal counsellor in both the *parlement* of Toulouse and senate of Milan.[57] In his treatise, *La grant monarchie de France* (written 1515; printed 1519), Seyssel endorsed monarchy (and specifically, French monarchy) as the best form of government and heredity as the best form of succession.[58] However, he was concerned to adumbrate the moral, religious and (most particularly) institutional bridles on monarchical power that would ensure monarchs ruled for the common benefit.[59] The principal institutional bridle comprised a three-tiered structure of counselling. At the centre was the *conseil secret*, a group of three or four intimate counsellors who discussed key issues with the king prior to their introduction to the second tier, the *conseil ordinaire*.[60] This second body was to meet daily (or at least three times a week) and was limited to ten to twelve members, though it could consult with experts on an *ad hoc* basis. Seyssel argued that the king should attend, partly to keep order but also because his grasp of political issues would be greater than if he relied on the reports and summaries of others.[61] The final tier was the *conseil générale*, a great council of princes of the blood, nobles, bishops, great officers of state and, under certain circumstances, the estates. Its function was only to give counsel or assent on major political changes, such as war.[62] Unsurprisingly, seeing *La monarchie* was written as a guide for Francis I, Seyssel's *conseil secret* had clear parallels with Francis I's *conseil des affaires*. But crucially, like Elyot's

56 Conrad, 'Problem of counsel', pp. 77–8.
57 Claude de Seyssel, *La grant monarchie de France composee par missure Claude de Seyssel lors euersque de Marseille et a present Archeuesque de Thurin adressant au roy tres crestien francoys premier de ce nom* (Paris, 1519); Seyssel, *The monarchy of France*, trans. J. H. Hexter, edited, annotated and introduced by Donald R. Kelley with additional translations by Michael Sherman (New Haven and London, 1981), pp. 3–6.
58 Seyssel's endorsement of heredity retained a caveat in that he endorsed the Salic Law. Seyssel, *La grant monarchie*, fos. i^r–viii^v (Seyssel, *Monarchy of France*, pp. 38–49); Brendan Bradshaw, 'Transalpine humanism', in J. H. Burns and Mark Goldie (eds.), *The Cambridge history of political thought, 1450–1700* (Cambridge, 1991; 1996 edn), pp. 128–9.
59 Bradshaw, 'Transalpine humanism', p. 129.
60 Seyssel, *La grant monarchie*, fo. xxi^r–xxi^v (Seyssel, *Monarchy of France*, pp. 76–7).
61 Seyssel, *La grant monarchie*, fos. xx^r–xxi^v (Seyssel, *Monarchy of France*, pp. 74–6).
62 Seyssel, *La grant monarchie*, fos. xix^v–xx^r (Seyssel, *Monarchy of France*, pp. 73–4).

consilium amicorum, the *conseil secret* bore close resemblance to the probouleutic groups used by Henry VIII, Mary and Elizabeth.[63]

These parallels suggest that Elizabeth's use of probouleutic groups cannot be attributed solely to her gender: they were used extensively by kings too. Yet, neither does it seem fair to attribute their adoption to an unthinking following of convention. Seyssel argued that the *conseil secret* was an essential part of governance because it allowed the king to discuss important matters among a few well-chosen counsellors, prior to wider debate. This was not only more effective – because decisions could be reached quicker and more easily – but, more crucially, it preserved confidentiality for important or sensitive issues.[64] Significantly, it was for the most sensitive issues of Elizabeth's reign that probouleutic groups were adopted: marriage, Mary Stuart and financial aid to Scotland and the Netherlands. They did not fully prevent issues from being debated widely at or outwith the court, as was demonstrated in 1579 by the circulation of Sussex's letter on the Anjou match and the failure of Elizabeth's injunctions against discussion of the match in sermons.[65] But they did enable issues of particular personal and political sensitivity to be examined thoroughly, by trusted advisers, without *officially* opening up debate or comprising Elizabeth's *imperium.* Such a requirement was not a product of Elizabeth's gender – the need to ensure she would not be bullied by male counsellors – but of the sensitivity of the issues under debate.

Indeed, the practical advantages of informal, non-institutionalised ways of taking counsel seem to have been central to their adoption by Elizabeth. Probouleutic, *ad hoc* and extra-conciliar counsel allowed Elizabeth both to take counsel on sensitive issues without opening up debate and pursue negotiations with more flexibility. The latter is highlighted by distinctions made by contemporaries, like Sir Thomas Sherley, between 'pryvate frendes' and 'cooncellors'.[66] Acting, or pretending to

---

63 Seyssel, *La grant monarchie,* prologue (Seyssel, *Monarchy of France,* pp. 31–7).

64 Seyssel, *La grant monarchie,* fos. xxi[v]–xxi[v], xxii[v]–xxiii[v] (Seyssel, *Monarchy of France,* pp. 76–7, 79–81).

65 LPL, Talbot Papers 3197, fo. 307r; Katherine Duncan-Jones and Jan van Dorsten (eds.), *The miscellaneous prose works of Sir Philip Sidney* (Oxford, 1973), pp. 33–4; [Sir Thomas Cecil] to Elizabeth, 28 Jan. 1580, CP148, fos. 19r–22v; John Stubbe, *The discouerie of a gaping gulf whereinto England is like to be swallowed by an other French mariage* (London, 1579; *STC* 23400); Edmund Spenser, *The shepheardes calendar* (London, 1579; *STC* 23089).

66 In 1586, Sir Thomas Sherley reminded Leicester to write to the privy council (as a body) as well as to 'pryvate frendes', 'for I have been so sayd vnto by some of your lords frendes that in these cases they are to deale [with?] your lord as cooncellors & not as private frendes'. Sherley pointed out, 'that private letters be nott taken knowledge of in cooncell'. Sherley to Leicester, 21 Mar. 1586, Cotton Galba C. 9, fo. 139v. See also Cotton Galba C. 9, fo. 123r.

act, in a 'private' capacity enabled counsellors, agents and ambassadors to discuss issues 'off the record' and pursue avenues without committing themselves or their masters. In 1571, both Walsingham (then resident ambassador to France) and Catherine de Médici made plays on talking as 'a pryvatt person' rather than 'a pvblycke person'.[67] On 9 February, Walsingham asked Catherine if she 'woolde receive at my handes as from a pryvatt person' his views on the importance of concluding an Anglo-French alliance, 'not having commission as a pvblycke person *to saye any more* then that which concerned La roches attempt.'[68] In June, Catherine asked Walsingham how best to bring a marriage between Elizabeth and Henry, duke of Anjou, to a speedy conclusion. Walsingham replied he 'was not able to advice in so weyghtye a cavse' but would give advice, if requested, as a 'privat man'.[69] Elizabeth made similar use of these dynamics in 1578 when she ordered Walsingham to have a 'private conference' with Francis, duke of Anjou, to ascertain his true feelings about the proposed match: it would enable the duke to reveal 'the verie secrete of his mynde and disposicon'.[70]

Acting as a 'privat man' enabled Walsingham to speak more freely: to talk beyond his commission, to talk frankly and reveal the contents of private conversations; it also enabled him to reveal sticking points and offer advice on how to resolve them.[71] Talking 'off the record' in this way was fundamental to the functioning of the polity, so that reactions to policies or means to implement policy could be probed prior to more formal and potentially binding negotiations. This was particularly important over sensitive issues like Elizabeth's marriage which, in 1571, raised important questions about religion and the unification of the crowns (if Charles IX died without a legitimate male heir) and promised to transform England's diplomatic alliances away from the Habsburgs. Catherine was equally unwilling to make negotiations public before she was more certain of their success, especially as Henry, duke of Anjou, was unenthusiastic about the match.[72]

Gender formed an important politico-cultural milieu for Elizabeth's relations with her counsellors. She was acutely aware that many believed

---

67 Walsingham to Cecil, 9 Feb. 1571, SP70/116, fos. 74r–5v; same to same, 21 Jun. 1571, SP70/118, fos. 110r–114v; same to same, 8 Oct. 1571, SP70/120, fos. 64r–67v.
68 SP70/116, fo. 74r. See also PRO, SP70/120, fo. 64r.
69 SP70/118, fo. 110v.
70 Wilson to Walsingham, 21 Jul. 1578, SP83/7/76.
71 SP70/116, fo. 74r; SP70/120, fo. 64r; PRO, SP70/118, fo. 110r.
72 Doran, *Monarchy and matrimony*, pp. 99–105.

her gender disabled her from exercising her queenship legitimately. Indeed, this is probably why Elizabeth was so keen to dismiss it as an irrelevance. However, it was not the only factor that shaped her political relationships. Elizabeth's perspective of her own power, and the means by which she exercised it, were strongly rooted in established theories of monarchical governance and English and continental practice: divine right, absoluteness, and concepts of counsel that represented counsellors as the *amici principis* and extolled the use of a *consilium amicorum* or *conseil secret*. But the parallels existed because contemporary theory reflected faithfully the realities of sixteenth-century politics. Informal means of counselling, especially probouleutic groups, were not adopted by Elizabeth to alleviate the perceived problems posed by her gender, to prevent her male counsellors from bullying her or to present a more acceptable face of female monarchy. They were utilised because, in the politically sensitive climate of the late sixteenth century, they offered the most effective means of addressing the problems the regime faced and the practical conditions imposed by a personal monarchy that was subject to the schedule, health and preferences of the queen. Equally, the crown's perspective was only one side of the story. Did gender define counsellors' responses and, if so, in what ways?

COUNSELLORS' VIEWS OF COUNSEL AND QUEENSHIP

Patrick Collinson's definition of Elizabethan England as a 'monarchical republic' has proved highly influential in reshaping our understanding of politics and political culture.[73] It has formed the foundation of John Guy's argument that Elizabeth's reign can be divided into two periods, each with a distinctive political agenda and dominant creed.[74] In turn, Guy's characterisation of the 'first reign' (1558–c.1585/7) as dominated by the theory of the 'mixed polity' has been taken up by Anne McLaren, though she has disputed the *terminus ad quem* and argued that gender, not religion, was the key driving force behind the development of quasi-republican ideas.[75] All three have defined counsellors as conciliarists, wholly committed to the concept of 'mixed monarchy', and focused attention on conflicts with Elizabeth where quasi-republican ideas were expressed. Yet, the flexible approach to policy-making taken by

---

73 Collinson, 'Monarchical republic'.
74 Guy, 'The 1590s'.
75 McLaren, *Political culture*.

counsellors – adopting probouleutic, *ad hoc* and extra-conciliar methods of counsel – immediately raises questions about the validity of such a monochromatic characterisation. McLaren's failure to map and test her 'providential' and corporate model of queenship on to real politics, other than parliamentary 'speech acts', only reinforces this: the hegemony of 'mixed monarchy', driven by attitudes towards gender, is never convincingly proved to have shaped the actions either of Elizabeth or the privy council. How can relationships between Elizabeth and counsellors be defined and what factors shaped them?

Though counsellors willingly and voluntarily assimilated themselves into Elizabeth's preferred methods of probouleutic, *ad hoc* and extra-conciliar counselling, policy-making remained characterised by deep tensions between the queen and her counsellors, with the latter trying to assert control over the process. Members of Elizabeth's network sought to manage incoming information. While ambassador to France in 1571 to negotiate the French marriage, Thomas Sackville wrote 'private' letters to Burghley and Leicester, emphasising how badly the negotiations were proceeding, but was more positive in his letters to Elizabeth which were little more than general summaries.[76] In 1572, Sir Thomas Smith, when special ambassador to France, marked two letters to Elizabeth 'a' and 'b': Burghley was only to consider delivering letter 'b' to her when he had managed to appraise her of the contents of letter 'a'.[77] In 1586, Hatton and Walsingham doctored a letter from Leicester, 'blotting out some thinges which they thwoght wold be offencyve, and mending some other partes as they thowght best', before giving it to Elizabeth, hoping to delay Heneage's dispatch to the Netherlands.[78]

If the purpose of such action was to manipulate Elizabeth into making and implementing key decisions, then counsellors criticised her more directly for refusing or failing to accept their advice. In 1569 Knollys complained to Elizabeth that it was 'not possible for your Maiesties most faithfull Counsellors to governe your state well vnlesse you shall Resolvtelie followe their opinions in waightie affairs'.[79] Nearly a decade later, and concerned by a perceived intensification of Catholic conspiracy

76 Walsingham to Burghley, 27 Jul. 1571, SP70/119, fo. 45r (private); same to same, 27 Jul. 1571, SP70/119, fo. 43r–43v (for Elizabeth); same to same, 31 Dec. 1571, SP70/121, fo. 128r (private); same to same, 31 Dec. 1571, SP70/121, fo. 124r–124v (for Elizabeth).
77 Smith to Burghley, 9 Jan. 1572, SP70/122, fo. 36r; same to Elizabeth, 5 Jan. 1572, SP70/122, fos. 13r–16v (letter 'a': see endorsement on fo. 16v); same to same, 8 Jan. 1572, SP70/122, fos. 27r–32v (letter 'b': see endorsement on fo. 32v).
78 Cotton Galba C. 9, fo. 79v.
79 Knollys to Elizabeth, 17 Jan. 1569, SP12/49/28, fo. 57v.

against England, he told Wilson, 'I do knoe that it is fytt for all men to gyve place to her estate: But I do knoe also that yf her majestie do not suppresse and svbiectt hir owne wyll & hir owne affections vnto sownde advice of open cownsayle, in matters towchyng the preventyng of hir danger, that hir majestie wol be vtterly overthrowne.' In a postscript, Knollys expressly told Wilson to 'hyde nothyng of my letter from hir majestie.'[80] In a barrage of criticism that passed between Elizabeth and Walsingham (and Somers), during the latter's embassy to France in the summer of 1581, Walsingham attacked her 'lothness to spend' and the way she conducted the Anjou marriage negotiations.[81] After negotiations were halted because an alleged conversation between Elizabeth and Marchaumont (Francis, duke of Anjou's agent) prior to 17 August (confirmed by the French ambassador to England, Mauvissière, on the 17th and conveyed to Henry III), in which Elizabeth had indicated she was inclined to the marriage if Henry would assume the full financial burden of Anjou's involvement in the Dutch Revolt, Walsingham told Elizabeth that her conduct was an unfit way for her to proceed. She should not allow the French ambassador to write of her resolutions without her knowledge and she should certainly inform her own ambassadors of her decisions.[82] Already aggrieved by the lack of direction given him, he told her that, if she continued to conduct diplomacy in this way, he had no interest in fulfilling his responsibilities to serve her in a diplomatic capacity, 'I shoold . . . repvte yt a greater favor to be commytted to the tower'.[83]

Walsingham's frustration accorded with others' who sought to withdraw their service from areas of policy with which they were in disagreement. Stephen Alford has convincingly shown how, in December 1559, Burghley sought not to resign from government but to be removed from involvement in Scottish policy because he disagreed profoundly with Elizabeth's refusal to back intervention in Scotland and because he could not with his 'conscience gyve any contrary advise'.[84] Similarly, in 1586, Burghley told Elizabeth that 'both afor God and man', he wanted to 'be fre from the shame and perrill that I sawe cold not be avoided' if she did

80 Harleian 6992, fo. 89r.
81 Somers to Burghley, 28 Aug. 1581, Cotton Galba E. 6, fo. 97r–97v (and draft: SP78/6/27, fo. 61r–61v); Walsingham to Elizabeth, 10 Aug. 1581, SP78/6/4, fo. 12v.
82 Walsingham to Elizabeth, 16 Aug. 1581, SP78/6/13, fo. 34r–34v; same to same, 12 Sept. 1581, CP12, fos. 3r–8v; Walsingham, Cobham and Somers to Burghley, 27 Aug. 1581, Harleian 6265, fos. 64v–65v; Walsingham to same, 21 Aug. 1581, SP78/6/20, fo. 47r.
83 SP78/6/20, fo. 47r. See similar comments in CP12, fos. 3r–5v.
84 Cecil to Elizabeth, [1559], Lansdowne 102, fo. 1r; Alford, *Early Elizabethan polity*, pp. 69–70.

not consent to Leicester retaining his position as governor-general in the Netherlands. Where in 1559 he had sought to retire from involvement in Anglo-Scottish affairs, now he appeared to seek withdrawal from governance altogether, asking to be 'discharged of the place I held'.[85]

Probouleutic, *ad hoc* and extra-conciliar counselling also stimulated tensions. In 1569, Knollys complained directly to Elizabeth that her discussions with the bishop of Ross, one of Mary's privy councillors and a trusted adviser, had so convinced Mary that Elizabeth 'wold haue hyr a Quene styll' that a favourable resolution (for the English) would be very hard to come by.[86] Both Heneage and Randolph were targets of hostility for offering extra-conciliar counsel.[87] In memoranda, reports and digests, Burghley often referred to what extant evidence suggests were probouleutic groups as meetings of 'the Counsell'.[88] This may not be significant. His reference to 'hir Counsell' in an entry for June 1571 in a digest of the French marriage negotiations written in 1579 may have been nothing more than a justifiable slip of memory after eight years (though it is possible Burghley began the digest – or a version of it – in 1573).[89] Other references may be a sign that Burghley saw no distinction between the probouleutic group and the privy council (other than in their responsibilities) or be mere shorthand, irritating for historians trying to reconstruct modes of counselling but understandable to contemporaries who knew what they were talking about. Yet, they may also signify Burghley's deeper concerns about the structure of Elizabethan counselling: the imposition of a conciliar structure on to the probouleutic group to refashion the process of debate retrospectively to fit more closely with the ideal of the 'mixed polity' that formed a central element of his political make-up.[90] This would seem to be supported by his attempt to open up debate on the Anjou marriage on 3 May 1579, contrary to Elizabeth's clear instructions: did he think that, as a proposed remedy to the succession problem (and potentially effecting the exercise of Protestantism in

85 Cotton Galba, C. 9, fo. 153r–153v.
86 Knollys to Elizabeth, 1 Jan. 1569, CP155, fo. 74r.
87 CP157, fo. 55r; Hunsdon to Walsingham, 30 Mar. 1581, Harleian MS 6999, fo. 138r–138v; Huntingdon to same, 2 Apr. 1581, Harleian MS 6999, fo. 152r; Walsingham to Randolph, 3 Feb. 1581, Cotton Caligula C. 6, fo. 128r; SP52/29/46; M. M. Leimon, 'Sir Francis Walsingham and the Anjou marriage plan, 1574–1581' (Ph.D. thesis, Cambridge, 1989), ch. 9.
88 Cotton MS Caligula C. 2, fo. 63r; The matters for treatises of Mariadg, 1579, CP148, fos. 69r, 75v; SP70/137, fos. 25r–26v; The some of the opinion of the Counsell, 16 Jan 1576, Cotton Galba C. 5, fos. 86r–87v.
89 Harleian 6991, fo. 19v.
90 Alford, *Early Elizabethan polity*, ch. 1 and passim.

England because Anjou was Catholic), debate should not be limited to a small clique?[91]

Tensions over methods of counselling and Elizabeth's failure or refusal to listen to and accept counsel had clear roots in late medieval and early modern theories of counsel and in attitudes towards gender, both of which had been imbued by counsellors.[92] Burghley justified advising against Elizabeth's opposition to Leicester's assumption of the governor-generalship of the Netherlands in 1586, 'as a Counsellor, that for the discharge of my Conscience and of my oth, of hir Counsellor, I cold not forbeare, to lett her know that this coyrss . . . was lyk to endavnger hir, in honor suerty and proffitt'.[93] In 1578, Knollys drew on negative stereotypes of women as weak and unable to control their passions, to strike a contrast between Elizabeth's failure to accept counsel and good advice. He demanded that the queen must 'suppresse and svbiectt hir owne wyll & hir owne affections vnto sownde advice of open cownsayle'.[94] '[W]yll' and 'affections' were emotive, unreasoned and transitory states associated with women and which encouraged flattery, characteristic of tyranny and the antithesis of good counsel, inherent in 'sownde advice' and 'saffe counsayle'.

However, gendered criticism of Elizabeth's role in policy-making was actually occasional. It was articulated by Knollys in January 1569 (over Mary and the Northern Rising) and January 1578 (the defeat of the Dutch at Gembloux and a perceived intensification of the Catholic threat), but was absent from conflicts over, for example, the Lords of the Congregation in December 1559, the French marriage negotiations in 1571–2 and August 1581 and the Dutch Revolt in February and March 1586. The uniform thread in all these cases, including Knollys's attacks, was a conflict over the problems facing the regime and how they should be remedied: specifically, the perceived threat of Catholic conspiracy, sponsored by France, Spain and the Papacy and supported by English Catholics, to oust Elizabeth from the throne and replace her with Mary Stuart, in addition to the related issues of Elizabeth's marriage and the succession, which weakened the Protestant succession, and the fate of the Dutch

---

91 CP148, fos. 42r–43v.
92 For the different theories of counsel, see Guy, 'Rhetoric of counsel', pp. 294–300 and, on classical-humanist counsel specifically, see Skinner, *Reason and rhetoric*, pp. 68–70.
93 Burghley to Leicester, 31 Mar. 1586, Cotton MS Galba, C. 9, fo. 151r–153v. For information on the humanist education of some of Elizabeth's counsellors and agents, see Hudson, *Cambridge connection*, pp. 43–59; Taviner, 'Robert Beale', p. 52.
94 Harleian 6992, fo. 89r; John Knox, *The first blast of the trumpet against the monstrvovs regiment of women* (Geneva, 1558; *STC* 15070).

revolt. The Netherlands was perceived as an important strategic entry point into England for Spanish forces; counsellors were also keen to support their Protestant brothers in their fight against Catholic 'tyranny', as they had been in Scotland in 1559 and France in 1562–3. Elizabeth was simply more lukewarm in her commitment to the Protestant cause than Burghley, Walsingham and others. As a result, religion, rather than gender, lay at the heart of divisions between them. Attitudes towards gender formed a politico-cultural milieu for their relationships and counsellors both had genuine anxieties about how queenship should function and sought to privilege the role of (male) counsellors in response. But, ultimately, these issues were subsidiary to the confessional divisions in England and on the continent and counsellors' desire to preserve Protestantism in England.[95]

Equally, relationships between Elizabeth and her counsellors were not uniformly hostile. It has already been noted that counsellors voluntarily participated in the very forms of counsel that were sometimes a source of their criticism and frustration. Moreover, though they sought to mediate her receipt of information, manipulated it to encourage her to make specific decisions and criticised her refusal always to accept their advice, they were neither able nor willing to dictate policy to Elizabeth or 'bounce' her into action on all issues all of the time. Susan Doran, for instance, has argued that their decision to offer Elizabeth their individual opinions on the Anjou marriage in October 1579 was a deliberate device to prevent her from concluding the marriage by denying her the conciliar support she required.[96] But there is no reason to dismiss the message as disingenuous. Both Burghley and Sussex had explicitly recognised that only Elizabeth could take the decision because marriage was a personal issue and Elizabeth was the one who would have to live with Anjou. As Sussex argued, 'her hart is to be gyded by godes dyrectyon and her awne . . . by cause no man can knowe the Inward dyrectyon of her harte . . . [neither] can eny man gyve councell therin'.[97]

This was perhaps hardly surprising on an issue with such a strong personal import, but similar attitudes were evident in other cases. In 1569, during the Northern Rising, while Knollys admonished Elizabeth that she must 'Resolutelie followe their opinions in waightie affairs', Burghley

95 Harleian 6992, fo. 100v.
96 Doran, *Monarchy and matrimony*, pp. 173–4.
97 Ibid., p. 173; SP78/3/17, fo. 34r; CP148, fo. 12r. This example is discussed at more length in Mears, '"Personal rule" of Elizabeth I', ch. 3.

told Sadler 'our partes is to counsell, and after to obay the commandor'.[98] He had said much the same to Smith in 1563: 'she is resolved, as I see to pass an other wey, and chang hir Courss. I must obey, and conform my self thervnto and so must yow, prayeng God that therof may follow that which hir Majesty desyreth and looketh for.'[99] Significantly, when Burghley disagreed with Elizabeth's refusal to aid the Protestant Lords of the Congregation in 1559, he decided to resolve the conflict between his oath to serve her as a counsellor and his own conscience by withdrawing from involvement in Anglo-Scottish affairs, not by trying to 'bounce' her into action.[100]

Neither was counsel always delivered in the combative tone of Knollys's letters of 1569 and 1578. Both Burghley, writing in 1569 to advise on proposals for a marriage between the fourth duke of Norfolk and Mary Stuart (which would neutralise the threat Mary posed to the English crown and, it was hoped, circumscribe her room for manoeuvre if she succeeded Elizabeth, especially on reconciling England back to Rome[101]), and Sir Nicholas Bacon, writing on Catholic conspiracy when too ill to attend the court in 1577, were more deferential. Committed as he was to resolving the succession and diminishing the threat posed by Mary (and already prepared to think in terms of her trial and execution) Burghley nevertheless merely listed the positive and negative consequences from dynastic and political settlements to the succession. He was concerned that an unsuccessful trial for treason of Norfolk would be damaging, but he was only 'bold to wish that your Majesty wold shew your intention only to inquire of the fact and the Circumstancees and not by any speche to note the same as treason.' Moreover, his advice was couched in deferential terms: 'Hervppon vnder your Majesties fauor and gret clemency I am bold to shew my opinion'.[102] Bacon, having deprecated his own knowledge and understanding, explicitly refused to present himself as an authoritative counsellor: the 'remedies that I can thinke of be these: nevertheless submitting them with all humbleness to your maiesties most grave, & wyse considerations.'[103] Even Knollys sought to moderate his harsh tone in 1578, 'Hir majestie knoethe that I am loathe to

---

98 Alford, *Early Elizabethan polity*, p. 33; Additional 33593, fo. 129.
99 Cecil to Smith, 16 Dec. 1563, Lansdowne 102, fo. 83r.
100 Lansdowne 102, fo. 1r.
101 For a full description of the 'Norfolk marriage plan', see Alford, *Early Elizabethan polity*, pp. 199–205.
102 Cotton Caligula C. 1, fo. 456r.
103 Additional 15891, fo. 4r.

offend hyr . . . And indede my speache hathe no grace worthie of hir majestie ears, God hathe denied it me, [Therefore] I do vtter my vnworthie speache vnto hir majestie'.[104]

Likewise, while in 1578 Knollys suggested that Elizabeth's style of governance potentially encouraged flattery, counsellors' attitudes to 'bad counsel', and Elizabeth's susceptibility to it, were ambiguous. Writing to Leicester on 26 April 1586, Walsingham reported that Elizabeth had suddenly changed her mind against continuing to support the Netherlands after consultations with Walsingham and Burghley who had 'protested . . . [that] if she dyd goo forwarde with the resolution, yt woold utterly overthrowghe the cause.' 'Svrely there is somme trecherye emongest owre selves,' Walsingham suggested, 'for I can not thinke that she woold doe this of [her] owne heade.' Walsingham thought there were grounds for his suspicions. Though only he and Burghley had been at the audience, Walsingham understood 'that ther are bad offices don from thence [the Netherlands] by secreat letters sent hether' which suggested that the States were unable to furnish agreed financial contributions. Matters were not helped by Leicester's own reports that he received such payments very slowly. Where Knollys blamed Elizabeth's refusal to accept advice on her 'wyll' and 'affections', which encouraged others to offer bad, flattering counsel, Walsingham found it hard to believe that she could fail to be persuaded by his and Burghley's 'good counsel'. He had to locate such failure not in gendered assumptions about governance or in rhetorical 'bad counsel' but in divisions amongst Elizabeth's servants at court and in the Netherlands. The blame rested with them, not the queen.[105]

COUNSEL, CONSULTATION AND THE 'COUNSEL OF MANNERS'

Counsellors' positive and deferential responses to Elizabeth's queenship undermine Collinson's, Guy's and Alford's emphasis on the 'mixed polity' as the dominant political creed, not only of individual counsellors but of the early and mid-Elizabethan polity itself. They also question Anne McLaren's argument that counsellors perceived themselves as, and justified their actions in terms of being, 'godly watchmen'.[106] Counsellors were less willing to pursue their claims to be authoritative counsellors, and

104 Harleian 6992, fo. 89r.
105 Walsingham to Leicester, 26 Apr. 1586, Cotton Galba C. 9, fo. 195r–195v.
106 McLaren, *Political culture*, pp. 48, 36–41.

press Elizabeth to listen to, and accept, their advice, than has been thought. Furthermore, it also questions the extent to which Elizabethan politics was adversarial. There were tensions and conflicts, but debate and policy-making could go smoothly too and counsellors would step back from pressing a particular line. If recent foci on gendered criticism, humanist concepts of counsel and ideas of the 'mixed polity' (as defined by St German and utilised by John Aylmer in his *An harborowe for faithfull and trewe subiectes* (1559) to 'defend' female monarchy) have emphasised combative and adversarial relations, how can we conceptualise this less confrontational style of politics?

Ciceronian concepts of citizenship and counsel, notions of the 'mixed polity' and attitudes to gender were specific elements in a wider political theory about monarchy and counsel. They defined particular attributes of a counsellor and his relationship with the monarch, or dealt with issues which real events had made problematic, like gender. At a more general level, counsel was defined in broader terms as a collaborative exercise between monarch and counsellors; it was for Sir Thomas Elyot, in Fred Conrad's words, 'a necessarily collegial enterprise'.[107] The purpose of counsel was to maintain, preserve, and at times correct, princely virtue: the prince's ability to identify the common benefit and realise it, on which the polity relied for good governance. This was achieved through conversation between the king and the *amici principis*: literally the 'king's friends', but glossed by contemporaries like Elyot as 'the kinges councellours and companions'.[108] It had three constituent parts: it had to be appropriate in substance, delivered at the right time and in a soothing manner.[109]

The act of counselling was defined as a reciprocal action: a dialogue. Elyot made this clear in *The gouernour* when he made a distinction between 'counsel' – a generic term referring to 'the sentence or aduise particularly gyuen by euery man for that purpose assembled' – and 'consultation', the act of giving and receiving advice.[110] 'Consultation' was a conference between the prince and those present, in which issues were tossed in the mind and weighed. Its purpose was not only to examine matters thoroughly but also to convince both the prince and those

---

107 Conrad, 'Problem of counsel', p. 89.
108 Ibid., pp. 76–8, 80–1.
109 Ibid., p. 87.
110 Elyot, *The gouernour*, fo. 252v.

appointed to implement policy that the chosen course was the best one. Active dialogue also enabled the prince and counsellors to examine how best to implement chosen policies and plan for unforeseen circumstances. In fact, Elyot argued that these two latter points were too often neglected, 'to the no little detriment of infinite persones, but also to the subuersion of most noble publike weales.'[111]

As Conrad noted nearly a decade ago, theorists, like Elyot, Sir Thomas More, Erasmus and Baldesar Castiglione, were also more interested in the 'counsel of manners' than 'counsel concerning business'. The 'counsel of manners' focused on how counsel was offered, rather than by whom and whether it had to be accepted. Counsellors were supposed to tell the monarch necessary hard truths but their advice was to be offered at the right time, place and in a soothing manner. They were, as has already been noted, the *amici principis* who were deputed to maintain the 'psychological well-being' of the monarch.[112] Drawing on classical sources, like Cicero, Plutarch and Isocrates, Elyot argued that vice or 'affections' could be moderated by counsel or conversation. These ideas were well established in the mental world of Elizabethans. *The gouernour* went through eight editions between 1531 and 1580 and concepts of the *amici* appeared in works beyond those of the humanist elite, like Richard Edwards's tragedy *Damon and Pithias* (performed at Whitehall in 1564; printed 1571):

> The strongest garde that Kynges can have,
> Are constant friends their state to save . . .
> True friends talke truly, they glose for no gayne.[113]

The emphasis on counsel as a collaborative activity and on the 'counsel of manners', by theorists like Elyot, reflects Elizabethan practice more subtly than some earlier characterisations of the Elizabethan polity. Probouleutic, *ad hoc* and extra-conciliar counsel all provided opportunities for issues to be examined actively and weighed in the mind. Elizabeth attended probouleutic meetings held on 29 April 1570 and on or before 15 January 1576 and was present at discussions on 18 September 1580.[114] In

---

111 Ibid., fos. 252v–253r.
112 Conrad, 'Problem of counsel', pp. 75–6, 87–91.
113 Richard Edwards, *The excellent comedie of two the most faithfullest freendes, Damon and Pithias* (London, 1571; *STC* 7514), sig. Hii[r].
114 Cotton Caligula C. 2, fos. 63r–65v; SP70/137, fos. 25r–26v; SP52/28/85; Cotton Caligula C. 6, fo. 82r–82v.

November 1572, Leicester talked 'to and fro' with her about the impact of the death of the earl of Mar, Regent of Scotland.[115] In a short series of consultations between 9 and 13 August 1581, Elizabeth, Burghley, Leicester, Sussex and Hatton actively debated Walsingham's alleged peremptory offer to Henry III of an offensive and defensive league in lieu of a marriage between Elizabeth and Henry's brother, Anjou, and its financial cost.[116] Each was forced to parry constantly, as they reacted to each other's opinions. On the 9th, Elizabeth was convinced by Burghley that Walsingham had followed her instructions, but was increasingly concerned about the financial burden the league might impose. Backed by Leicester, Sussex and Hatton, Burghley advised, 'there could be no great matter managed that was free from charge.' In response, thinking Walsingham was hostile to the marriage, Elizabeth tested her counsellors' opinions, pretending to read to Burghley a commendation of the duke in one of his letters. 'I sawe not the wordes written,' Burghley reported to Walsingham, '[but] I answeared that allwayes yow aboue anie other of her servants had euer commended him moste'.[117] On the 10th, Elizabeth returned to her dissatisfaction with Walsingham's proceedings; Burghley parried by defending the Secretary and reminding Elizabeth of her decision that Walsingham was to negotiate a non-dynastic alliance instead of the marriage.[118] Still unconvinced, Elizabeth 'changed her opinion': though 'she had rather be at the charges of a warre with a marriage then without a marriage', she instructed Walsingham to negotiate a non-dynastic defensive and offensive league, with a secret treaty of aid for Anjou.[119]

Counsellors sought to time their advice correctly and offer it in a soothing manner. In September 1577, Bacon justified counselling Elizabeth because he perceived that the danger she faced had risen to too high a pitch.[120] He invoked terms of 'love' and 'allegyance', which emphasised the companionate, but ultimately inferior, nature of his relationship with Elizabeth. He offered counsel because he was 'bounden' to Elizabeth by 'myne allegyance & a number of benefittes'. '[My] body, suche as yt is, every day and hower, is & ever shalbe at your maiesties

115 CP7, fo. 57r.
116 Harleian 6265, fos. 52r–53r; Burghley to Walsingham, 11 Aug. 1581, Harleian 6265, fo. 53r–53v; same to same, 13 Aug. 1581, Harleian 6265, fos. 54v–55r.
117 Harleian 6265, fo. 52r–52v.
118 Ibid.; Harleian 6265, fo. 53r; Burghley to Walsingham, 13 Aug. 1581, Harleian 6265, fo. 54v.
119 Harleian 6265, fo. 53r.
120 Additional 15891, fo. 4r–4v.

commaundement'.[121] They also sought to convince Elizabeth that the best course had been adopted; to reconcile the private and public wills of the monarch and maintain their 'psychological well-being' as contemporary theory expected. In June 1578, Wilson reported to Davison that counsellors, committed to supporting the Dutch rebels as a means to occupy Philip's resources and establish a buffer from Catholic invasion, had persuaded Elizabeth to honour earlier loans promised to the States. She had been 'inwardly moved to doe good' and 'satisfied in conscience, how to deale'.[122]

If Elizabethan policy-making can be better conceived in terms of 'consultation' rather than 'counsel' and the 'counsel of manners' rather than 'counsel concerning business', it is not without its problems. The 'counsel of manners' mixed awkwardly with ideas of Ciceronian citizenship, attitudes towards gender and Protestant commitment to create a web of competing influences and demands on individuals. In his criticism of Elizabeth in 1578, Knollys was torn between his acknowledgement of her sovereign status and the authority it conferred on her to govern policy on the one hand – 'I do knoe that it is fytt for all men to gyve place to her estate' – and, on the other, his growing anxiety over Catholic conspiracy and duty as a counsellor to help in the remedying of such danger.[123] The diverse responses of men like Burghley, Bacon, Walsingham and Knollys were manifestations not only of how these competing factors jostled with each other but how their impact was fluid and changeable. In March 1586, for instance, Burghley's Protestant conviction, his commitment to the Dutch cause and his self-perception as a classical-humanist counsellor appear to have been the principal determinants of how he perceived the dangers facing the realm and how they could best be resolved. They provoked him actively to seek withdrawal from governance. Conversely, in 1559, 1563, 1569 and 1579 these very strong influences were tempered by loyalty to Elizabeth, causing him to express explicitly the limitations of counsellors' powers and the supremacy of Elizabeth's authority.

These difficulties in part reflected both the complexities of political theory and practice and the weaknesses of contemporary theory itself, which identified good governance with the good prince and provided little, other than his own virtue, to ensure he fulfilled his responsibility.

121 Ibid. See also Cotton Caligula C. 1, fo. 456r.
122 Watts, *Henry VI*, pp. 27–8; Wilson to Davison, 5 Jun. 1578, SP83/7/5.
123 Harleian 6992, fo. 89r.

Who defined what was good for the common weal: counsellors, like Burghley, Walsingham and Leicester who identified it as the preservation of Protestantism, or Elizabeth?[124] But the conceptualisation of counsel as a collegial enterprise and the emphasis on the 'counsel of manners' remains a vital way of understanding Elizabethan politics because it reflected reality. Politics was not static but changeable and contingent. Policy had to be constantly reviewed as the political landscape changed, as new information was received and, especially in the case of marriage negotiations, in reaction to proceedings at foreign courts. This was not only apparent in the debates between Elizabeth, Burghley, Leicester, Sussex and Hatton in August 1581, over Walsingham's embassy to France, but also in Elizabeth's *volte face* against supporting an invasion of Scotland to oust Lennox in 1581. With her subsequent failure to pursue a mediated settlement, this stimulated a significant reappraisal of policy that advocated an Anglo-French alliance to help remedy problems caused by the unsettled succession; it was not fully worked out before the arrival of the French commissioners in April.[125] Political debate was also contingent on Elizabeth's schedule: even important letters could be left unread while she went hunting; consultation and decision-making could be delayed by illness.[126] In November 1572, Leicester had to wait before discussing Mar's death with Elizabeth because, at six o'clock, she 'was at her wonted repose'.[127] Discussion and counsel, in these circumstances, had to be flexible and informal.

The mutability of politics was reinforced by ideological conflicts between Elizabeth and counsellors on key issues: marriage and succession, Mary Stuart, Catholic conspiracy and the Dutch revolt. These issues were not only central to the political agenda, but were personally and politically sensitive. Marriage had an obvious personal import for Elizabeth; resolving politically the threat posed by Mary Stuart to the crown was also problematic. To condone Mary's deposition and seek her trial and possible execution would not only be to kill a fellow, divinely appointed monarch – something which Elizabeth appears to have been very loathe to do – but would also sanction precisely the action that councillors perceived the Catholic princes were plotting against her. To develop stronger ties with the fledgling Jacobean regime could confer legitimacy on it. This

124 Burghley to Walsingham, 20 Jun. 1586, Cotton Galba C. 9, fo. 275r.
125 Mears, '"Personal rule" of Elizabeth I', chs. 5 and 6.
126 *CSP Spanish*, II, p. 6; Walsingham to Davison, 11 Oct. 1578, SP83/9/59, fo. 1r; SP83/8/14, fo. 3r.
127 CP7, fo. 57r.

would further sanction Mary's deposition and could also denote tacit recognition of James's claim as Elizabeth's heir which, in turn, could further strengthen Mary's claims to the throne. These seem the precise reasons why Elizabeth baulked at agreeing to a strengthening of Anglo-Scottish amity, offered by Dunfermline in July 1578. As Walsingham observed, she thought it was 'dishonorable' to conclude an alliance with James whilst Mary was still alive.[128] Similarly, intervention in Scotland and the Netherlands, the acceptance of gages for the repayment of loans and Leicester's acceptance of the governor-generalship in 1586 set precedents for the encouragement of domestic subversion by foreign princes and the transfer of allegiance and lordship from a legitimate monarch to a foreign prince. As with action against Mary, this effectually condoned practices the English feared the Catholic princes were operating against them.[129]

Elizabethan policy-making was characterised by tension and conflict, more because of ideological differences between Elizabeth and her counsellors than attitudes towards gender. And, when these tensions boiled over, relationships between individuals could become hostile and uncomfortable. Equally, however, policy-making was also characterised by smoother relationships and a less adversarial give-and-take in political debate, particularly because counsellors recognised the limits of their roles and were deferential to Elizabeth. Attitudes towards gender and ideas of the 'mixed polity' and Ciceronian citizenship were crucial elements, helping to define individuals' perceptions of their roles and to shape their relationships with others. But they do not encapsulate the nature of Elizabethan policy-making completely. In both theory and practice, collegiality, rather than conflict, was the standard to which contemporaries strived and, on many occasions, achieved. Criticism and argument were inherent in Elizabethan political debate, but Elyot's emphasis on 'consultation' and the 'counsel of manners' represents an important and neglected dimension to any reconstruction of Elizabethan politics.

CONCLUSION

Elizabeth's education, her view of counsel and counsellors and the wider context of English and continental theory and practice are vital to understanding her queenship. Attitudes towards gender did shape the

---

128 Additional 15891, fo. 48r; SP83/7/91, fo. 1r.
129 Walsingham to Bowes, 6 Sept. 1580, SP52/28/83, fo. 235r–235v.

politico-cultural environment of the late sixteenth century; deep differences of political conviction (issues, remedies and creeds) also shaped the exercise of Elizabeth's queenship in crucial ways. Moreover, the latter were reinforced by the former. Entrenched gender assumptions privileged the role of (male) counsellors and provided a stimulus for arguments that Elizabeth should listen *and accept* advice; they also provided a language to criticise Elizabeth's exercise of her queenship when conflict arose over political issues. But neither worked in isolation. Important though it was, gender did not eclipse concepts and practices of counsel and governance established prior to 1553; rather it competed with them. Pervasive as concepts of Ciceronian citizenship and the 'mixed polity' were, Elizabeth's and counsellors' mental landscapes ranged over classical, medieval and Renaissance ideas of consultation, the 'counsel of manners' and the concept of counsellors as the *amici principis* as well as continuing commitment to loyalty, obedience and an acknowledgement of individuals as subjects as well as citizens.

To understand how these competing, and at times, conflicting influences operated it is necessary to make three fundamental changes to our conception of Elizabethan politics and the relationships between queen and counsellors. First, in its ideal form, politics was seen as a collegial enterprise and one in which collegiality or friendship was fundamental to the correct functioning of the polity. Second, though English and continental political culture was vital in shaping political consciousness – providing, as Quentin Skinner has argued, the range and limits of ideas available to those involved in the practical politics – we must take greater note than hitherto of the practical characteristics of politics and the real-life conditions to which they were subject.[130] Third, we must acknowledge the contingent nature of politics and political relationships and recognise that counsellors in particular constantly renegotiated their positions as they juggled competing intellectual and practical influences.

Early and mid-Elizabethan policy-making was recognised by both Elizabeth and counsellors as a collaborative exercise, though one in which ultimate supremacy lay with the crown. Collegiality was part of their entrenched mental world and was realised through strong social and familial connections across the political network, shared education and

---

130 Quentin Skinner, 'Meaning and understanding in the history of ideas', *History and Theory*, 8 (1969), pp. 3–53 and reprinted in James Tully (ed.), *Meaning and context: Quentin Skinner and his critics* (Cambridge and Oxford, 1988), pp. 29–67 (see especially pp. 56–9 in the Tully edition); Skinner, 'Some problems in the analysis of political thought and action', in Tully (ed.), *Meaning and context*, pp. 107–12.

outlooks. Though classical, medieval and Renaissance theory was essential in shaping (and reflecting) this mental world, the practical conditions of Elizabethan politics – its mutability and the sensitive nature of key issues – were the ultimate arbiters of practice. Central elements of Elizabeth's queenship – probouleutic groups, *ad hoc* and extra-conciliar counsel – were shaped more by present practical needs than issues of gender. Yet, though Elizabethan politics were collegial, they were by no means always harmonious: the very existence of competing influences of kinship, gender, obedience, confessionalisation and citizenship created opportunities for conflict. Counsellors' responses, however, were to juggle these factors and renegotiate their positions rather than develop an entrenched, adversarial position against the queen.

CHAPTER 4

News and political debate at the Elizabethan court

Political debate at the Elizabethan court is traditionally seen as highly restricted. Wallace MacCaffrey argued that the political omnipotence of the queen and privy council 'denied [courtiers] any major role in power-brokering or decision-making'.[1] Simon Adams noted that Burghley disliked those outside the privy council discussing politics and, with Leicester, occasionally sought to limit such debate.[2] However, evidence of networks between Elizabeth's trusted advisers and other, less favoured, courtiers raises the possibility that political debate was more widespread. The examples of Sir Walter Mildmay, William Davison, Edmund Tremayne and Robert Beale reviewed in chapter 2 demonstrate both that Elizabeth's trusted advisers discussed issues with those outside the queen's network and that the information and news those courtiers were able to provide could make a significant contribution to policy-making. News and debate straddled the boundaries between Elizabeth's network and those of her advisers and restrictions on political debate, if they existed, neither worked nor, perhaps, were enforced.

The nature of political debate at court has important repercussions for our understanding of alternative ways in which counsel was offered at court. Particularly since the publication of Norbert Elias's *The court society* (written in the 1920s; published in 1969) and Stephen Orgel's *The illusion of power* (1975), literary scholars and historians have become increasingly attuned to the ways contemporaries used court etiquette and entertainments to embody monarchical power or offer counsel to the king.[3] Historians have also pointed to the use of other forms of visual arts.

---

1 McCaffrey, *Making of policy*, pp. 431–2.
2 Adams, 'Eliza enthroned', pp. 62–3.
3 Elias, *Die höfische Gesellschaft*; Elias, *The court society*, trans. Jephcott; Orgel, *Illusion of power*. For a brief historiographical commentary, see Bevington and Holbrook, 'Introduction', in Bevington and Holbrook (eds.), *Politics of the Stuart court masque*, pp. 3–8 and Adamson, 'Making of the *ancien-régime* court', pp. 7–41.

Margaret Aston has suggested that the anonymous painting 'Edward VI and the pope' may have been commissioned to counsel either Elizabeth to reform the church fully or the fourth duke of Norfolk not to marry Mary Stuart.[4] John King's reappraisal of Elizabethan portraiture has suggested that images of Elizabeth as a perpetual virgin from the mid-1570s sought to discourage her from marriage, especially during the Anjou negotiations, and to redefine her failure to marry and resolve the succession in a positive light.[5] Similarly, as the focus of court studies has shifted from drama and literature to explore religious ritual and ceremony, sermons have not only been identified as vehicles for counsel but, it has been argued, ones of greater importance because they were staged more regularly.[6] In Peter McCullough's words, 'The court pulpit was a site of conflict not consensus': 'Court preachers were just as likely to come to court trying to influence royal opinion as they were to parrot them.'[7]

Influenced by the work of drama and literary scholars, historians have become increasingly sensitive to issues of dramaturgy and audience reaction when glossing political drama and sermons.[8] Using a rare, eye-witness account of the first performance of Thomas Sackville's and Thomas Norton's *Gorboduc*, at the Inner Temple in December 1561 or January 1562, Norman Jones, Paul Whitfield White and Greg Walker have demonstrated that the eye-witness read the play as a commentary on the rival suits of Robert Dudley, later the earl of Leicester, and Eric XIV of Sweden for Elizabeth's hand.[9] This work has contributed to a growing critique of Orgel's arguments that the audience was always a model one. Audiences did not always recognise or accept the message the patron or

4 Margaret Aston, *The king's bedpost: Reformation and iconography in a Tudor group portrait* (Cambridge, 1993).
5 John N. King, 'Queen Elizabeth I: representations of the Virgin Queen', *Renaissance Quarterly*, 43 (1990), pp. 30–74.
6 Adamson, 'Making of the *ancien-régime* court', pp. 7–41; Margaret Christian, 'Elizabeth's preachers and the government of women: defining and correcting a queen', *Sixteenth Century Journal*, 24 (1993), pp. 561–76; P. E. McCullough, *Sermons at court: politics and religion in Elizabethan and Jacobean preaching* (Cambridge, 1998).
7 McCullough, *Sermons at court*, p. 5.
8 Some key subsequent works on dramaturgy are John Astington, *English court theatre, 1558–1640* (Cambridge, 1999); Paul Whitfield White, 'Politics, topical meaning, and English theatre audiences, 1485–1575', *Research Opportunities in Renaissance Drama*, 34 (1995), pp. 41–54; Andrew Gurr, *Play-going in Shakespeare's London* (Cambridge, 1987), pp. 80–111; Helen Cooper, 'Location and meaning in masque, morality and royal entertainment', in David Lindley (ed.), *The court masque* (Manchester, 1984), pp. 135–48.
9 Norman Jones and Paul Whitfield White, '*Gorboduc* and royal marriage politics: an Elizabethan playgoer's report of the premiere performance', *English Literary Renaissance*, 26 (1996), pp. 3–16; Greg Walker, *The politics of performance in early Renaissance drama* (Cambridge, 1998), ch. 6. See below, n. 102.

author intended.[10] Practical problems have been highlighted: Sir John Harrington recorded that the bishop of Durham, Matthew Hutton's, sermon in the Chapel Royal in Whitehall in 1593 was so crowded that he 'heard it not well, but was faine to take much of it on trust on other mens report'.[11] It has also become apparent that historians should not rely on the printed text as evidence: printed versions of *Gorboduc* (1565; 1570), John Lyly's *Endymion* (1591), bishop Richard Curteys of Chichester's sermon at Greenwich in 1574 and Canterbury preacher, John Walsall's at Paul's Cross in 1578 all appear to have been different from the texts as performed or delivered.[12]

However, despite these advances, little attention has been paid to placing topical drama, art and sermons into the wider context of court politics. Too often they are assumed to be alternatives to conventional counsel, invoked when issues were too sensitive or Elizabeth too resilient to pressure for direct advice-giving to work. Thus, they have not only reinforced depictions of political debate at court as restricted but that it was also unidirectional. Though Orgel's argument that court drama upheld and embodied monarchical power has been challenged, a consensus remains that plays and sermons were directed at the monarch, even if they, or courtiers, did not accept the message conveyed.[13]

This picture seems at odds with wider evidence. One the one hand, it appears to exaggerate the importance of drama, sermons and art as political commentaries and means by which courtiers could participate in policy-making. Though we can only identify the content of a small fraction of the 160 plays and masques performed at court between 1558 and 1588,[14] and the hundreds of sermons, those offering specific counsel to the monarch appear to have been in the minority. On the other, it is divorced from a growing body of evidence that suggests that political debate was both widespread and not always directed towards the queen. In November 1567, for example, a 'Warnynge' was issued to the household officers supervising bouge at court 'to cause ther Guests to use

10 Gurr, *Play-going*, pp. 107–11; Whitfield White, 'Politics, topical meaning', pp. 45–6.
11 Cited by McCullough, *Sermons at court*, p. 39.
12 Jones and Whitfield White, '*Gorboduc* and royal marriage politics', pp. 12–14; Walker, *Politics of performance*, pp. 213–20; John Lyly, *Endymion*, ed. David Bevington (Manchester and New York, 1996), p. 4; Richard Curteys, *A sermon preached at Grenevviche, before the Queenes maiestie . . . the 14. day of Marche 1573* (London, 1574; *STC* 6135), sig. Aii[r]; John Walsall, *A sermon preached at Paul's Crosse by Iohn Walsall, one of the preachers of Christ his Church in Canterburie 5 October 1578* (London, [1578?]; *STC* 24995), sig. Aii[r].
13 Bevington and Holbrook, 'Introduction', pp. 3–8.
14 See E. K. Chambers, *The Elizabethan stage* (4 vols., Oxford, 1923), IV, pp. 77–104.

modest Speches upon the Affayres of the Realme.' There is little sense that these individuals sought to counsel the queen, but rather to discuss issues amongst themselves. Interestingly, officers were not required to prevent such debate.[15]

It is with these issues that this chapter is concerned. Widening the perspective of the previous two, it seeks to explore the nature of political debate at court, placing the paradigm of policy-making outlined in chapters 2 and 3 into the wider context of the court itself. By showing that political debate extended beyond Elizabeth's network of trusted advisers and their own contacts, to courtiers otherwise excluded from policy-making, it disputes notions that political debate at court was restricted. It also suggests that debate was not unidirectional. Challenging both Orgel and his critics, it argues that court debate was not solely concerned with embodying, challenging or counselling the monarch but could be conducted in a sphere independent of the crown, for courtiers' own political, personal and ideological reasons. Moreover, in exploring the vehicles for court debate and the social status of its participants, the chapter raises important questions about our understanding of the 'public sphere': whether conditions existed for a 'public sphere' in the Elizabethan realms and what its relationship was with the court.

THE CIRCULATION OF NEWS AND DISCUSSION OF ISSUES AMONG ELIZABETHAN COURTIERS

Though the circulation of news in the early modern period has been a growing area of research since the publication of key articles by Fritz Levy and Richard Cust, attention has focused on news outwith the court. Little, if any, attention has been paid to news within the physical environs of the court or between it and courtiers when they were absent abroad or on their country estates.[16] Moreover, the circulation of news has been defined as an exclusively male activity: women have been regarded as excluded from, or peripheral to, the main centres of news – the royal court, St Paul's and the Inns of Court – and uninterested in political events, preferring insubstantial 'gossip'.[17] The former not only seems to

---

15 Murdin (ed.), *Collection of state papers*, p. 764.
16 For a definition of the court, see above, pp. 8–9. Levy, 'How information spread', pp. 20–3; Levy, 'Decorum of news', pp. 17–21; Cust, 'News and politics', pp. 60–90.
17 For example, Ian Atherton, 'The itch grown a disease: manuscript transmission of news in the seventeenth century', in Joad Raymond (ed.), *News, newspapers and society in early modern Britain* (London, 1999), pp. 39–65.

reinforce notions that political debate at court was highly circumscribed, but has created an important gap in our understanding of the circulation of news: if debate at court was restricted, how did those outwith the court obtain their information? Assumptions that women were neither involved nor interested in news are also increasingly out of step with growing recognition of the political roles played by aristocratic and gentle women at court and in the localities, as demonstrated by the seminal work of Barbara Harris and others.[18]

As has been seen, letters and memoranda circulated amongst members of Elizabeth's network and those of her trusted advisers.[19] Political issues were discussed by the same individuals; indeed, the extent of this practice is likely to be greater than extant evidence suggests because much would have been communicated verbally, by those physically at court. Yet, it is also clear that debate extended beyond these networks, to other courtiers. In 1580, John Dee discussed Elizabeth's title to Friesland and Greenland with Burghley in the privy chamber; later the same year, he learned news from Ireland, 'of the Italiens overthrow whom the Pope sent'.[20] His access to the court also enabled him to witness events: he noted on 12 July 1581 that, 'the Erle of Lecester fell fowly out with the Erle of Sussex, Lord Chamberlayn, calling each other traytor, whereupon both were commanded to kepe to theyr chambers at Greenwich, wher the court was'.[21] Successive earls of Rutland received news from court and elsewhere. The second earl received reports of English intervention in Scotland in 1560 from John Sydenham; on Anglo-Scottish relations from Thomas Randolph and on the French wars from his brother-in-law, the earl of Shrewsbury, and Sir John Mason, Treasurer of the Chamber and a diplomat.[22] His eldest son received regular reports from his uncle, Roger Manners, one of Elizabeth's esquires of the body, including on the Anjou match, the Dutch revolt, Scottish events and conspiracies against the queen.[23] He also exchanged newsletters with Sir Christopher Wray, Chief

18 See above, ch. 1, n. 45.
19 See above, ch. 2.
20 *The private diary of Dr John Dee and the catalogue of his library of manuscripts from the original manuscripts in the Ashmolean Museum at Oxford, and Trinity College, Library, Cambridge*, ed. James Orchard Halliwell (Camden Society, 19; London, 1842), p. 10.
21 *Diary of John Dee*, pp. 10–11.
22 John Sydenham to the earl of Rutland, 8 July 1560, *HMC Rutland*, I, pp. 71–2; Randolph to same, 30 Nov. 1562, ibid., p. 83; same to same, 10 June 1563, ibid., pp. 84–7; Shrewsbury to same, 18 July 1562, ibid., p. 81; Sir John Mason to same, 29 July 1562, ibid., p. 82.
23 Roger Manners to Rutland, 22 Nov. 1581, *HMC Rutland*, I, p. 129; same to same, 26 Oct. 1582, ibid., p. 143; same to same, 2 June 1583, ibid., pp. 150–1; same to same, 25 Nov. 1583, ibid., p. 155; same to same, 20 Dec. 1583, ibid., p. 156.

Justice of Queen's Bench, and was in touch with Walsingham, Sussex and Robert Beale, among others.[24] In December 1581, for example, Beale appraised him of the progress of the Anjou marriage negotiations, telling him that they had been conditional on Henry III declaring war on Philip II and paying Anjou's charges. Beale speculated that one of Henry's ambassadors, Pinart, had either misunderstood the terms or did not have the authority to agree to them.[25] The fourth earl was already part of a news network on his accession to the title, even though he had not been expected to accede and was, in Lawrence Stone's words, 'a bluff, simple country gentleman': he had been receiving reports on the court, the Low Countries, France and other events from at least the early 1570s.[26]

Philip Gawdy reported news to his parents from court in the mid-1580s, though it is unclear whether he was able to use his father's earlier contacts with the Bacons and others.[27] In November 1587, 'being at the courte vppon Sonday last', he reported to his father the appointment of Sir Amias Paulet as a one of the peace commissioners to the Netherlands, and, of much interest to Bassingborne Gawdy, on the competition for the shrievalties of Norfolk and Suffolk.[28] A week later, he reported that the duke of Parma, governor-general of the Netherlands, had arrived in Dunkirk, 'suspected for No good to vs' and, on 1 December, 'of [the] landing of certeyne Spanyardes in Ireland and of winning of a Castle wher they shold have taken Mr Denny a prisoner. But it is very vnlike to be true and yet reported in moste places, and in the best of places'.[29] Bassingborne Gawdy also received news on Anjou's visit to England in 1581 and the progress of the Dutch revolt in 1588 from his half-brother, Anthony.[30]

24 For example, Sir Christopher Wray to Rutland, 29 Sept. 1582, *HMC Rutland*, I, pp. 141–2; same to same, 3 Apr. 1583, ibid., p. 148; same to same, 9 Sept. 1583, ibid., p. 152; Walsingham to same, 1 Mar. 1574, ibid., p. 100; same to same, 15 Sept. 1582, ibid., p. 140; same to same, 26 Sept. 1582, ibid., p. 141; same to same, 10 Jan. 1584, ibid., p. 158; Sussex to same, 25 July 1580, ibid., p. 120.
25 Beale to Rutland, 18 Dec. 1581, *HMC Rutland*, I, pp. 130–1. See also, same to same, 18 Sept. 1581, ibid., p. 128 and passim.
26 Lawrence Stone, *Family and fortune: studies in aristocratic finance in the sixteenth and seventeenth centuries* (Oxford, 1973), p. 175; Thomas Morgan to John Manners, 5 Dec. 1570, *HMC Rutland*, I, p. 91; John Manners to Rutland, 15 Feb. 1571, ibid., p. 91 and passim.
27 Hasler, II, p. 176.
28 Philip Gawdy to Bassingborne Gawdy, 16 Nov. 1587, Egerton 2804, fos. 35r–36r.
29 Philip Gawdy to Bassingborne Gawdy, 24 Nov. 1587, Egerton 2804, fos. 37r–38r; same to same, 1 Dec. 1587, Egerton 2804, fos. 39r–40r. See also same to same, 8 Dec. [1587], Egerton 2804, fo. 42r–42v; same to same, 14 Dec. 1587, Egerton 2804, fo. 45r; same to same, 9 Feb. [1588], Egerton 2804, fo. 48r; same to same, 8 May [1588?], Egerton 2804, fos. 50r–51r; same to same, 18 June [1587?], Egerton 2804, fo. 54r; same to same, 6 Apr. [1588?], Egerton 2804, fo. 60r.
30 Anthony Gawdy to Bassingborne Gawdy, 20 Oct. [1581], *HMC Gawdy*, p. 17; same to same, 20 May [1588], ibid., pp. 29–30. Anthony Gawdy also reported to his nephew, Bassingborne Gawdy the younger: see same to Bassingborne Gawdy the younger, 15 Feb. 1588, ibid., p. 29.

The social penetration of news could also run deep. R. Brakinbury corresponded with both the third earl of Rutland and the Heneages. In March 1574, he reported to the earl 'strange news, but not to be credited' that Henry III had imprisoned the Huguenot leaders, the princes of Navarre and Condé and Francis, duc de Montmorency, and that Amsterdam had surrendered to the Spanish. Two years later, he reported again on French and Dutch affairs, as well as rumours that Mary Sidney, daughter of Sir Henry and Lady Mary, was to be married to the earl of Pembroke.[31] In 1583, he received a letter from Heneage, though its contents are unknown.[32] He was probably Richard Brackenbury, a gentleman usher of the chamber who was deputed to attend ambassadors and visitors, make the royal palaces ready for residence and prepare lodgings for the queen while she was on progress. He was also occasionally paid riding charges, though it is unclear from the accounts whether this was through his duties as a gentleman usher or because he also acted as an extraordinary messenger.[33]

News and political debate were not the preserve of male courtiers and household servants. In 1566, de Silva discussed who was to be sent as ambassador to the Imperial court with Burghley's wife, Lady Mildred Cecil.[34] Elizabeth Talbot, countess of Shrewsbury (more commonly known as Bess of Hardwick), had an extensive network of contacts at court – including Burghley, Leicester, Elizabeth Wingfield (Mother of the Maids, and wife of Sir Anthony Wingfield, a gentleman usher to Elizabeth) and her stepdaughter-in-law, Anne Herbert – from whom she was able to solicit or receive both domestic and continental news.[35] In addition, she was supplied news by her son-in-law, Gilbert, and his wife; servants such as Hugh Fitzwilliam as well as via letters sent to her husband, the earl of Shrewsbury, which he shared with her.[36] In the early

31 Brakinbury to Rutland, 22 Mar. 1574 and 12 Dec. 1576, *HMC Rutland*, I, pp. 101, 110.
32 *HMC Finch*, I, p. 25.
33 For example, E351/541, fo. 209r; E351/542, fos. 6v, 7r, 18v–19r, 31r–31v, 43r. For riding charges, see E351/541, fo. 213v, E351/542, fos. 11r, 24r, 35r.
34 De Silva to Philip II, 10 July 1564, *CSP Spanish*, I, p. 367; same to same, 22 Apr. 1566, *CSP Spanish*, I, p. 544.
35 For example, the earl of Shrewsbury to the countess of Shrewsbury, 10 Oct. 1580, Folger X.d.428 (104); Elizabeth Wingfield to the same, 21 Oct. [1568], Folger X.d.428 (129); Anne Talbot to same, 29 May [1575], Folger X.d.428 (122).
36 For example, Gilbert and Mary Talbot to the countess of Shrewsbury, 1 Jul. 1589, Folger X.d.428 (115); Hugh Fitzwilliam to same, 28 Jul. 1570, Folger X.d.428 (28); same to same, 21 Sept. 1571, Folger X.d.428 (29); same to same, 3 Feb. 1574, Folger X.d.428 (30); the earl of Shrewsbury to same, [Spring 1574?], Folger X.d.428 (93); Folger X.d.428 (104). James Daybell, '"Suche newes as on the Quenes hye wayes we have mett": the news and intelligence networks of Elizabeth Talbot, countess of Shrewsbury (c.1527–1608)', in Daybell (ed.), *Women and politics*, pp. 114–31.

1570s, the countess of Huntingdon was in contact with George Blyth, a former deputy regius professor of Greek at Cambridge and a member of the household of his relative, Burghley.[37] Towards the end of Elizabeth's reign, Lady Knyvett received reports from her brother, Thomas Fortescue, and from Rauf Rabbards; Joan Thynne from her husband, John, when he was at court.[38]

Letters to and from women did bristle with court 'gossip': reports of Elizabeth's health, her progresses, who was in or out of royal favour, aristocratic marriages and appointments. In October 1589, Thomas Fortescue told Lady Knyvett that John Fortescue had been made one of the under-treasurers of the Exchequer; that his son, Francis, had married a daughter of John Manners of Haddon Hall, and that Lady Bromley had married one of Raleigh's men, without advice or consent.[39] Bess of Hardwick's contacts at court reported on the queen's health and aristocratic marriages; much of her correspondence with her friends in the privy chamber, like Elizabeth Wingfield and Lady Dorothy Stafford, in the latter years of the reign concerned how the queen reacted to her gifts and how she stood in royal favour.[40]

But they also contained much information on domestic and continental political events. Fitzwilliam's letters to Bess in the early 1570s reported on the French civil war, Spanish attacks on the Moors and the Dutch revolt as well as an extensive account of the duke of Norfolk's arrest.[41] Later, in 1589, Bess's daughter and son-in-law spared her none of the gory details in recounting Henry III's assassination:

[the] cruell varlett (with a longe sharpe pointed knyfe that he hadd in his wyde sleve for that purpose) stabbed the kynge into the syde therwith . . . the king havynge sum glimpse of the knyfe <styck> stroke it sumwhat donne with his arme / wherby it proced not so depe into his boddy but that there was hope of his recovery / the kynge him selfe wrested that knyfe oute of the vyllanes hande (sum sayes he pulled it out of his owne boddy) but certayne it is that the kynge stabbed the varlett two or three tymes into the face & hedd therewith.[42]

37 Additional 46367, fo. 54v; R. C. Barnett, *Place, profit, and power: a study of the servants of William Cecil, Elizabethan statesmen* (Chapel Hill, NC, 1969), pp. 40–2; Hasler, I, p. 452.
38 Egerton 2714, fo. 73r. See also Egerton 2714, fo. 29r; John Thynne to Joan Thynne, 13 Feb. 1601, in Alison Wall (ed.), *Two Elizabethan women: correspondence of Joan and Maria Thynne, 1575–1611* (Wiltshire Record Society, 38; Devises, 1983), pp. 17–18.
39 Thomas Fortescue to Lady Knyvett, 21 Oct. 1589, Egerton 2713, fo. 261r–261v; Hasler, II, pp. 147, 148–51.
40 Elizabeth Wingfield to the countess of Shrewsbury, 8 Dec. [c.1585?], Folger X.d.428 (131); Lady Dorothy Stafford to same, 13 Jan. 1601, Folger X.d.428 (120).
41 Hugh Fitzwilliam to the countess of Shrewsbury, 28 Jul. 1570, Folger X.d.428 (28); same to same, 3 Feb. 1574, Folger X.d.428 (30); same to same, 21 Sept. 1571, Folger X.d.428 (29).
42 Folger X.d.428 (115).

In June 1574, the countess of Huntingdon was told by George Blyth, 'Hear is no news but the expectacion of the Spa[nish?] fleet and of the Comminge of the king of Polonia into Fraunce with the consequence of the Queen Motheres Regence and the restraint of the Princes theire.'[43] Philip Gawdy reported to his mother, Lady Anne, in April 1581, that the French ambassadors were due to arrive shortly.[44] In February 1587, he reported rumours that Mary Stuart had either attempted to escape by concealing herself up a chimney or that 'she is executed', 'But the truethe [is] not directly knowen'.[45] Rabbards's reports to Lady Knyvett included not only news of the second earl of Essex's standing at court – he 'hath bynne long at hys owne Lybertie bvt yet kepth in svm thynke he is forgotten of the worlde, and others that he is contente to be forgotten' – but also foreign news, 'the peace hangs in Svbtile ballens not knowne which waye they wyll wag'.[46] Joan Thynne received an extensive account of Essex's revolt and its aftermath from her husband. 'Good pug,' he wrote, 'On Sunday last was such a hurly-burly in London and at the Court as I never saw. The Earl of Essex, accompanied with sixty gentle-men of account went into London . . . and made the citizens to assist them.' Having recounted the manoeuvres of Essex and his followers, Thynne concluded, 'All the earls are sent for up to try these earls and it is thought that much expedition shall be used in the trial and execution in secret.'[47]

Moreover, 'gossip' was neither the preserve of women nor trivial. Male courtiers appear to have been just as interested in dynastic alliances, the queen's health and other news as their female counterparts. Much of the third earl of Rutland's correspondence (from male and female corres-pondents) recorded information otherwise termed 'gossip': in 1576 alone, he was informed of an affair between John Savage and one of his mother's relatives, Elizabeth's reaction to Mary Shelton's marriage (one of her maids of honour) and the marriage of the earl of Hertford.[48] Philip Gawdy reported the tilts staged at court in the winter of 1587 and the visits Elizabeth had made to the Lord Admiral and Walsingham.[49] In a personal monarchy, in which issues of access and favour were central, and

43 Additional 46367, fo. 54v.
44 Philip Gawdy to Lady Anne Gawdy, 7 Apr. 1581, Egerton 2804, fo. 7r.
45 Philip Gawdy to Lady Anne Gawdy, 8 Feb. [1587], Egerton 2804, fo. 19r–19v.
46 Egerton 2714, fo. 73r. See also Egerton 2714, fo. 29r.
47 Wall (ed.), *Two Elizabethan women*, pp. 17–18.
48 Sir William Cordell to Rutland, 13 Jan. 1576, *HMC Rutland*, I, p. 107; ibid., pp. 107, 110; Thomas Screven to same, 16 Feb. 1577, ibid., p. 111.
49 Egerton 2804, fos. 37r–38r.

where familial networks were essential both for governance and the maintenance of family fortunes, Elizabeth's health and moods, fluctuations in royal favour, as well as dynastic alliances and appointments were of crucial importance.

Letters appear to have been a common way that courtiers obtained news but two other methods were also used. First, news was disseminated orally, though our evidence tends to come second-hand, when it was reported to a third party in a letter. For instance, Gilbert and Mary Talbot wrote to Bess of Hardwick in 1589 of 'Suche newes as on the *Quenes* hye wayes [around Dunstable] we have mett with'. This included the appointments of Thomas Snagge (a Bedfordshire lawyer) and the earl of Derby as Speaker of the Commons and Lord Steward respectively; rumours that little would be achieved at the session and that there had still been no news of the earl of Arundel's arraignment.[50] Second, there is evidence that courtiers also obtained small news pamphlets. Two inventories of books owned by Francis, second earl of Bedford, taken in 1584 and totalling 221 books, record a large number of small news pamphlets, including *24. of August. 1578. A discourse of the present state of the wars in the lowe countryes* (1578); Thomas Churchyard's *A scourge for rebels . . . touching the trobles of Ireland* (1584), and the unidentified 'Of ij adulterers in St Brides'.[51] Lady Mary Grey owned 'The edict of pacification' – probably *The edict or proclamation set forthe by the French Kinge vpon the pacifying of the troubles in Fraunce* (1576) – as well as John Field's *An admonition to the parliament* (1572) and Thomas Cartwright's *A replye to an ansvvere made by M. Doctor Whitgifte* (1573) and *The second replie of Thomas Cartwright: agaynst Maister Doctor Whitgiftes second answer* (1575).[52] All these examples demonstrate that courtiers obtained news from outside the court.

The circulation of news was, therefore, widespread; neither was it exclusively a male activity. Women were not excluded, but were an integral part. Information was shared between men and women, and their

---

50 Gilbert and Mary Talbot to the countess of Shrewsbury, Feb. 1589, Folger X.d.428 (114).

51 M. St Clare Byrne and Gladys Scott Thomson, '"My lord's books": the library of Francis, second earl of Bedford, in 1584', *Review of English Studies*, 7 (1931), pp. 399–400, 405, nos. 55, 77, 183; *24. of August. 1578. A discourse of the present state of the wars in the lowe countryes* ([London], 1578; *STC* 18438); Thomas Churchyard, *A scourge for rebels . . . touching the trobles of Ireland* (London, 1584; *STC* 5255).

52 Burgon, *Sir Thomas Gresham*, II, 415–16; *The edict or proclamation set forthe by the French Kinge vpon the pacifying of the troubles in Fraunce* (London, 1576; *STC* 13091); John Field, *An admonition to the parliament* ([Hemel Hempstead?], 1572; *STC* 10847); Thomas Cartwright, *A replye to an ansvvere made of M. Doctor Whitgifte agaynste the admonition to the parliament* ([Hemel Hempstead?], 1573; *STC* 4711); Cartwright, *The second replie of Thomas Cartwright: agaynst Maister Doctor Whitgiftes second answer* ([Heidelberg], 1575; *STC* 4714).

networks of contacts comprised both genders. The third earl of Rutland's correspondents included Elizabeth Stafford, Eleanor, Lady Savage, and Eleanor Bridges as well as his uncle, Roger Manners, Burghley, Sussex, Walsingham, Robert Beale, Sir William Cordell, George Delves, Thomas Screven (his agent or solicitor) and Brackinbury.[53] Bess of Hardwick's ranged from Lord Burghley, the earls of Leicester, Cumberland, Arundel and Rutland, Gilbert Talbot and Hugh Fitzwilliam to the countesses of Kent and Pembroke, Elizabeth Wingfield, Mary Scudamore, Lady Dorothy Stafford and Frances Cobham.[54] The Talbots, Gawdys and Heneages shared news between spouses; the Heneages' circle of correspondents included not only leading counsellors, like Burghley, Smith and Hatton, but other courtiers like Cordell, Lady Leighton and the countess of Warwick.[55]

COURTIERS' MOTIVES FOR POLITICAL PARTICIPATION

Contemporaries rarely articulated why they sought news, leaving historians to surmise and assume. Much emphasis has been placed on inquisitiveness and acquisitiveness. People sought news either to keep abreast of events whilst away from the court or because they were consumers and news was a commodity. Inquisitiveness has been defined, by both contemporaries and modern historians, as a trivial motive: Sir Thomas Cornwallis, former controller of the household under Mary, justified his desire for news to his agent, John Hobart, as 'a fancye commenly incident to oulde menn'.[56] This was not necessarily true: as members of the political elite, courtiers had as much reason to want to keep abreast of political events as have members of modern democracies. Yet, courtiers' motives for seeking and disseminating news, as well as discussing political issues, ranged more widely.

Using Bess of Hardwick's correspondence between 1569 and 1574, James Daybell has demonstrated that news-gathering was intimately tied to courtiers' political position and standing at court. Wife of Mary

---

53 *HMC Rutland*, I, pp. 91–213.
54 Folger X.d.428 passim; Daybell, '"Suche newes"', passim.
55 Egerton 2804, fo. 7r; Cecil to Heneage, 9 Aug 1569, *HMC Finch*, I, p. 6; Smith to same, 16 Sept 1572, ibid., pp. 20–1; Sir Christopher Hatton to same, 25 Sept 1577, ibid., pp. 22–3; Cordell to Lady Heneage, 13 Dec 1569, ibid., pp. 7–8; ibid., pp. 24–5; W. Poyntz to Lady Heneage, 23 July 1583, ibid., pp. 25–6.
56 Sir Thomas Cornwallis to John Hobart, 14 May 1592, Bodleian Library, Oxford, Tanner MS 286, fo. 130r, quoted in James Scott-Warren, 'News, sociability, and book-buying in early modern England: the letters of Sir Thomas Cornwallis', *The Library*, 7th series, 1 (2000), p. 388.

Stuart's keeper, the earl of Shrewsbury, and largely absent from court, Bess needed to keep abreast of domestic and foreign events, including the Northern Rising, the Ridolphi Plot and the Norfolk marriage plan in which Mary was implicated.[57] Moreover, when suspicions grew not only that one of Shrewsbury's servants, Hersey Lassels, was too favourable to Mary, but the countess was also, Bess had to transmit news and information back to the court in order to protect herself from further accusations.[58]

Utilitarian motives, however, were more multi-dimensional than this. First, as demonstrated by the Gawdys and Thynnes, news-gathering was both an offshoot of, and integral to, the existence of local feuds with other gentry families in their localities as well as one's position at court. The Gawdys were closely allied to the Bacons, Knyvetts and Wyndhams who contested political dominance of Norfolk and Suffolk with the more established Heveninghams (with the Cleres, Heydons and Lovells) after the fall of the fourth duke of Norfolk in 1572 left a power vacuum.[59] The Thynnes were involved in a long-standing conflict with the Marvins to establish pre-eminence in Wiltshire, as well as a protracted battle to evict Lord Lovell from Caus Castle.[60] The presence of family members at court – Philip Gawdy and, more occasionally, Sir John Thynne himself – was not merely a testimony to the dynasty's political significance. It provided the means to pursue local rivalries on national scale: whether this was, as in the Gawdys' case, appraising the head of the household of the appointments to the Norfolk and Suffolk shrievalties (central to the establishment of local dominance) or seeking to prevent the appointment of rivals (especially Thomas Lovell), as Philip Gawdy attempted in 1587–8.[61] But it also provided families with access to wider news from the court and abroad. Even for dynasties untroubled by local rivalries, news of county appointments was vital. Roger Manners was at pains to inform the third earl of Rutland of the competition for the shrievalty of Nottinghamshire in 1582, though he stood 'so indifferent, [and] mind[ed] not to deal' in it.[62]

---

57 For the Norfolk marriage plan, see above p. 94 and Alford, *Early Elizabethan polity*, pp. 199–205.
58 Daybell, '"Suche newes"', pp. 122–4.
59 Hassell Smith, *County and court*, chs. 8–9.
60 Wall (ed.), *Two Elizabethan women*, pp. xvii–xx, xxii–xxiv; Wall, 'For love, money, or politics? A clandestine marriage and the Elizabethan Court of Arches', *Historical Journal*, 38 (1995), pp. 511–33.
61 Hassell Smith, *County and court*, pp. 183–7; Egerton 2804, fos. 35r–36r; Egerton 2804, fo. 39v; Egerton 2804, fo. 42r.
62 Manners to Rutland, 29 Nov. and 6 Dec. 1582, *HMC Rutland*, I, pp. 144–5.

Second, the integration of younger men into news networks appears to have been a further stage in their political education and career. During and after his sojourn on the continent, the third earl of Rutland was quickly integrated into a news network that included leading courtiers like Burghley, Leicester, Walsingham and Sussex, as well as his uncle, Roger Manners. Walsingham was at pains to emphasise that he would keep the young earl informed of events – on 31 March 1574, he wrote, 'You shall be made partaker of such news [on the French wars] as we receive' – a zeal reinforced by Manners some years later.[63] It is difficult not to see these efforts as an attempt by Burghley and others to groom the young earl for a political career. Burghley was highly interested in cultivating the aristocracy politically. Rutland had become one of his wards in 1563, though Burghley's mistrust of the dowager countess seems to have been as, if not more, important than his political motives. The earl then pursued an education conventional for governors: Oxford, Cambridge, possibly Lincoln's Inn, followed by military service during the Northern Rising. Burghley instructed him on how to make best use of his European tour in the 1570s; advice that the earl followed, noting down military techniques and reporting on events at the French court.[64] Conversely, Rutland held no official position that made knowledge of, for instance, wider European affairs vital: he was only a member of the Council of the North and lord lieutenant of Nottinghamshire. And, though his aristocratic status may have contributed to courtiers' eagerness to integrate him into their circle, this was balanced by the political legacy the earl inherited: his father had been president of the Council of the North.

If didactic motives were behind participation in the circulation of news, then this was not necessarily imposed on individuals by leading courtiers. One of the most important correspondents for successive earls of Rutland was their agent and solicitor, Thomas Screven. His letters from court to the third earl were particularly illuminating, covering not only court news but also detailed information on Norfolk's execution, a proposed treaty of peace between the Dutch and Spanish, and the French wars.[65] Whether such information was solicited by the earls, or volunteered by Screven, its

---

63 Walsingham to Rutland, 31 Mar. 1574, *HMC Rutland*, I, p. 102; Manners to same, 28 Jul. 1580, ibid., p. 120.
64 Stone, *Family and fortune*, p. 172; Notes taken by the earl of Rutland on his journey from Calais to Amiens, 31 Jan.–Feb. 1571, *HMC Rutland*, I, p. 91; Burghley to Rutland, 2 Mar. 1571, ibid., p. 91; Rutland to Leicester, 28 Apr. 1571, ibid., p. 92.
65 Screven to Rutland, 21 Jan. 1572, 27 Feb. 1572, 16 Feb. 1577, 11 Nov. 1577, *HMC Rutland*, I, pp. 97, 98, 111, 115.

purpose may have been to inculcate the receivers with political knowledge and experience, either as they fashioned themselves as governors or Screven sought to. Certainly, when the fifth earl was arrested for his involvement in Essex's revolt in 1601, Screven was not only central in conveying, unwillingly, the details of events to the rest of the Manners family, but also directly advised the earl. Visiting him in the Tower on 10 March 1601, he 'spake pleasantly [but made] him beleave they were come to warne him to be [ready] for his triall as [on] the morow'.[66]

Access to, and interest in, domestic and foreign news was not necessarily motivated by utilitarian motives; it was also fed by ideological beliefs. The countess of Huntington's interest in Henry III's arrival in France and the expectation of a Spanish invasion probably stemmed from her Protestant commitment: she had had a godly upbringing and, in adulthood, was an important patron of puritan clerics and a well-known, regular dedicatee of godly sermons and devotional works.[67] Bess of Hardwick's interest in the Northern Rising, the Norfolk marriage plan and the Ridolphi Plot may also have had a confessional dimension. Though evidence of her religious affiliation is limited, we know that she moved in a circle of committed Protestants (including Catherine, dowager duchess of Suffolk, John Dudley, duke of Northumberland, and the Greys) in the 1550s, extending this through, for example, her marriage to Sir William St Loe in 1559.[68] Philip and Anthony Gawdy's reports on the Anjou marriage negotiations and the Dutch revolt may also have been partly stimulated by the family's confessional affiliation: Philip's father, Bassingborne, was a puritan.[69] Ideological motives, in fact, chimed with utilitarian ones: the local rivalries in Norfolk and Suffolk between the Bacons and Heveninghams, in which the Gawdys were involved, had confessional and constitutional overtones. The Bacons and their allies, like the Gawdys, represented both a puritan interest and an emphasis on the common law and the 'mixed polity'. The Heveninghams supported centralised prerogative governance and opposed the dominance of the common law and its principles. Some of the latter's allies, such as the Gawdys' rival, Thomas Lovell, were Catholics; others, like Sir Christopher Heydon, flirted only briefly with Protestant ideas. Indeed,

66 Screven to Manners, 11 Mar. 1601, *HMC Rutland*, I, p. 373.
67 Additional 46367, fo. 54v; Claire Cross, *The puritan earl: the life of Henry Hastings, third earl of Huntingdon, 1536–1595* (London, Toronto and New York, 1966), ch. 2, esp. pp. 23, 26–8, 273.
68 David N. Durant, *Bess of Hardwick: portrait of an Elizabethan dynast* (London, 1977), pp. 15–18, 20, 23–4, 26, 27–8, 34.
69 Hassell Smith, *County and court*, pp. 177–8.

confessional clashes were an important part of local conflicts in Elizabethan Norfolk.[70]

Equally, news of political events or court 'gossip' was not always
conveyed for its political, practical or ideological import. This comes
across most forcefully in one of Brakinbury's early letters to the third
earl of Rutland. Despite the large social gulf between the two men,
Brakinbury joked with the earl,

> When you come to the Court, you will scarce be known; so little account do
> these ladies make of us married men, and specially of those that be absent, for
> 'from newe fountains the water seemethe the sweytest.' You should be here a
> month before you could learn to speak to one and not offend the other.[71]

Brakinbury's jocular tone, the way he associates himself with the earl
('us married men') and the gossipy nature of his letter suggests that the
dissemination of news was also a product of courtiers' friendships: something that was conveyed as individuals kept in touch with each other.
Both continental and domestic events (including reports on changing
social alliances at court), involving their family, friends and colleagues,
were part of courtiers' everyday lives. Reporting on them was to appraise
the receiver of their kith and kin's activities and to share in their personal
experiences as much as political debate.

Though the reasons for courtiers' participation in the dissemination of
news were varied, and could owe as much to local rivalries or personal
friendships as to ideological or practical political agendas, they tell us
much about political debate at court. Political participation in the sixteenth century has usually been attributed either to traditions of noble
counsel or, more recently, to newer, classical-humanist concepts of citizenship. However, access to news was also an important foundation stone:
not only could it signify interest in political events and issues but it
provided courtiers with the means to participate in debate. Whether we,
with hindsight, would perceive their information as accurate or not, the
knowledge courtiers derived of events and issues from the circulation of
news identified to them what problems faced the regime and others, what
the subjects of debate were, and informed them of changes to or consoli-
dations in social and dynastic alliances. It provided them with the actual
tools for debate – political knowledge – without which, traditions of
noble counsel or classical-humanist concepts of citizenship would have
been redundant. The circulation of news, and particularly its wide

---

70 Ibid., pp. 181–92, 166–7, 163–6, 184–5 and ch. 10.
71 *HMC Rutland*, I, p. 101.

dissemination, was thus central to the existence of political debate at court: the discussion of events and issues, as well as their mere reporting.

THE TRANSMISSION OF NEWS AND THE SOCIAL STATUS OF PARTICIPANTS

If the dissemination of news, one of the central foundations of political participation, was wider than previously thought – both empirically and in terms of gender – then this raises further questions about how restricted political debate was at court. Courtiers' news networks comprised primarily family, kin, friends and servants. Sir Walter Mildmay's son, Anthony, conveyed news to his father when he accompanied Randolph on embassy to Scotland and Walsingham and Cobham to the Netherlands in 1578.[72] Philip Gawdy was the main provider of news for his Norfolk-based family; Roger Manners sent news to his nephew, the earl of Rutland; the earl exchanged information with his brother, John Manners, as well as the earl of Shrewsbury, his uncle by marriage. Gilbert Talbot was an important correspondent for his mother-in-law, Bess of Hardwick. It is possible that Hugh Fitzwilliam derived some of his information about Norfolk's arrest, which he reported to Elizabeth Talbot, from his 'cosen', Henry Skipworth, who was appointed to guard the duke.[73] The roles of younger relatives as providers of news, particularly on embassies, may have been a widespread practice: we know that two of Hunsdon's relatives (probably his sons, Edmund and Robert) and one of Sir Amias Paulet's (a George Paulet or Pawlet) were employed as messengers between the court, counsellors and agents or ambassadors, but we lack extant letters from them to Hunsdon or Paulet indicating they exploited their positions to provide news for their relatives.[74]

Ties of friendship were also important. Cecil's, Smith's and Hatton's letters to Heneage probably owed as much to his friendship with all three men as to his position as Treasurer of the Chamber and an intimate of the queen.[75] Bess of Hardwick's contacts drew as much on friends, like Lady Dorothy Stafford, as on relatives, like Elizabeth Wingfield.[76] Even those who may have been professional or semi-professional providers of news were

---

72 NRO, Fitzwilliam (Milton) Political 222; NRO, Fitzwilliam (Milton) Political 220, fo. 1r; NRO, Fitzwilliam (Milton) Political 220, fos. 1v–2r; SP83/9/3ε.
73 Folger X.d.428 (29).
74 See, for example: George Pawlet, E351/541, fos. 210r, 211r, 211v, 212r, 223r, 223v and E351/542, fo. 7v; Humphrey Mildmay, E351/542, fo. 33v; Henry Cheke, E351/541, fo. 22v.
75 For Smith and Heneage's friendship, see Dewar, *Sir Thomas Smith*, pp. 121–3, 131, 181–2.
76 Daybell, '"Suche newes"', pp. 122, 126.

often distant relatives or servants. Hugh Fitzwilliam was a distant relative of Bess's; John Kniveton, one of the earl of Shrewsbury's main providers of news (whose letters were also given to Bess) was a household servant.[77]

It has been remarked that news networks at court were characterised by a transmission of information that moved upwards socially: from social inferior to superior.[78] This can certainly be seen in the networks of the Mildmays, Gawdys and Talbots, as well as in more fragmentary evidence. They all used their sons to convey news to parents or other older relatives, such as Philip Gawdy's uncle, Anthony.[79] Bess of Hardwick and Lady Heneage received news from distant and/or socially inferior, relatives: Hugh Fitzwilliam, Elizabeth Wingfield and William Poyntz.[80] Successive earls of Rutland corresponded with their solicitor, Thomas Screven.[81] The third earl was also in touch with the clerk of the privy council, Robert Beale, and one Brakinbury, possibly Richard Brakenbury, a gentleman usher of the chamber. The countess of Huntingdon received letters from George Blyth.

Ian Atherton and James Daybell have argued this was because news was a 'gift', which cemented relationships between provider and recipient or offered news in tacit exchange for support or protection.[82] This is supported by examples in the Talbot correspondence: in 1607, George Chaworth wrote to Bess reminding her that he had supplied her with news in his previous letter and then presented her with a request that she speak to his uncle about his inheritance.[83] But broader social and practical factors appear to have been more important. Supplying news was perceived as a filial duty: Gilbert Talbot stated he discharged his 'duty by wrytyng' to his mother-in-law; Philip Gawdy's regular references to parental expectations that he will convey news frequently convey a similar sense.[84] Equally, servants, like Screven, articulated a clear commitment

---

77 Folger X.d.428 (93); Daybell, '"Suche newes"', p. 123.
78 For instance, Daybell, '"Suche newes"', pp. 120–1.
79 Egerton 2804, fo. 36r.
80 Hugh Fitzwilliam may have been the Hugh Fitzwilliam who served as Secretary to Sir Thomas Hoby, ambassador to France (1566), and as Chargé d'affaires in France (1566–7).
81 Manners to Rutland, 21 Dec. [1582], *HMC Rutland*, I, p. 147.
82 Atherton, '"The itch grown a disease"', pp. 50–1; Daybell, '"Suche newes"', p. 121. See also Scott-Warren, 'News, sociability, and book-buying', pp. 388–9, on the circulation of news cementing kinship links and other relationships.
83 George Chaworth to Elizabeth, countess of Shrewsbury, 13 Feb. 1607, Folger X.d.428 (15); Daybell, '"Suche newes"', p. 121.
84 Gilbert Talbot to countess of Shrewsbury, 28 Jun. 1574, Folger X.d.428 (107); Philip Gawdy to Bassingborne Gawdy, 12 Apr. 1581, Egerton 2804, fo. 9r; same to same, 21 May [1587], Egerton 2804, fo. 23r; same to Lady Anne Gawdy, 26 May [1587], Egerton 2804, fos. 25r–26r; same to Bassingborne Gawdy, 27 Oct. 1587, Egerton 2804, fo. 29r.

and loyalty to the families they served. On the arrest of the fifth earl of
Rutland in 1601, Screven lamented how this 'late wofull accident'
impugned the 'most noble howse and blooded, never yet spotted since
it tooke beinge'.[85]

Social inferiors could also be well placed to gain court news. Those who
held household posts, like Richard Brakenbury, had immediate access to
the court. As a gentleman usher of the chamber, Brakenbury was involved
in managing courtiers' access to public and private rooms in the royal
palaces; he thus knew who was at court, who was in favour and could
observe fluctuating alliances. He was also deputed to attend ambassadors,
make the royal palaces ready for residence and prepare lodgings for the
queen while she was on progress, giving him further potentially valuable
access to sources of foreign news. In 1577–8, he accompanied Sussex when
he met the Spanish ambassador, Bernardino de Mendoza, at Gravesend
and attended on him for fifteen days; the same year, he was paid for
attending on the French ambassador, Bacqueville, for seventy days.[86] The
following year, he attended on both Simier, Anjou's agent, and Casimir;
in 1581, he attended on the French commissioners who had come to treat
for Elizabeth's marriage to Anjou.[87] Moreover, if the riding charges paid
to him were because he acted as an extraordinary messenger, this could
have widened his access to news further: messengers were often asked to
convey (often sensitive) information verbally.[88]

Equally, aristocratic and gentle sons were well placed to gain news from
the court as it became increasingly common for families to send them to
the Inns of Court as a 'finishing school'. Philip Gawdy, for instance, was
at Clifford's Inn in the early 1580s from where a number of his early letters
were written.[89] As will be seen in chapter 6, the Inns were themselves
important sites for the circulation of news and public political debate,
but, physically close to the court, they also acted as a way to gain access to
the royal court and its news. Moreover, sons' attendance at the Inns may
have reinforced filial responsibilities to supply their parents with news:
after all, their time in London was at parental expense.

In addition, both the growing emphasis on political education by
classical-humanist writers and practitioners, as well as a more overt
development of skills, knowledge and contacts to gain political or

85 Screven to John Manners, 23 Feb. 1601, *HMC Rutland*, I, p. 366.
86 E351/541, fo. 209r; E351/542, fo. 19r.
87 E351/542, fos. 6v, 19r.
88 See above, n. 33.
89 Egerton 2804, fos. 7r–7v; Egerton 2804, fo. 9r.

diplomatic careers by the lesser gentry stimulated youths and/or social inferiors to offer news and information to courtiers. Young men, like Anthony Mildmay, were able to accompany ambassadors on embassy. Those without these connections, like Beale or Daniel Rogers, developed a wide range of continental contacts (from whom news could be gained) as part of a conscious attempt to establish diplomatic or political careers. Such contacts could, and were, used to obtain news. Beale's and Rogers's extensive network of European contacts included George Buchanan, Hubert Languet, Petrus Ramus, Hadrianus Junius, Justus Lipsius and Jacob Sturm.[90]

However, the socially upward nature of news transmission has also been exaggerated and evidence of courtiers corresponding with their social equals and superiors ignored. Bess of Hardwick may have used Elizabeth Wingfield and Hugh Fitzwilliam to obtain news, but her contacts also included the earls of Leicester, Cumberland and Arundel and the countesses of Pembroke and Kent. The Heneages' included fellow knights, Sir Thomas Smith and Sir Christopher Hatton, as well as Lord Burghley. Moreover, though letters provide the greatest and easiest means of exploring the dissemination of news, they seem to privilege transmission over long physical distances which may have been more characteristic of the work of socially inferior providers who were not always able to meet directly with their patrons or who sought to exploit patrons' temporary physical distance from the court. If we reconstruct the different ways in which news was disseminated amongst courtiers a different picture is revealed. News was learned by direct observation: John Dee witnessed the argument between Leicester and Sussex in 1581; Gawdy observed everything from tilts and the bestowing of knighthoods to Elizabeth's removes. As has already been noted, much must also have been conveyed verbally, though extant indirect evidence is fragmentary. We do know that Philip Gawdy spoke to Sir Thomas Leighton about his embassy to France and reported other news derived from the 'common report' or 'hearsay' at court.[91] Moreover, Gawdy often stated explicitly if his information came from 'hearsaye', suggesting that much else was drawn from

---

90 Taviner, 'Robert Beale', pp. 64–5, 89–91, 170–81, 192, 201, 207–8; van Dorsten, *Poets, patrons and professors*, pp. 19–29, 42–3.
91 Though Philip Gawdy's letter mentioning Leighton is dated [1587?] by *HMC*, it is most likely to date from 1588 because Leighton's embassies to France occurred 1 Apr 1585–June? 1585 and late May 1588–c.1 Jul. 1588: Bell (ed.), *Handlist of British diplomatic representatives*, pp. 96–7. Egerton MS 2804, fo. 54r; Egerton 2804, fo. 36r; Egerton 2804, fo. 51r; Philip Gawdy to Bassingborne Gawdy the younger, 11 Nov. 1587, Egerton 2804, fo. 33r.

conversation with courtiers.[92] Indeed, it would seem odd if those with access to court and with ties of kin or friendship with leading counsellors and servants did not make extensive use of verbal communication.

Moreover, though some providers of news may have been socially inferior to those with whom they were in contact, their position at court could bestow on them a greater political significance. As clerk of the privy council, a temporary replacement for Walsingham on embassy to Scotland and an important member of Walsingham's network, Beale's political significance not only outweighed his social status but, in some respects, that of the third earl of Rutland with whom he corresponded. Roger Manners may have been socially inferior to his nephew but, as an esquire of the body to Elizabeth, he had access to information that few could rival.[93] Indeed, Walsingham and Burghley believed no man could obtain better information than Manners.[94] Similarly, Bess of Hardwick may have matched better than her half-sister, Elizabeth Wingfield, but the latter's position as Mother of the maids in the privy chamber gave her valuable access to and knowledge of the queen that the countess was keen to exploit.

If the transmission of news was regularly, rather than exclusively, socially upward, this still has important ramifications for our understanding of political debate at court. First, it underlines how pervasive the dissemination of news and the discussion of political issues was at court. A wide variety of news was communicated among courtiers, male and female, across the social ranks; between those at the centre of Elizabeth's network – including leading counsellors and her privy chamber servants – and those well beyond it. Second, it suggests that political debate at court was not as restricted as has been thought. Not only did aristocratic courtiers, like Rutland and Bess of Hardwick, gain information but so too did lesser men and women, like Hugh Fitzwilliam, Philip Gawdy, Thomas Screven and Joan Thynne. If debate was so restricted at court, how did the likes of Fitzwilliam and Screven obtain information to pass on to Elizabeth Talbot or the earl of Rutland? Third, it suggests that the willingness or ability of the regime to censor debate has been exaggerated. The 'warnynge' issued to those supervising bouge at court at Hampton Court in 1567 seems unexceptional in these circumstances:

92 Egerton 2804, fo. 19r–19v; Egerton 2804, fo. 36r; Egerton 2804, fo. 51r.
93 Lisle Cecil John, 'Roger Manners, Elizabethan courtier', *Huntington Library Quarterly*, 12 (1948–9), pp. 59–63.
94 Walsingham to Rutland, 24 Apr. 1576, *HMC Rutland*, I, p. 108; Burghley to same, 27 Mar. 1586, ibid., p. 192.

the limitations placed on debate there were minor, a question of tone rather than substance.

COURTIERS' POLITICAL PARTICIPATION: DEBATE AND COUNSELLING

The wider circulation of news – empirically, socially and in terms of gender – has important consequences for our understanding of political participation at court. We are very familiar with the active role played by a small number of courtiers who offered counsel to Elizabeth, usually in what has been defined as less conventional ways: drama, sermons and art. But this involved few people and appeared to be directed solely at the monarch, contributing little to political discourse amongst courtiers. Evidence of the circulation of news, however, would suggest that courtiers participated in political debate in a greater variety of ways – through conversation and letters – and, if the example of the 'warnynge' given at Hampton Court is representative, were not primarily concerned with counselling Elizabeth. In what ways did courtiers participate in political discourse, at what levels and with whom? What consequences does this pose for our understanding of court politics: was debate unidirectional, focused on the monarch, as Orgel has argued?

Though little evidence survives, what we know of the circulation of news suggests that courtiers' principal form of participation revolved around the dissemination of news and its discussion orally or in letters. It appears to have been the most encompassing form of participation, socially and in terms of gender and regularity. News circulated amongst aristocrats, like the Shrewsburys and Rutlands, the gentry, like the Gawdys and Thynnes, and to their servants and lesser individuals like Fitzwilliam, Screven and Brakinbury. It is harder to pin down actual discussions – conducted verbally, they will survive, at best, second-hand in letters and other reports – but there are suggestive signs. In 1581, in order to verify the truth of reports that the French ambassadors would shortly arrive, Philip Gawdy appears to have consulted widely: 'by reason of so many sundry reportes yet the last that I heard'.[95] He talked directly with Sir Thomas Leighton on the latter's return from France, probably in the summer of 1587, understanding 'the manner of his being there' as a result.[96]

95 Egerton 2804, fo. 7r.
96 Egerton 2804, fo. 54r.

The dominant positions of oral debate and letters were partly practical. News was obtained through family, friends, colleagues and servants rather than through a centralised agency; personal communication, whether through speech or letter, was the main means available to communicate it. Moreover, though Leicester, Warwick, Sussex, Derby, Lord Admiral Howard, Lord Hunsdon and the countess of Essex had their own acting companies, discussing political issues with fellow courtiers either directly in speech or in letters was quicker, easier and cheaper than commissioning and sponsoring a play. Even the Gawdys were able to afford to use a private carrier: Philip promised to send letters this way rather than wait for the regular post.[97]

Equally, though we have no direct evidence, what we know of printed news pamphlets and of Elizabeth's preferred means of receiving counsel suggests that the dominance of oral communication and letters may have also been because they were deemed to be more appropriate vehicles for news and debate. First, from a courtiers' perspective, letters and conversation were able to convey information relatively quickly, retaining the topicality of issues which, as will be seen in chapter 5, was a valued criterion and key selling point for printed news pamphlets. They were also able to convey effectively information that is often termed 'gossip' – births, deaths, marriages and *mésalliances*. As events of both political and familial import, they were deemed to be the concern only of the political elite at court, and not of Elizabeth's subjects as a whole. Conversation and letters could direct or circulate this information at the 'correct' audience; they also allowed for easy rectification if information proved wrong or changed.

Second, Elizabeth's reactions to receiving counsel from those outside her circle of trusted advisers suggests that she was not opposed to political debate at court but expected it to be conducted in certain ways. For instance, while she had John Stubbe, author of the controversial pamphlets against the Anjou match *The discoverie of a gaping gulf* (1579), tried at Queen's Bench and sentenced to have his right hand cut off with a cleaver, she took no action against either Sir Philip Sidney or Sir Thomas Cecil, Burghley's eldest son, who wrote letters of advice to her on the match at the same time.[98] There is no evidence that Sidney's absence from court

---

97 Egerton 2804, fo. 29r; Egerton 2804, fo. 33r.
98 Sir Philip Sidney to Elizabeth, c.Nov. 1579–Oct. 1580, Harleian 1323, fos. 44r–56v (and see Duncan-Jones and van Dorsten (eds.), *Miscellaneous prose*); CP148, fos. 19r–22v. For full details of this episode see my, 'Counsel, public debate, and queenship', pp. 629–50 and below, ch. 6.

during the first half of 1580 was an exile imposed by an angry queen.[99] The difference in tone between the pamphlet and the letters was an important factor: whereas Cecil and Sidney were deferential, Stubbe levelled personal criticisms against Anjou and questioned Elizabeth's ability to make a decision on the grounds of her gender.[100] But the social standing of the three men and their chosen form of communication were highly influential. As courtiers and sons of the nobility or gentry, Cecil and Sidney could present their advice in traditional terms of noble counsel; as an ordinary subject, Stubbe could not.[101] Though the existence of multiple copies of Sidney's letter suggest it circulated at court, his and Cecil's choice of letter-form for their advice meant its dissemination was restricted to the queen, and possibly other courtiers; Stubbe's printed pamphlet was available to all who could buy a copy.

Elizabeth's preference for political debate to be conducted only by courtiers, within the confines of the court, and preferably not subjecting her to open pressure, were conditions to which conversation and letters were well-suited. They enabled courtiers to discuss political issues without reference to the queen. When courtiers did address Elizabeth directly, verbally or in a letter of advice, she was able to receive counsel without an audience hanging on her reaction, as at a play or sermon. Moreover, though we have seen that the circulation of news was socially broad, political debate conducted by conversation and in letters remained, in theory at least, circumscribed to courtiers and did not extend to the general public.

In both its frequency of use and its acceptability, political debate conducted verbally or in letters surpassed counselling Elizabeth indirectly through the visual arts, as a form of political participation. Drama, sermons and art were recognised as legitimate and effective means of counselling, particularly on sensitive subjects like Elizabeth's marriage and the succession. It was part of early modern political culture, as articulated by scholars like Erasmus, in which counsellors were encouraged to advise in subtle and entertaining ways to persuade the monarch almost without them realising it. Advice and political commentary were cloaked in plays like Norton's and Sackville's *Gorboduc* (1561–2) and Thomas Hughes

---

99 Duncan-Jones and van Dorsten (eds.), *Miscellaneous prose*, pp. 34–5.
100 Harleian 1323, fos. 44r–56v; CP148, fos. 19r–22v; John Stubbs, *The discoverie of a gaping gulf whereinto England is like to be swallowed by an other French mariage* (London, 1579; *STC* 23400), sigs. D8v–E6v.
101 Mears, 'Counsel, public debate and queenship', pp. 646–7.

et al.'s The misfortunes of Arthur (1588)[102] as well as sermons. In April 1579, Gilbert Talbot reported to his father that

The preachers have bene somewhat too busye to applye their sermonds to tende to covertly agaynste this marryage, many of them inveyinge greatly therat, tyll the laste weke her matie gave expresse comandement that none of them sholde hereafter preache upon any suche texte as the lyke myghte be inferred.[103]

Thomas Drant censured Elizabeth for too lenient treatment of the Northern rebels and counselled greater preparedness against Catholic subversion and invasion in his sermon at Windsor in January 1570.[104] Richard Fletcher defended the execution of Mary Stuart and called for harsher policies towards English Catholics in a sermon delivered immediately after the execution, probably in February 1587.[105] The anonymous group portrait, 'Edward VI and the Pope', may have been commissioned in the late 1560s or early 1570s either to advise Elizabeth to reform the church fully or the fourth duke of Norfolk against marrying Mary Stuart.[106]

However, few courtiers were able to counsel Elizabeth even indirectly. It was primarily the preserve of chaplains and bishops, like Thomas Drant (chaplain to Bishop Grindal of London and a court preacher) and Richard Fletcher (one of Grindal's successors at London), who were not only able to turn exhortatory sermons to political ends but had more opportunities

---

102 The literature in this field is extensive but see the following selection of primary and secondary works on the plays cited and others: Ernest William Talbert, 'The political import and the first two audiences of *Gorboduc*', in Thomas P. Harrison, Archibald H. Hill, Ernest C. Mossner and James Sledd (eds.), *Studies in honor of DeWitt T. Staines* (Austin, TX, 1967), pp. 89–115; Marie Axton, 'Robert Dudley and the Inner Temple Revels', *Historical Journal*, 13 (1970), pp. 365–78; D. S. Bland, 'Arthur Broke's *Masque of beauty and desire*: a reconstruction', *Research Opportunities in Renaissance Drama*, 19 (1976), pp. 49–55; Jones and Whitfield White, '*Gorboduc* and royal marriage politics', pp. 3–16; Walker, *Politics of performance*, ch. 6; de Silva to Philip II, 14 Apr. 1567, *CSP Spanish*, I, pp. 632–4; Norman Council, '*O Dea certe*: the allegory of *The fortress of perfect beauty*', *Huntington Library Quarterly*, 39 (1976), pp. 329–42; H. R. Woudhuysen, 'Leicester's literary patronage: a study of the English court, 1578–82', (D.Phil. thesis, Oxford, 1980); *The misfortunes of Arthur: a critical, old-spelling edition*, ed. Brian Jay Corrigan (New York and London, 1992).

103 Talbot to Shrewsbury, 4 Apr. 1579, Talbot MS F/307, in Lodge, *Illustrations of British History*, pp. 212–13.

104 Thomas Drant, *Two sermons preached the one at S. Maries Spittle on Tuesday in Easter weeke 1570 and the other at the court at Windsor the Sonday after twelfth day, being the viij of Ianuary, before in the yeare 1569* (London, 1570; *STC* 7171.5), sigs. Ii[v], Ivii[r]–Kiv[v].

105 McCullough, *Sermons at court*, pp. 84–90; I McCullough, 'Out of Egypt: Richard Fletcher's sermon before Elizabeth I after the execution of Mary Queen of Scots', in Julia M. Walker (ed.), *Dissing Elizabeth: negative representations of Gloriana* (Durham, NC and London, 1998), pp. 118–49.

106 Aston, *King's bedpost*, passim.

to do so. Though there were fewer sermons at the Elizabethan court than its Jacobean successor, they still occurred on weekdays, Sundays and during Lent. Moreover, as Sunday sermons were free-standing, rather than part of the service, their texts did not necessarily follow the day's lesson, providing more scope to tackle topical issues. Equally, though more than 160 plays were performed at court in the first thirty years of the reign, extant evidence suggests that few of them addressed political themes or were conceived as plays of counsel. Moreover, many of the most prominent examples of counselling plays, like Norton's and Sackville's *Gorboduc* or Hughes *et al.*'s *The misfortunes of Arthur* were products of the Inns of Court. A letter from Francis Bacon to Burghley suggests that *The misfortunes of Arthur* was written purposely for the court, but *Gorboduc* was not and it remains unclear why it was performed at court: it is usually attributed to Leicester's patronage but there is no evidence to support this.[107] Counselling works of art are even more rare; indeed, because the identity of the patron or artist of 'Edward VI and the Pope' remains a mystery, it is difficult to know if this was even a court production.

However, if the importance of drama, sermons and art as means for courtiers to act politically has been exaggerated, then they were still an integral part of court debate, raising questions about how far such debate was directed solely towards the monarch. First, courtiers could be as much the targets of patrons', playwrights', preachers' and painters' counsel as the monarch. Richard Curteys's sermon on the need for greater patronage of a preaching ministry, delivered at Greenwich in 1574, is often glossed as a direct criticism of Elizabeth. Certainly, he reminded Elizabeth of her own mortality towards the end of his sermon:

I am a gentleman, a Noble man, I came in with the conqueror, I can fetche my pedigree long before the Conquest, a kyng was my father, a Queene was my mother, a king my brother, a Queene my sister: yet must you saye, 'The grave is my house, darknesse is my bed'.[108]

Yet, Curteys implicated the nobility and gentry in his criticisms of lay patrons. 'Wee of the Churche of Englande, are vnthankfull to God for oure Treasures and Jewels, for oure houses and landes, our vnitie and peace'.[109] In particular, he criticised courtiers for failing to honour their

---

107 Francis Bacon to Burghley, n.d., cited in *Misfortunes of Arthur*, ed. Corrigan, p. 1; Ian Archer *et al.* (eds.), *Religion, politics and society, in sixteenth-century England* (Camden Society, fifth series, 22; Cambridge and London, 2003), pp. 49–50.
108 Curteys, *A sermon preached at Grenevviche*, sig. Cviii[v].
109 Ibid., sig. Civ[r].

responsibilities to provide hospitality, alms and support education, leaving these duties to the clergy:

They think that Job should pray and sacrifice for them. The spirituall men (say they) shoulde keepe hospitalitie, the spirituall men shoulde see the people taught, shoulde giue almes . . . most true: and therefore, should Gentlemen, and Noble men keepe hospitalitie, shoulde see the people taught, giue almes.[110]

Similar themes were apparent in his Lent sermon preached the following year, when he called the nobility the 'posts of the Christian Church and common welth', the ministers the rails and the people the pales.[111]

Second, politically engaged drama did not just seek to offer advice; it also explored broader issues facing the Elizabethan regime and encouraged courtiers to reflect on them. John Lyly's *Sapho and Phao* has traditionally been seen as an attempt to counsel Elizabeth on the Anjou match but recent reassessments of the date of its first performance have pointed to 1584, a few months prior to Anjou's death, rather than 1582 when the negotiations remained fitfully, if not seriously, alive.[112] Rather than seeking to counsel Elizabeth, the play explored, in front of courtiers, the issue of a queen conquering her passions that, until so recently, had been of crucial importance to the political agenda. Lyly's seemingly deliberate choice of the obscure legend of Sappho in 1584 is otherwise difficult to explain. Certainly, his choice contrasted strongly with that for *Campaspe*, probably also first performed in 1584, which had circulated in popular ballad form since the 1560s.[113]

This approach to political issues was strongly characteristic of Lyly's plays: *Campaspe* (1584) and *Endymion* (1588) addressed peace versus war, the duties of citizenship (including the antithesis between the court and the country), military honour versus courtiership, as well as courtly manners and courtly love.[114] But it is also evident in other works. *Gorboduc* explored the nature of counsel and the relationship between monarchs

---

110 Ibid., sig. Cv[r].

111 Richard Curteys, *A sermon preached before the Queenes Maiestie at Richmond the 6. of Marche last past* (London, 1575; *STC* 6139), sig. Civ[r].

112 John Lyly, *'Campaspe' and 'Sapho and Phao'*, ed. G. K. Hunter and David Bevington (Manchester and New York, 1991), pp. 4–5.

113 The Stationers' Register records a balled entitled 'The history of Alexander Campaspe, and Appelles' for 1565–6, though the ballad is no longer extant. *'Campaspe' and 'Sappho and Phao'*, ed. Hunter and Bevington, pp. 152–3, 166, 5–6.

114 *'Campaspe' and 'Sappho and Phao'*, ed. Hunter and Bevington, pp. 5–6, 16, 156, 177–8; *Endymion*, ed. Bevington, pp. 11–12.

and their counsellors.[115] *The misfortunes of Arthur* dealt with the antithesis between peace and war and the nature of kingship and governance, including the roles of the nobility and citizenry.[116] Indeed, it is hard not to see, in *The misfortunes of Arthur*, that the discussion of whether to avenge the blood of one's family was an attempt to explore the consequences for Elizabeth of Mary's execution the previous year.[117]

This discursive function was central and integral to these plays, dictating their structure and style. All of them deliberately subordinated plot and melodrama to dialogue in order to explore their political themes fully and to allow them to come to the fore. Dialogue and soliloquies were used to present different viewpoints to educate the audience.[118] Physical action was often sidelined: in *The misfortunes of Arthur*, for instance, violence was off-stage to allow debates on kingship and governance to dominate the audience's attention.[119] And, particularly in Lyly's plays, issues were divided into a thesis and antithesis, and characters were often paired or grouped together, reinforcing the sense of arguing *in utramque partem* (or pro and contra).[120] In *Endymion*, for instance, Endymion and Cynthia were paired to explore the antithesis between love and one's higher political, religious or moral calling, while the group comprising Endymion, Eumenides and Semele was used to explore the theme of love and friendship.[121] It was an approach that not only drew on dramatic traditions of the Italian *comedia nova* or *trattati d'amore* and English medieval guild drama, but also had close parallels with Elizabethan court fashions in rhetoric and oratory, specifically Elizabeth's favoured preaching style, *pronunciationem aulicam* and *ingenium aulicam* (courtly delivery and courtly wit), practised by her favourite preachers, like Thomas Dove and Alexander Nowell.[122]

115 Jessica Lynn Winston, 'Literature and politics at the early Elizabethan Inns of Court' (Ph.D. thesis, University of California, Santa Barbara, 2002), pp. 160–6; Winston, 'Expanding the political nation: *Gorboduc* at the Inns of Court and succession revisited', *Early Theatre*, 8 (forthcoming: 2005). I would like to thank Jessica for giving me a copy of her article prior to publication.

116 *Misfortunes of Arthur*, ed. Corrigan, pp. 26–31, 155–9, 170, 108–14, 125, 141–2, 161.

117 Ibid., pp. 134–5.

118 *'Campaspe' and 'Sappho and Phao'*, ed. Hunter and Bevington, p. 173.

119 *Misfortunes of Arthur*, ed. Corrigan, pp. 31–6.

120 Joel B. Altman, '*Quaestiones copiosae*: pastoral and courtly in John Lyly', in Altman (ed.), *The Tudor play of mind: rhetorical inquiry and the development of Elizabethan drama* (Berkeley, CA and London, 1978), pp. 196–228.

121 *Endymion*, ed. Bevington, pp. 38–42.

122 McCullough, *Sermons at court*, pp. 78–9.

Directed at Elizabeth, these plays were 'Mirrors for princes', demonstrating for what she should strive.[123] But, for courtiers, plays like *Sapho and Phao* and *The misfortunes of Arthur* were, in effect, dramatic versions of the pro and contra memoranda that some of Elizabeth's most trusted advisers, like Burghley, used to explore issues prior to giving advice.[124] They covered similar issues, either directly or from alternative angles: Elizabeth's marriage (e.g. *Sapho and Phao*) or the nature of monarchy, counsel and citizenship (e.g. *Gorboduc, Campaspe*). In their subject matter, structure and style, they encouraged courtiers to explore broad, relevant, political issues actively from a range of perspectives, to examine issues from all angles and to come to conclusions about the right course of action, even though their opinions would not necessarily be sought by Elizabeth. In doing so, they contributed directly to courtiers' political discourse conducted in more conventional ways, through conversation and letters. Not only did they address some of the same issues on which news circulated – Elizabeth's marriage, the fate of Mary Stuart – but they encouraged courtiers to engage actively in exploring and evaluating them. Where the reporting of news highlighted what events were of interest, drama *in utramque partem* could help define what problems these events raised and how they might be resolved.

Third, courtiers do not seem to have glossed performances of politically engaged drama and sermons, like *The misfortunes of Arthur* or Fletcher's sermon after Mary Stuart's execution, solely in terms of the monarch's reaction, as Orgel and others have argued.[125] Rather, they also interpreted them in terms of their own political knowledge, suggesting that their experiences may then have become part of, and influenced, wider court political discourse. This is suggested by the eyewitness account of the first

---

123 For example, in *Campaspe* Hepheston chides Alexander for being more interested in love than war:

> I cannot tell, Alexander, whether the report be
> more shameful to be heard or the cause more sorrowful to be
> believed. What, is the son of Philip, King of Macedon,
> become the subject of Campaspe, the captive of Thebes?
> (*Campaspe*, II. 2. 33–6)

124 Skinner, *Reason and rhetoric*, chs. 1, 2; Alford, *Early Elizabethan polity*, pp. 14–28 and passim; Mears, '"Personal rule" of Elizabeth I', ch. 3 and see above, ch. 3.

125 Orgel, *Illusion of power*, pp. 9–16 and ch. 2; Jonathon Goldberg, *James I and the politics of literature: Jonson, Shakespeare, Donne, and their contemporaries* (Stanford, CA, 1989), passim.

performance of *Gorboduc* (1561–2).[126] Though the performance took place at the Inner Temple, not the court, it is possible that the author of the account was a minor courtier. Simon Adams has suggested the author was John Hales who, on his return to England in 1559, resumed his duties as Clerk of the Hanaper, until his arrest in 1564 for writing 'The declaration of the succession of the crown imperial of England'. He was also well connected to other members of the court, including Sir Ralph Sadler, Robert Beale and Roger Ascham.[127]

The eyewitness glossed *Gorboduc* topically, perceiving it primarily as a commentary on Elizabeth's marriage and the rival suits of Leicester and Eric XIV of Sweden. He commented, 'Many thinges were handled of mariage and that the matter was to be debated in parliament . . . And many thinges were saied for the Succession to putt thinges in certenty.' In particular, he highlighted the second dumb show in which a king, offered a clear glass and a golden cup, trampled the glass one underfoot and took the golden one, which was full of poison. This he glossed as, 'men refused the certen and tooke the vncerten, wherby was ment that yt was better for the Quene to marye with the Lord Robert knowen then with the king of Sweden.'[128] Though it appears that the version of the play may have differed slightly from that which was published in 1565 and 1570,[129] *Gorboduc* nevertheless ranged more widely than the eyewitness's account suggests. Jessica Winston has pointed out how preoccupied the play was with the issue of counsel, exploring different forms in relation to monarchical power.[130]

The eyewitness's reading seems to have been shaped by contemporary events. At court, Sir Thomas Smith, who had received Eric's brother, John of Finland, in 1559 wrote his 'Orations for and against the Queen's marriage' at this time and was involved in an informal discussion with a friend about the Swedish match.[131] In the City, joint woodcut portraits of Eric and Elizabeth circulated as (premature) wedding souvenirs.[132] Moreover, at the beginning of December, Eric's ambassador, Nicholas

126 'A "journall" of matters of state happened from time to time as well within and without the realme from and before the death of King Edw. the 6th until the yere 1562', c.1562, Additional 48023 fo. 359v; modern edition: Archer *et al.* (eds.), *Religion, politics and society*, pp. 36–122.
127 Archer *et al.* (eds.), *Religion, politics and society*, pp. 45–51, 51 (fn. 55); Hasler, II, pp. 238–9.
128 Additional 48023, fo. 359v.
129 Jones and Whitfield White, '*Gorboduc* and royal marriage politics', pp. 12–14; Walker, *Politics of performance*, pp. 213–20.
130 Winston, 'Literature and politics', pp. 160–81; Winston, 'Expanding the political nation'.
131 John Strype, *The life of the learned Sir Thomas Smith, kt. DCL* (new edn, Oxford, 1820), pp. 59 (fn. B), 60–4, 184–259.
132 Jones and Whitfield White, '*Gorboduc* and royal marriage politics', p. 9.

Guildernstern, had asked Elizabeth to confirm the terms of the marriage, to issue Eric a passport to visit and to confirm whether, if they married and had issue, Elizabeth would go with Eric to Sweden. Crucially, the eyewitness appears to have known of Guilderstern's request, and Elizabeth's response: he recorded it in his journal prior to the entry on *Gorboduc*.[133]

We do not know exactly how, or when, the 'journall' was compiled: internal references do suggest that it was the basis for a fuller account,[134] though it is unclear to what degree the author recorded events contemporaneously. However, throughout the text, the author displays a wide-ranging knowledge of events which, in conjunction with his possible court connections, suggests that he may have been able to gather news as events happened. If so, this would suggest that he read *Gorboduc* topically, focusing on the marriage itself because his knowledge of contemporary events – particularly Guilderstern's negotiations – made this aspect of particular relevance. In turn, this would indicate that courtiers were not merely concerned with the monarch's reaction, but interpreted performances according to their knowledge of contemporary events and issues. Furthermore, though evidence is lacking, it may also suggest that their interpretations then entered the political discourse as they reported and reflected on performances to their friends, relatives, masters and mistresses.

Courtiers thus participated in political discourse and activity in a variety of ways. It is most likely that direct conversation was the predominant means, though little evidence of this remains extant. Drama, sermons and art offered some courtiers the opportunity to counsel Elizabeth, but they were more important either as a means of counselling *courtiers* or to explore and debate topical issues, often *in utramque partem*, before and for a courtier audience. These different forms appear to have been highly integrated, not only into each other, but also into the fabric of court life. Political discourse conducted in drama, sermons and art addressed many of the same issues articulated verbally or in letters. They seem to have been glossed according to the audience members' political knowledge, and it is possible that the interpretations courtiers placed on them entered their political discourse, as they reported on and discussed plays and sermons.

133 Additional 48023, fo. 358r.
134 For example, 'Enquire of Mr Askam for the copie of the articles of griefes, that the Scottes had against the French which were by him translated into Laten and sent to king Phillipp.' Additional 48023, fo. 352v.

Integrated though these different forms were, the preponderance of oral communication and letters over politically engaged drama, sermons and art challenges current theories that political debate at court was solely or primarily directed towards the monarch. Counselling plays, sermons, art – and letters – appear to have been relatively rare and courtiers' principal engagement in politics seems to have been through disseminating news and discussing issues among themselves. Political debate was thus conducted largely independently of the monarch and it did not seek primarily to influence their actions. Participation could be stimulated by ideological concerns, but these did not often translate into a policy-making agenda on which courtiers were able or willing to act. Similarly, the discussion of issues and events appears to have been a important consequence of the thirst for news which was itself stimulated by a range of personal factors, whether these were local rivalries or individuals' political standing or education.

COURTIERS' POLITICAL PARTICIPATION: SELF-FASHIONING

However, though the relative importance of counselling drama and sermons in courtiers' political participation seems to have been exaggerated, it may also be as big a mistake to see courtiers' participation as wholly reactive: responding to issues that had been made a subject of debate by others, either in conversation, correspondence or as audiences. Margaret Aston's reading of the group portrait, 'Edward VI and the pope', is highly convincing but it is worth contrasting it with another painting, emanating from a broadly similar social and political milieu (as far as that of the group portrait's can be ascertained) and utilising the same imagery: a series of wall-paintings depicting King Hezekiah at Sir Thomas Smith's house, Hill Hall, in Essex (Plate 4.1). This series of paintings provides a case-study which suggests that courtiers may have patronised clear, ideological messages to articulate their own political beliefs as much as to counsel the queen.

Smith's Hezekiah series was based primarily, but freely, on Bernard Salomon's woodcuts for *La sainte Bible en François* (Lyon, 1554) and was located in a small, first-floor room in the corner of the west end of the north range.[135] It depicted, on the east wall, Ahaz closing the Temple,

---

135 Richard Simpson, 'Sir Thomas Smith and the wall-paintings at Hill Hall, Essex: scholarly theory and design in the sixteenth century', *Journal of the British Archaeological Association*, 130 (1977), pp. 12–14.

Plate 4.1 'Hezekiah opening up the Temple', mural, Hill Hall, Essex. Reproduced by permission of English Heritage. NMR.

Hezekiah breaking into the Temple (Plate 4.1) and the destruction of the idols. On the south wall and side of the chimneystack was the destruction of Sennacherib's army by the Angel of the Lord. The accompanying text above the paintings has been lost.[136] Despite the interest in domestic and ecclesiastical wall-paintings in the late nineteenth and early twentieth centuries, little research has been conducted on the purposes or meaning of this, or other, murals, apart from the decorative.[137] Both the Hezekiah series, and its companion ('Cupid and Psyche') in adjoining rooms, have traditionally been glossed as indicative only of Smith's intellectual and aesthetic interests: visual realisations of his belief, derived from works by Roger Ascham and Guillaume Budé, that iconography was a development

136 *Essex domestic wall-paintings, 14th–18th century* (University of Essex Exhibition Catalogue, 1989), pp. 16–17.
137 James Sutton, 'The decorative program at Elizabethan Theobalds: educating an heir and promoting a dynasty', *Studies in the Decorative Arts*, 7 (1999–2000), pp. 33–64.

of history and that its study was a means to ascertain representational truth in art.[138]

The similarities with 'Edward VI and the pope' are striking. First, they appear to have been commissioned at a similar time: the Hezekiah series dates from between 1568 and 1569;[139] Aston has dated 'Edward VI and the pope' to the late 1560s or early 1570s, on account of the apparent use of drawings by Maarten van Heemskerck or engravings by Philip Galle for key compositional elements.[140] Second, there are subtle similarities in content. Aston has argued that, in the context of the date of its composition, the central position occupied by Edward VI in the group portrait recalled images of Hezekiah, who was represented explicitly in Smith's wall-paintings. By presenting Elizabeth with a depiction of Edward, who had been likened to the reforming Old Testament king, Josiah, Aston argued that 'Edward VI and the pope' invoked contemporary images of Elizabeth as another reforming king, Hezekiah.[141] Third, therefore, the pictures can be glossed in similar terms: as a call to Elizabeth to act like Edward/Josiah/Hezekiah and reform the church fully, purifying it of images, idols and other superstitions.[142] In Smith's series, 'Ahaz closing the Temple' represented the rejection of the true (Protestant) faith and the reconciliation to Rome in 1553. 'Hezekiah opening up the Temple' (Plate 4.1) celebrated not only the return of true religion, but (damaged) background details depicted the destruction of images and idols. This was reinforced by the third scene, now much damaged, 'The destruction of images', which depicts at least three figures with hammers raised to smash idols and a broken altar in the centre.[143]

138 Simpson, 'Sir Thomas Smith', pp. 4–11. See also J. F. A. Roberts, 'English wall-paintings after Italian engravings', *Burlington Magazine*, 28 (1941), p. 86.
139 Simpson, 'Sir Thomas Smith', pp. 2–4; Tobit Curteis, 'The Elizabethan wall-paintings of Hill Hall: influences and techniques', in Ashok Roy and Penry Smith (eds.), *Painting techniques: history, materials and studio practice. Contributions to the Dublin congress, 7–11 September 1998* (London, 1998), pp. 131–4. For earlier arguments about the dating of the series, see: P. J. Drury, '"A fayre house, buylt by Sir Thomas Smith": the development of Hill Hall, Essex, 1557–81', *Journal of the British Archaeological Association*, 136 (1983), pp. 108, 119.
140 Aston, *King's bedpost*, pp. 54–93.
141 Ibid., pp. 97–107, 113–27; William Keating Clay (ed.), *Liturgical services: liturgies and occasional forms of prayer set forth in the reign of Queen Elizabeth* (Parker Society; Cambridge, 1847), pp. 549–4; Edwin Sandys, *Sermons made by the Most Reuerende Father in God, Edwin, Archbishop of Yorke* (London, 1585; STC 21713), pp. 42, 49, 52–77; Alexandra Walsham, '"A very Deborah"? The myth of Elizabeth I as a providential monarch', in Doran and Freeman (eds.), *Myth of Elizabeth* pp. 143–68 and p. 165 (fn. 26).
142 Aston, *King's bedpost*, pp. 97–134, 206–7.
143 *Essex domestic wall-paintings*, p. 16.

However, whereas Aston has argued that 'Edward VI and the pope' may have been commissioned to counsel Elizabeth directly, this does not seem to have been the purpose of the Hezekiah murals. They were located in a small room in a corner of the north range of the house. Though we do not know the purpose of the room – it has been suggested that, because Hezekiah was a patron of literature, it may have been a study[144] – it seems to be too small and too private a part of the house for Elizabeth to have viewed it. Moreover, there is no evidence that Elizabeth visited Hill Hall and thus was able to see the murals. Her only recorded visit to one of Smith's houses occurred in August 1565 and was to Ankerwycke in Berkshire.[145]

It is possible, therefore, that the murals were commissioned to articulate Smith's own outlook. There are signs that Smith may have been directly involved in conceiving and designing both the Hezekiah and Cupid and Psyche series. Inventories of his books in 1566 and 1576 show he owned key books on architecture and art, including five editions of Vitruvius, Philibert de l'Orme's *Nouvelles inventions pur bien bastir* (Paris, 1561), John Shute's *The first and chief groundes of architecture* (London, 1563), Jacques Androuet du Cerceau's *Livres d'achitecture* (Paris, 1559), Albrecht Dürer's *De symmetria*, Conrad Gesner's *Icones Avium* and Paolo Giovio's *Dialogo dell' Impresse militari et amorose*. While on embassy to France in 1563, Smith frequently met Anne de Montmorency and visited his house at Écouen, which was decorated with cycles of Cupid and Psyche and Old Testament scenes. These two factors may even have combined: Richard Simpson has suggested that the book 'Pictura psyches' recorded in Smith's inventory of 1576 may have been a bound volume of pictures by Michael Coxie, Agostino Veneziano and the Master of the Die on whose designs Montmorency's 'Cupid and Psyche' were based. No other collection is known.[146]

If the murals were designed to articulate Smith's outlook, then two, mutually exclusive, messages are possible. First, Smith may have sought to align himself with the moderate puritans and their programme of further reform. This is indicated not only by the depiction of Hezekiah, but also by the paintings on the south wall and side of the chimneystack showing the destruction of Sennacherib's army. Sennacherib, king of Assyria,

---

144 Ibid.
145 Cole, *Portable queen*, Appendices 1 and 6.
146 Simpson, 'Sir Thomas Smith', pp. 4–14; Drury, '"A fayre house, buylt by Sir Thomas Smith"', p. 120.

invaded Judah twice: the second time treacherously, after Hezekiah had paid him tribute. Hezekiah prayed to God to save Judah, which he did by sending an angel to destroy most of the Assyrian army. In this context, the paintings depicted not only a reforming king, but one who owed his survival to divine providence (which must be repaid). This was exactly the message that John Foxe in the 'Book of martyrs' and other moderate puritans pressed in the late 1560s and early 1570s.[147] Such a reading also emphasises the need to stand firm against Catholic threats from abroad – a message also conveyed in Drant's sermon of 1570 – even if their forces, like Sennacherib's, appeared insurmountable: God would intervene.[148] Alternatively, it has been suggested that Smith may have chosen to decorate this room, which may have been a library, with a figure acknowledged as a patron of literature: Hezekiah.[149]

The former scenario makes the greatest sense of the use of imagery and its similarity, not only with 'Edward VI and the pope' but also with other contemporary sermons and printed texts. It also evades some of the problems of glossing the murals as indicative of literary interests. First, Hezekiah was an obscure choice to represent literary patronage, in comparison to a more well-known figure, like Jerome or Thomas Aquinas. Second, the literary reading is reliant on categorising the room in which the series appears as a library, a definition derived from identifying Hezekiah as a literary patron.[150] Yet, the first scenario contrasts with both some contemporary criticisms of Smith's religious belief – especially in Edward's reign and during his embassy to France in the early 1560s – and the conclusions of his modern biographer, Mary Dewar, who concluded, '[Smith's] outlook was secular, his own religious temperament distinctly cool.'[151]

There are signs that Smith's religious affiliation was more radical than Dewar argues. We know that, during the parliamentary debates on the first Edwardian prayer book in December 1548, Smith made a lengthy and damning critique of Catholicism and Catholic beliefs.[152] Aspersions cast on his commitment to Protestantism during his embassy to France were

---

147 For example, Thomas S. Freeman, '"As true a subiect being prisoner": John Foxe's notes on the imprisonment of Princess Elizabeth, 1554–5', *English Historical Review*, 117 (2002), pp. 104–16; Freeman, 'Providence and prescription', pp. 27–55; Walsham, '"A very Deborah?"', pp. 143–68.
148 For Hezekiah's reforming zeal and his response to Sennacherib's invasions, see 2 Kings, 18–20.
149 This is suggested by the curators of the exhibition on domestic wall-paintings at the University of Essex, 1989: *Essex domestic wall-paintings*, p. 16.
150 Ibid.
151 Dewar, *Sir Thomas Smith*, pp. 39–40, 91–2, 38.
152 Ibid., pp. 39–40.

partly products both of conflicts with his predecessor, Throckmorton, who was strongly committed to the Huguenots' cause, and Smith's reliance on the Cardinal of Ferrara for information. The former owed much, as Dewar attests, to personal rivalries; the latter may have been more a sign of Smith's lack of diplomatic skill than of his religious affiliation. Certainly, he demonstrated a fervent – if still politically misguided – commitment to the Huguenots in the early months of 1563.[153] We also know that he owned a copy of the icon of Elizabethan Protestantism, Foxe's 'Book of martyrs', probably the edition of 1570, the first to be published in two volumes. It was this edition that, according to Thomas Freeman, marked a decisive change in the depiction of Elizabeth: criticising her failure to live up to moderate puritans' hope of further church reform.[154]

Moreover, the use of the image of Hezekiah as a reformer and a model for Elizabeth's queenship was well established by the late 1560s when the series was commissioned. In August 1564, *Ezekias* was performed in Elizabeth's presence by members of King's College, Cambridge, though it was not a new play: it was written some time before 1540 by Nicholas Udall, headmaster of Eton, who had died in 1556. John Jewel placed a strong emphasis on Hezekiah in his *An apologie, or aunswer in defence of the Church of England* (1562); a similar emphasis was apparent in marginalia in 2 Kings (where Hezekiah's history was recounted) in the Bishop's Bible, which pointed to the duty of monarch to root out idolatry. The epistle of the Geneva Bible (1560) exhorted Elizabeth to be like Josiah and root out superstition; Hezekiah, along with other reforming kings, was held up as an example to her.[155]

These signs make it hard not to see the Hezekiah series as an articulation of Smith's politico-religious outlook, and one that was more radical than Dewar has suggested. Hezekiah was just too pervasive an image of a religious reformer in Elizabethan England for other analogies to work effectively. Laying aside the circular and problematic nature of readings that the series depicted literary interests, Smith would have been

153 Ibid., pp. 94–6.
154 The information derives from Smith's will, which states that the copy was in two volumes. As the will was dated 2 April 1576, it seems unlikely that the edition was from 1576. Dewar, *Sir Thomas Smith*, p. 203. For information on the changes in the depiction of Elizabeth in the four editions of Foxe, see Freeman, '"As true a subiect being prisoner"', pp. 104–16; Freeman, 'Providence and prescription', pp. 27–55.
155 Aston, *King's bedpost*, pp. 113–27.

swimming against too strong an iconographical tide to have chosen Hezekiah to represent learning.

If the Hezekiah series did articulate Smith's politico-religious outlook, aligning himself with the moderate puritans at a time of growing tensions between them and Elizabeth, then his audience is unknown. Though it does not appear to have been Elizabeth, it could have been privy councillors and courtiers, especially those, like Burghley and Heneage who were actively canvassing for his return to court at the time.[156] Alternatively, there may not have been an audience: situated in a small, seemingly private room, the series may have been a case of self-fashioning for Smith's own consumption. This period, after all, was one when Smith was virtually in retirement.[157]

There are signs that Smith's actions are representative of those of courtiers more generally, even to their choice of media through which to articulate their outlooks. James Sutton has already drawn attention to how Burghley utilised murals at Theobalds to record and publicise his family's achievements.[158] Similar motives may have been behind the depiction of the Spanish Armada, possibly in a frieze around an interior wall, in the summerhouse at Beddington, Surrey, owned by Sir Peter Carew, and in a series of tapestries owned by Lord Howard of Effingham. Both were likely to have been commissioned to celebrate the men's involvement: though aged about fifty-eight, Carew had served in the English fleet; Howard was Lord Admiral.[159] But there are also signs, derived from commissions of murals depicting the Spanish Armada for church walls or on personal tombs, as well as in examples of needlework, in the first half of the seventeenth century that visual images were used to articulate individuals' politico-religious affiliation and to inculcate a similar view in fellow parishioners.[160] Three parishes with murals of the

---

156 Dewar, *Sir Thomas Smith*, p. 121.
157 Ibid.
158 Sutton, 'Decorative program', passim.
159 John Aubrey, *The natural history and antiquities of the county of Surrey* (2 vols., Dorking, 1975), II, p. 161; Arthur M. Hind, *Engraving in England in the sixteenth and seventeenth centuries* (3 vols., Cambridge, 1952–64), I, p. 25; Felipe Fernández-Armesto, *The Spanish Armada: the experience of war in 1588* (Oxford, 1988), p. 174. Neither Carew's frieze nor Howard's tapestries remain extant: the tapestries were destroyed by fire in 1834.
160 This was part of the substance of my paper 'Wall-paintings of the Spanish Armada and the popularity of James VI and I in England', given at the conference, 'James VI and I – Quatercentenary perspectives', University of Reading, 10 July 2003. I am currently preparing a larger article on the functions of Elizabethan and early Jacobean wall-paintings which will address this point more fully.

Armada in their churches – Gaywood, near King's Lynn; Preston, Suffolk; and Bratoft, Lincolnshire – all had Protestant affiliations. Thomas Hares, rector of Gaywood, who allegedly commissioned the mural, came from a family of committed Protestants and was educated at Trinity College, Cambridge, which had one of the largest puritan communities in Elizabethan Cambridge.[161] Robert Ryece, lay patron of Preston, commissioned the Suffolk mural; he was also a committed protestant.[162] Though we know little of Bratoft's minister in the early seventeenth century, Leonard Ithell, non-conformity was widespread in Jacobean Lincolnshire as revealed in William Chaderton's episcopal visitation of 1604 and by petitions against the Hampton Court conference by both clergy and the laity in the winter of 1604–5.[163]

As with politically engaged drama and sermons, these were not methods that were open to all but they could say as much about an individual's self-presentation as did, for example, the countess of Huntingdon's correspondence with George Blyth. Moreover, it reinforces the extent to which political debate at court was not focused solely on the monarch. Even for a man like Smith, who had the queen's ear, his engagement with issues was not merely or solely directed at counselling the queen and shaping policy. Participation in political debate could be self-centred, aimed at discussing issues to which one was personally or ideologically committed with one's contemporaries and articulating one's beliefs and self-image to the outside world.

161 Francis W. Steer, 'Painting in a Norfolk church of Queen Elizabeth at Tilbury', *Essex Review*, 53 (1944), pp. 1–4; Arthur Chilton, 'Queen Elizabeth at Tilbury', *Essex Review*, 53 (1944), p. 68; Consignation Book, 1627, NRO, DN/Reg 16/Book 22 (3rd series) (via the *Clergymen of the Church of England Database*, for which I would like to thank Stephen Taylor, Ken Fincham and Arthur Burns for access prior to publication); Francis Blomefield (and Charles Parkin), *An essay towards a topographical history of the county of Norfolk* (11 vols., London, 1805–10), VIII, p. 425; John le Neve, *Monumenta Anglicana* (5 vols. in 4, London, 1717–19), I, p. 36.

162 Robert Ryece, 'The breviary of Suffolk', 1618, Harleian 3873/2, fos. 10r–72v; C. G. Harlow, 'Robert Ryece of Preston, 1555–1638', *Proceedings of the Suffolk Institute of Archaeology*, 32 (1971–3), pp. 56–68; H. M. Cautley, *Royal arms and commandments in our churches* (Ipswich, 1934), p. 85; *Alumni Cantabrigienses*, ed. John Venn and J. A. Venn (10 vols., Cambridge, 1922–54), IV, p. 422.

163 Anna Hulbert, 'Report on Bratoft, Lincolnshire, allegory of the Spanish Armada, August 1977', Wall Paintings Survey, Courtauld Institute, London; *The state of the church in the reigns of Elizabeth and James I*, ed. C. W. Foster (Lincoln Record Society, 23; Lincoln, 1926), pp. 179, 387, 303, 399, 418; *Alumni Cantabrigienses*, II, p. 452; *Lincolnshire pedigrees: volume II*, ed. A. R. Maddison, (Harleian Society publications, 52; London, 1903), p. 544; Clive Holmes, *Seventeenth-century Lincolnshire* (*History of Lincolnshire*, ed. Joan Thirsk, vol. VII; Lincoln, 1980), pp. 92–3.

POLITICAL DEBATE IN THE COURT AND THE
PUBLIC SPHERE

In February 1589, as they travelled through Bedfordshire, Gilbert and Mary Talbot wrote to Bess of Hardwick 'all the Quenes hye wayes hathe afforded vs of newes'. Though they appeared to be grudging over how little news they were able to glean, their haul was not unimpressive: they reported that Elizabeth had attended parliament on the first day of the session, that Thomas Snagge had been appointed Speaker of the Commons and the earl of Derby as Lord Steward. One of Gilbert's servants had learned that there was a general feeling that little would be achieved in the session and that it would be prorogued shortly. There was still no news as to whether the earl of Arundel was to be arraigned.[164]

In conjunction with the social diversity of those who were able to gain news at or from the court, the physically wide circulation of news and the nature of political participation at court, the vignette of the Talbots gathering news at Dunstable to pass on to the countess raises questions about the relationship between political debate at court and that, if any, outside it. The desire for news by courtiers, especially when they were absent from court, indicates that news was deliberately disseminated from the physical environs of the court to the homes and estates of the nobility, gentry and household officials. This widened the physical theatre in which news circulated, facilitating it being 'leaked' or transmitted to others. The availability of news at court also appears to have been relatively wide socially so that its direct dissemination to non-courtiers became easier. Equally, the court held no monopoly of news. News circulated in the counties either verbally, as the Talbots' letter illustrates, or in printed pamphlets, like those evident in Bedford's and Lady Mary Grey's book inventories; letters may also have circulated. All of these circumstances point to the possibility of the existence of a 'public sphere'; the availability of news being an essential prerequisite for its existence according to Habermas. And, the apparently symbiotic relationship between the court and the world outside it in the dissemination of news suggests that the relationship between the two was close.

These images are at odds with current perceptions of the public sphere. In his highly influential *Strukturwandel der Öffentlichkeit* (*The structural transformation of the public sphere*), Jürgen Habermas defined the public sphere as the critical-rational debate of political issues by a social,

---

164 Folger X.d.428 (114).

professional, educated male elite, primarily conducted in coffee houses and emerging in the late seventeenth and early eighteenth centuries in Britain.[165] Moreover, he, and those who have followed him, defined the court and the public sphere as distinct and opposing entities. The stimulus for the development of the public sphere, according to Habermas, came only partly from the growing privacy of the court, and primarily from commercial pressures leading to the development of long-distance trade, commercialisation, capitalism and the development of printed newsletters and newspapers.[166] The centrality of newsletters and newspapers, developed from and by mercantile news networks, was thus wholly independent from the activities of the court.[167] This polarity between the court and public sphere was reinforced by Habermas's emphasis on the ideological stance taken by the public sphere which he defined as largely in opposition to the government.

The nature of political debate at the Elizabethan court casts doubt on some of these assumptions. By demonstrating that the circulation of news at court was socially broad, and relatively physically extensive, it questions the extent to which both the origins of the public sphere can only be dated to the late seventeenth century and that it was an entity distinct from the court. It suggests that news was more widely available to a broad social range prior to the emergence of newsletters and newspapers. This is reinforced by the snapshots provided by the Talbots' letter from Dunstable and Bedford's and Grey's book inventories. Wider circulation of news opens up the possibilities of the existence of public debate: if news was available to subjects, surely they talked about it? But it also indicates that the circulation of news outside the court may well have been related to that at court. Not only was the court a source of news events, but it was also an important conduit for domestic and foreign news because courtiers sought and disseminated news and travelled physically between the court and the provinces. Thus, the court and public sphere may not have been distinct, opposing entities.

If the dissemination of news among courtiers and the nature of political debate at court raise possibilities that a public sphere existed in the late sixteenth century, then a whole host of other questions are raised. Did the court monopolise the dissemination of news into the provinces, or were there other sources of news? How extensive was participation,

---

165 Habermas, *Structural transformation*, passim.
166 Ibid., pp. 9–25.
167 Ibid., pp. 16, 20–2.

geographically, socially and in terms of gender? We have already seen that, at court, women participated in the circulation of news and discussion of ideas. Was this merely because of their social status and their access to the court, or was political participation in the provinces less gender exclusive than is often thought? Was public debate limited either to the more populated areas of England, and specifically London and the south-east, or was there debate in Wales and Ireland? If so, were the means of news circulation, the subjects of debate and the manner of debate the same? Moreover, if political debate did exist in Elizabeth's realms beyond the immediate physical and social environs of the court, did it constitute a 'public sphere' as defined by Habermas or his critics?

These are the questions that concern the remainder of this book. As I have done with debate at court, I begin by exploring the circulation of news outside the court's environs, across the whole of Elizabeth's realms. By examining both the different media that contemporaries used to circulate news and its actual dissemination across Elizabeth's realms, I am able to show that the circulation of news, an important foundation stone for political debate, was widespread, socially, geographically and in terms of gender. Taking existing definitions of the 'public sphere' from Habermas and his critics as a starting point, I then explore the nature of Elizabethan public debate, how far it matches current models of the 'public sphere', in what ways it differs and what these differences can contribute to the way we conceptualise the 'public sphere' as a whole. The relationship between the public sphere and the court remains a central issue within this, as does what could be defined as 'elite' and 'popular' perceptions of the queen and her governance in the final chapter. Though the issues that Elizabethans debated are explored in both the examination of news and the nature of the public sphere, the final chapter investigates debate on one theme – Elizabeth and her queenship – and seeks to chart both the similarities and differences in views and reactions between otherwise diverse groups of people.

CHAPTER 5

The circulation of news in the Elizabethan realms

On 20 December 1569, a 'wench' told Harry Shadwell, a twenty-six-year-old vintner, and his fellow prisoners at the Counter (one of the London prisons) that Scottish troops had mustered to support Elizabeth against the Northern rebels. The following day, as Shadwell returned with his keeper from being questioned at the bishop of London's palace, his waterman, Richard Whittacres, informed him that the Scottish troops had numbered 10,000 and that the Rising had started because the northern earls (Northumberland and Westmorland) 'beare a grudge to my Lord Robert [Dudley] and . . . *his* brother'.[1] Entering the Counter, Shadwell was asked by Harry White 'what good newes[?]' Shadwell replied that 15,000 troops had been mustered for Elizabeth, and all but forty slain. Moreover, 'I harde the Reebells hadd sent a letter vnto the Duke of Alba: And the Duke of Alba hathe directed the coppies of the same to the Pope'. '[It] will prove now', Shadwell continued, 'as the Duke of Alba hathe . . . made his promise that he will come and paye his souldiours there wages in cheapsyde And farther that he will make the Queenes maiestie to come . . . *vppon* Candlemas daye nexte And here Masse'.[2] Later that evening, as Shadwell's companions continued to discuss this news, the young vintner repeated his statement, learned partly from 'ii gentlemen', that the earls had written to Alva asking him to persuade the pope to send them aid immediately.[3] Under examination on 24 December, Shadwell denied he had made any such reports and 'prayed god' that the rumours circulating in Cheapside about the payment of Alva's soldiers 'should *not* nowe come to passe'.[4]

---

1 Depositions of Thomas Lees, Harry Whyte and others, 23 Dec. 1569, SP12/60/48, fo. 136r; Examination of Richard Whittacres, 27 Dec. 1569, PRO, SP12/60/54, fo. 152r.
2 SP12/60/48, fo. 136r–136v; Examination of Harry Shadwell, 24 Dec. 1569, SP12/60/49, fo. 138r.
3 SP12/60/48, fo. 137r.
4 SP12/60/49, fo. 138r–138v.

For Jürgen Habermas, the circulation of news was a prerequisite for the emergence of the bourgeois public sphere in the late seventeenth and early eighteenth centuries.[5] Both he and early modern historians identified print – pamphlets, newsletters and newspapers – as the main vehicle for news.[6] Indeed, they have tended to define or privilege print as a 'formal' vehicle for news and other means, such as letters and oral communication, as 'informal' vehicles. By emphasising the role of print, historians have concluded that the circulation of news in the late sixteenth century was limited and the existence of a public sphere negligible. In seminal articles, Fritz Levy argued that small, printed pamphlets were not produced on a large scale until the outbreak of war with Spain in 1585, making the circulation of news prior to this date limited.[7] Moreover, with the exception of broadsides printed during and after the Northern Rising, news in print was restricted to a social and educated elite, who could afford, obtain and read pamphlets.[8] He concluded that, even at an elite level, printed news did not contribute to the establishment of a public sphere in Elizabethan England because pamphlets were *ad hoc*, irregular, they concentrated on key events and were often imbued with government propaganda.[9] His arguments have been influential, attaining the status of orthodoxy: they are supported, in full or part, by Alexandra Halasz's[10] and Joad Raymond's studies of the rise of pamphlet production as well as Lisa Ferraro Parmelee's exploration of the dissemination in England of pamphlets on the French Wars of Religion.[11]

However, the discussion of the Northern Rising in and around the Counter in December 1569 contests these notions. It challenges Levy's, Halasz's and Raymond's emphasis on printed pamphlets by pointing to the importance of oral communication of news. It also suggests that the desire for, and access to, news was not only socially broader than Levy and Raymond indicate but may have been characteristic of women as well as men. Shadwell and his fellow inmates initially learned about the Scottish

---

5 Habermas, *Structural transformation*, pp. 20–4.
6 Ibid., pp. 20–4; Levy, 'How information spread', pp. 20–3; Levy, 'Decorum of news', pp. 17–21. See also Cust, 'News and politics', pp. 60–90.
7 Levy, 'How information spread', p. 20; Levy, 'Decorum of news', pp. 18–19.
8 Levy, 'Decorum of news', pp. 18–19.
9 Ibid., pp. 17–21.
10 Halasz, *Marketplace of print*, pp. 15–16, 23–34, 162–4, 166–78. Levy has challenged Halasz's arguments in his 'Decorum of news', pp. 33–4.
11 Lisa Ferraro Parmelee, 'Printers, patrons, readers and spies: importation of French propaganda in late Elizabethan England', *Sixteenth Century Journal*, 25 (1994), pp. 853–7; Parmelee, *Good newes from Fraunce: French Anti-league propaganda in late Elizabethan England* (Rochester, NY and Woodbridge, Suffolk, 1996), ch. 2; Raymond, *Pamphlets and pamphleteering*, pp. 15–16 and ch. 4.

troops from a 'wench'. Though illustrating the circulation of news in London, the penetration of news into the environs of the Counter, which might be regarded as isolated from the outside world, raises the possibility that news may not have been geographically limited. These issues have also been highlighted by Adam Fox's work on oral culture in Tudor England and Thomas Cogswell's vivid sketch of news networks in Jacobean London.[12]

This chapter seeks to resolve the apparent contradictions between current understanding of news, news media and circulation and the contemporary evidence, as a necessary precursor to assessing whether a public sphere existed in the Elizabethan realms. It examines whether print was the most important vehicle for news in the late sixteenth century and explores what other formats were used. To achieve this, it addresses early modern news on its own terms, as contemporaries saw it. First, and most importantly, it does not define news solely as major domestic and foreign political events that we know, with hindsight, were 'true'. Rather, it acknowledges what contemporaries found newsworthy or believed to be true, even if it was later proved false: murders, witchcraft trials, accounts of monstrous births, reports of Elizabeth's illegitimate pregnancies or children. After all, rumour is just news proved wrong by hindsight. Second, it neither assumes the centrality of print nor distinguishes between print as a 'formal' vehicle of news and oral and manuscript communication as 'informal', with the implication that 'informal' vehicles were less reliable and accurate. Similarly, though I address questions raised by recent literature that compares early modern news against the characteristics of later newspapers – topicality, precise periodicity, seriality, physical continuity, consecutive numbering and stable titles – I do not use these characteristics to measure my texts because, though important, they are ultimately anachronistic. Third, the chapter addresses how widely (and differently) news circulated in terms of social status, gender and geography and whether different formats had different audiences. It does not assume that there were distinctions between elite and popular news networks because recent research has undermined arguments that there were distinct 'elite' and 'popular' cultures, suggesting instead that cultural practices were shaped more by gender and geography

---

12 Adam Fox, 'Rumour, news and popular political opinion in Elizabethan and early Stuart England', *Historical Journal*, 40 (1993), pp. 597–620; Fox, *Oral and literate culture in England, 1500–1700* (Oxford, 2000), ch. 7; Thomas Cogswell, *The blessed revolution: English politics and the coming of war, 1621–1624* (Cambridge, 1989), pp. 20–7.

than social status.[13] To achieve this, I take a different approach to Halasz, Lake and Questier and explore the physical distribution of texts through inventories and accounts. Lake's and Questier's study of murder pamphlets demonstrates how much useful information about news and its circulation can be derived from textual analysis of the pamphlets themselves. But textual analysis is less effective in providing insights into the social, gender and regional composition of pamphlets' audiences.[14]

My approach has its problems, largely posed by extant sources.[15] Whilst printed pamphlets are relatively easy to trace, existing physically or recorded in the Stationers' Register, evidence of oral and manuscript communication is more fragmentary, scattered across letters, diaries and court records. Whilst these do shed light on how widely news circulated socially and on the involvement of women, they do not provide a quantitative picture of the geographical range. For instance, as outlined in chapter 1, assize records, which reveal much about political debate through cases of seditious and slanderous words, are only extant for the home counties and south-eastern circuit for Elizabeth's reign. The ramifications of this for our understanding of the public sphere will be addressed in the next chapter. Exploring the dissemination of printed texts is also problematic: library inventories often exist only for more wealthy and educated citizens, and, like probate inventories (which can reveal the reading tastes of less wealthy individuals), rarely record small pamphlets and broadsides which were ephemeral and of little financial value. However, though booksellers' inventories and accounts are more rare, crucially a number exist for provincial English sellers, providing some indication of book availability in the counties as well as London. There are also a number of indirect, but specific, references to the importation of books into Ireland.

ELIZABETHAN NEWS PAMPHLETS

A pamphlet was a small, quarto book of between one and twelve sheets (eight to ninety-six pages), often sold stitched but uncut.[16] Though Levy,

---

13 For example, see Amussen, 'The gendering of popular culture'; Underdown, 'Regional cultures?'
14 Lake with Questier, *Anti-Christ's lewd hat.*
15 For a detailed discussion of primary sources relevant to the public sphere, and their problems, see above, ch. 1.
16 Raymond, *Pamphlets and pamphleteering*, pp. 5, 81. Raymond argues that 'pamphlet' took on a specific meaning from the 1580s – a small, topical and scandalous book – derived partly from eighteenth-century commentaries and from contemporary works, like the Martin Marprelate

Parmelee, Halasz and Raymond have emphasised their importance over broadsides and ballads as conveyers of news, broadsides (whether ballads or prose) were also common vehicles. The production of news pamphlets did escalate after 1585 as a result of both the Spanish war and the importation and translation of material on the Wars of Religion, principally by the stationer, Edward Aggas. But production of both news pamphlets and broadsides in the first thirty years of Elizabeth's reign was not negligible. Counting the smaller pamphlets alone (of up to thirty-two pages), which were cheaper and hence more accessible to a wider audience,[17] there were at least eighty separate titles published between 1558 and 1589. There are also more than fifty-one longer pamphlets. A further 140 pamphlets of unknown size are recorded in the registers of the Stationers' Company between 1558 and 1586 but which are no longer extant. At least thirty-seven news broadsides and ballads remain extant (1558–89), with a further 151 (including epitaphs) recorded in the registers (1558–86).[18] Moreover, these figures are likely to be underestimates. It is widely accepted that individual titles of pamphlets, and to a far greater extent, broadsides have not survived in anything like their original numbers: Tessa Watt has estimated that only about 250 of an estimated 3,000 ballad titles are extant.[19] The Stationers' Register does not provide a comprehensive picture of titles published because it only became obligatory to register titles in 1585. While the numbers of titles that were registered but not actually printed is likely to be negligible, it is possible that other pamphlets and broadsides existed but leave no trace in either physical copies or in the register.

Recent research has tended to measure early modern news against the characteristics of modern news media: topicality, precise periodicity, seriality, physical continuity, consecutive numbering and stable titles.[20] Yet, of these, contemporaries only seemed to value topicality and, if Philip Gawdy's comment to his parents is significant, it was less topicality itself than knowing something that others did not that was important. He wrote in November 1587, 'some Newes cam out of Flaunders very latly

---

tracts. While it is clear that topicality and calumny were important characteristics of pamphlets from the 1580s, to define pamphlets solely in these terms is to ignore the fact that the majority of texts between eight and ninety-six pages were not scandal sheets. Ibid., ch. 1 and passim.

17 See below, n. 102.

18 Note that it is not always possible to distinguish between broadsides and pamphlets in the Stationers' Register and so these figures are approximate.

19 Watt, *Cheap print*, pp. 11–37, 40–2. For manuscript collections see, for example, the commonplace book of Richard Sheale of Tamworth, Staffs, described in ibid., pp. 16–21.

20 For example, Raymond, *Pamphlets and pamphleteering*, ch. 4.

yesternight, but unknowen to any but the best.'[21] Rather, Elizabethan news pamphlets need to be measured against the qualities contemporaries (producers and consumers) valued: the range of news reported, the information conveyed, veracity of reports and the interpretative framework in which news was presented, as well as topicality.

The range of news topics covered was broad, addressing issues and events of national or continental significance: the Northern Rising in 1569;[22] the murder of Mary Stuart's second husband, Henry, Lord Darnley (1567);[23] the proposed match between Norfolk and Mary Stuart;[24] the execution of John Felton, who brought the papal bull, *Regnans in excelsis* to England (1570);[25] the death of James Fitzmaurice in the Desmond Rebellion in Ireland in 1579;[26] the capture, trial and execution of conspirators, including Anthony Babington[27] and Francis Throckmorton,[28] and of Jesuit priests.[29] Though the Wars of Religion generated a large body of material,[30] other foreign events were also

21 Egerton 2804, fos. 37r–38r.
22 William Gibson, *A discription of Nortons falcehod of York shyre* (London, [1570]; *STC* 11843); W[illiam] S[erres], *An answere to the proclamation of the rebels of the North* (London, 1569; *STC* 22234).
23 H.C., *A dolefull ditty, or sorowful sonet of the Lord Darly* (London, 1579; *STC* 4270.5). See also the broadsides printed in Scotland on the murder of the earl of Moray (Robert Sempill, *The deploration of the cruel murther of James Erle of Murray* (Edinburgh, 1570; *STC* 22192a.5)) and other Scottish broadsides, including Robert Sempill, *The Kingis complaint* (Edinburgh, 1567; *STC* 22200); Semphill, *The poysonit schot* (Edinburgh, 1570; *STC* 22204); Semphill, *Ane premonitioun to the barnis of Leith* (Edinburgh, 1572; *STC* 22204.5).
24 Thomas Norton, *A discourse touching the pretended match betwene the Duke of Norfolk and the Quene of Scottes* (London, 1569; *STC* 13869).
25 F.G., *The end and confession of Iohn Felton* (London, 1570; *STC* 11493).
26 Thomas Churchyard, *A most true reporte of Iames Fitz Morrice Death* (London, [1579]; *STC* 5244). See also Churchyard, *A scourge for rebels* (1584).
27 Thomas Nelson, *A proper newe ballad declaring the substance of all the late pretended treasons against the Queenes Maiestie* (London, 1586; *STC* 18426.5). See also Thomas Deloney, *A most ioyfull song* (London, 1586; *STC* 6557.6).
28 Q.Z., *A discouerie of the treasons practised and attempted against the Queenes Maiestie and the realme, by Francis Throckmorton* (London, 1584; *STC* 24050.5).
29 *A declaration of the Queenes Maiesties most gratious dealing with William Marsden and Robert Anderton* (London, 1586; *STC* 8157); *A true report of the inditement, arraignement, conuiction, condemnation, and execution of Iohn Weldon, William Hartley, and Robert Sutton* (London, 1588; *STC* 25229.3); William Tedder and Anthony Tyrrell, *The recantations as they were seueralie pronounced by William Tedder and Anthony Tyrrell* (London, 1588; *STC* 23859.3).
30 Including *The destruction and sacke cruelly committed by the duke of Guyse* (London, [1562]; *STC* 11312); *A summe of the Guisian ambassage to the bishop of Rome* (London, 1579; *STC* 6319); Edward Aggas, *A declaration set forth by the French king* (London, 1585; *STC* 13092); Philippe de Mornay, *A necessary discourse concerning the right which the house of Guyze pretendeth to the crown of France* (London, 1586; *STC* 12508); *The French kinges declaration vpon the riot, felonie, and rebelleion of the duke of Mayenne* (London, 1589; *STC* 13098.5); *The declarations as well of the French King, as the King of Navarre* (London, 1589; *STC* 13098.8).

reported including the siege of Jula in Hungary (August 1566);[31] the siege
of Polotsk in Lithuania (1579),[32] as well as defences of William of
Orange's resistance against Philip II.[33] Domestic events, including witch
trials,[34] extreme weather conditions,[35] and the birth of malformed animals
and children were also reported,[36] as were similar events on the continent.[37] There were also reports on Elizabeth's progresses and her appearance at Tilbury in 1588.[38] Moreover, reports sought to convey factual
information, detailing, for instance, the precise chronology of events at
the siege of Polotsk,[39] or translating proclamations and edicts, such as *The
proclamation and edict of the Archbyshop, and Prince Elector of Cvlleyn*
(1583) and *The edict, for the reunitying of his subiectes in the Catholique,
Apostolique and Romishe Churche* (1585).[40]

31 *Newes from Vienna* (London, 1566; *STC* 24716).
32 *A true reporte of the taking of the great towne and castell of Polotzko* (London, 1579; *STC* 20092.5).
33 *A declaration and publication of the most worthy Prince of Orange* (London, 1568; *STC* 25708); *An
    aduise and answer of my lord ye Prince of Orenge* (London, 1577; *STC* 25710.5); *Antwerpes vnity*
    (London, 1579; *STC* 25711).
34 John Philips, *The examination and confession of certaine wytches at Chensforde in the countie of
    Essex* (London, 1566; *STC* 19869.5); *A rehearsall both straunge and true, of hainous horrible actes
    commited by . . . four notorious witches* (London, 1579; *STC* 23267); *A detection of damnable
    drifttes, practiced by three witches* (London, 1579; *STC* 5115); *The apprehension and confession of
    three notorious witches* (London, 1589; *STC* 5114). Philip's *Examination and confession* contains
    three, separately paginated pieces viz. *The examination and confession*, *The second examination
    and confession of mother Agnes Waterhouse and Jone her daughter*, and *The ende and last confession
    of mother Waterhouse at her death, whiche was the xxix daye of Julye. Anno 1566*. Though *STC*
    catalogues them as one text, and only one title was registered with the Stationers' Company
    (*The examination of certen wyches at Chensforde befor the queens majesties Jugdges in the countye of
    Essex*), it is possible that they were marketed separately, as suggested by Shaaber (though the
    Stationers' Registers do not include entries for all three titles as he suggests). E. A. Arber (ed.),
    Transcripts of the registers of the Company of Stationers of London, 1554–1640 (5 vols., London,
    1875–94), I, p. 328; Matthias A. Shaaber, *Some forerunners of the newspaper in England, 1476–1622*
    (Philadelphia and London, 1929), pp. 302–4.
35 *A straunge and terrible wunder wrought very late in the parish church of Bongay* (London, 1577;
    STC 11050); D. Sterrie, *A briefe sonet declaring the lamentation of Beckles* (London, 1586; *STC*
    23259).
36 John Mellys, *The true description of two monsterous children* (London, 1566; *STC* 17803); C. R., *A
    true discription of this marueilous straunge fishes* (London, 1569; *STC* 20570).
37 *A true and perfect discourse of three great accidents that chaunced in Italie within twentie and sixe
    dayes* (London, 1588; *STC* 14285); Cornelius Pet, *An example of Gods iudgement shew[n] vpon two
    children* (London, 1582; *STC* 10608.5).
38 *A famous dittie of the ioyfull receauyng of the Queens most excellent maiestie, by the worthy citizens of
    London the xij day of Nouember 1584* (London, 1584; *STC* 12798); Thomas Deloney, *The Queens
    visiting of the campe at Tilsburie* (London, 1588; *STC* 6565).
39 *True reporte of the taking of . . . Polotzko* (1579).
40 *The proclamation and edict of the Archbyshop, and Prince Elector of Cvlleyn* (London, 1583; *STC*
    11694); *Edict du roy sur la reunion de ses subiects, a l'eglise catholique* [with an English translation,
    The edict, for the reunitying of his subiectes in the Catholique, Apostolique and Romishe Churche by
    Hector Rowland] (London, 1585; *STC* 13092.5).

Reports could be highly topical. The *Breefe discourse of the taking of Edmund Campion* (1581) and *Master Campion the seditious Jesuit is welcome to London* (1581) were entered in the Stationers' Register within two days of Campion's detention in the Tower.[41] Anthony Munday's *A breefe and true reporte of the execution of certayne traytours at Tiborne* (1582) was registered the day after the last execution, though it appears to have been prepared earlier.[42] Four pamphlets and ballads on the earthquake in April 1580 were registered within days of the event.[43] *A true discription of this maruelous straunge fishe* (1569) was printed within a fortnight of the fish's capture on 16 June. Topicality was not confined to domestic events. The edict of Nemours, signed by Henry III on 7 July 1585 and read and published in the *parlement* of Rouen on 23 July, was printed in England a fortnight later.[44] *The true coppie of a letter written from the Leager by Arnham* ([1591]) was registered in England in two days, while *Newes from the Englishe armye out of Britanne the thirde of June 1591* (1591) was entered twelve days after it had been sent from the front, and two days since it had arrived in England.[45]

Authors and printers also sought to emphasise the veracity of their accounts. At its simplest, this was achieved by utilising phrases such as 'A true report' or 'A true discourse' as part of the title,[46] but witnesses and authorities could also be invoked. The author of *A declaration of the fauourable dealing . . . for the examination of certaine Traitours* (1583) stated he had consulted 'a very honest Gentleman whom I know to haue good sufficient means to deliuer the trueth against such forgers of lyes'.[47] A broadside report about Margaret vergh Gryffyth, who had a curved horn on her forehead, was vetted prior to publication by 'a learned

---

41 Arber (ed.), *Registers of the Company of Stationers*, II, p. 397.
42 Anthony Munday, *A breefe and true reporte of the execution of certayne traytours at Tiborne* (London, 1582; *STC* 18261).
43 *A godly newe ballat moving vs to repent by ye example of ye erthquake*; *A true report of this erthquake in London*; Thomas Churchyard, *A warning to the wise . . . written of the late earthquake* (London, 1580; *STC* 5259) and *A fatherlye admonycon and lovinge warnynge to England* were all entered in the Stationers' Register between 7 and 8 April 1580 with a number of other works following over the next month. Arber (ed.), *Registers of the Company of Stationers*, II, pp. 368–70.
44 *Edict du roy* (1585). The continental calendar was ten days ahead of the English calendar.
45 Arber (ed.), *Registers of the Company of Stationers*, II, pp. 590, 583; *The true coppie of a letter written from the leager by Arnham* (London, [1591]; *STC* 781).
46 For example, *A true discourse of the late battaile fought betweene our Englishmen, and the Prince of Parma* (London, 1585; *STC* 17156); *A true report of the taking of Marseilles by the fauourers of the league* (London, 1585; *STC* 17468); *True report of the inditement . . . of Iohn Weldon* (1588).
47 Thomas Norton, *A declaration of the fauourable dealing . . . for the examination of certaine Traitours* (London, 1583; *STC* 4901), sig. Aii^r.

Preacher'.[48] Though these devices were conventional and commonplace, they were not without substance. Only one instance of 'news' being manufactured or recycled can be identified for the period 1558 to 1589: *A detection of damnable driftes*, recounting a witchcraft trial in April 1579, was a partial reprint of *The examination and confession of certaine wytches at Chensforde* (1566) with the names, place and date changed.[49]

News was, however, reported in moral and political interpretative frameworks. These ranged from works that were little more than government propaganda – like Thomas Norton's *A discourse touching the pretended match between the Duke of Norfolke and the Queene of Scottes* (1569)[50] – to more independent works – like Bishop Pilkington's *The true report of the burnyng of the steple and church of Poules* (1561)[51] – which were by no means shorn of editorial comment or ideological bias. Pamphlets could convey also a more general moral message, such as *A true description of two monstrous children* (1566). This broadside explicitly rejected that the birth of the children was a punishment for their parents; rather they were 'lessons for vs all, / which dayly doe offend'. Readers were exhorted to 'amend your state / and call to God for grace . . . while you haue time and space'.[52]

These frameworks – which differ little from the commentary, spin and bias of modern journalism – suggest that news was not perceived as unmediated information to be collected for its own sake. Events were infused with meaning and the purpose of reading news was to obtain and learn from it. In other words, news was consciously situated in a public sphere of knowledge and the application of meaning to persons or realms. Yet equally, there were perils to communicating news and its meaning: who identified the meaning and how could they be sure that the reader would recognise it? The interpretative frameworks, particularly the preliminary material, provided the reader with the direction to understand

---

48 *A myraculous, and monstrous, but yet most true, and certayne discourse, of a woman (now to be seene in London) of the age of threescore yeares* . . . (London, 1588; *STC* 6910.7).
49 *Detection of damnable driftes* (1579); Philips, *Examination and confession of certaine wytches* (1566). *A detection of damnable driftes* lacks the allegations against Mother Waterhouse and her daughter, Jone, 'The second examination and confession of mother agnes Waterhouse & Jone her daughter' and 'The ende and last confession of mother waterhouse at her death'. However, the final two pieces may to have been issued separately (see above, n. 34).
50 Norton, *Discourse touching the pretended match* (1569), especially sigs. Aii^v–Avi^v.
51 James Pilkington, *The true report of the burnyng of the steple and church of Poules* (London, 1561; *STC* 19930). See also, Q.Z., *Discouerie of the treasons practised . . . by Francis Throckmorton* (1584), sigs. Ai^r–Ai^v; *A ballat intituled Northomberland newes* (London, [1570]; *STC* 7554); Deloney, *A most ioyfull Songe* (1586).
52 Mellys, *True description of two monsterous children* (1566).

the significance of events, guiding them to the 'right' conclusion. Crucially, this was not just characteristic of some texts directly or indirectly produced by the regime – such as *The recantations . . . by Wylliam Tedder and Anthony Tyrrell* (1588) – but of independent works, like *An advertisement to the King of Navarre* (1585). The author of the latter warned his readers to judge this 'lewd and slaunderous Pamphlet' carefully because it maliciously attacked the Huguenot leader, Navarre's, 'very modest and dutifull declaration'.[53]

THE DISSEMINATION OF NEWS PAMPHLETS IN THE ELIZABETHAN REALMS

If in number and substance, pamphlets and broadsides were more important vehicles for news prior to 1585 than Levy and others have suggested, then this is reinforced by what we can learn of their dissemination. As the centre of printing for England, Wales and Ireland,[54] the availability of news pamphlets and broadsides was at its greatest in London. They were sold primarily in St Paul's churchyard, the main marketplace for books and pamphlets, where printers and booksellers had stalls, but were also available from shops in places like neighbouring Paternoster Row.[55] An extant inventory of Henry Bynneman's stock in 1583 provides a window into what was available. Many pamphlets Bynneman printed in the final years before his death in 1583, like *A briefe discourse of the most haynous and traytorlike fact of Thomas Appeltree* (1579), Arthur Golding's *A discourse vpon the earthquake* (1580) and *A true discourse of the assault committed vpon . . . William Prince of Orange* (1582) are not listed, suggesting they may have sold out.[56] Copies of earlier pamphlets

---

53 André Maillard, *An advertisement to the King of Navarre . . . Truly translated according to the copy printed in French* (London, 1585; *STC* 13127), sigs. Aiii^r–Aiv^v.

54 On the decline of regional printing presses in England after the establishment of uniform liturgical practice in 1539, see Stacey Gee, 'The printers, stationers and bookbinders of York before 1557', *Transactions of the Cambridge Bibliographical Society*, 12 (2000), pp. 27–54. Two (illicit) presses existed in Wales in the 1580s: see John Penry, *A viewe of some part of such publike wants & disorders* ([Coventry], 1589; *STC* 19613), p. 68; Martin Marprelate, *O read ouer d. John Bridges* ([East Moseley, Surrey], 1588; *STC* 17453), p. 23; Ifano Jones, *A history of printing and printing in Wales to 1810* (Cardiff, 1925), pp. 16–22. For the history of printing in Ireland, see below, nn. 90–3.

55 C. Paul Christianson, 'The stationers of Paternoster Row, 1534–1557', *Papers of the Bibliographical Society of America*, 87 (1993), pp. 81–91.

56 Other recent printed works were recorded in the inventory for the main shop. Note, however, that some news pamphlets may have been stocked in Bynneman's two other shops, in St Gregory's, where the stock was not itemised individually in the extant inventories. Mark Eccles, 'Bynneman's books', *The Library*, fifth series, 12 (1957), pp. 84–7.

remained: Golding's *A briefe discourse of the late murther of master G Saunders* (1577),[57] Thomas Churchyard's *A discourse of the queens maiesties entertainement in Suffolke and Norfolke* ([1578])[58] and an unidentified work called 'the murders of ffrance' (possibly the English translation of François Hotman's *De furibus Gallicis*, Geoffrey Fenton's *A discourse of the ciuiles warres in Fraunce* or a now lost work printed by Bynneman).[59] But these appear to have been the residue of successful titles. Though it is difficult to establish average print-runs, it is thought that books were printed in batches of 250 and in runs of between 250 and 1,500.[60] With remaining copies totalling 350, 41 and 182 respectively, it appears that there was a market even for long works like Churchyard's eighty-eight-page *Discourse*.

Crucially, personal diaries, extant booksellers' and library inventories, financial accounts and probate inventories demonstrate that pamphlets and broadsides were widely available in England and, possibly, Wales. Edward Wingfield, of Kimbolton Castle, Huntingdon, owned a copy of 'Newes from the Turk', possibly *A discourse of the bloody and cruel battaile, of late lost by the great Turke Sultan Selim* (1579), *Newes from Vienna, the 5. day of August* (1566) or *A copy of the last aduertisement that came from Malta* (1565).[61] William Carnsew of Bokelly, an established but not wealthy member of the Cornish gentry, read of the 'Pacyfficacions pro-claymyd in Fraunce . . . prentyd in Englyshe' as well as 'the Franche storyes' on 26 January 1577.[62] The former was probably the lengthy *Edict*

57 Arthur Golding, *A briefe discourse of the late murther of master G Saunders* (London, 1577; *STC* 11986); Eccles, 'Bynneman's books', p. 89, no. 121; Barnard and Bell, 'Henry Bynneman', p. 33, no. 121.

58 Thomas Churchyard, *A discourse of the queens maiesties entertainement in Suffolke and Norfolke* (London, [1578]; *STC* 5226); Eccles, 'Bynneman's books', p. 86, no. 99; Barnard and Bell, 'Henry Bynneman', p. 31, no. 99.

59 Eccles, 'Bynneman's books', p. 86, no. 117; Barnard and Bell, 'Henry Bynneman', pp. 36–7, no. 117. Another (probate) inventory, that for Nicholas Clifton, a stationer of St Aldgate's (d. 1578), gives further evidence of the availability of news pamphlets. It includes 'Alarum to Englande foreshowing', as well as older books on Wyatt's Rebellion and the examination of John Bradford. Strickland Gibson (ed.), *Abstracts from the wills and testamentary documents of binders, printers and stationers of Oxford, from 1493 to 1638* (London, 1907), pp. 15, 13, 16.

60 Raymond, *Pamphlets and pamphleteering*, p. 80. Print-runs of less than 250 made composition costs expensive and less commercially viable; runs of more than 1,250–1,500 without resetting the type were disallowed by the Stationers' Company except for primers, proclamations etc. Arber (ed.), *Registers of the Company of Stationers*, II, p. 43. I would like to thank Ian Gadd for this reference and for information on print-runs of proclamations.

61 Henry R. Plomer, 'Some Elizabethan book sales', *The Library*, third series, 7 (1916), p. 327. *Newes from Vienna* (1566); *A copy of the last aduertisement that came from Malta* (London, 1565; *STC* 17214); *A discourse of the bloody and cruel battaile, of late lost by the great Turke Sultan Selim* (London, 1579; *STC* 22180).

62 'Carnsew's diary', p. 29.

or proclamation set forthe by the French Kinge vpon the pacifying of the troubles in Fraunce (1576); the latter may have been a lengthy work like Henri Estienne's *A mervaylous discourse upon the lyfe . . . of Katherine de Medicis* (1575) or Jean de Serres's *The fourth parte of the comentaries of the ciuill warres in Fraunce* (1576) or a shorter pamphlet like *The protestation of the most high and mightie Prince Frauncis . . . translated out of the frenche* (1575).[63] On 29 January 1577, Carnsew read 'the storye of the Turkys newlye sett oute this yere';[64] on 2 December 1577, he read about 'the Synkyng of Temar in Hungarye';[65] 'newes of Fraunce and Flanders' on 12 December 'and other occurencys' on 31 December[66] though, as none of these can be identified with printed texts, it is unclear whether they were pamphlets.

John Denys, a French binder and bookseller in Cambridge, stocked 'the trouble of France' and 'A discourse of the Frenche affaires', possibly Jennar's translation of de Rondard's *Discourse of the present troubles in France* (1561) and *Discourse of the ciuil wars and troubles in France* ([1570]) respectively.[67] William Knowsley, also of Cambridge, sold copies of 'Kinge of navarr', an unidentified ballad or broadside now no longer extant.[68] Knowsley obtained at least some of his stock from Thomas Chard (or Chare) of London who worked in partnership with Edward Aggas. Aggas was a trained printer but does not appear to have operated a press, concentrating on importing, translating and producing reports on the Huguenots' actions in the French Wars of Religion. Indeed, it is

63 Ibid., p. 32. *The edict or proclamation set forthe by the French Kinge* (1576); Henri Estienne, *A mervaylous discourse upon the lyfe . . . of Katherine de Medicis* ([London], 1575; *STC* 10550); Jean de Serres, *The fourth parte of the comentaries of the ciuill warres in Fraunce*, trans. Thomas Tymme (London, 1576; *STC* 22243); *The protestation of the most high and mightie Prince Frauncis . . . translated out of the frenche* (London, 1575; *STC* 11311).

64 'Carnsew's diary', p. 34. Unidentified: neither *STC* nor the Stationers' Company Register records any works on the Turks, printed in 1577.

65 'Carnsew's diary', p. 56. Unidentified, possibly a reference to the capture of Temesvar, Hungary, by the Turks in 1552 but *STC* records no extant books on this.

66 'Carnsew's diary', p. 57. *STC* records no other French news, other than the works like *The edict or proclamation set forthe by the French Kinge* (1576), *The protestation of the most high and mightie Prince Frauncis* (1575) and others already cited. If the 'newes of Fraunce and Flanders' were separate items, those on Flanders could be *An aduise and answer of my lord ye Prince of Orenge* (1577) or, less likely, *A iustification of the Prince of Orendge agaynst the false sclaunders* (London, 1575; *STC* 25712).

67 George J. Gray and W. M. Palmer (eds.), *Abstracts from the wills and testamentary documents of binders, printers and stationers of Cambridge, from 1504 to 1699* (London, 1915), pp. 60–1, 51–2.

68 Donald Paige, 'An additional letter and booklist of Thomas Chard, stationer of London', *The Library*, fourth series, 21 (1940), pp. 28, 30. 'King of navarr' is likely to be a broadside because Knowsley's twelve copies were valued at 12 pence in total. See also Robert Jahn, 'Letters and booklists of Thomas Chard (or Chare) of London, 1583–4', *The Library*, fourth series, 4 (1924), pp. 219–37.

possible that the working relationship between Chard and Aggas may have facilitated the dissemination of these pamphlets in Cambridge and East Anglia.[69] In 1569, Robert Scott of Norwich obtained four dozen ballads on the life of Edmund Bonner to sell, as well as copies of 'Diriges of Bonner', probably Lemeke Avale's *A commemoration or dirige of Bastarde Edmonde Boner* (1569).[70] The following year, he bought from London twenty-five copies of a ballad on the Northern Rising and six 'pictures of monstrous fishes', probably *A moste true and maruelous straunge wonder . . . of xviii monstrous fishes taken in Suffolke at Downam bridge* (1568).[71] At his death in 1585, Roger Ward of Shrewsbury's stock included recent titles such as, *A true reporte of a conference had betwixt Doctour Fulke, and the Papists being at Wisbich Castle* (1581);[72] *A declaration of the recantation of Iohn Nichols* (1581);[73] Munday's *A breefe aunswer made vnto two seditious pamphlets* (1582); [74] and *A true discourse of the assault committed vpon . . . William, Prince of Orange* (1582).[75] His stock also included older pamphlets and broadsides, such as *The disclosing of a late counterfeited possession by the deuyl* (1574);[76] Churchyard's *The most true reporte of Iames Fitz Morrice death* (1579);[77] *Of two woonderful popish monsters* (1579);[78] and *A reply . . . to a late rayling . . . libel of the papists* (1579).[79]

69 Paige, 'Additional letter and booklist', pp. 31–45.

70 Plomer, 'Elizabethan book sales', pp. 321–3; Lemeke Avale, *A commemoration or dirige of Bastarde Edmonde Boner* (London, 1569; *STC* 977). The ballad on Bonner's life was probably Thomas Broke, *An epitaphe declaryng the lyfe and ende of D. Edmund Boner &c* (London, 1569; *STC* 3817.4).

71 Plomer, 'Elizabethan book sales', pp. 321–3; *A moste true and maruelous straunge wonder . . . of xviii monstrous fishes taken in Suffolke at Downam bridge* (London, 1568; *STC* 12186). The specific ballad on the Rising that Scott bought has not been identified.

72 *A true reporte of a conference had betwixt Doctour Fulke, and the Papists being at Wisbich Castle* (London, 1581; *STC* 11457); Alexander Rodger, 'Roger Ward's Shrewsbury stock: an inventory of 1585', *The Library*, fifth series, 13 (1958), p. 256, no. 292; p. 257, no. 340.

73 *A declaration of the recantation of Iohn Nichols* (London, 1581; *STC* 18533); Rodger, 'Roger Ward', p. 258, no. 347.

74 Anthony Munday, *A breefe aunswer made vnto two seditious pamphlets . . . Contayning a defence of Edmund Campion* (London, 1582; *STC* 18262); Rodger, 'Roger Ward', p. 258, no. 379.

75 *A true discourse of the assault committed vpon the person of the most noble prince, William, Prince of Orange* (London, 1582; *STC* 25713); Rodger, 'Roger Ward', p. 257, no. 323; Byrne and Thomson, '"My lord's books"', p. 399, no. 61.

76 *The disclosing of a late counterfeited possession by the deuyl in two maydens within the citie of London* (London, 1574; *STC* 3738); Rodger, 'Roger Ward', p. 257, no. 335.

77 Churchyard, *True reporte of Iames Fitz Morrice death* (1579) or *A ballat of Fitzmorris* (licensed to Richard Jones, 4 Sept. 1579); Rodger, 'Roger Ward', p. 257, no. 313; Arber (ed.), *Registers of the Company of Stationers*, II, p. 359.

78 Philip Melancthon, *Of two woonderful popish monsters* (London, 1579; *STC* 17797); Rodger, 'Roger Ward', p. 252, no. 83.

79 *A reply . . . to a late rayling . . . libel of the papists set vpon postes, and also in Paules church in London* (London, 1579; *STC* 19179); Rodger, 'Roger Ward', p. 251, no. 63.

Equally, booksellers' inventories are likely to underestimate the dissemination of pamphlets in the provinces because the main purveyors of books outside London were probably travelling chapmen, rather than sedentary specialists.[80] Certainly, the existence of a provincial market is reinforced by evidence of the printing of regional news stories for local markets – as distinct from stories with a national appeal[81] – such as *The first anointed Queen I am, within this town which euer came*, a simple broadsheet printed by John Allde in 1573, probably produced for Elizabeth's visit to Rye in August 1573,[82] and *A new Yorkshyre song* (1584), probably a special commission.[83]

Roger Ward of Shrewsbury's stock is particularly significant because it may point to the availability of news pamphlets and broadsides in Wales where evidence of the dissemination of books, beyond the academic libraries of men like Sir John Stradling and Jaspar Gryffyth (rector of Longston, Montgomeryshire and warden of Ruthin Hospital), is limited.[84] Most of Wales's trade by land – in cloth and livestock – was routed through Shrewsbury, though Oswestry and Leominster were also important.[85] There were also close political and administrative links with Shrewsbury through the Council of the Marches of Wales. Indeed, Monmouthshire had only two representatives on the Council compared to Shropshire's twenty-two.[86] It is likely that Shrewsbury acted as the main market or nexus for book-buying for Wales, but, as demonstrated by Gryffyth's library, books may have also been obtained directly from London.[87] Ward's stock suggests that news pamphlets, from *A declaration of the recantation of Iohn Nichols* to *Of two woonderful popish monsters*, may have circulated in Wales. The dissemination of news pamphlets and broadsides in Wales may have been further facilitated by well-established

80 Arber (ed.), *Registers of the Company of Stationers*, I, p. 184 (fine for hawking books on the streets of London); Watt, *Cheap print*, pp. 264–6.
81 For example, I.P., *A meruaylous straunge deformed swine* (London, 1570; *STC* 19071) and *A straunge and terrible wunder* (1577).
82 *The first anointed Queene I am, within this town which euer came* (London?, 1573; *STC* 7582.5). See the notes in *Early English Books Online* or on the microfilm (reel 1709:08).
83 William Elderton, *A new Yorkshyre song* (London, 1584; *STC* 7559).
84 Graham C. G. Thomas, 'The Stradling library at St Donats, Glamorgan', *National Library of Wales*, 24 (1986), pp. 402–19; Richard Ovenden, 'Jaspar Gryffyth and his books', *British Library Journal*, 20 (1994), pp. 107–39.
85 Glanmor Williams, *Recovery, reorientation and Reformation: Wales, c.1415–1625* (Oxford, 1987), pp. 401–2.
86 Ben Howell, *Law and disorder in Tudor Monmouthshire* (Cardiff, 1995), pp. xliii–xlv.
87 Ovenden, 'Jaspar Gryffyth', pp. 112, 115–16.

maritime trading links between a number of Welsh ports and Bristol, Gloucester, Chester (via Beaumaris) and other English ports.[88] There is more direct evidence of the dissemination of printed news and information in Ireland. As for Wales, research over the past thirty years has emphasised that Ireland was a dynamic, rather than static, political society with members of its elite absorbed politically, culturally and intellectually in the Renaissance.[89] Initial attempts to establish printing in Ireland in the early sixteenth century failed,[90] while the bulk of the work conducted by the Queen's Printers – Humphrey Powell (1550–c.1567),[91] William Kearney (1591–c.1599)[92] and John Francton (c.1600–c.1619)[93] – focused on the Book of Common Prayer and proclamations on Irish affairs.[94] However, there is evidence that English

---

88 For trade to English ports, see E. A. Lewis (ed.), *The Welsh port books, 1550–1603* (Cymmrodorion Record Society, 12; London, 1927), pp. 7, 30–6, 61–7, 111–16, 126–35, 263–5 and passim; Williams, *Recovery, reorientation and Reformation*, pp. 401–3; Howell, *Law and disorder*, p. lxx.

89 Williams, *Recovery, reorientation and Reformation*; Glanmor Williams and Robert Owen Jones (eds.), *The Celts and the Renaissance: tradition and innovation* (Cardiff, 1990), especially R. Geraint Gruffydd's essay 'The Renaissance and Welsh literature', pp. 17–39; J. G. Jones, 'The Welsh poets and their patrons, c.1550–1640', *Welsh History Review*, 14 (1979), pp. 245–77. For Ireland: Katherine Simms, *From kings to warlords: the changing political structure of Gaelic Ireland in the later Middle Ages* (Woodbridge, Suffolk, 1987); Nicholas Canny, *The Elizabethan conquest of Ireland: a pattern established, 1565–1576* (Hassocks, 1976); Brendan Bradshaw, 'The Elizabethans and the Irish', *Studies*, 66 (1977), pp. 38–50; Bradshaw, 'The Elizabethans and the Irish: a muddled model', *Studies*, 70 (1981), pp. 233–44; R. D. Edwards, 'Ireland, Elizabeth I and the Counter-Reformation', in Bindoff, Hurstfield and Williams (eds.), *Elizabethan government and society*, pp. 315–39; Brendan Bradshaw, 'Manus "the Magnificent": O'Donnell as Renaissance prince', in Art Cosgrove and Donal McCartney (eds.), *Studies in Irish History* (Dublin, 1979), pp. 15–36; John J. Silke, 'Irish scholarship and the Renaissance', *Studies in the Renaissance*, 20 (1973), pp. 169–206; Helga Hammerstein, 'Aspects of the continental education of Irish students in the reign of Queen Elizabeth I', in T. D. Williams (ed.), *Historical Studies: papers read before the Irish conference of historians*, 8 (1971), pp. 137–53.

90 Desmond Clarke and P. J. Madden, 'Printing in Ireland', *An Leabharlann*, 12 (1954), p. 115.

91 E. R. McClintock Dix, 'Humphrey Powell, the first Dublin printer', *Proceedings of the Royal Irish Academy*, 27 (1907), section C, pp. 213–16; Dix, 'Humphrey Powell, Dublin's first printer: some new information', *Bibliographic Society of Ireland Publications*, 4 (1928), pp. 77–80; *HMC Report on the manuscripts of the Lord De L'Isle and Dudley* (6 vols., London, 1925–66), I, p. 397; N. B. White, 'Elizabethan Dublin printing', *Irish Book Lover*, 21 (1933), p. 113; David B. Quinn, 'Information about Dublin printers, 1556–1573, in English financial records', *Irish Book Lover*, 27 (1942), pp. 112–14.

92 E. R. McClintock Dix, 'William Kearney, the second earliest known printer in Dublin', *Proceedings of the Royal Irish Academy*, 28 (1908), section C, pp. 157–61; Robert Munter, *A dictionary of the print trade in Ireland, 1550–1775* (New York, 1988), p. 152.

93 Munter, *Dictionary of the print trade*, pp. 107–8; Henry Plomer, 'John Francton and his successors', *Irish Book Lover*, 3 (1911), pp. 109–10; E. R. McClintock Dix, 'Initial letters used by John Francton, printer at Dublin', *Irish Book Lover*, 3 (1911), pp. 58–9.

94 For example, *A proclamacyon set fourth by the Erle of Sussex* (Dublin, 1561; *STC* 14138); *A proclamacyon. Sett furthe by the Lorde Justice* (Dublin, 1564; *STC* 14139); Lord Deputy and the Privy Council of Ireland to Elizabeth, 17 Apr. 1562, SP63/5/85, fo. 223. For evidence of printed

pamphlets, on Irish affairs as well as English and continental events, were imported to and circulated in Ireland. In January 1572, an English ship brought 'newse in print, that Sir Thomas Smyth hathe the gyft of part of Vlster and the Ardes and his sonne is coming ovar with a grete number of men to possesse and habyte the same' to an unidentified port in the north.[95] Probably referring to *The offer and order giuen forthe by Sir Thomas Smyth Knighte* (s.n.), this 'newse' quickly circulated: Brian Mac Phelim O'Neill, chieftain of the Clandeboy O'Neills, complained to the privy council in England of the grant.[96] In June, 'a nother prynted booke of the said Thomas Smythes enterprise' had been brought from England, probably *A letter sent by I.B. Gentleman vnto his very frende Maystet R.C. Esquire* (1572).[97] In May 1572, copies of 'a declaracion of the victorye againste the Turckes in a littell booke' were imported to Limerick. This was either the slightly outdated *[C]ertayn and tru good neus, from the seyge of the isle Malta* (1565) or *Newes from Vienna the 5. day of August* (1566), titles that were circulating in England.[98] In 1581, Edward Bulger of Dublin was arrested in Chester for attempting to convey 'Pamphilettes' (Robert Persons's *A brief discours contayning certayne reasons why Catholiques refuse to goe to church* (1580) and, possibly, *A briefe censure vppon two bookes written in answere to M. Edmunde Campions offer of disputation* (1581)) into Ireland on behalf of two Catholics, John Finglas and Richard Talbot.[99]

proclamations no longer extant but traceable in financial accounts, see White, 'Elizabethan Dublin printing', p. 113; Quinn, 'Information about Dublin printers', pp. 113, 114 (fn. 7).

95 William Piers to [Fitzwilliam], 2 Jan. 1572, SP63/35/2, fo. 19r.

96 Though Piers did not identify the 'newse in print', it is most likely to be the single sheet *The offer and order giuen forthe by Sir Thomas Smyth Knighte* (London, s.n.; *STC* 22868.5). SP63/35/2, fo. 19r–19v; Brian Mac Phelim O'Neill to the privy council, 27 Mar. 1572, SP63/35/45, fo. 164r. O'Neill knew of Smith's order prior to Piers writing to Fitzwilliam on 3 January, though it is unclear if he obtained actual copies.

97 Fitzwilliam and the privy council of Ireland to the privy council, 28 June 1572, SP63/36/48, fos. 167v–168r; *A letter sent by I. B. Gentleman vnto his very frende Maystet R. C. Esquire* (London, 1572; *STC* 1048). Note that this reprints *The offer and order* (s.n.) from sig. G3v.

98 Interrogatories ministered vnto the within sworne persones, May 1572, SP63/36/29, fos. 109v–110r; *[C]ertayn and tru good nues, from the seyge of the isle Malta* (London, 1565; *STC* 17213.5); *Newes from Vienna* (1566).

99 William Byrd, mayor of Chester, and Chancellor Gerard to Leicester, 17 Feb. 1581, SP63/80/60, fo. 171r–171v; John Finglas to Richard Brette, 2 Jan. 1581, SP63/80/60.I, fo. 173r; Richard Talbott to Walter Sutton, 29 Jan. 1581, SP63/80/60.VI, fo. 180r; The examynacion of Edward Bulger, 15 Feb. 1581, SP63/80/60.VIII, fo. 183r; The examinacion taken of John Finglas, gent., 22 Feb. 1581, SP63/80/72, fo. 209r–209v; Robert Persons, *A brief discours contayning certayne reasons why Catholiques refuse to goe to church* (Douai [i.e. East Ham], 1580; *STC* 19394). The identification of the second book is unclear. Finglas wrote, 'ther was an offer of disputacion made by one campyon a Jesuite that kepeth heare in England from place to place secretlye thervnto/whervnto was written towe bokes in answer the one by m chark thither by mr Hammond to which was

These snapshots are reinforced by evidence from the port books, which show a constant traffic of (primarily educational, grammar and service) books, not only to Dublin, but also to provincial ports.[100]

Evidence of the dissemination of printed news pamphlets supports broader studies that have increasingly shown that there was not necessarily a clear-cut distinction between 'elite' and 'popular' readers. As noted in chapter 4, the second earl of Bedford owned a large number of small news pamphlets, including *24. of August. 1578. A discourse of the present state of the wars in the lowe countryes* (1578); Churchyard's *A scourge for rebels . . . touching the trobles of Ireland* (1584); and the unidentified 'Of ij adulterers in St Brides'.[101] Lady Mary Grey probably owned *The edict or proclamation set forthe by the French Kinge vpon the pacifying of the troubles in Fraunce* (1576).[102] Gentlemen like Wingfield and Carnsew also read and owned small pamphlets, like 'Newes from the Turk' and 'Pacyfficacions proclaymyd in Fraunce . . . prentyd in Englyshe'. Nor were they items that were beyond the price range of yeomen, artisans and shopkeepers, though probate inventories rarely allow us to trace individual ownership. Modern estimates of the cost of pamphlets suggest they may cost between two and nine pence, broadsides as little as a halfpenny.[103] Broadsides and small pamphlets were not, therefore, the preserve of a poorer, less educated audience.

---

this short replye made which I have sent you <by this> herin inclosed.' This would suggest it was Persons, *A briefe censure vppon two bookes written in answere to M. Edmunde Campions offer of disputation* (Douai [i.e. Stonor Park, Pyrton], 1581; *STC* 19393). However, that was not published until some time in 1581 while Finglas's books were sent on 2 January 1581. It is possible, therefore, that Finglas's letters and the related investigations have been misdated and actually refer to 1581 Old Style, i.e. January 1582.

100 For example: Port of Bristol: Bristol: Customer Overseas Outwards, Easter 1574-Michaelmas 1574, E190/1129/6, fo. 8v; Port of Bristol: Bristol: Controller Overseas Outwards, Michaelmas 1574–Easter 1575, E190/1129/5, fo. 9r; Port of Bristol: Bristol: Customer Overseas Outwards, Michaelmas 1575–Easter 1576, E190/1129/10, fo. 9r; Port of Bristol: Bristol: Customer Overseas Outwards, Michaelmas 1576–Easter 1577, E190/1129/16, fo. 7r; M. Pollard, *Dublin's trade in books, 1550–1800* (Oxford, 1989), pp. 36–7. See also: Quinn, 'Information about Dublin printers', pp. 113–14, 114–15 (fn. 3). For earlier evidence of the importation of books to Ireland, including ballads or broadsides, see Leslie Martin Oliver, 'A bookseller's account book, 1545', *Harvard Library Bulletin*, 16 (1968), pp. 139–55 and M. Pollard, 'James Dartas, an early Dublin stationer', *Irish Book Lover*, 2 (1976), pp. 227–8.

101 Byrne and Thomson, '"My lord's books"', pp. 399–400, 405, nos. 55, 77, 183; *24. of August. 1578* (1578); Churchyard, *A scourge for rebels* (1584).

102 Burgon, *Sir Thomas Gresham*, II, pp. 415–16.

103 Watt, *Cheap print*, pp. 261–4; Barnard and Bell, 'Henry Bynneman', pp. 8–9; Raymond, *Pamphlets and pamphleteering*, p. 39.

ORAL CIRCULATION OF NEWS

Vibrant as the market in printed news was – Henry Bynneman alleged he had printed *A true discourse of the late voyages of discouerie for finding of a passage to Cathaya* (1578) to 'satisfye the greedy expectation' of news[104] – it was only one vehicle among many that disseminated news among Elizabethan men and women. News also circulated orally as well as in manuscript form, whether as letters or as manuscript pamphlets.

At an elite level, the nobility and gentry utilised household servants to convey verbal messages and information. The clearest examples derive from Ireland. In early 1571, James Fitzmaurice's servant (or son) arrived from Spain and 'reportyd prively' to William Fitzjames 'that ther is great company of shippes redy to come in to the haven of dangyn [i.e. Dingle]'. Another man reported to Fitzjames that he had witnessed Fitzmaurice assault Sir Thomas Fitzgerald of Desmond, killing forty of Desmond's men.[105] Turlough Luineach O'Neill, Shane's successor as leader of the Tyrone O'Neills, sent a 'horseboy' to enquire of the earl of Desmond 'in what estate he was in' in June 1572.[106] But, as Harry Shadwell's activities make clear, oral communication was important for other Elizabethans. In Cheapside in 1559, Thomas Holland, vicar of Little Burstead in Essex, was told by a former vicar that a man had been sent to the Tower 'for saeng the queens maiestie was with childe'.[107] In 1569, rumours circulated in County Carlow, south of the Pale in Leinster, that Elizabeth and the earl of Ormond were to be murdered. They may have been started by Sir Edmund Butler, the earl's brother and heir.[108] News also circulated in Ireland of Burghley's death in 1584, while it was reported in England that Ormond had been overthrown; both reports proved false.[109] Henry Machyn's diary and the 'Journall of matters of state' (which includes the account of the first performance of *Gorboduc*) brim with references to the 'common talcke' and the 'common brute'. In 1561, the 'common talcke is that the king of Sweden is solicited to marriage with the

---

104 George Best, *A true discourse of the late voyages of discouerie for finding of a passage to Cathaya* (London, 1578; *STC* 1972), sigs. Biii^r–Biv^r.
105 Fitzwilliam to Burghley, 1 May 1571, SP63/32/18, fo. 71r. Mary O'Dowd (ed.), *Calendar of State Papers Ireland: Tudor period, 1571–1575* (Kew and Dublin, 2000), p. 17, identifies the bearer of the first news as Fitzwilliam's son, but the original document appears to say 'James fytz morrys mane' suggesting a servant.
106 Warham St Leger to Burghley, 3 June 1571, SP63/32/50, fo. 148r.
107 [unknown] to the privy council, 15 June 1560, SP12/12/51, fo. 36r.
108 Edward Langham to Sir Henry Sidney, 22 June 1569, SP63/28/48, fo. 106r.
109 Earl of Ormond to Burghley, 22 July 1580, SP63/74/55, fo. 102r.

Scottyshe Quene'; the following January, 'there was a grete talcke in London of the fall of money'.[110] In Ireland in 1562, there were common 'brutes' that the Viceroy, the earl of Sussex, would be replaced.[111]

Vehicles which now survive in printed or manuscript form, circulated principally orally: proclamations, publicising news and royal orders,[112] and ballads, polemically charged accounts mainly of politico-religious or moral issues, which were performed publicly and privately by harpers, minstrels, cantabanqui, ballad sellers and customers.[113] Their impact is testified to by John Carre, a haymaker, who had told his friends in 1584 that 'the king of Scottes shalbe your gouernour' having learned this 'news' from a song.[114] In 1568, the Council of the Marches of Wales set up a commission to regulate travelling minstrels and musicians, principally at the Caerwys Eisteddfod, but also across North Wales generally.[115] Sermons were also used to convey both information and government directives: in his sermon at Paul's Cross on 9 April 1559, William Bill explained why the Catholic bishops had been imprisoned in the Tower.[116] On 22 June 1561, the dean of Durham preached against 'a nothe boke that ys prynted, and [bade every] man be ware of yt, for yt ys vere herese'.[117]

Church services themselves were also able to disseminate news, especially when the service followed the structure laid out in special prayer books published to pray, or provide thanks, for divine intervention in key domestic and continental events, such as the earthquake in London (1580), the Parry and Babington plots (1585, 1586), the sieges of Malta (1565) and Jula, Hungary (1566) by the Turks, and the St Bartholomew's Day Massacre (1572).[118] They not only made parishioners aware of specific

110 Additional 48023, fos. 358r, 360r. See also, fo. 355r–355v, 362r and the many examples in Machyn's diary (though it is not always clear if they were all oral circulation): *Machyn's diary*, pp. 213–15, 220–1, 223, 230–1, 245, 259, 265–8, 270, 275, 298, 300–2.
111 SP63/5/85, fo. 223r. See also, privy council of Ireland to Elizabeth, 12 June 1561, SP63/4/3, fo. 3r–3v; Sussex to Cecil, 19 Aug. 1561, SP63/4/37, fo. 80r.
112 *Machyn's diary*, pp. 229, 278, 311–12; George Owen, Lord of Kemeys, *The Taylor's cussion*, ed. Emily Pritchard (Olwen Powys) (London, 1906), pp. 94–5; SP63/4/3, fo. 3r; SP63/5/85, fo. 223r.
113 For example: *The plagues of Northomberland* (London, 1570; *STC* 1421); Gibson, *Nortons falcehod* ([1570]); *Most ioyfull Songe* (1586); *The shape of ii monsters* (London, 1562; *STC* 11485); Watt, *Cheap print*, pp. 11–37, 40–2.
114 ASSI 35/26/7, m. 25. See also Thexaminations of John Thipthorp, Thomas Nashe [and others], 3 July 1584, SP12/172/7, fo. 10r.
115 Council of the Marches of Wales to the Commissioners of the Caerwys Eisteddfod, 1568, *HMC Report on manuscripts in the Welsh language* (6 vols. in 2, London, 1898–1910) I:i, pp. 291–2.
116 *Machyn's diary*, p. 194.
117 Ibid., p. 261.
118 I have discussed this in a paper 'All the news that's fit to preach: prayer books and the public sphere in Elizabethan England' at the Sixteenth-Century Studies Conference in Toronto in 2004 and at the Ecclesiastical History Seminar at the Institute of Historical Research in 2005

events but were able to convey detailed information: *The order of prayer
. . . to auert Gods wrath from vs, threatned by the late terrible earthquake*
(1580) contained a report of the earthquake that had struck on 6 April,
and the physical and human destruction it had caused. It also placed
the event within the context of other English and continental earth-
quakes, famines, weather and monstrous births.[119] *An order of praier
and thankes-giuing* (1585) contained an extract of William Parry's
confession.[120]

Whether in the shape of ballads or dialogue, proclamations or prayer
books, the circulation of news orally was geographically wide. 'What
news?' was a common question, asked particularly of those on the road
or who came from London, and some artisans and traders, like John
Bradburie, an Oxford tailor, were paid to convey messages.[121] William
Carnsew of Bokelly, Cornwall, heard of the proposed promotion of the
bishop of Exeter to Salisbury, the return of the Spanish ambassador,
Mendoza, to the royal court and, at Port Eliot, that 'the Londoners
shyppes were restored by the prynce of orenge that that flanders was
yeldyd hoollye to hyme', though this proved untrue.[122] In Monmouth, in
1571–2, rumours that Charles Somerset and William Morgan would
be elected knights of the shire circulated by the 'voyce' or 'common
intelligence'.[123] In April 1569, Sir William Fitzwilliam, Vice-Treasurer and
Treasurer at war in Ireland, heard 'great brutes' of 'the prynce of condes
being slayne and of other great matters against hym and the admiral

and intend to develop it further in an article. *The order of prayer . . . to auert Gods wrath from vs,
threatned by the late terrible earthquake* (London, 1580; *STC* 16512); *An order of praier and
thankes-giuing for the preseruation of the quene maiesties life and salfetie* (London, 1585; *STC*
16516); *An order of prayer and thankesgiuing, for the preseruation of her maiestie and the realme,
from the bloodie practises of the pope* (London, 1586; *STC* 16517); *A fourme to be vsed in common
prayer . . . for the deliuery of those christians that are nowe invaded by the Turke* (London, [1565];
STC 16508); *A shorte forme of thankesgeuing for the delyuerie of the isle of Malta from the Turkes*
(London, 1565; *STC* 16509); *A fourme to be vsed in common prayer . . . for the preseruation of those
christians and their countries that are nowe invaded by the Turke* (London, [1566]; *STC* 16510); *A
fourme of common prayer to be vsed . . . and necessarie for the present tyme and state* (London, 1572;
STC 16511). All are printed in Clay (ed.), *Liturgies.*
119 *The order of prayer* (1580), and printed in Clay (ed.), *Liturgies*, pp. 564–6, 569–70.
120 *An order of praier and thankes-giuing* (1585), and printed in Clay (ed.), *Liturgies*, pp. 583–5.
121 The saying of Anne Dowe of Burndwood wydowe, 28 Jul. 1560, PRO, SP12/13/21.I, fos. 56r–58v;
ASSI 35/29/1, m. 33; Thomas Bette, *A nevve ballade intitvled, agaynst Rebellious and false Rumours*
(London, 1570; *STC* 1979); E. R. Brinkworth (ed.), *The archdeacon's court: liber actorum, 1584* (2
vols., Oxfordshire Record Society, 23–4, 1942–6), II, p. 131.
122 'Carnsew's diary', pp. 32, 36, 51–2, 30 (fn. 36).
123 William Morgan of Llantarnam, esq. vs. Thomas Herbert of Mynstow [i.e. Monmouth], sheriff,
13–14 Elizabeth I, STAC5/M31/39.

[Coligny]'.[124] At Kinsale, Athlone and Galway, merchants reported news of Don John's victory over the Turks at Lepanto.[125] In 1572, James Welshe of Waterford reported that King Sebastian of Portugal had mustered an army of 70,000 men rumoured to be destined for Africa, La Rochelle or Ireland, and that Coligny had been appointed general of troops to be sent into Flanders.[126]

Special prayer books were widely distributed by bishops, via apparitors and sumners, for compulsory purchase by parishes. Though there is no evidence of their circulation in Wales and Ireland, churchwardens' accounts show that copies of prayer books on the siege of Malta by the Turks were purchased by, for instance, Morebath, Devon,[127] Ludlow, Shropshire,[128] Wootton St Lawrence, Hampshire,[129] St Andrew, Canterbury,[130] as well as many London parishes, including St Botolph Aldersgate,[131] St Benet Gracechurch Street[132] and St Matthew Friday Street.[133] Those on the earthquake of 1580 were purchased by Prescot, Lancashire,[134] St Michael's, Chagford, Devon,[135] St Michael in Bedwardine, Worcester,[136] Mere, Wiltshire,[137] Wootton St Lawrence, Hampshire,[138] St Botolph Aldgate, London[139] and Holy Trinity Minories.[140] Whilst purchase does not denote that the

---

124 Fitzwilliam to Cecil, 11 Apr. 1569, SP63/28/1, fo. 1v.
125 Thexaminacion of Walter Frence, 30 Mar. 1572, SP63/35/46, fo. 166r–166v; John Craston to [unknown], 13 Apr. 1572, SP63/36/1, fo. 1r; Domenic Browne to Sir Edward Fitton, 14 Apr. 1572, [Fitzwilliam's copy], SP63/36/2.I, fo. 4r–4v. Craston was probably John Crofton, clerk of the council in Connacht.
126 George Wyse to Fitzwilliam, 20 July 1572, SP63/37/13.I, fo. 13r. For other examples, see Patrick White to Walsingham, 29 June 1580, SP63/73/69, fo. 162r–162v.
127 J. Erskine Binney (ed.), *The accounts of the wardens of the parish of Morebath, Devon, 1520–1573* (Devon Notes and Queries Supplement; Exeter, 1904), p. 228.
128 Thomas Wright (ed.), *Churchwardens' accounts of the town of Ludlow in Shropshire from 1540 to the end of the reign of Queen Elizabeth* (Camden Society, os, 102; London, 1869), p. 122.
129 J. F. Williams (ed.), *The early churchwardens' accounts of Hampshire* (Winchester and London, 1913), p. 184.
130 Charles Cotton, 'Churchwardens' accounts of the parish of St Andrew, Canterbury, from AD 1485 to AD 1625. Part IV: 1553-4 – 1596', *Archaeologia Cantiana*, 35 (1921), p. 58.
131 Guildhall MS 1454/69.
132 Guildhall MS 1568/1 (part 1), p. 177.
133 Guildhall MS 1016/1, fo. 37r.
134 F. A. Bailey (ed.), *The churchwardens' accounts of Prescot, Lancashire, 1523–1607* (Lancashire and Cheshire Record Society, 104; Preston, 1953), p. 84.
135 Francis Mardon Osborne (ed.), *The churchwardens' accounts of St Michael's church, Chagford, 1480–1600* (Chagford, 1979), p. 239.
136 John Amphlett, *The churchwardens' accounts of St Michael's in Bedwardine, Worcester, from 1539 to 1603* (Worcestershire Historical Society; Oxford, 1896), p. 87.
137 Thomas H. Baker, 'The churchwardens' accounts of Mere', *Wiltshire Archaeological and Natural History Magazine*, 35 (1907–8), p. 69.
138 Williams (ed.), *Churchwardens' accounts of Hampshire*, p. 196.
139 Guildhall MS 1235/1 (part 1), fo. 154v.
140 LPL MS 3390, fo. 55v.

parish used the prayer books – their purchase was compulsory, though it seems as if some parishes avoided the apparitor or were left out of his circuit – it seems unlikely that they were all left mouldering in a corner after the apparitor's departure.

OTHER MEDIA FOR THE DISSEMINATION OF NEWS

Though oral circulation seems to have been the most common, and most geographically widespread, vehicle for news, other forms were also evident. As was the case for the circulation of news in and around the court, non-courtiers were able to observe events. Machyn recorded Elizabeth's removes between palaces or the houses of courtiers; royal entertainments on the river; the movements of privy councillors, ambassadors (English and foreign) and foreign visitors; as well as the opening and closing of parliament.[141] The elaborate obsequies organised for Henry II of France on 8 September 1559, and attended by leading courtiers, reinforced and further disseminated news of Henry's death already circulating orally.[142] Though opportunities for observing court news could be limited – restricted to Elizabeth's removes and royal, public entertainments – observations favoured sensational and/or local news. Malformed animals and children were often put on public display.[143] Machyn observed and recorded a large number of skimmington rides, pillories, murders, accidents and suicides that occurred in London.[144]

As Carnsew's diary shows, letter-writing was central to the circulation of news among the gentry: in January 1577 alone, he received or wrote letters, on the 7th, 8th, 9th, 12th, 16th, 17th and 25th.[145] Bassingborne Gawdy, and his wife, Lady Anne, in Norfolk eagerly awaited news conveyed by their son, Philip, in London. In May 1587, they had to be content with a report of a duel between Sir William Waldegrave and Lord Windsor, the arrest of some Jesuits and the imprisonment of two lawyers for 'to lyberall speaches', until 'further tyme may minister further cause of

---

141 For example, *Machyn's diary*, pp. 191, 195–9, 225, 234, 261–4, 270, 275.

142 Ibid., pp. 209–10.

143 Ibid., pp. 280–1, 284, 311; *True discription of this marueilous straunge fishes* (1569); *A miraculous . . . discourse of a woman* (1588). The pig may be one of those pictured in *The shape of ii monsters* (*STC* 11485). It is not described, but the other pig, with a malformed head and legs, is stated as having been born on 7 May 1562 at Charing Cross. Machyn's entry is undated but is in between entries for 9 and 11 May.

144 *Machyn's diary*, pp. 196–7, 219, 252, 220.

145 'Carnsew's diary', pp. 31–2.

writing.'[146] The Gawdys used both the regular carrier and sent letters privately.[147] Though news was principally conveyed from the centre to the provinces, some, like Sir Thomas Cornwallis, sent their London correspondents local news.[148] Philip Gawdy waited eagerly for news from Norfolk.[149]

News pamphlets were not confined to print, but also circulated in manuscript. These included those that were also available in print: Bedford appears to have owned manuscript copies of Dudley Fenner's *The ansuuere copies vnto the confutation of Iohn Nichols his recantation* and Nowell's *A true report of the disputation . . . with Ed. Campion Iesuit,* both circulating in print.[150] But also material, usually defined by the regime as critical and seditious, only in manuscript. In July 1582, the Attorney-General, Sir John Popham, forwarded a 'seditious pamphlet' to Walsingham that had been discovered by Dr John Hammond (Chancellor of the diocese of London and a leading member of the High Commission, examining Jesuits and seminary priests) in the church porch of St Giles without Cripplegate: a densely written, two-page attack on *A particular declaration or testimony, of the vndutifull and traitorous affection borne against her Maiestie by Edmund Campion* (1582) and Anthony Munday's *The Englyshe Romayne life* (1582).[151]

Though, as Peter Lake has shown, there could be a close relationship between domestic news pamphlets – especially those reporting murders – and drama, the stage was relatively insignificant as a medium for news.[152] Plays were able to convey information about political events. Christopher Marlowe's *The massacre at Paris* recounted events in the French wars, from the St Bartholomew's Day Massacre to the assassination of Henry III in 1589. John Lyly's *Sappho and Phao, Campaspe* and *Endymion,* which explored broad political issues like peace versus war and the ideal of citizenship and were first performed at court, were also performed at

---

146 Egerton 2804, fo. 23r.
147 Egerton 2804, fo. 26r; Egerton 2804, fo. 29r; Egerton 2804, fo. 33r.
148 Scott-Warren, 'News, sociability and book-buying', pp. 389–90.
149 Egerton 2804, fos. 35r–36r.
150 The description 'parchm[ent]' after entries 42, 44 and 47 of Bedford's inventory suggests that these may have been manuscript copies. Byrne and Thomson, '"My lord's books"', pp. 398–9, nos. 42, 44, 47. Dudley Fenner, *The ansuuere copies vnto the confutation of Iohn Nichols his recantation* (London, 1583; *STC* 10764.3); Alexander Nowell, *A true report of the disputation or rather priuate conference had in the Tower of London, with Ed. Campion Iesuite* (London, 1581; *STC* 18744).
151 Dr John Hammond to Sir John Popham, 6 July 1582, SP12/154/53.I, fo. 96r; *Censvre vpon the Aunsweres of Mr Bosgrave and Mr Orton,* nd, SP12/154/53.II, fos. 97r–97v.
152 Lake with Questier, *Anti-christ's lewd hat,* chs. 1 and 10.

the public theatre of Blackfriars in the early to mid-1580s.[153] Indeed, Paul Kocher's little-known work on the literary sources for *The massacre at Paris* has demonstrated both the congruence between the play, key histories and small pamphlets and the array of factual and polemical information conveyed by Marlowe.[154] However, plays lacked topicality and were rarely the format in which reports circulated first. *The massacre at Paris* was probably not performed until January 1593, four years after the most recent event it depicted and nearly twenty after the massacre itself.[155] Domestic events, such as the murder of Thomas Arden of Faversham (1551) and of a London merchant, George Saunders (1573), were not transformed into plays until forty and twenty-six years after the event respectively, even though accounts of both murders had circulated some years prior to this.[156]

PHYSICAL SPACE AND THE ORAL DISSEMINATION OF NEWS

Though the oral circulation of news was geographically wide, its heart in London was St Paul's churchyard. John Keyle discussed the Swedish marriage negotiations with a Mr Allen and an unidentified Frenchman while he was 'walkinge in pwles [sic]'.[157] It was a recognised centre for news of all kinds, acting as an employment exchange for the clergy and, at Paul's Cross, a mouthpiece for the government.[158] Bishop Pilkington of Durham went so far as to complain that, 'The South Alley [is] for Usurye and Popery, the North for Simony, and the Horse Fair in the middest for all kinds of bargains'.[159] But news also travelled down the arteries leading from St Paul's: southwards to Paul's Wharf and the river – as demonstrated by Shadwell's conversations with Whittacres – and eastward down Cheapside and into Lombard Street and Cornhill (site of the Royal

---

153 Altman, '*Quaestiones Copiosae*'. See above, ch. 4.
154 Paul H. Kocher, 'Fransçois Hotman and Marlowe's *Massacre at Paris*', *Publications of the Modern Language Association*, 56 (1941), pp. 349–68; Kocher, 'Contemporary pamphlet backgrounds for Marlowe's *Massacre at Paris*,' *Modern Language Quarterly*, 8 (1947), pp. 151–73.
155 *The complete works of Christopher Marlowe*, ed. Fredson Bowes (2 vols., Cambridge, 1973), I, p. 357.
156 *The lamentable and true tragedie of M. arden of Feuersham* (London, 1592; STC 733); Raphael Holinshed, *The firste volume of the chronicles of England, Scotlande, and Irelande* (London, 1577; STC 13568a); Golding, *The late murther of master G Saunders* (1577).
157 Interogatories ministred vnto John Keale, 6 Aug. 1562, SP70/40, fo. 77r.
158 Anthonie Anderson, *A sermon preached at Paules Cross* (London, 1581; STC 570), sig. Gii^r; Joseph Hall, *Virgidemiarum* (London, 1597; STC 12716), pp. 39–40.
159 James Pilkington, *The burnynge of Paules Church* (London, 1563; STC 19931), sigs. Giii^r–Giii^v.

Exchange). Though there are no direct references to it in the extant sources, Leadenhall may also have been significant. As an important marketplace, an arsenal and a site where triumphs were organised and poor relief distributed, it was a common location for public gatherings.[160] Cheapside and Lombard Street were two of the main points at which proclamations were published.[161] Both Lombard Street and the Royal Exchange probably derived their significance from their roles as meeting places for English and foreign merchants and, particularly in the case of Lombard Street, as a centre for mercantile transactions.[162] Merchants were active newsmongers, while the establishment in Lombard Street and the Royal Exchange of two daily times for business (nine o'clock in the morning and evening for Lombard Street; noon and six o'clock at the Exchange) facilitated the dissemination of news beyond the mercantile community, comparable to the establishment of noon as the best time to obtain news at St Paul's. Lombard Street was closed to traffic and the times were known as the 'street time', 'in the street' or 'at the street hour'.[163]

Both in the City of London and in the English provinces, the parish church operated as the main nexus for news and information; there is less evidence for Wales and Ireland.[164] Not only were they the forum for sermons and services conducted according to the special prayer books, but proclamations were often read out in church. Proclamations and orders about the plague (1564) and weights and measures (1587–8) were purchased 'to be red in the churche' and 'to [be] set up in a table' by the

160 Jean Imray, 'The origins of the Royal Exchange', in Saunders (ed.), *The Royal Exchange*, pp. 20–2.
161 *Machyn's diary*, p. 229; [unknown] to the privy council, 15 June 1560, SP12/12/51, fo. 36r; Interogatories ministered vnto James Goldborne and his answers to the same, 6 Aug. 1562, SP70/40, fo. 61v.
162 Caroline Barron, Christopher Coleman and Claire Gobbi (eds.), 'The London journal of Alessandro Magno, 1562', *The London Journal*, 9 (1983), pp. 147, 152 (fn. 33).
163 Imray, 'Royal Exchange', p. 20; Burgon, *Sir Thomas Gresham*, II, p. 345; *Machyn's diary*, p. 229; Cogswell, *Blessed revolution*, pp. 20–9. The Italians referred to these times as 'at Rialto', 'at san Marco' or 'at the Rialto hour': Barron *et al.* 'Alessandro Magno', p. 147.
164 The failure to establish Protestantism firmly at grassroots level in Ireland and, to a lesser extent, Wales, along with weak English control of Ireland, the poverty of most Irish and Welsh parishes and the prevalence of Welsh and Gaelic probably precluded prayer books, for instance, having a major impact even if they were distributed there. Extant editions of two prayer books explicitly state they were published for specific dioceses – *An order of praier and thankes-giuing for the preseruation of the quene maiesties life and salfetie* for Winchester and *A fourme to be vsed in common prayer . . . for the deliuery of those christians that are nowe invaded by the Turke* – for Norwich (STC 16508.3) and Salisbury (STC 16508.7) – but there is no evidence that Welsh or Gaelic editions were printed of any special prayer book.

churchwardens of St Mary Woolnoth, St Botolph Aldgate and St Peter Westcheap, London.[165] Financial collections among clergy and laity were made in London and provincial parishes like St Ewen, Bristol, Worfield, Shropshire, and Kilkhampton, Cornwall, for repairs to St Paul's (1580),[166] to redeem Daniel Rogers, imprisoned while on embassy to Rudolph II and the duke of Saxony in 1580,[167] for the relief of Geneva when it was under siege from the duke of Savoy in 1583[168] and for the redeeming of merchants in Spain.[169] Such collections brought foreign news into even small, poor parishes, like Ridge in Hertfordshire.[170] Some events were also marked with peals of bells, both indicating that news penetrated local parishes and acting as means to disseminate it further to other inhabitants. The defeat of the Turks at Lepanto in 1572 was celebrated at St Michael Cornhill[171] and Lambeth, Surrey;[172] the capture of the Babington conspirators in 1586 at St Christopher le Stocks,[173] Lambeth,[174] St Peter,

165 Guildhall MS 1002/1a, fos. 119v, 255r; Guildhall MS 1235/1 (part 1), fo. 77v; Guildhall MS 1235/1 (part 2), fo. 19v; Guildhall MS 645/1, fo. 127v; *A proclamation for waightes* (London, 1587; STC 8167). It is unclear if the 'admonytion' about the plague at St Mary Woolnoth was a proclamation or some other order. It was paid for on 8 Mar. 1563 [Old Style], which would seem to be too late for it to be either the proclamations adjourning Michaelmas term (21 Sept. 1563) or adjourning Hilary term to Hertford Castle (10 Dec. 1563) yet too early for Cancelling Maundy ceremony (23 Mar. 1564).

166 H. R. Wilton Hall (ed.), *Records of the old Archdeaconry of St Albans: a calendar of papers*, AD 1575 to AD 1637 (St Albans and Hertfordshire Architectural and Archaeological Society; St Albans, 1908), pp. 39–41.

167 CUL MS Mm.1.29, fo. 44r; Wilton Hall, *Records of the old Archdeaconry of St Albans*, pp. 45, 47. Rogers was licensed by the privy council to raise the cost of his ransom from a levy on the clergy. Earle's reference is unclear as to whether the collection was aimed at clergy or their congregation: van Dorsten, *Poets, patrons and professors*, pp. 68–75.

168 Betty R. Masters and Elizabeth Ralph (eds.), *The church book of St Ewen's, Bristol, 1454–1584* (Publications of the Bristol and Gloucestershire Archaeological Society Records Section, 6; London and Ashford, 1967), p. 248; Wilton Hall (ed.), *Records of the old Archdeaconry of St Albans*, pp. 22–4.

169 Ivon L. Gregory, 'Kilkhampton churchwardens' accounts, 1560–1605', *Devon and Cornwall Notes and Queries*, 24 (1950–1), p. 39. For other collections, see *Machyn's diary*, pp. 304–5; Wilton Hall (ed.), *Records of the old Archdeaconry of St Albans*, pp. 13, 16–17, 45, 47–9; Williams (ed.), *Churchwardens' accounts of Hampshire*, p. 66; H. B. Walters, 'The churchwardens' accounts of the parish of Worfield. Part VI, 1572–1603', *Transactions of the Shropshire Archaeological and Natural History Society*, third series, 10 (1910), p. 68; Osborne, *Churchwardens' accounts of St Michael's church, Chagford*, p. 235.

170 Wilton Hall (ed.), *Archdeaconry of St Albans*, p. 24.

171 Alford James Waterlow (ed.), *The accounts of the churchwardens of the parish of St Michael, Cornhill in the city of London, from 1456 to 1608* (n.p., 1883), p. 166.

172 Charles Drew (ed.), *Lambeth churchwardens' accounts, 1504–1645, and vestry book, 1610* (Surrey Record Society, 18; Frome and London, 1941), p. 111.

173 Edwin Freshfield (ed.), *Accomptes of the churchwardens of the paryshe of St Cristofer's in London, 1575 to 1662* (London, 1885), p. 17.

174 Drew (ed.), *Lambeth churchwardens' accounts*, p. 162.

Hertfordshire[175] and Prescot, Lancashire[176] and the execution of Mary Stuart in 1587 at St Christopher le Stocks,[177] St Mary Woolchurch,[178] St Botolph Aldgate,[179] St Peters Westcheap[180] and St Thomas, Salisbury.[181] Drawing together local inhabitants, church services were also occasions at which news and gossip could be exchanged: Carnsew noted for 1 July 1577, 'At cherche. Talkyd of divers thynges.'[182]

Other locations were also important. Ports were important nexi of news, especially those involved in continental trade. Limerick, Athlone, Galway, Kinsale and Waterford, as well as Dublin, were important nexi for Ireland, communicating news not only to the immediate population, but via the regime's network of provincial governors, to the Lord Deputies and back to London.[183] London, as well as provincial ports, like Chester and Bristol, operated in similar ways and, though there is no explicit evidence, it is likely that Welsh ports – such as Swansea and Carmarthen – which were involved in continental trade, were also important.[184]

Inns and taverns – the precursors of coffee houses – also acted as important foci.[185] As major commercial centres and staging posts for travellers, larger establishments were able to operate as news hubs and there is evidence to suggest that, like later coffee houses, they provided printed news for customers to read, often in the form of broadsides pasted on the walls.[186] Inns acted as 'post offices', where private and official letters could be deposited for collection – Edmund Manninge collected his letters from John Welchman's inn in Deddington[187] – and as market-places for ballad sellers.[188] As social centres for both the local elite and

175 Anthony Palmer (ed.), *Tudor churchwardens' accounts* (Hertfordshire Record Society Publication, 1; Cambridge, 1985), p. 130.
176 Bailey (ed.), *Churchwardens' accounts of Prescot*, p. 101.
177 Freshfield (ed.), *Accomptes of the churchwardens of . . . St Cristofer's*, p. 17.
178 Guildhall MS 1013/1, fo. 48r.
179 Guildhall MS 1235/1 (part 2), fo. 11v.
180 Guildhall MS 645/1, fo. 123r.
181 H. J. Fowle Swayne (ed.), *Churchwardens' accounts for S. Edmund and S. Thomas, Sarum, 1443–1702* (Wiltshire Record Society; Salisbury, 1896), p. 296.
182 'Carnsew's diary', p. 44.
183 See above, nn. 124–5.
184 Lewis (ed.), *Welsh port books*, pp. 6, 110, 117, 262 and passim.
185 For coffee houses, see Habermas, *Structural transformation*, passim.; Pincus, '"Coffee politicians does create"', pp. 807–34; Cowan, 'What was masculine about the public sphere?', pp. 127–57; Cowan, 'The rise of the coffeehouse reconsidered', *Historical Journal*, 47 (2004), pp. 21–46.
186 Fox, *Oral and literate culture*, p. 352; Watt, *Cheap print*, pp. 193–6.
187 Brinkworth (ed.), *Archdeacon's court*, p. 230.
188 Peter Clark, *The English alehouse: a social history, 1200–1830* (London and New York, 1983), p. 155.

poor, taverns, inns and alehouses were sites where political debate was likely to take place.[189] Moreover, both licensed and unlicensed establishments were geographically widespread and extensive in number: Peter Clark has estimated that there were approximately 24,000 in England alone by the middle of Elizabeth's reign.[190] A crack-down on unlicensed premises around Abergavenny and Usk in 1578, revealed fifteen and nine unlicensed alehouses respectively.[191] Quarter Sessions records for Caernarfonshire are littered with recognises for unlicensed alehouses.[192] County towns, and other major urban centres, were also important: in 1596, Thomas Wendon asked his neighbours if anyone had been to Colchester and heard any news.[193]

PRINTED VERSUS NON-PRINTED FORMS OF COMMUNICATION

Historians have sought to minimise the role of oral and non-printed vehicles for news. Contrasting them to the 'formal' vehicle of print, they have argued that the ability of oral and manuscript communications to convey substantial accounts and their social and geographical exclusivity means they were less significant than printed pamphlets. Levy has argued that the significance of letters has been exaggerated as they conveyed only limited information: Philip Gawdy's correspondence comprised 'little more than one-liners'.[194] Both Levy and Steve Pincus have argued that oral communication was restrictive, because it depended on individuals' access to news networks, which tended to be socially elitist and exclusive to men.[195]

These arguments cannot be sustained fully. The accessibility of printed news was affected by literacy and language. Research suggests that, though skills in reading and writing appeared to increase during the sixteenth century, literacy varied substantially between occupations, genders, regions and between urban and rural dwellers. Those groups with the highest literacy rates, like the gentry and clergy, were those that

189 Ibid., pp. 158–160.
190 Ibid., pp. 41–3.
191 Howell, *Law and disorder*, pp. 59–60, 63, 71. See also *Calendar of Salusbury correspondence, 1553–c.1700, principally from the Lleweni, Rûg and Bagot collections*, ed. W. J. Smith (Board of Celtic Studies, History and Law Series, 14; Cardiff, 1954), p. 23.
192 For instance: Caernarfonshire Record Office, XQS/1569/50, XQS/1575/120, XQS/1575/138, XQS/1578/12, XQS/1578/13, XQS/1578/16.
193 Examination of Thomas Wendon, 3 July 1596, SP12/259/51; Fox, *Oral and literate culture*, p. 350.
194 Levy, 'Decorum of news', p. 20.
195 Ibid., pp. 20–1; Pincus, '"Coffee politicians does create"', pp. 818–19.

Table 5.1. *Rates of illiteracy in England in the early seventeenth century*

Occupation/gender	% illiterate: rural dwellers	% illiterate: urban dwellers
Clergy and profession	0	0
Gentry	2	2
Yeomen	33	30
Bakers	27	26
Weavers	49	34
Tailors	51	43
Labourers	85	78
Miners	96	[Data not available]
Women (all classes)	90	60

Source: David Cressy, 'Literacy in context: meaning and measurement in early modern England', in John Brewer and Roy Porter (eds.), *Consumption and the world of goods* (London and New York, 1993), p. 315.

represented the smallest sections of the population, while those, like labourers, who comprised a large section of the population, had the lowest literacy. Female literacy, especially in rural areas, was very high (see table 5.1).[196]

Low literacy rates were compensated for by contemporary reading practices which facilitated communication between the literate and the illiterate, giving illiterate men and women indirect access to the printed word. Reading was often communal, with younger people reading to parents and other adults, while those who were illiterate could buy texts for others to read to them.[197] Indeed, there is evidence to suggest that even private reading was performed aloud: in 1570, Arthur Chapman of Wolsingham, County Durham, was told by his minister to read more quietly as he was disturbing the church service.[198]

196 David Cressy, 'Literacy in context: meaning and measurement in early modern England', in John Brewer and Roy Porter (eds.), *Consumption and the world of goods* (London and New York, 1993), pp. 313–15; Tim Harris, "The problem of "popular political culture" in seventeenth-century London', *History of European Ideas*, 10 (1989), pp. 50–1; Fox, *Oral and literate culture*, pp. 12–14. For a more extensive survey see Cressy, *Literacy and the social order: reading and writing in Tudor and Stuart England* (Cambridge, 1980) and for the historiography of literacy studies, see W. B. Stephens, 'Literacy in England, Scotland and Wales, 1500–1900', *History of Education Quarterly*, 30 (1990), pp. 545–71, though note that Stephens does not actually discuss Wales.
197 Fox, *Oral and literate culture*, pp. 37–9.
198 Ibid., p. 37.

Equally, however, the vast majority of news pamphlets, broadsides and proclamations were printed in English, though it was not the universal language in Elizabeth's realms.[199] The Act of Union (1536) effectually established English as the official language of Tudor Wales and reinforced the voluntary adoption of English by the Welsh gentry, but the majority of the population (farmers, craftsmen and labourers) continued to speak only Welsh.[200] As is evident from the Herberts, earls of Pembroke, even at an elite level full adoption of English could be slow and it appears that gentlewomen were not encouraged to learn English until the early seventeenth century.[201] In Ireland, Irish remained the predominant language; written English was used by the New English, Anglo-Irish and some Irish Gaels but spoken English was largely limited to Dublin, the English baronies of Forth and Bargy in Wexford, the Fingall district (north of Dublin) and some towns, like Waterford and Cork. Moreover, Forth, Bargy and Fingall developed distinctive dialects, with many borrowings from Irish and different accenting. Growing polarisation between the Gaelic Irish and Anglo-Irish on one hand, and the New English on the other, resulted in people refusing to speak English or Irish, even when they knew it: Fynes Morison alleged that the women of Cork and Waterford were prevented from speaking English to Englishmen by their husbands.[202] Indeed, even in parts of England, English was not necessarily the first language: Cornish was spoken in Cornwall, though this gradually declined with the establishment of the liturgical service in English.[203]

Conversely, oral and manuscript media covered a diverse range of news, was accessible to a wide social range of people and was able to overcome linguistic barriers. Local news – of marriages, deaths, births, accidents, murders, suicides, skimmingtons and pillories – fill the diaries of men like Machyn and Carnsew and circulated to and from the centre and the localities.[204] National and continental news also circulated widely

199 For instance, it was only at the end of the reign that proclamations for Ireland were printed in Gaelic: State Papers Ireland indicated that *The Queenes maiesties proclamation against the Earle of Tirone* (Dublin, 1595; *STC* 14145), now extant only in English, was also printed in Gaelic (recorded by *STC* as *STC* 14146).
200 W. Ogwen Williams, 'The survival of the Welsh language after the Union of England and Wales: the first phase, 1536–1642', *Welsh History Review*, 2 (1964), pp. 67–93.
201 Ibid., pp. 81–4.
202 Brian Ó Cuív, 'The Irish language in the early modern period', and Alan Bliss, 'The English language in early modern Ireland', in T. W. Moody, F. X. Martin and F. J. Byrne (eds.), *A new history of Ireland III: Early modern Ireland, 1534–1691* (Oxford, 1976, 1991 edn), pp. 509–45 and 546–60 respectively.
203 Williams, 'Survival of the Welsh language', p. 75.
204 *Machyn's diary*, pp. 193, 196–7, 199, 208–9, 219, 241, 246, 259; 'Carnsew's diary', p. 55.

in oral form. London abounded with news of Elizabeth's marriage negotiations, the devaluation of the coinage and the Northern Rising. Machyn
noted of the burial of Leicester's first wife, Amy Robsart (but not her
actual death), the death of Jane Seymour (one of Elizabeth's maids of
honour), the earl of Hertford's arrival at the Tower and the birth of both
of his children by Lady Catherine Grey, a fight between Lord Montague
and Lord Delaware and their subsequent imprisonment, and the arrival of
Shane O'Neill at court in January 1562.[205] Robert Taylor, a labourer from
Chelmsford, Essex, had learned of the adoption of the English service in
the Chapel Royal by August 1560, calling it 'but palterye'.[206] In Cornwall,
Carnsew learned of the Peace of Monsieur (1576), the taking of nine
English ships by the Dutch (1576), the pacification of Ghent (8 November
1576) and the sacking of Antwerp by the Spanish (the 'Spanish
fury', November 1576).[207] Ballads on the Spanish Armada circulated
in Pembrokeshire and Cardiganshire.[208] News of the Turks' defeat at
Lepanto, a planned invasion by Thomas Stuckley (1572), King Sebastian
of Portugal's crusade against the Moors, and Fitzmaurice's and Sanders's
planned invasion of Ireland (1579) reached the Irish ports of Kinsale,
Athlone, Galway and Waterford by word of mouth.[209]

Neither was the news conveyed in letters narrow or insubstantial.
Letters could convey continental news and rumours: a man identified
only as 'E.R.' wrote to Richard Glascocke, a merchant in London, from
Ireland in 1579 about naval preparations at Naples and Biscay against
England under the commandment of James Fitzmaurice and Nicholas
Sanders. He also reported that Francis, duke of Anjou, aimed to conquer
the Flemish frontier; that Cardinal Granvelle was to serve as Viceroy in
Spain; and on the wedding of the Spanish Infanta to the Emperor.[210] John
Finglas reported Campion's offer to the government of a disputation to
Richard Brette of Luttrelston, Ireland.[211] The Gawdys in Norfolk learned
about a whole range of events, from the appointment of the sheriff of
Norfolk in 1587 to the conduct of Leicester's campaign in the Netherlands
from the letters of their son.[212]

205 *Machyn's diary*, pp. 242–3, 253–4, 267–8, 270, 274–5, 300.
206 Ibid., p. 197; PRO, ASSI 35/3/2, m. 10.
207 'Carnsew's diary', pp. 29–30, 37. See also pp. 36, 51, 54, 56, 57.
208 Owen, *The taylor's cussion*, fo. 5v.
209 SP63/35/46, fo. 166r–166v; SP63/36/1, fo. 1r; SP63/36/2.I, fo. 4r–4v; SP63/37/13.I, fo. 13r; E. R. to
      Richard Glascocke, 17 July 1579, SP63/67/31, fo. 66r; Patrick White to Walsingham, 29 June
      1580, SP63/73/69, fo. 162r–162v.
210 SP63/67/31, fo. 66r.
211 SP63/80/60.I, fo. 173r.
212 Egerton 2804, passim.

Oral news networks were not as socially – or ethnically – exclusive as
Pincus and Levy have suggested. Though St Paul's, Lombard Street and
the Royal Exchange were populated by an educated, social and mercantile
elite, access was not denied to men of lower social status or of different
nationality. Lawrence Perrye, a servant of an Essex lawyer, who was
reported in 1587 to the privy council for alleging that James VI was
coming to England to avenge the death of his mother, 'may be fond or
ells in Paules church where his maisteres accustometh dailye to walke.'[213]
The Venetian merchant, Alessandro Magno's, description of the news
network at Lombard Street indicates that foreign merchants were an
established part of the networks focused on Lombard Street.[214] Watermen,
like Whittacres, learned news as it travelled down to Paul's Wharf and the
river; news penetrated the gates of the Counter.

Outside London, the importance of the parish church, alehouse, the
port or county town as sites for news meant that access to news could be
socially broad. Special prayer books were used and financial collections
made in small, rural, relatively poor parishes like Morebath, Devon and
Ridge, Hertfordshire. Most of the landlords of unlicensed alehouses in
Abergavenny and Usk in 1578 were yeomen, labourers or spinsters.
Indeed, cases of seditious and slanderous words brought before the privy
council or local assizes in the south-east, demonstrate both that news and
political debate were conducted in streets, fields, homes and workshops
and that they were socially inclusive. For example, Perrye's allegations
against James VI were made in the house of Mrs Gray in Curringham,
Essex.[215] John Whyte, alias Snellynge, had prophesied Elizabeth's death,
standing in a shoemaker's workshop in the presence of shoemakers, their
apprentices and a blacksmith.[216] Carnsew learned of Mendoza's return
to the court from John Goldsmythe, the son of the vicar of St Kew;
of unspecified French news from his servant, Thomas Roche; and news
about Orange from Sir John Danvers's servant.[217] If these men conveyed news to the gentleman Carnsew, what was to stop them from
communicating it to their own friends and relatives?

213 Edward Ryche to Henry Grey of Pirgo, 5 Mar. 1587, SP12/199/14.I, fo. 27r; Thexamination of
John Hammond of Curringham, 5 Mar. 1587, SP12/199/14.II, fo. 28r. Fox argues that Perrye was
repeating news that Baude had heard at St Paul's but this is not stated in either document: Fox,
Oral and literate culture, pp. 346–7.
214 Stowe stated that the Italian merchants met at the west end of Lombard Street in a house between
Cornhill and Lombard Street. Barron *et al.* (eds.), 'Alessandro Magno', pp. 147, 152 (fn. 33).
215 SP12/199/14.II, fo. 28r.
216 Examynacions taken by me Arthur Herrys, 22 Oct. 1586, SP12/194/57.I, fos. 88r–89r.
217 'Carnsew's diary', pp. 36–7, 51–2.

Oral communication could also reach parts of Elizabeth's realms that other forms were unable, or less able, to do. It responded to the linguistic challenges posed by Wales and Ireland by communicating news and information in Welsh and Gaelic, which were poorly served, if at all, by printed pamphlets and broadsides. There is fragmentary evidence that proclamations and instructions, such as for the suppression of felonies in Merionethshire, were verbally proclaimed in Welsh at local quarter sessions.[218] Similar practices may have been adopted in Ireland.

What evidence exists of the exclusivity of oral and manuscript news networks points rather to the deliberate exclusion of others from knowledge and channelling of information through particular networks of correspondents for political reasons. For instance, though Turlough Luineach O'Neill's 'horseboy' reported his message fully to the earl of Desmond as instructed, when examined by the Lord Deputy, Warham St Leger, the boy 'denyed to haue don any suche messadge, counterfeiting hym self to be drunk' and gave false information about an alleged sojourn in England in Sussex's household.[219] Conversely, Sir Edward Fitton, president of Connaught and Thomond, would 'trust no body nether the byshopes who be heer of consell to kno it [a letter by Domenic Browne about Stuckley's proposed invasion of Ireland] nor eny clarcke to wryghte it but my on hand hath scryblest it' before sending the copy to Lord Deputy Fitzwilliam.[220] English news networks in Ireland relied on English provincial governors and Anglo-Irish officials, like Browne and George Wyse (mayor of Waterford). Yet, equally, these networks were not impenetrable: Browne's and Wyse's news, for example, all derived from reports made by local Irish merchants arriving home from the continent. Moreover, the impact of political, religious and ethnic divisions on channels of communication can be exaggerated: there is a plethora of letters in State Papers Ireland, between Gaelic chieftains, like Brian MacPhelim O'Neill of Clandeboy, Anglo-Irish lords, like Ormond and Kildare, and various local and central English governors.

---

218 'Instructions from the Councell of Marches to suppresse felonyes in Merionethshire', n.d., National Library of Wales, Peniarth MS 410 D, part I, transcribed in Peter R. Roberts, 'Elizabethan "overseers" in Merioneth', *Journal of the Merioneth Historical and Record Society*, 4 (1961–64), pp. 7–13, see p. 12 (article 29); Williams, 'Survival of the Welsh language', p. 72.

219 SP63/32/50, fo. 148r. Desmond appears to have conveyed Turlough Luineach's message to St Leger, but either he did not do so fully or St Leger sought further information and hence examined the boy.

220 Fitton to Fitzwilliam, 12 Apr. 1572, [Fitzwilliam's copy], SP63/36/2.II, fo. 4v. Fitzwilliam then copied the letter in his own hand, to send to Elizabeth though it is unclear whether this was for the same reason as Fitton did so or just to retain Fitton's original in the council's archive.

The privileging of print, therefore, seems erroneous: oral and manuscript forms of communication were as, and probably more, important in
the circulation of news in Elizabethan England, Wales and Ireland. Hard
and fast distinctions between different media also detract from the fact
that printed and non-printed media interacted, practically and stylistic-
ally. Ballads, songs, prayers and sermons were all primarily oral performances, but were also disseminated in printed form. Information derived
from printed pamphlets could be disseminated further, or be corrected,
by oral communication: news of Sir Thomas Smith's venture in Ulster
may have partly arrived in Ireland via print, but it spread further orally.[221]
Carnsew read about the Peace of Monsieur but 'was then Infformyd that
it was not then stablyste becawse the 8 townys were nott delyveryd.'[222]
News initially received orally could be transmitted by letter or print:
verbal reports by Irish merchants were written up and sent as letters to
local governors and the Lord Deputy.[223] Letters could be accompanied by
printed pamphlets or broadsides: in November 1587, Philip Gawdy sent
his brother and parents respectively two proclamations 'in the very prime'
and two books, including one that had been distributed at a tilt at
court.[224] Margaret Hill sent Richard Carnsew a copy of a newsbook on
Essex's execution in 1601.[225] News pamphlets, like *A true report of the
taking of Marseilles* (1585), *A true and perfect discourse of three great accidents
that chaunced in Italie* (1588) and *A true discourse of the late battaile fought
betweene our Englishmen, and the Prince of Parma* (1585), were often
written in letter-form.[226] Partly a literary device to make a new genre of
writing more familiar by utilising traditional forms of communication, it
also established an air of reality and a claim to veracity by posing as an
alleged eyewitness report. In the words of the author of *A true discourse*, it
enabled readers to be 'fully certified of the truth'.[227]

---

221 SP63/35/2, fo. 19r; SP63/35/45, fo. 164r.
222 'Carnsew's diary', p. 29.
223 See also SP63/36/1, fo. 1r.
224 Egerton 2804, fo. 33r; Egerton 2804, fo. 37r.
225 Levy, 'Decorum of news', p. 26.
226 *True report of the taking of Marseilles* (1585); *True and perfect discourse of three great accidents*
     (1588); W.M., *A true discourse of the late battaile fought betweene our Englishmen, and the Prince of
     Parma* (London, 1585; *STC* 17156). See also *The true copie of a letter from the Queenes Maiestie . . .
     vpon the apprehension of diuers persons, detected of a most wicked conspiracie* (London, 1586; *STC*
     7577); William Cecil, *The copie of letter sent out of England to Don Bernardin Mendoza* (London,
     1588; *STC* 15412); *A letter written by a French gentleman to a friend of his at Rome* (London, 1587;
     STC 19078.6); Q. Z., *Discouerie of the treasons practised . . . by Francis Throckmorton* (1584).
227 *True discourse of the late battaile* (1585), sig. Aiv^r.

There is also little sense in which print was 'formal' (with its implication of superiority) and oral or manuscript communication 'informal'. Print was only 'formal' in the sense that it was able to convey to a wider audience a fixed account, but it could not dictate dissemination nor govern the responses of its readership. Indeed, the privileging of print as the 'formal', superior form of news communication seems to owe more to the pervasiveness of newspapers (as well as television and the internet) as purveyors of news in the modern age.

NEWS MEDIA, SOCIAL STATUS AND GENDER

Broad distinctions between different types of media are less significant than between the relative importance of different media to different social and ethnic groups. The circulation of court news could be dependent on one's access to the court: Philip Gawdy and John Wynn of Gwydir were able to convey court news because they had access to court, or knew others who did.[228] Carnsew learned of 'doctor Julio [Guilio Borgarucci, Elizabeth's physician] and howe he fleed into Fraunce' from Lord Mountjoy, a friend of both Carnsew and Borgarucci.[229] Carnsew's diary demonstrates that the gentry had access to a well-used postal network, within Cornwall as well as between the county and Oxford and London, prior to the establishment of royal postal routes in 1579.[230] In contrast, letters do not appear to have been important vehicles for news below gentry level: the earliest examples date from the early seventeenth century.[231] This may be merely because, lacking facilities and interest, the correspondence of yeomen, artisans and others has not survived as it has for the nobility and gentry. It may also be because letters were beyond the literate and financial reach of men and women further down the social scale. Cressy

228 Wynn's contact was Sir Richard Bulkeley, a member of the royal household, who also wrote to John and his father, Maurice Wynn, directly: *Calendar of Wynn (of Gwydir) Papers, 1515–1690, in the National Library of Wales and elsewhere* (Aberystwyth, Cardiff and London, 1926), pp. 14–15, 126.
229 'Carnsew's diary', p. 51.
230 The postal service used by Carnsew does not appear to have been significantly hindered by the fact that Bokelly was north and east of the route established by the crown in 1579, nor by geographical obstacles, like the Tamar estuary, which slowed communication between Devon and Cornwall. 'Carnsew's diary', passim.; Mark Brayshay, 'Royal post-horse routes in England and Wales: the evolution of the network in the later-sixteenth and early-seventeenth century', *Journal of Historical Geography*, 17 (1991), p. 385; Mark Brayshay, Philip Harrison and Brian Chalkley, 'Knowledge, nationhood and governance: the speed of the royal post in early modern England', *Journal of Historical Geography*, 24 (1998), p. 279. See also David B. Cornelius, *Devon and Cornwall: a postal history, 1500–1791* (Postal History Society, 31; Reigate, 1973), pp. 1–2.
231 Fox, *Oral and literate culture*, pp. 373–4.

has noted, for instance, that those with limited literacy skills tended only to be able to read print rather than handwriting.[232] The cost of sending letters is difficult to gauge as there is little extant evidence on private carriers or the use of the 'through post' (a messenger hiring horses) for 'bye letters' (private correspondence). Crofts argues that 'through post' was charged at 1.5 pence per mile in 1584, making the cost of sending letters from London to Bristol, Chester and Berwick 29s 3d, 36s 8d and 72s 4d respectively; it was presumably cheaper to get a postboy already travelling the route to carry additional letters.[233]

Social status and financial wealth were not the only factors that governed Elizabethans' access to news and the media they used. Language and geography were also crucial. The dominance of the Welsh and Gaelic languages in Wales and Ireland respectively meant that the impact of print, especially below gentry level, was minimal: the Elizabethan printing trade was dominated by London and was nearly exclusively English-speaking. If this meant that oral communication was of greater importance in Wales and Ireland, then the precise impact of oral news could still be varied. It is difficult to gauge, for example, the exact importance of proclamations and instructions as forms of news because, though there is evidence that they were proclaimed in the vernacular, it is unclear how extensive this practice was. Similarly, geography and landscape affected the routes on which and the speed with which news could travel. Physical distance from London and the continent could have little impact: letters facilitated communication between Elizabeth's realms and between them and the continent; merchants were key purveyors of news; and many ports in England, Wales and Ireland had good British and continental trading links. But equally, it cannot be denied that access to news and the quantity of news available was substantially higher in London than in, say, remote northern parishes. Royal post-routes were established between Dover, London and Berwick as early as 1512, with a branch from Newcastle to Carlisle in 1566, but routes to the south-west were not established until 1579 and those to Ireland, via Liverpool, Chester or Holyhead, were temporary and *ad hoc*. An extensive network – of seventy-nine routes covering 1,200 miles – was not established until the 1590s. The average delivery time of official letters from London to Dover, Salisbury and

---

232 Cressy, 'Literacy in context', p. 312.
233 The high cost of 'through post' was partly because the messenger had to pay for a guide. J. Crofts, *Packhorse, wagon and post: land carriage and communications under the Tudors and Stuarts* (London and Toronto, 1967), pp. 78–9, 95–6, 94–5. See also chs. 8–17.

Chester were approximately ten, fifteen and thirty hours respectively with return journeys of fourteen and a half, twenty and thirty-seven and a half hours. It is more difficult to gauge how far private letters enjoyed the same service.[234] Physical terrain, like mountains and rivers, could restrict communication or isolate whole areas.[235] News was likely to circulate more quickly and easily to and between urban areas than rural ones, where there was a higher density of population, better communication links with other towns etc.

It is much more difficult to assess how important a factor gender was in governing people's access to news because our evidence is limited and patchy. Certainly, women were not excluded either from the circulation of news or participation in debate; indeed, the pervasiveness of news in parish churches, streets, fields and homes meant that they could not have escaped it. Lady Anne Bacon's letters to her son, Anthony, mixed advice on religion, health, politics and social life with local gossip.[236] Anne Gawdy was often a recipient of her son's letters, containing news, which she was expected to read and pass on to her husband. Carnsew's diary shows that social visiting, which facilitated the circulation of news orally and in print, was not confined to men: Mrs Carnsew regularly visited Penvose, Ogbear Hall, Boscastle and Erth Baton, while female friends and relatives, like Jane Penkevall, Ann Tremayne, Mrs Arundell of Treryce and Mrs Cosworth, visited Bokelly.[237] Lower down the social scale, cases of seditious and slanderous words point to women's involvement in conveying news and participation in political discussions in their own homes and outside. Mrs Keale of Rochford Green, Essex, and Anne Dowe, a widow, alleged in 1560 that Elizabeth was pregnant by Dudley. Joan Lister, an Essex spinster, was indicted for arguing that Elizabeth could not be governor of the realm (it is unclear if she meant monarch or Supreme Governor) 'bycause she is but a woman'.[238] Sybill Horte of Winterborne, Gloucestershire, discussed the dearth of corn and 'the Rebelles as were at London', with her servant, John Toye, and a labourer,

234 Brayshay, 'Royal post-horse routes', pp. 375–85, 386–7; Brayshay *et al.*, 'Knowledge, nationhood and governance', pp. 270–7.
235 Brayshay *et al.*, 'Knowledge, nationhood and governance', p. 279.
236 Lynne Magnusson, 'Widowhood and the politics of reception: Anne Bacon's epistolary advice', paper at 'Rethinking women and politics in early modern England' conference, University of Reading, 16 July 2001.
237 'Carnsew's diary', pp. 31, 32, 38, 40, 42, 43, 44, 47.
238 ASSI 35/28/5, m. 31. See also ASSI 35/1/6, mm. 12 and 14 (where no reason is stated). Other cases of women being indicted for seditious and slanderous words include ASSI 35/27/8, m. 31, ASSI 35/19/4, m. 31.

Simon Yomans.[239] Elizabeth Langford took part in a conversation during haymaking in 1584 about a captain who 'woulde destroye manie Scottes if he weare in Scotland' and heard John Carre's allegations that 'the king of Scottes shalbe your gouernour.'[240]

If the circulation of news in Elizabethan England, Wales and Ireland was far wider and more pervasive than previous historians have acknowledged, then the social, financial, linguistic and geographical factors which appear to have governed it raise questions for our understanding of the public sphere. The circulation of news was not uniform but governed by one's social status, financial wealth, geographical location and linguistic ability. In effect, this created a whole series of smaller news networks, comprising individuals' networks of correspondents (personal or official), neighbours, friends, as well as parish ministers, merchants, booksellers, peddlers or travellers met on the street. To what extent did these multiple news networks facilitate the establishment of an Elizabethan public sphere and shape its nature?

---

239 The informacion of Sibill Horte, 24 Aug. 1586, PRO, SP12/192/50, fo. 80r; The examynacion of Symon Yomans, 24 Aug. 1586, PRO, SP12/192/51, fo. 81r.
240 SP12/172/7, fo. 10r. See also ASSI 35/26/7, m. 25.

CHAPTER 6

The Elizabethan public sphere

Elizabethan Maldon, a sizeable port and a parliamentary borough, was alive with politico-religious debate and action. In 1572, Thomas Playfere, a labourer, was indicted for declaring, 'Lett the parliament begynne' because the earl of Shrewsbury would 'stand vp for heyre apparent, beate hym downe who will'. He also alleged that Elizabeth had had two children by Leicester.[1] In August 1577, both in Maldon and surrounding towns and villages, Robert Blosse (or Mantell) 'did give out & saye that kinge *Edward* was alyve' and claimed he was Edward himself.[2] Found guilty at the Essex assizes a year later, he was imprisoned in Colchester gaol but escaped and continued to spread his rumours. He was tried again in 1581, confessed, and was sentenced to be hanged, drawn and quartered.[3] It was not his only brush with the law: earlier, in 1572, he had been questioned by William Fleetwood in London for alleging that Elizabeth had had four children by Leicester.[4] In April 1588, a dispute broke out at All Saints with St Peter between two vicars over whether local preachers prayed fervently for the queen and whether Elizabeth could rightly style herself Queen of France.[5]

Interest in the succession, Elizabeth's sexuality and her royal title was not confined to Maldon; they were subjects of public debate across Elizabeth's realms. In conjunction with evidence of the socially and geographically wide circulation of news it suggests, on the one hand, that

---

1 ASSI 35/22/10, mm. 11, 14.
2 ASSI 35/20/5, m. 36; *APC,* X, p. 223. Blosse appears to have been the son of a London goldsmith (Levin, *'Heart and stomach of a king',* p. 101), but seems to have resided in or around Maldon in the late 1570s and early 1580s. Two further indictments in 1581 (ASSI 35/23/1, mm. 48, 49) state that he was recently of Maldon though, in fact, he had been imprisoned in Colchester gaol at some point between 1578 and 1581.
3 ASSI 35/23/1, m. 49; ASSI 35/23/1, m. 48.
4 The examination of Robert Blosse, 20 Oct. 1572, Lansdowne 16/8, fo. 17r.
5 The deposicion of diuerse persones against Marke Wiersdale, 29 Apr. 1588, SP12/178/27, fos. 52r–53r.

a public sphere may have existed in the late sixteenth century. On the other, it raises questions about whether such a public sphere can be defined in Habermasian terms: as an identifiable group of individuals, meeting in specific physical locations for debate, with access to the same information and having common political interests and responses. Different issues were discussed by different people whilst similar topics could be discussed by socially and physically disparate groups, unaware of each other's existence. It raises the possibility that the Elizabethan public sphere has to be defined in terms of multiple spheres and some account has to be made of the existence of shared discourses, even if actual debate was conducted by isolated groups.

These questions have also been asked by historians who have challenged Habermas's definition of the public sphere. The wider social, gender and political composition of the public sphere, established by Steve Pincus and Brian Cowan, have made it harder to sustain the concept of a single public sphere.[6] So too has the identification of religion and science both as important factors in stimulating participation in the public sphere and as subjects of debate in their own right.[7] Nancy Fraser, Keith Michael Baker, Geoff Eley and Nicholas Garnham have all posited the need to think in terms of multiple, often contending or overlapping, public spheres.[8] However, Craig Calhoun, in his introduction to a seminal collection of essays on the public sphere, has argued that the model of multiple spheres risks neglecting the 'communicative relationships' between individual spheres. He suggests we need to think instead in terms of a 'field of discursive connections' that linked together individual spheres. This 'field' was a network that communicated a fairly even flow of information, but which had 'clusters of relatively greater density of communication' within the overall framework. These clusters were shaped by geographical and population factors (cities and neighbourhoods) and/or organised by gender, profession, ideology or by issue.[9]

---

6 Pincus, '"Coffee politicians does create"', pp. 807–34; Cowan, 'What was masculine about the public sphere?', pp. 127–57.
7 Zaret, 'Religion, science, and printing', pp. 216–24.
8 Calhoun, 'Introduction', p. 37; Nancy Fraser, 'Rethinking the public sphere: a contribution to the critique of actually existing democracy', Keith Michael Baker, 'Defining the public sphere in eighteenth-century France: variations on a theme by Habermas', Geoff Eley, 'Nations, publics, and political cultures: placing Habermas in the nineteenth century', Nicholas Garnham, 'The media and the public sphere', all in Calhoun (ed.), *Habermas and the public sphere*, pp. 109–42, 181–211, 289–339, 359–76 respectively.
9 Calhoun, 'Introduction', pp. 37–8.

The issue to which Calhoun points, but does not articulate explicitly, is: what is the relationship between the situated (physically located) model of the public sphere and the unsituated model (a discourse or 'field of discursive connections')? Indeed, by emphasising 'information' and 'communication', it is unclear whether Calhoun sees the 'clusters' as situated, public spheres or as discourses. For Habermas, the physical location of the public sphere – in coffee houses – was one of its central characteristics. However, the wide variety of physical spaces in which news was learned, and hence discussed, in the Elizabethan realms – St Paul's churchyard, Lombard Street, Cheapside; provincial towns, markets and ports; parish churches, homes, workshops, prisons, streets and fields – might suggest that physical location is of minor importance in the early period. This is reinforced by Alexandra Halasz's argument that an unsituated public sphere existed in early modern England, created by the 'marketplace of print' which stimulated a discourse between authors, printers, sellers and customers.[10] By highlighting the existence of shared discourse among people not necessarily in physical proximity to each other, her definition is closer to Calhoun's 'field of discursive connections'. It opens up the possibility that, in order to reconcile evidence both of situated debate and shared discourses across physically disparate groups, the Elizabethan public sphere should be defined in Calhoun's terms as a network of clusters, characterised by varying 'densities' of debate, shaped by social, economic, geographical, ideological, professional and other factors.

However, there are serious problems with Halasz's definition of the public sphere. First, she has assumed that all purchasers of pamphlets read them, making them participants in the discourse. But this cannot be proved, not least because Halasz is not interested in exploring the dissemination of texts.[11] Second, the nature of readers' participation is unclear. Even when purchasers did read the pamphlets, the opportunities for participating *actively* in the discourse were limited in the terms defined by Halasz. By characterising the public sphere as an unsituated discourse in print, Halasz implies that printed pamphlets were the only medium for participating actively in debate. This restricts the scope of the public sphere to an educated, literate elite willing and able to publish their ideas and ignores evidence of verbal debate among a wide variety of people. This is an important limitation of Halasz's model because, whatever the

10 Halasz, *Marketplace of print*, pp. 15–16, 23–7, 28–34, 162–4, 166–78.
11 Though Halasz does review, briefly, the physical dissemination of texts, she does not see it as central to her argument. Ibid., pp. 8–12.

criticisms levelled at the *composition* of the Habermasian public sphere, there is an unspoken consensus that the *discussion* of political issues was an inherent part of the public sphere.

The diversity of public debate suggests that the Elizabethan public sphere actually comprised multiple spheres, but how were they related? This chapter seeks to define the exact nature of these spheres by exploring situated public spheres, unsituated discourses and their relationship. In particular, it asks whether Calhoun's model of a 'field of discursive connections' highlights the multiplicity of public spheres and the importance of shared discourses at the expense of the physically located communities in which debate was experienced. To reconstruct the Elizabethan public sphere comprehensively is beyond the scope of a single chapter, especially when extant sources for lower social levels are limited.[12] So, case studies have been used to sketch its nature, incorporating its social, geographical and ideological diversity. The chapter also addresses two further important challenges to Habermas: that the subjects of debate were not fixed and what factors stimulated participation. It does not deal either with Habermas's emphasis on the rational-critical nature of debate or that public debate was always in opposition to the regime. If, as argued in chapter 5, we must adopt contemporaries' views of newsworthiness – which included stories of murders, monstrous births and Elizabeth's alleged pregnancies – then we must also acknowledge that these were legitimate subjects of debate. Though the nature of extant sources tends to privilege opinions hostile to the regime, there is no reason why public debate should be defined wholly in these terms. Less critical responses will be examined in chapter 7.

SITUATED PUBLIC SPHERES

In December 1561 or early January 1562, Norton's and Sackville's play, *Gorboduc*, was performed at the Inner Temple, one of the Inns of Court, before an audience of the privy council, members of the Inner Temple and Gray's Inn and, possibly, female courtiers. On 18 January, it was performed again, before the queen, at court at Whitehall.[13] As discussed in chapter 4, in examining the related issues of Elizabeth's marriage and the succession, *Gorboduc* addressed two of the central themes of the

---

12 For a detailed discussion of the source problems, see above, ch. 1.
13 For further discussion of *Gorboduc* and a select bibliography of the key secondary works on it, see above, ch. 4.

Elizabethan political agenda during the first thirty years of the reign. It was not an isolated instance at the Inns of Court. Five years later, in 1566, Lincoln's Inn hosted a 'moot' on the same topics, including an examination of Mary Stuart's claim to the throne. Burghley intervened to stop the debate and one of the Inn's governors, William Thornton, was imprisoned.[14] In 1579, an alumnus of Lincoln's Inn, John Stubbe, wrote a controversial pamphlet against Elizabeth's proposed marriage to Francis, duke of Anjou – *The discoverie of a gaping gulf* – for which he, along with William Page, an MP who had attempted to distribute fifty copies to the West Country, had his right hand publicly severed with a cleaver. The indictment at Queen's Bench alleged the pamphlet had been written in Lincoln's Inn, where Stubbe had been appointed steward the previous year.[15] Both James Dalton, a bencher of the Inn, and Robert Monson, a former member of the Inn and judge of Common Pleas, questioned the legality of Stubbe's sentence.[16]

The Inns of Court represent one of the clearest examples of a situated public sphere in the late sixteenth century. Broad political issues, as well as specific policies, were debated orally or examined in print. As Jessica Winston has shown, *Gorboduc* addressed the themes of counsel and governance far more than it did marriage and the succession.[17] Rebellion, foreign wars, civil strife, as well as the nature and responsibilities of kings, counsellors, magistrates and citizens were all explored in translations of classical texts or vernacular treatises – including Goddred Gilby's translation of Cicero's *Ad Quintum* (1561) and George Gascoigne's *The glasse of government* (1575) – the production of which students from the Inns dominated.[18] Adopting the vernacular and utilising cheaper, quarto formats, these texts also explicitly sought to disseminate political ideas to a wider, non-Latinate audience, beyond the immediate governing elite.[19] The Inns were considered to be springboards to court service and, indeed, both translations and vernacular treatises were partly conceived as ways for their authors to assert their claims to exercise political authority.[20] Moreover, professional lawyers, trained at the Inns, were directly involved

14 Murdin (ed.), *Collection of state papers*, p. 762.
15 Mears, 'Counsel, public debate, and queenship', pp. 629–50; Coram Rege Roll, Michaelmas term 21–22 Elizabeth, KB27/1271 (Crown side), m. 3v.
16 William Camden, *Annales, or the historie of the most renowned and victorious princesse Elizabeth* (3rd edn, London, 1635), p. 239; Hasler, III, pp. 66–7. Dalton was committed to the Tower.
17 Winston, 'Literature and politics', pp. 142–81.
18 Ibid., pp. 31–4, 106–7, 158–9, 70–85, 108–31, 69–83.
19 Ibid., pp. 70–3, 87–98, 118–21, 129–31.
20 Ibid., pp. 33–4.

in national, city and local politics and governance, comprising the third largest occupational group among borough members in parliament and dominating City government.[21]

The Inns of Court were also physically situated and had strong institutional identities. They were in relatively close proximity to each other, dotted between the river and Holborn, around Temple Bar, Fleet Street and Holborn itself. Individually, they had jurisdiction over the nearby Inns of Chancery: Middle Temple, for example, had jurisdiction over New Inn. Physical proximity and institutional connections were reinforced by shared living quarters, education and, at some Inns, strong regional bias in membership. Many students were accommodated within the Inns, while alumni retained rights of membership, and hence residence. Though there was no fixed curriculum or standardised teaching procedures, from the 1560s a growing proportion of students had received a classical-humanist education before proceeding to the Inns, creating a shared educational experience and fostering a common political outlook.[22] There were strong regional connections at individual Inns: Lincoln's Inn, for example, drew a high proportion of its students from London, Essex, East Anglia and the West Country. These were reinforced by admission policies and financial concessions awarded to sons of alumni, particularly from gentry families.[23] Membership of the Inns created and sustained friendships between members.[24]

Though the Inns were a highly developed form of the situated public sphere, they were not unique. Peter Lake and Michael Questier have drawn attention to the central role played by prisons and execution scaffolds as sites of public debate, especially for English Catholics and foreign missionaries. Prisons, whether in London or places like Wisbech or Beaumaris castles, were 'the ideological nerve centre, the lungs of the catholic community'.[25] Not only were they the centre of Catholics' and missionaries' news networks and sites for individual conversions and debate – for instance, John Foxe visited the seminary priest, William Tedder, in 1583 – but they were also locations of both private and public debates, some of which were publicised in printed pamphlets, most

21 Hasler, I, pp. 56, 45; Ian Archer, 'Popular politics in the sixteenth and early seventeenth centuries', in P. Griffiths and M. Jenner (eds.), *Londinopolis* (Manchester, 2000), pp. 28–9.
22 Wilfred R. Prest, *The Inns of Court under Elizabeth I and the early Stuarts, 1590–1640* (London, 1972), chs. 6 and 7, especially pp. 143–4, 137–41; Winston, 'Literature and politics', pp. 3–4, 8–10.
23 Prest, *Inns of Court*, pp. 32–7.
24 Winston, 'Literature and politics', pp. 55–61.
25 Lake with Questier, *Anti-christ's lewd hat*, pp. 199–205.

notably between Edmund Campion, Ralph Sherwin and Alexander Nowell, William Fulke, William Charke and others in August and September 1581.[26] Similarly, execution scaffolds were public stages on which condemned Catholics could define themselves as martyrs, testify to the truth of their faith and contest that of Protestantism. They exploited the etiquette of the scaffold to demonstrate that they faced death willingly and were assured of salvation; they competed with Protestant clergy to convert their fellow condemned in their final moments.[27] Scaffolds, in particular, were interactive sites where the assembled audience were able to communicate with, or participate in, the debate and action. On the one hand, the crowd drowned out the prayers of John Hewett, William Hartley and Robert Sutton in 1588; on the other, they prevented Stephen Rousman from being butchered with a rusty knife in Gloucester in 1586.[28]

Equally, political debate among provincial, minor gentry could also be physically situated, circumscribed by geography as well as social and economic factors. William Carnsew discussed political issues in his own house at Bokelly in Cornwall, in the homes of his friends and neighbours (including George Grenville of Penhale, St Trudy, and Lord Mountjoy) and at local markets and ports.[29] Thomas Owen, the eldest son of Owen ap Gruffydd ap Morris and a recusant, was politically active in and around his estate of Plas Du, in Llanarmon, Caernarfonshire. He allowed clandestine masses to be sung in his house; he entertained fellow recusants and seminary priests and allegedly accompanied the latter in missions to nearby Chirkland, Bromfield and Creuddyn.[30] Activity outside the immediate environs of Plas Du was conditioned by his familial and social connections. It was alleged that he escaped investigation for recusancy by the Council of the Marches of Wales in 1578 because some of his friends, imprisoned in Ludlow on separate charges, learned of the commission before it was issued and 'some of their wyves reported the same'.[31] He was able to worship at the homes of relatives and friends in

26 Ibid., pp. 209–11; Thomas M. McCoog, SJ, '"Playing the champion": the role of disputation in the Jesuit mission', in McCoog (ed.), *The reckoned expense: Edmund Campion and the early English Jesuits* (Woodbridge, 1996), pp. 135–6.
27 Lake with Questier, *Anti-christ's lewd hat*, pp. 215–25 and ch. 7.
28 Ibid., pp. 271–2 and ch. 7.
29 'Carnsew's diary', pp. 56, 51, 32, 37, 35.
30 E. Gwynne Jones, 'The Lleyn recusancy case, 1578–1581', *Transactions of the Honourable Society of Cymmrodorion* (1936), pp. 102–4 (note that the *Transactions* do not have volume numbers); STAC5/O7/22, Thomas Owen vs. Robert Vaughan, 22 Elizabeth I.
31 Gwynne Jones, 'Lleyn recusancy case', pp. 99–100.

England, including the Houghtons of Lea Hall, Preston, and Viscount Montague of Cowdray, Sussex. A similar picture is painted by fellow Caernarfonshire recusant, Robert Pugh of Penrhyn.[32]

Identifying situated public spheres at non-elite level is significantly more difficult. Extant sources of political debate are dominated by cases of seditious or slanderous words. These tend to reveal isolated cases and there is usually insufficient evidence available to explore the wider context in which these cases occurred and, hence, to reconstruct the nature of the public sphere. However, the patterns of debate that can be discerned across these cases suggest that labourers, artisans, yeomen and their families discussed news and issues primarily in the physically circumscribed area of their local community: in their homes, workshops, streets, fields and the local parish church.[33] Anne Dowe, an itinerant widow in Essex, discussed Elizabeth's relationship with Leicester in the home of a Mrs Keale of Rochford Green; Simon Yomans discussed the Northern Rising in his mistress's house in Winterborne, Gloucestershire.[34] Giles Fezard, of Downhyde St Mary, Wiltshire, was alleged to have said 'the duke of Guies was a very knave and a traytor' in the street of an unidentified parish in the early years of Elizabeth's reign.[35] Instances where debate clearly travelled beyond a parish are relatively rare and, as in the case of Anne Dowe – whose news about Elizabeth's alleged pregnancy in 1560 was discussed in Rochford and Danbury (ten miles north-west of Rochford) – did so through the agency of those who travelled between parishes and towns.[36]

However, physically situated public spheres did not have to be physically compact communities, like the Inns of Court or the local parish. The Palesmen of Ireland formed a coherent, identifiable political group, united by a common concern over the cess and billeting, who petitioned Elizabeth and the Lord Deputies in the 1560s and 1570s and organised campaigns of civil disobedience.[37] But they were both geographically

---

32 See E. Gwynne Jones, 'Robert Pugh of Penrhyn Creuddyn', *Transactions of the Caernarvonshire Historical Society*, 4 (1942–3), pp. 10–19; Jones, 'The duality of Robert ap Hugh of Penrhyn Creudynn', *Transactions of the Caernarvonshire Historical Society*, 17 (1956), pp. 54–63.

33 See also, SP12/194/57.I, fos. 88r–89r; SP12/172/7, fo. 10r; ASSI 35/26/7, m. 25.

34 SP12/13/21.I, fos. 56r–57r; SP12/192/50, fo. 80r; SP12/192/51, fo. 81r.

35 Attorney General vs. jury of Wiltshire, 5 Elizabeth I, STAC5/A8/5; Attorney General vs. Fessard and Sherwood, n.d., STAC5/A52/17.

36 SP12/13/21.I, fos. 56r–58r.

37 A boke comprehending dyuers articles specifying the miserable state of the Englishe pale of Ireland, [before 21 Mar.] 1562, SP63/5/51, fos. 133r–136v; My Lord of Sussex's interrogations, [21 Mar.] 1562, SP63/5/52, fos. 138r–140r; The gentilmen of Irelandes Aunswere, [21 Mar.] 1562, SP63/5/54, fos. 145r–149r; The reply of the gentlemen of Ireland and the students of the Inns of

dispersed as well as socially, ethnically and politically diverse. Meath was the county hit hardest by the cess, but petitioners were drawn from across the Pale. They included long-established Pale families (like the Barnewells and Fitzsimmons), officeholders (including Sir Thomas Cusacke, Sir John and Oliver Plunkett, and James Dowdall), the Anglo-Irish nobility (particularly Viscount Baltinglas, Viscount Gormanston and Baron Delvin) and New English settlers and officials (including John Parker, Walter Peppard and Francis Agard) who quickly identified with Pale interests.[38] Irish students at the Inns of Court (often from prominent Pale families) were also involved.[39] Indeed, petitioners consciously sought the support of English settlers to demonstrate that their grievances were not ethnically or confessionally motivated, nor a minority opinion.[40]

If political grievances allowed the Palesmen to transcend geographical, social, ethnic and factional boundaries, then their organisation further hardened a physically dispersed group into a tight-knit political community. Their petitions were not *ad hoc* and random: as Ciaran Brady has argued, delegates travelled throughout the Pale to collect signatures for the petitions, often specifically choosing individuals to demonstrate the wide geographical and ethnic opposition to the cess and billeting.[41] Meetings also appear to have been held, usually by Baron Delvin or Viscount Gormanston, to appoint delegates for collecting signatures and presenting petitions to the regime. Collective action was also organised, including instances of civil disobedience in which many refused to collect or deliver the cess. Pamphlets and doggerels may also have circulated.[42]

These examples suggest that physical situation was an essential characteristic of individual public spheres that made up a larger, Elizabethan

Court, [21 Mar.] 1562, SP63/5/58, fos. 168r–169v; Oliver Plunkett *et al.* to Elizabeth, 27 May 1562, SP63/6/12, fo. 22r–23r; same to Leicester, 27 May 1562, SP63/6/13, fos. 24r–24v; A slanderous book, June 1562, SP63/6/37, fos. 75r–90r, esp. 77v, 82v; Sussex to Elizabeth, 6 Sept. 1562, SP63/7/4, fos. 7r–8v; Articles of interrogatorye ministred by therle of Sussex, 2 Sept. 1562, SP63/7/4.I, fos. 9r–10r; Baltinglas to Elizabeth, 10 Jan. 1576, SP63/57/1, fo. 1r–1v; Petition of the inhabitants to Sir Henry Sidney, [1576–7], SP63/57/1.I; Baltinglas and others to the privy council of England, 11 Jan. 1576, SP63/57/4, fo. 7r–7v; Elizabeth to Lord Deputy Sidney and the privy council of Ireland, 14 May 1577, SP63/58/20, fos. 67r–68v; privy council of England to Sidney, 14 May 1577, SP63/58/21, fos. 70r–71; Submission by the Lord Deputy, [20 June 1577], SP63/57/51, fo. 146r; Brady, *Chief governors*, pp. 102–3, 216–27.
38 The thirteenth earl of Desmond was involved, with Archbishop Dowdall of Armagh, in criticising Sussex's exploitation of the cess in 1557–8. The earl of Kildare may have formented or supported grievances against Sussex secretly. Brady, *Chief governors*, pp. 89–93, 102–3, 212–14, 235–7.
39 SP63/5/51, fo. 136r.
40 Brady, *Chief governors*, pp. 237–8.
41 Ibid., pp. 237–40.
42 Ibid.

whole: debate was conducted primarily through face-to-face conversation. Physical location was usually compact, but individual public spheres could cover a wide geographic range if, like the Palesmen, they were organised. Immediately, this undermines Halasz's emphasis on the role of print in the public sphere. Though it was a forum for the dissemination and discussion of ideas, its impact as a medium for public discourse was limited, partly because the circulation of pamphlets could be limited but mainly because they offered few opportunities for readers to participate actively in debate. More generally, these examples reinforce the picture painted by the circulation of news in chapter 5: that the Elizabethan public sphere as a whole was characterised by great diversity in its participants and the subjects of debate. It strengthens the notion that the Elizabethan public sphere has to be defined as comprising multiple spheres. Conversely, it intensifies the need to explore how, if at all, these disparate individual spheres were connected to each other.

However, if multiple, situated, public spheres existed in the Elizabethan realms, then the inner coherence of these individual spheres can be exaggerated. The Inns of Court were actually socially, confessionally and politically divided. Social tensions between professional lawyers and gentlemen using the Inns as a finishing school escalated in the late sixteenth century.[43] The Inns were hives of religious dissent, as a string of arrests for possession of seditious texts between 1568 and 1570 testified. Middle Temple and Inner Temple were particularly slow to heed the privy council's demands for greater conformity.[44] Though the Inns dominated the production of vernacular political treatises and translations of classical texts, their students espoused no uniform political doctrine, as demonstrated by John Stubbe's *A gaping gulf* (1579), and *A briefe discovrse of royall monarchie* (1581) by Charles Merbury of Gray's Inn. The former propounded the theory of the 'mixed polity'; the latter was closer to 'imperial monarchy'.[45]

---

43 Prest, *Inns of Court*, pp. 23–4, 40–6.
44 The Inns were also targets for continental missionaries because they were outside City and suburban jurisdiction, were close to centres of recusancy (Lincoln's Inn Fields, Drury Lane, Holborn, Covent Garden and St Giles) and were convenient meeting places where strangers could blend easily into the constant flow of students, clients, lawyers and servants. R. M. Fisher, 'Privy council coercion and religious conformity at the Inns of Court, 1569–84', *Recusant History*, 15 (1979–81), pp. 306–11; Prest, *Inns of Court*, pp. 174–7, 186.
45 Stubbs, *A gaping gulf* (1579), esp. sigs. A2v–A3r, F4r, E1v; Merbury, *Briefe discovrse of royall monarchie* (1581), sigs. ⁺iii– iiiᵛ, pp. 2–5, 7, 8, 18–38, 41–7; Mears, 'Counsel, public debate, and queenship', pp. 629–50; Guy, 'Tudor monarchy and its critiques', pp. 87–8.

UNSITUATED DISCOURSES

If Stubbe and Merbury demonstrate how political ideology could cut through physically located public spheres, then the isolation of individual spheres from each other can be exaggerated. In their own ways, the 'moot' at Lincoln's Inn in 1566 and Anne Dowe's discussion of Elizabeth's relationship with Leicester both contributed to the debate on the succession, though the two were entirely unconnected. Common subjects of debate are crucial to an understanding of the multiple model of the Elizabethan public sphere. Physical situation defined the heart of the Elizabethan public spheres, but unsituated discourses were its arterial system, reaching out from one sphere to another and providing an overarching framework that linked disparate and distinct spheres together.

The two most important unsituated discourses, as far as extant evidence shows, were the debates on the nature of the Elizabethan church and of Elizabeth's queenship. Both encompassed a broad social, gender and geographical range of participants, linking together diverse, distinct individual spheres. The debate on the English church conducted by the clerical and lay elite across the confessional spectrum, and their actions in pushing Elizabeth for more or less reform, are well documented.[46] But

46 The literature on puritans' demands for reform is extensive, but see in particular: Collinson, *Puritan movement*, passim; Aston, *King's bedpost*, pp. 106–7, 97–105, 108–12; David J. Crankshaw, 'Preparations for the Canterbury Provincial Convocation of 1562–3: a question of attribution', in Wabuda and Litzenberger (eds.), *Belief and practice in Reformation England*, pp. 60–93; Usher, 'Deanery of Bocking', pp. 434–55; Freeman, '"The reformation of the church in this parliament"', pp. 131–47; Patrick Collinson, 'The downfall of Archbishop Grindal and its place in Elizabethan political and ecclesiastical history', in Peter Clark, A. G. R. Smith and Nicholas Tyacke (eds.), *The English Commonwealth, 1547–1640* (Leicester, 1979), pp. 39–57; Lake, *Moderate puritans*; John Guy, 'The Elizabethan establishment of the ecclesiastical polity', in Guy (ed.), *Reign of Elizabeth I*, pp. 126–49; Patrick Collinson, 'Ecclesiastical vitriol: religious satire in the 1590s and the invention of puritanism', in Guy (ed.), *Reign of Elizabeth I*, pp. 150–70; John Bossy, *The English catholic community, 1570–1850* (London, 1975); Patrick McGrath, 'Elizabethan Catholicism: a reconsideration', *Journal of Ecclesiastical History*, 35 (1984), pp. 414–28; McGrath and J. Rowe, 'The imprisonment of catholics for religion under Elizabeth I', *Recusant History*, 20 (1991), pp. 415–35; Christopher Haigh, 'Catholicism in early modern England: Bossy and beyond', *Historical Journal*, 45 (2002), pp. 481–94; A. Pritchard, *Catholic loyalism in Elizabethan England* (London, 1979); Alexandra Walsham, *Church papists* (London, 1993); Walsham, '"Yielding to the extremity of the time": conformity, orthodoxy and the post-Reformation catholic community', in Peter Lake and Michael Questier (eds.), *Conformity and orthodoxy in the English Church, c.1560–1660* (Woodbridge, Suffolk, 2000); Michael L. Carafiello, *Robert Persons and English Catholicism, 1580–1610* (London, 1998); Thomas M. McCoog, SJ, *The Society of Jesus in Ireland, Scotland and England, 1541–1588: 'our way of proceeding'* (Leiden, 1996); Michael C. Questier (ed.), *Newsletters from the archpresbyterate of George Birkhead* (Camden Society, fifth series, 12; Cambridge and London, 1998); Questier, *Conversion, politics and religion in England, 1580–1625* (Cambridge, 1996).

many of the same issues were the source of complaint and resistance for ordinary Elizabethans, creating a shared discourse amongst socially diverse and geographically dispersed people. Prefiguring the physical attacks on the crucifix and candlesticks on the altar in the Chapel Royal in 1562 and 1567, Robert Taylor, a labourer from Chelmsford, Essex, publicly criticised Elizabeth's religious practice, stating 'that Service that the quene *hadd* and did vse in her Chappell was but palterye'.[47] Owen Ridley, a cleric of Battersea, spoke out openly and at length against crossing at baptism, one of the major issues of debate during the first meeting of Convocation. It was like the 'other superstitious and divellyshe ceremonyes vsed by the papistes in the celebracion of that sacrament to witt, salt, creeme, spittle, oyle, and candles' and he 'dyd wonder and greatlye marvell' at learned men who supported its continuation.[48] In 1587, Thomas Baslyn, a schoolmaster from an unidentified parish in Wiltshire, refused to allow his local minister to baptise his daughter using the sacrament as laid out in the Book of Common Prayer (i.e. with the sign of the cross).[49] Many, from Edward Andrewes, a Norfolk gentleman, to Thomas Greene, a Cornish labourer, were indicted for defaming the Book of Common Prayer and/or interrupting divine service.[50]

Conversely, John Ripton, a smith from East Tilbury, Essex, 'trusted to haue the pluckinge of twentie suche knaves as the vicar of Easte Tilberye was oute of their howses by the hoddes' and soon see the return of Catholics to their benefices.[51] Samuel Pilkington, of Westgate, Kent, was indicted in 1584 for stating 'he hoped to see the daye that the pope of Rome should haue as great Authorytye & beare as great swaye in Inglande as euer he dyd in Rome'.[52] Christopher Dearling, minister of Upton Lovell, Wiltshire, was indicted in 1585 for preaching 'seditious doctryn . . . [and] maintain[ing] purgatorie' at Heytesbury.[53] An anonymous writer deposited a manuscript attacking *A particular declaration or testimony, of the vndutifull and traitorous affection borne against her*

---

47 Aston, *King's bedpost*, pp. 106–7, 97–105, 108–12; ASSI 35/3/2, m. 10.
48 ASSI 35/30/6, m. 6.
49 *Wiltshire County Records: minutes of proceedings in sessions, 1563 and 1574 to 1592*, ed. H. C. Johnson (Devizes, 1949), p. 123. For other cases see, for example: PRO, ASSI 35/23/2, m. 30; Litzenberger, 'Defining the Church of England', pp. 147–9; Litzenberger, *The English Reformation and the laity: Gloucestershire, 1540–1580* (Cambridge, 1997), pp. 147–8, 150–1.
50 Attorney-General vs. Andrewes, 28 Elizabeth I, KB27/1296 (2) (Crown side), m. 22; Attorney-General vs. Hyll, 28 Elizabeth I, KB27/1296 (2) (Crown side), m. 10. See also, ASSI 35/18/5, m. 17; ASSI 35/24/2, m. 53.
51 ASSI 35/16/2, m. 50.
52 ASSI 35/26/4, m. 20.
53 *Wiltshire County Records*, p. 103.

Maiestie by Edmund Campion (1582) and Anthony Munday's *The Englyshe Romayne life* (1582) in the porch of the church of St Giles Cripplegate.[54]

Public perceptions of Elizabeth's queenship will be explored more fully in the following chapter, but it needs to be noted here that her political legitimacy, her gender and her exercise of governance were discussed across the social spectrum. Elizabeth's gender was not only the subject of John Knox's *The first blast of the trumpet against the monstrous regiment of women* (1558) and John Aylmer's *An harborowe for faithfull and trewe subiectes* (1559)[55] but was queried by ordinary Elizabethans. Joan Lister, a spinster from Cobham, denied Elizabeth could be governor of the realm 'bycause she is but a woman'.[56] Mary Cleere of Kent alleged, 'it did not become women to make knightes'.[57] In 1559, Peter Hall, a cleric, and John Hall, a labourer, both from Halden, Kent, were indicted at the local assizes for stating, 'That the Quene was not worthie to beare Rule, or to be supreame hed of the Churche'.[58] Similar views were expressed by Stephen Slater, a weaver from Smithfield. He praised Philip II for being 'a father to Ingland and did better loue an Inglyshe man then the Quenes majesties did'.[59] Thomas Davye, a labourer from Cudford, Sussex, was indicted in 1583 for saying, 'A great manye haue gone out of this realme & resisted the Crowne and so would I, yf I could haue free passage for a time.' He asserted that he would resist the 'quene and the Crowne' and that 'if he might haue free passage out of this realme, he would refuse the queene and the crowne for a time'.[60] At the arrest of Nicholas Kelsham for debt in 1584, Peter Barker, a yeoman of Christchurch, Kent, allegedly retorted 'Gypp mr Bayly [i.e. Under-Bailiff Crayford] & gypp Mrs Queene' as well as 'many other scandalous words'.[61]

---

54 SP12/154/53, fo. 95r; SP12/154/53.I, fo. 96r; SP12/154/53.II, fo. 97r–97v; *A particular declaration or testimony, of the vndutifull and traitorous affection borne against her Maiestie by Edmund Campion* (London, 1582; STC 4536); Anthony Munday, *The Englyshe Romayne life. Discouering: the liues of the English men at Roome* (London, 1582; STC 18272). The 'Censvre' does not identify *A particular declaration* explicitly, but it seems to be the likeliest source of the comments from the description ('a late declaration published by autorytye of the answeres to certayne articles') and the references to the contents of the preface.
55 Jordan, 'Woman's rule', pp. 417–51; Amanda Shephard, *Gender and authority in sixteenth-century England: the Knox debate* (Keele, 1994).
56 ASSI 35/28/5, m. 31. It is unclear if, by 'governor', Lister meant Elizabeth could not be queen or, specifically, Supreme Governor of the church. See also, McLaren, *Political culture*, pp. 12–17.
57 ASSI 35/19/4, m. 31.
58 ASSI 35/1/6, mm. 12, 14.
59 ASSI 35/27/2, m. 47.
60 ASSI 35/25/7, m. 29.
61 ASSI 35/26/4, m. 12.

Debates on the nature of the Elizabethan church and of Elizabeth's queenship were 'discursive connections': common themes discussed by diverse, physically distant groups of people. The former, in the shape of confessional affiliation, was also a 'discursive connection' because it was a factor that stimulated participation in public debate. Both worked on a broad social and geographic canvas, but such connections did always not need to function at this level. Similarities across four indictments at the Essex assizes between 1579 and 1586 show that real events provoking debate – including the Northern Rising and the fate of the earl of Westmorland – may have acted as a 'discursive connection' between unrelated individuals within a narrower, county-wide network. In 1581, David Brown, a husbandman of East Tilbury, was indicted at Brentwood for alleging, on 20 January 1581, that 'ther is no other chrisrian prince [i.e. Elizabeth] that hathe suche crewell lawes as to burne [i.e. bore?] men throwe their eares which are nowe vsed in this Realme.' Her cruelty, Brown argued, set 'all nacions in our neckes'. He argued that the earl of Westmorland would invade England, from Ireland, to reclaim his estates. '[A] greate part of his soldyers,' Brown alleged, 'are suche as haue ben burned [i.e. bored?] throwe the eares allredye'.[62] Five years later, William Medcalfe, a labourer from Coggleshall, was indicted for declaring that Westmorland was going to invade England with the help of Philip II:

with fyftene or else twentye thowsand Inglyshe men, wherof a great parte are bored throwghe the eares, of which the quene hathe a letter of their severall names . . . and she maye loke on them to her shame . . . [Westmorland] putt his truste in god to be revenged of the deathe & blud of the late duke of Norfolk.[63]

The common theme of ear burning or boring in these two cases, which were otherwise unconnected in time and place, suggests they may have been part of a specific shared discourse among ordinary Elizabethans in Essex on the Northern Rising and the rebellion of Westmorland and Northumberland. This seems more likely in the light of the indictment at Chelmsford assizes of Gregory Clover, a yeoman from Colchester, and Thomas Wixstead, a saltpetreman from Dedham, in 1579. Clover was alleged to have declared, 'my lord of Warwick and my lord of leycester are traytor[s] & comm of a traytors blode And that yf they had right they had loste ther heddes so well as others for making awaye of kinge Edward.' He was also accused of trying to stimulate a connection between Oxford and

62 ASSI 35/23/1, m. 36.
63 ASSI 35/28/1, m. 32.

the Dudleys.[64] Presumably in response to Clover or inciting his reply, Wixstead was alleged to have said, 'my lorde of Oxforde was not worthey to wype the lorde of warwickes shoes And that the said Earle of Oxforde was confederate with the duke of Norfoulk And [Norfolk] was as well worthey to loose his hedde'.[65] They were both found guilty and sentenced to be set in the pillory in Colchester on a market day and have an ear nailed to the pillory.[66]

Many cases extant in the local assize records for the Home Counties and south-eastern circuits under Elizabeth do not record a verdict or, where they do, specify the sentence. But Clover and Wixstead's cases are the only two that record a sentence where ears were nailed to the pillory. It is, therefore, possible that the references to burned or bored ears in Brown's and Medcalfe's statements reflected an existing discourse in Essex, critical of Elizabethan justice, at least partly provoked by Clover's and Wixstead's sentences. All four cases were geographically dispersed across Essex and there was no common ideological or confessional stance between the men. Both Clover and Wixstead may have been Protestants: Clover's accusations against the Dudleys for furthering Edward VI's death may be symptomatic of support for the Edwardian regime and church; Wixstead appeared to have little time for Norfolk who might popularly be perceived as an ally of the Catholic Mary Stuart. Conversely, Brown was clearly a conservative, or Catholic: at the same assizes in 1581, he was indicted for declaring, 'yt was a merry worlde when the shervyce was vsed in the latten tunge'.[67] Medcalfe's support of Westmorland may be similarly symptomatic of religious conservatism; clearly, he supported Norfolk in contrast to Wixstead. With no obvious connection between the cases, it is possible that Brown and Medcalfe created a discourse (or drew on an existing one in Essex) derived from knowledge of Clover's and Wixstead's fates which they used to demonstrate the injustice and cruelty of the regime, even though its victims stood for very different opinions than Brown and Medcalfe. It suggests that not only did unsituated discourses operate at more local levels, but that they intersected with each other, perhaps forming new discourses. Clover's and Wixstead's debate on Oxford, Norfolk and the Dudleys merged with that of Brown and Medcalfe on the Northern Rising and the earls of Westmorland and

64 ASSI 35/21/7, m. 19.
65 ASSI 35/21/7, m. 20.
66 ASSI 35/21/7, mm. 19 and 20.
67 ASSI 35/23/1, m. 36.

Northumberland, via the punishments meted out to Clover and Wixstead and the common figure of Norfolk.

Whether operating at a national or local level, unsituated discourses are vital to our understanding of the multiple model of the Elizabethan public sphere. There were common themes of debate in public discourse which can be seen as linking otherwise separate, individual situated public spheres. Yet, defining the Elizabethan public sphere solely as a set of unsituated discourses is as problematic as defining it as a set of physically located spheres. As Brown's and Medcalfe's discourse in Essex demonstrates, unsituated discourses remained dependent on real people to give them life, and, hence, were conditioned as much by social, economic, political, ethnic and geographical factors as the situated public sphere. Brown's and Medcalfe's statements appear to have relied on their access both to rumours about Westmorland and, possibly, to knowledge of Clover's and Wixstead's experience. Moreover, though there is a significant amount of evidence showing, for instance, that matters such as crossing at baptism, the Book of Common Prayer and Elizabeth's own religious practice were matters of debate for a wide social and geographically located range of Elizabethans, these discourses cannot truly be regarded as 'shared' because participants did not always fully interact with, or were aware of, each other.

THE INTERPLAY BETWEEN PUBLIC SPHERES AND UNSITUATED DISCOURSES

If the Elizabethan public sphere was characterised by both multiple, situated spheres and unsituated discourses, what was the relationship between them? Calhoun has defined the public sphere as 'a field of discursive connections' comprising 'clusters of relatively greater density of communication', but this seems inappropriate for the Elizabethan realms.[68] Whilst it highlights the existence of common issues of debate, reflects that individual public spheres can be conceived of as linked by such issues and notes that the intensity (or existence) of debate varied, it defines both the public sphere and the debates that comprise it as unsituated discourses. This diminishes the significance of physical location to which the examples of the Inns of Court and the Palesmen point. It also implies too much coherence and uniformity. First, by seeing the public sphere as a network of discourses, it suggests that diverse

---

68 Calhoun, 'Introduction', pp. 37–8.

individuals were involved in *shared* discourses. However, though there were themes in Elizabethan public debate, such as religion and queenship, that were discussed by a wide range of people these were only *common* themes not a *shared* discourse. Owen Ridley and Thomas Baslyn, who objected to crossing at baptism, or Edward Andrewes and Thomas Greene, who were accused of defaming the Book of Common Prayer, were unknown to each other. The 'shared' nature of their discourse is only abstract or imposed as a conceptualisation by later historians. Second, the 'field of discursive connections' implies that the subjects of debate were uniform, relevant to all. Topics of debate in the Elizabethan period were more haphazard: religion may have been of concern to many, but the cess was only of concern to the Palesmen among whom it was the principal subject of debate.

Instead, we need to understand the multiple model of the Elizabethan public sphere as comprising a diverse range of individual, situated public spheres over which lay an arterial network of common themes of debate. The individual spheres were not so much 'clusters of communication', as clusters or communities of debate. Debate was experienced primarily through face-to-face debate among real people gathered together in a physical location. It was conditioned by social, economic, ideological and geographic factors. The arterial network comprised common themes of debate – including religion and queenship – but it was haphazard. Branches could break off or end in discursive cul-de-sacs: not all issues (such as the cess and billeting) were of concern to everyone and, once again, participants' involvement was conditioned by geographical, social, professional and other factors that barred their access to others.

The interplay between individual situated spheres and the arterial network of common discourses can be illustrated through a microstudy of John Stubbe, a London lawyer, educated at Cambridge and Lincoln's Inn and living in London in the 1560s and 1570s. Stubbe is best known for his pamphlet, *The discoverie of a gaping gulf* (1579), that attacked the proposed marriage between Elizabeth and Francis, duke of Anjou, addressing its perceived political and confessional consequences. Stubbe argued that the marriage would not provide England with a strong ally and that, as Anjou was Henry III's heir presumptive, England was likely to be absorbed into France. He argued that the marriage of a Protestant to a Catholic was a breach of divine law and it would not provide England with a (Protestant) heir. He attacked Anjou's faith and family, particularly Catherine de Médici. And, in both presuming to comment on the marriage and stating that Elizabeth, as a woman, needed to follow the advice of her counsellors, it articulated the theory of the 'mixed polity': that Elizabeth should govern under the guidance of her male counsellors, particularly on such a sensitive and important issue as marriage.[69]

Stubbe's pamphlet has traditionally been perceived as a commission, by either Leicester or Walsingham, to articulate opposition to the match and to attempt to 'bounce' Elizabeth into refusing it by applying pressure of 'popular opinion'.[70] However, as I have argued elsewhere, though *The gaping gulf* shows that Stubbe was familiar with detailed points made by the earl of Sussex (the match's leading supporter) in both letters and memoranda, it is impossible to trace convincing connections between him, Leicester and Walsingham either directly or through a third party.[71] First, the only connection (to Leicester) was through Stubbe's printer, Hugh Singleton, via Edmund Spenser who was in Leicester's service at this time and whose *The shepherdes calendar* (which also commented on the marriage) was printed by Singleton. But there is no evidence to suggest that Singleton's involvement in *The gaping gulf* and *The shepherdes calendar* were part of a co-ordinated campaign. Second, there were closer connections to Burghley, through his secretaries Michael Hickes and Vincent Skinner, with whom Stubbe had attended Cambridge and Lincoln's Inn and may have collaborated on *The life off the 70. archbishopp off Canterbury Presentlye sitting Englished* in 1574.[72] Crucially, Sussex's letter to Elizabeth of August 1578 and a memorandum in his hand that repeats much of the information in the letter, are in Burghley's archive: both seem likely sources for Stubbe's familiarity with Sussex's arguments.[73] Third, though Elizabethan public debate has traditionally been seen

---

69 Stubbe, *A gaping gulf*, sigs. A2v–A3r, F4r, E1v and passim; *John Stubbs's 'Gaping Gulf' with letters and other relevant documents*, ed. Lloyd E. Berry (Charlottesville, VA, 1968).

70 H. J. Byrom, 'Edmund Spenser's first printer, Hugh Singleton', *The Library*, fourth series, 14 (1933), pp. 121–56; M. M. Leimon, 'Sir Francis Walsingham and the Anjou marriage plan, 1574–81' (Ph.D. thesis, Cambridge, 1989), pp. 124–5; Doran, *Monarchy and matrimony*, pp. 164–5, 170–1; Blair Worden, *The sound of virtue: Philip Sidney's* Arcadia *and Elizabethan politics* (New Haven and London, 1996), pp. 111–12, 185; Peter Lake and Michael Questier, 'Puritans, papists, and the "public sphere" in early modern England: the Edmund Campion affair in context', *Journal of Modern History*, 72 (2000), pp. 595–600.

71 Mears, 'Counsel, public debate and queenship', passim. For Stubbe's attack on Sussex's arguments, compare the earl's letters and memoranda (CP 148, fos. 12r–16v and CP10, fos. 30r–33v) with Stubbs, *A gaping gulf*, esp. sigs. B2v, C8v–D1r, D4v–D5v.

72 Hasler, III, pp. 390–1, 460; John Stubbe to Michael Hickes, 21 Mar. 1570, Lansdowne 12, fo. 117r; same to same, 1 Dec. 1580, Lansdowne 31, fo. 40r; same to same, 30 July 1582, Lansdowne 36, fos. 212r–13r; same to same, 14 Sept. 1589, Lansdowne 61, fo. 170r; Hickes to Stubbe, [Dec. or Jan. 1582], Lansdowne 107, fo. 168r–168v; same to same, n.d., Lansdowne 107, fo. 170r–170v; *The life off the 70. archbishopp off Canterbury. Englished* [trans. John Stubbs?], ([Zurich], 1574; *STC* 19292a).

73 CP 148, fos. 12r–16v; CP10, fos. 30r–33v.

as co-ordinated by the council to 'bounce' Elizabeth into action, Tom Freeman's work on Thomas Norton's role in the parliament of 1571 undermines how far we can conceive individuals as the council's puppets.[74]

Rather, it appears that *A gaping gulf* was an independent initiative by a man who was politically active, a committed Protestant and may have imbued Ciceronian ideas of citizenship, as well as those of the 'mixed polity'. His mental world can be gauged by his education and career. Educated at Cambridge and Lincoln's Inn, the latter's influence may have been crucial. Not only had Lincoln's Inn developed a strong Protestant identity from the start of Elizabeth's reign but the Inns were also institutions where, as we have seen, the concept of the 'mixed polity' was absorbed by many. The notion was derived partly from the work of Christopher St German, whose *Doctor and student* (1528 and 1530) and *New additions* (1531) were virtually 'set texts' at the Inns.[75] They also had a long tradition of political satire and complaint.[76] Moreover, *A gaping gulf* was not Stubbe's only foray into print to mount a politico-religious attack. *The life off the 70. archbishopp off Canterbury*, on which he is thought to have collaborated with Hickes and Skinner, was a faithful translation of Matthew Parker's *De antiquitate Britannicae ecclesiae & priuilegiis ecclesiae Cantuariensis* (1572–4) but with added marginalia that attacked Parker's hostility to the moderate puritans' calls for reform.[77] Though family connections were also important, Stubbe's commitment to the Protestant cause shaped his later activities. In 1585, he became secretary to his cousin by marriage, Peregrine Bertie, Lord Willoughby d'Eresby, governor of Bergen-op-Zoom in the Netherlands, relaying information on Dutch affairs between Willoughby and Burghley. In 1589, he went to fight with the Huguenots in France, dying the following year.[78]

---

74 See above, introduction and ch. 1; Freeman, '"The reformation of the church in this parliament"' pp. 131–47.

75 *John Stubbs's 'Gaping Gulf'*, ed. Berry, pp. xxii–xxiv; Fisher, 'Reformation in microcosm?', pp. 37–9, 47, 49; Guy, 'Tudor monarchy and its critiques', pp. 87–8.

76 John Taylor, *English historical literature in the fourteenth century* (Oxford, 1987), pp. 256, 236–7; T. F. Tout, 'Literature and learning in the English civil service in the fourteenth century', *Speculum*, 4 (1929), pp. 367, 369; Janet Coleman, *English literature in history, 1350–1400: medieval readers and writers* (London, 1981), pp. 94–130.

77 Matthew Parker, *De antiquitate Britannicae ecclesiae & priuilegiis ecclesiae Cantuariensis, cum archiepiscopis eiusdem 70* (London, 1572–4; *STC* 19292). See especially, *The life of the 70 archbishopp off Canterbury*, sigs. Aiii^r, Cii^r, Bviii^r, Civ^r–Civ^v.

78 *John Stubbs's 'Gaping Gulf'*, ed. Berry, pp. xlii–xlvi; Rafe Rokeby the younger, 'Oeconomia Rokebiorum', in *A history of Richmondshire*, ed. T. D. Whitaker (2 vols., London, 1823), I, pp. 174–5.

Stubbe's commitment to Protestantism, his belief that England was a 'mixed polity' in which governance was shared between monarch and councillors, his political activity (he was returned MP for Yarmouth in 1588, drafting a petition against Whitgift's subscription campaign[79]) and his willingness to articulate his views in print suggest that he was no council stool-pigeon in 1579. Rather, believing he had a duty to offer counsel, that Elizabeth had a responsibility to accept it and that, most importantly, the marriage was politically and confessionally dangerous, he wrote *A gaping gulf* of his own accord, exploiting his connections with Hickes and Skinner to obtain inside information.

Stubbe's significance is not just that he underlines how independent Elizabethan public debate was from the council. He also demonstrates how the individual, situated public sphere and the arterial network of common discourses interacted. *A gaping gulf* and *The life* can both be seen as part of unsituated discourses on, respectively, marriage and succession and on church reform. They were Stubbe's response to these issues, as much as were denials of Elizabeth's claim to the throne or demonstrations against the Book of Common Prayer. But *The life* in particular may have been a response to specific, localised events that Stubbe witnessed. Stubbe was based in London in the 1560s and, probably, the 1570s during the Vestiarian Controversy (1562–6) and Parker's enforcement of conformity: he entered Lincoln's Inn in 1562, was called to the bar in 1572 and held senior posts at the Inn in the late 1570s; the indictment against him for *A gaping gulf* also stated the pamphlet had been written at the Inn.[80] Thus, he experienced first hand the temporary suspension of thirty-seven London ministers in March 1566 when they refused to conform to the royal injunctions on clerical dress, the widespread despair it provoked among the godly laity, left bereft (in their eyes) of spiritual guidance at Easter and the subsequent development of underground congregations.[81]

Mixed with his own confessional commitment and the circle in which he moved, it may have been Stubbe's direct experience of the reform cause that shaped his participation in public debate, encouraging him, Hickes and Skinner to collaborate on their attack on Parker. The tone of the

---

79 Petition to parliament, Mar. 1589, Additional 48101, fo. 136r–136v.
80 Mears, 'Counsel, public debate and queenship', p. 639; KB27/1271 (Crown side), m. 3v.
81 Collinson, *Elizabethan Puritan Movement*, pp. 68–91; Usher, 'Deanery of Bocking', pp. 434–55; CUL, Mm.1.29, fos. 1v–3v; *Correspondence of Matthew Parker, DD, Archbishop of Canterbury*, ed. John Bruce and Thomas Thomason Perowne (Parker Society; Cambridge, 1853), pp. 275–9; *The remains of Edmund Grindal*, ed. William Nicholson (Parker Society; Cambridge, 1843), pp. 288–9.

The life contrasted greatly with that of Skinner's English translation of Gonsalvius's denunciation of the Spanish Inquisition, *Sanctae Inquisitionis Hispanicae artes aliquot detectae*, the second edition of which (1569) had been dedicated to Parker.[82] Thus, Stubbe's participation in public debate was both a product of his direct experiences, of the physical location in which he lived, and was part of a wider, unsituated discourse. It was part of an unsituated discourse because Stubbe chose to participate in debate by publishing a pamphlet, which is an unsituated discourse as defined by Halasz, and because his theme was a common one, which many discussed in different ways and from different perspectives.

The relationship between individual, situated spheres and the arterial network of unsituated discourses, however, goes further than this. Marriage, succession and the nature of the Elizabethan church were related issues. Whereas the former sought to preserve Protestantism by providing an heir of Elizabeth's body and hence nullifying Mary Stuart's claim to the throne, the latter sought to establish the Elizabethan church on what puritans perceived were truly reformed lines. They can, therefore, be regarded as different perspectives or angles on a wider theme: the Protestant identity of the Elizabethan realms, particularly England. Conversely, both the issues and Stubbe's pamphlets about them were also distinct. The focus of *A gaping gulf* was wide, concerned with England's broad confessional affiliation in the present and future, her relationship with other European powers and articulating an overt political ideology. That of *The life* was narrower, addressing the specific nature and internal organisation of the Elizabethan church in the present. In other words, Stubbe, and the situated sphere of which he was part, engaged in two discourses. The arterial network that lay over Stubbe's sphere comprised multiple branches which connected him to different parts of the broad Elizabethan public sphere.

THE SUBJECTS OF DEBATE

Though the structure and composition of the public sphere have been the main foci of challenges to Habermas's model, criticisms have also been levied both at how he defined the subjects of debate and how he explained

---

82 Reginaldus Gonsalvius Montanus, *A discovery and playne declaration of sundry subtill practises of the holye inquisition of Spayne. Set forth in Latine, and newly translated* [by V. Skinner] (London, 1568; *STC* 11996); Montanus, *A discovery and playne declaration . . .* (London, 1569; *STC* 11997), sigs. Aii[r]–Aii[v].

growing political awareness and participation. Habermas largely assumed that the subjects of debate were established prior to the development of the public sphere and were not questioned.[83] This has been challenged by Eley, Warner and Zaret who have also pointed to the importance of issues such as identity, nationalism, religion, science and gender as subjects of debate in their own right from the seventeenth century onwards and as factors in bringing new topics to the fore.[84]

There is little sense in which the subjects of Elizabethan debate were fixed prior to the establishment of the public sphere. Though evidence is fragmentary, what remains extant suggests that debate was often stimulated by specific events or wider issues that they prompted: Elizabeth's political legitimacy;[85] her marriage and the succession;[86] the fates of leading aristocrats (Norfolk, Westmorland, Northumberland, Hertford);[87] the debasement of the coinage; repairs to St Paul's Cathedral; executions, murders and suicides; malformed children and animals; the Irish cess, billeting and the plantations; the French Wars of Religion[88] and other foreign wars and battles. Indeed, the range of subjects of Elizabethan debate was far wider than either Habermas or his critics have noted for later periods.

Equally, there is evidence to show that issues identified by Zaret and others as subjects of debate from the seventeenth century also excited Elizabethan debate and that they could act to stimulate the introduction of new topics. Three broad issues stand out. First, Elizabeth's accession, the second female monarch in five years, reinforced the importance of the nature of queenship in the lexicon of sixteenth-century political debate. Responses to Elizabeth's queenship will be examined in the following chapter. Second, as we have seen, the nature of the Elizabethan church, whether defined by puritans as not godly enough, or by Catholics as heretical, was a subject of debate among the clergy and laity, across both the confessional spectrum and Elizabeth's realms.

---

83 Habermas, *Structural transformation*, p. 36.
84 Calhoun, 'Introduction', pp. 34–7; Eley, 'Nations, publics, and political cultures'; Zaret, 'Religion, science, and printing'; Michael Warner, 'The mass public and the mass subject', in Calhoun (ed.), *Habermas and the public sphere*, pp. 377–401.
85 For example: ASSI 35/1/6, mm. 12, 14; ASSI 35/19/4, m. 31.
86 For example, SP70/40, fos. 61r, 62r; Interogatories ministred vnto John keale and his answers to the same, 6 Aug. 1562, SP70/40, fos. 78r, 79r; ASSI35/22/10, m. 11; SP12/172/7, fo. 10r.
87 For example, ASSI 35/25/7, m. 6A; Attorney General vs. Kenelm and Berney, 14 Elizabeth I, KB27/1240 (Crown side), m. 2; ASSI 35/28/1, m. 32; SP12/60/48, fos. 136r–137v; SP12/60/49, fo. 138r–38v.
88 For instance, 'Carnsew's diary', p. 29 and the numerous printed pamphlets, as selectively listed in ch. 5.

Third, it seems that national identity was not just the preserve of nineteenth-century public discourse, but that it dominated the political culture of the Gaelic Irish as articulated in extant bardic poetry. Since at least the late 1970s, the value of bardic poetry, whether extant in the poem-books of individual lords/families (*duanairí*) or in miscellaneous collections, as historical evidence has been highly controversial. By defining early modern Gaelic bardic poetry as creatively static, cut off from innovation in other fields and in decline as a profession, literary scholars and historians like Tom Dunne, Bernadette Cunningham, Nicholas Canny and Michelle O Riordan have suggested that bardic poetry was unable to register contemporary responses to English conquest and governance, and, hence, issues of national political and religious change.[89] Conversely, Brendan Bradshaw's study of the *duanairí* of the O'Byrne sept of Colranell, County Wicklow – to which Dunne's article was a response – and Marc Caball's full-length study of Elizabethan and Jacobean poetry have challenged this orthodoxy, demonstrating a number of examples where bardic poetry responded directly to specific issues and events during the conquest.[90]

Any study of Gaelic poetry has to be sensitive to literary conventions and methodological problems. The function of poetry was to praise the virtues and actions of the chieftains to publicise and legitimate their rule. Hence, emphasising chieftains' financial generosity, sexual attractiveness, physical good looks and military prowess were essential components; they were also regularly compared favourably to their ancestors or ancient

89 T. J. Dunne, 'The Gaelic response to conquest and colonisation: the evidence of the poetry', *Studia Hibernica*, 20 (1980), pp. 7–30; Bernadette Cunningham, 'Native culture and political change in Ireland, 1580–1640', in Ciaran Brady and Raymond Gillespie (eds.), *Natives and newcomers: essays on the making of Irish colonial society, 1534–1641* (Bungay, Suffolk, 1986), pp. 148–70; Nicolas Canny, 'The formation of the Irish mind: religion, politics and Gaelic Irish literature, 1580–1750', *Past & Present*, 95 (1982), pp. 91–116; Michelle O Riordan, *The Gaelic mind and the collapse of the Gaelic world* (Cork, 1990); Katherine Simms, 'Bardic poetry as a historical source', in T. J. Dunne (ed.), *The writer as witness: literature as historical evidence* (*Historical Studies*, 16; Cork, 1987), pp. 58–75. For reviews of O Riordan's important, but controversial, work, see Breandán O'Buachalla, 'Poetry and politics in early modern Ireland', *Eighteenth Century Ireland*, 7 (1992), pp. 149–75; Marc Caball, '*The Gaelic mind and the collapse of the Gaelic world*: an appraisal', *Cambridge Medieval Celtic Studies*, 25 (1993), pp. 87–96; Brendan Bradshaw, 'The bardic response to conquest and colonisation', *Bullán: an Irish Studies Journal*, 1 (1994), pp. 119–22. See also Marc Caball, *Poets and politics: reaction and continuity in Irish poetry, 1558–1625* (Cork, 1998), pp. 6–13.

90 Brendan Bradshaw, 'Native reaction to the Westward enterprise: a case-study in Gaelic ideology', in K. R. Andrews, N. P. Canny and P. E. H. Hair (eds.), *The Westward enterprise: English activities in Ireland, the Atlantic, and America, 1480–1650* (Liverpool, 1978), pp. 65–80; Caball, *Poetry and politics*, passim.

heroes.[91] Methodologically, poems need to be explored in their entirety and within their political, social and cultural context; distinctions also need to be made between the *duanairí*, which tend to be conservative, and composite collections, which were less bound by literary conventions of style and content.[92] Three key problems of O Riordan's study are her selective quotation from poems, her failure to place them firmly within their political and cultural context and her exclusive focus on *duanairí*.[93]

Examined sensitively, it becomes clear from Gaelic bardic poetry that the English conquest of Ireland and the legitimacy of the English government were the main issues of debate among the Gaelic Irish and that a nascent national identity was being articulated. This is demonstrated in Brian Ó Gnímh's ''Na Bhrían táinig Aodh Eanghach' (e. 1570s), Uilliam Óg Mac an Bhaird's 'Gaoidhil meallta nó mac Néill' (e. 1570s), the anonymous 'An sluagh sidhe so i nEamhuin?' (c.1574–5), and Fearghal Óg Mac an Bhaird's 'Cia re bhfuil Éiri ac anmhuin?' (from the poembook of Cú Chonnacht Maguire, chieftain of the Maguires of Fermanagh, d. 1589).[94] 'Gaoidhil meallta nó mac Néill', dedicated to Turlough Luineach O'Neill, likened the Gaelic Irish to bees, lured out of their hive by the honey of the English:

> It is in this manner that the English host
> deals with the Gaoidhil of Ireland, the princely
> men of Lios Bhreagh are being driven from the
> native land of their ancestors.[95]

'An sluagh sidhe so i nEamhuin?' (c.1574–5), also dedicated to Turlough Luineach O'Neill, evoked an imaginary hosting of troops supplied by local Gaelic families, like the MacDonnells, Clandeboye O'Neills and O'Cahans, at Navan fort under O'Neill. The poet asserted the assembly was called in response to growing English hegemony in Ulster:

> That the land of their ancestors is under foreign oppression
> is the reason for the gathering of the noble families,
> the lord of their assembly remembers
> that the land of Ireland is fettered.[96]

91 O Riordan, *Gaelic mind*, pp. 27–32; Caball, *Poets and politics*, pp. 17–20. On the (changing) conventions by which the Welsh were praised by Celtic bards see Jones, 'The Welsh poets', pp. 248–9.
92 Caball, *Poets and politics*, pp. 89–90.
93 O'Buachalla, 'Poetry and politics', pp. 149–75; Caball, '*The Gaelic mind . . .* an appraisal', pp. 87–96.
94 Caball, *Poets and politics*.
95 Ibid. Translation is Dr Caball's.
96 Ibid., pp. 43–4. Translation is Dr Caball's.

English conquest and governance provided a new impetus or focus for
bardic poets to define, establish and extol the virtues of their patrons,
while existing literary conventions – notably the identification of Ireland
as a woman – provided easy and apposite ways to express the political
claims of the Gaelic chieftains against the English regime, as is demonstrated in the poem-books of Hugh MacShane O'Byrne and Feagh
MacHugh O'Byrne. Both these, and others, made claims to national
leadership, either by evoking the image of Ireland as a woman (and Hugh
MacShane as her lover), or of mythical leaders, notably Lugh Lámhfhada,
who rallied the nation against invaders and oppressors.[97] More significantly, Mac an Bhaird's 'Cia re bhfuil Éiri ac anmhuin?', 'Brath lendáin ac
Leic Lughaidh' and "Leath re Fódla fuil Uidhir' (all from the Maguire
poem-book) went beyond asserting Cú Chonnacht Maguire's claims to
national leadership and implied that Ireland had no leader or king. First,
by equating Ulster with the whole of Ireland, Mac an Bhaird implied that
Maguire's claims to leadership applied as much to Ireland as to Ulster.
Second, by deliberately using the archaic 'rí' ('king'), the poet argued
that Ireland lacked a legitimate monarch, asserted that Ireland could
function as a unitary state and claimed the crown for Maguire. 'Cia re
bhfuil Éiri ac anmhuin?' specifically states that Ireland has had no king
since Donnchadh in 1035 and that the crown was vacant:

> For whom is Ireland waiting? Claimants
> to her throne are slow to appear, for
> no lord inhabits her, the country of the
> wide territories with warm lakes . . .
> In Ireland of the shallow streams there
> was not a crowned lord who won
> acknowledgment after Donnchadh – it is
> not an omen of honour for Ireland.[98]

This was not an isolated occurrence. Though Flann Eoghan Mac
Craith's 'Í N-ainm a áirdmic' (c.1590) eulogised Elizabeth, it never called
her queen of Ireland, though later poems referred to James VI and I as
king.[99]

---

97 Bradshaw, 'Native reaction', pp. 73, 75–7. The poems are number 16, by Tadhg Dall Ó
hUiginn, in Hugh MacShane's poem-book and numbers 19, 24, 51 in Feagh MacHugh's.
98 Caball, *Poets and politics*, pp. 25–31. Translation is Dr Caball's.
99 John C. Mac Erlean (ed.), *Duanaire Dáibid uí bruadair (The poems of David Ó Bruadair), Part
III: containing poems from the year 1682 till the poet's death in 1698* (Irish Text Society, 18;
London, 1917), pp. 64–73.

Nationalist concerns may have dominated Irish public debate, but they may not have been just the preserve of the Gaelic elite. Though there is little evidence of its import among Welsh recusants, the dispute between Robert Wiersdale, vicar of All Saints with St Peter, Maldon, and Roger Nowell of Heybridge in 1588 over whether Essex ministers prayed for the queen fervently enough raises interesting points.[100] First, Nowell alleged that some preachers denied Elizabeth was queen of Ireland and France; a position with which, according to Nowell and three witnesses, Wiersdale agreed.[101] Though the veracity of these accusations and the grounds on which Elizabeth's titles were denied are unknown, it begs the question whether Wiersdale and his colleagues refused to recognise Henry VIII's declaration of Ireland as a kingdom in 1541 or whether they tacitly agreed with the Gaelic Irish. Second, Nowell himself only responded to Wiersdale's denial of Elizabeth's title to the French crown. He told Wiersdale, 'take heed what he sayde for Fraunce ys the Quenes Inheritance' and pointed to a statute for Edward III's that would prove him correct. Did his (or any of the five witnesses,) failure to dispute the allegation about the crown of Ireland signify agreement with Wiersdale, or simply a belief, imbued from contemporary pamphlet literature, that Ireland was a bog not worth arguing about?[102]

MOTIVATIONS FOR PARTICIPATION IN PUBLIC DEBATE

Habermas argued that the professional elite who became of members of the public sphere were politicised by the liberation of commodity exchange and social labour from government control. With greater distinctions between the 'private' (domestic household and family) and 'public', growing literacy, greater availability of (printed) news and the development of physical locations in which to discuss issues (coffee houses), commercial development transformed the nature of citizenship: engaging in critical, public debate replaced acting in common as a principal civic task.[103] By challenging Habermas's definition of the subjects of debate, Eley, Warner and Zaret also questioned Habermas's

---

100 SP12/178/27, fos. 52r–53r.
101 However, William Lee, servant of Dr Walker, who was conducting the examination of ministers that day testified that Wiersdale only disputed Elizabeth's title to France: SP12/178/27, fo. 52r.
102 SP12/178/27, fos. 52r–53r. For Machyn's description of Shane O'Neill as the 'wilde Yrish man', see 'Machyn's diary', p. 300 and for general views of the Irish, see Sheila T. Cavanagh, '"The fatal destiny of that land": Elizabethan views of Ireland', in A. Hadfield (ed.), *Representing Ireland: literature and the origins of conflict, 1534–1660* (Cambridge, 1993), pp. 116–31.
103 Habermas, *Structural transformation*, pp. 73–9, 43–51, 23–4, 41–3, 36–7, 51.

arguments on participation. They suggested that nationalism, religion, science and gender all stimulated individuals to become involved in public debate.[104] In particular, Zaret emphasised religion. The Reformation encouraged widespread participation in public debates, which, in conjunction the growing emphasis on parliamentary representation and the increasing numbers of contested elections under James I, stimulated appeals to popular opinion by the government and opposition during the Civil War, regicide and Restoration.[105] The importance of political enfranchisement has also been highlighted by Tim Harris. His study of London has shown that a high proportion of freemen, quicker access to freed status, the growth of municipal elections and the proliferation of local offices led to greater political awareness among the London populus, especially when combined with growing literacy and long-established traditions of informal policing.[106]

The politically enfranchised were likely to participate in public debate. Though, for instance, Palesmen had been eased out of many of the most important official positions and the percentage of them holding civil office declined from the 1540s, more than 50 per cent continued to hold office during Elizabeth's reign and they dominated local offices, like shrievalties and local commissions.[107] But though we are hampered by our inability to trace the lives of the many yeomen, labourers and spinsters recorded in assize indictments for talking about political issues, there appears to be little correlation between officeholding and participation in public debate. Officeholding by yeomen and others lower down the social scale, as well as by women, was highly circumscribed or nonexistent. Even at higher social levels, connections cannot always be made. William Carnsew's wide political interests cannot have been a product of officeholding because his formal involvement in local administration was limited: he was a JP only twice, in 1564 and 1571.[108]

In some cases, political impotency and the lack of enfranchisement may have stimulated localised discourses. A number of cases are extant which involved the verbal and physical abuse of political, administrative or legal figures or material representations of authority, such as writs. For example, John a Wood, a trugger from Maighfield, Sussex, was indicted

104 Calhoun, 'Introduction', pp. 34–7; Eley, 'Nations, publics, and political cultures'; Zaret, 'Religion, science, and printing'; Warner, 'The mass public and the mass subject'.
105 Zaret, 'Religion, science, and printing', pp. 216–24.
106 Harris, 'Problem of "popular political culture"', pp. 43–58.
107 Brady, *Chief governors*, pp. 213–14.
108 'Carnsew's diary', p. 14.

in March 1571 for seditious words against Lord Keeper Bacon, Sir William Cordell, Master of the Rolls, a judge, Richard Covert, and an unidentified man, John Thatcher:

It is pittye that there is not a payer of gallowes sett vp at westminster hall dore & the master of the roules hanged theron drawen & quartered & his skynne flawen from his backe, & mr Covent & Mr Thatcher be traytores & diuers of his neighbores to be dogges, murtherers periured persons, false packers of matters, It is pittye my lord keper is not hanged drawen & quartered for he is a traitor both to god and the quene & the Councell.[109]

In February 1572, William Kettell, a clothworker and merchant of Cannick Street and London, and his wife, Grace, responded angrily to being served writs of subpoena to answer allegations that William had spoken seditious and slanderous words against the queen.[110] William chased its deliverer, Richard Wollastone, 'a lone mile to home to haue donn him some greate hurte' while Grace 'brake the waxe that enclosed the same writ in a number of small peces . . . and veray errogantlie flonge the same amongst the same people and . . . afterwarde she flonge [it] vnder her fete and trode vppon the same'.[111] She alleged this was because, being presented with 'paperes' by an unknown man and 'being in some feare *of the sodden puttinge of a thing into her hande*' had 'lett the same fall' but their actions speak more of anger and personal invective: the charge appears to have been levied as part of an attempt to blacken William's character in a case of the alleged theft of bills and obligations valued at over £211.[112]

However, there is evidence to suggest that there was a growing sensitivity to social status in the mid- and late sixteenth century which may have stimulated political interest and participation. Re-evaluating the diary of Henry Machyn and its purpose in the context of the genre of chronicle writing, Ian Mortimer has suggested that Machyn was motivated to keep his diary because of his self-perception of his social status. He resorted to recording political events in his chronicle because he lacked other conventional credentials for membership of the mercantile class:

109 ASSI 35/13/3, m. 36. Though the indictment crossed out Thatcher's name, and inserted 'vno' rather than 'duam', it is clear from the report that Wood abused Thatcher too. Thatcher may have been a judge, another official or, possibly, the defendant or accused in a case in which Wood was involved and which may have prompted these allegations.
110 William Kettell was alleged to have said, 'yf the Quene of England had a sonn and were with him as his prentise he wowld make him to carrye the water tanckard'. Mounslowe vs. Kettell, [n.d., 1553–8], STAC4/11/42.
111 Hopton vs. Kettell, 1558–79, C3/95/94; STAC4/11/42.
112 Attorney General vs. Kettell, 14 Elizabeth I, STAC5/A15/4; C3/95/94.

officeholding and a high level of literacy. The son of a Leicestershire miller, Machyn, with his brother, became a moderately prosperous London citizen but one who remained an outsider to mercantile society. The diary allowed Henry to consolidate his credentials to that class by enabling him to record the London he knew and, more importantly, to stress his own place within its society. Machyn's choice of the chronicle format, and his decision to leave the manuscript in his will to William Hervey, Norroy king of arms and later Clarenceux king of arms – which suggests, Mortimer argues, a conscious desire for the chronicle to be kept for posterity – were both apposite and specific to Machyn's mercantile pretensions: the major readers and producers of chronicles were merchants.[113] Machyn's example suggests more broadly that political participation, whether active or in recording the news and events, could be stimulated by concerns about social status and a means to claim membership of higher social and professional groups.

Similarly, changes in *perceptions* of political roles and responsibilities may have had an impact. Habermas identified the significance of classical-humanism in its privileging of the gentry over the provincial nobility as governors and bureaucrats.[114] Yet, its real import appears to lie more in the model of citizenship that it promoted and the absorption of these ideas, directly and indirectly, by the gentry and professionals, including those who were not members of the Elizabethan regime. A growing number of students at the Elizabethan Inns of Court, an important situated public sphere, had received a classical-humanist education at school or university prior to their admission. Though we do not know precisely the substance of John Stubbe's education, for instance, his perception of counsel and citizenship articulated in *A gaping gulf* was strongly Ciceronian. Both classical-humanist ideals of citizenship and quasi-republican ideas appear to have penetrated urban elites in the English provinces, as is demonstrated by civic treatises and manuscripts advices like John Hooker's *Orders enacted for orphans* ([1575]), prepared for Exeter, John Barston's *Safegarde of societie*, drawn up in 1576 after the incorporation of Tewkesbury, and George Clarkson's advice submitted to the seventh earl of Northumberland in 1567.[115] They were also evident in

---

113 Ian Mortimer, 'Tudor chronicler or sixteenth-century diarist? Henry Machyn and the nature of his manuscript', *Sixteenth Century Journal*, 23 (2002), pp. 981–98.
114 Habermas, *Structural transformation*, p. 9.
115 Peltonen, *Classical humanism*, pp. 57–68; Mervyn James, 'The concept of order and the Northern Rising, 1569', in James (ed.), *Society, politics and culture: studies in early modern England* (Cambridge, 1986), pp. 278–85.

Ireland, articulated particularly clearly in treatises examining the need for reform in Ireland, such as Thomas Beacon's *Solon his follie* (1594).[116] Clarkson's advice to Northumberland is particularly important. There is no evidence that Clarkson had been educated at university or the Inns of Court, suggesting that classical-humanist ideas were pervasive, influencing people beyond those who were formally trained humanists.[117]

Changing perceptions of social status and political responsibilities only partly explain what motivated Elizabethans to participate in public discourse. They do not account fully for the variety of issues that were discussed or provide convincing explanations for many non-elite participants, despite the example of Clarkson. Confessional allegiance appears to have been a more important, and more universal, factor. Studies of puritans' demands for ecclesiastical reform in particular have demonstrated that religious belief motivated elite nonconformists. Though it is harder to establish the motivation of those lower down the social scale, there are signs that suggest religious affiliation stimulated political participation or debate. Thomas Baslyn's refusal to have his daughter baptised according to the Book of Common Prayer was clearly because of his puritan beliefs. A memorandum in the minutes of the assize proceedings notes that he believed the churching of women was 'a Juysh cerymonie' and the conformation of children was 'a tradition of man as he thincketh'. His wife was not churched and his children were not confirmed.[118] Wiersdale, the Essex minister who denied that Elizabeth was queen of Ireland and France, appears to have been a puritan, while his opponent, Nowell, was both more conformist and hostile to puritans: in 1582, he had been involved in a dispute with George Gifford, a puritan, when he had sought to prevent Gifford from preaching at Wiersdale's parish church of All Saints with St Peter, Maldon.[119] Thomas Owen's and Robert Pugh's actions in Wales were born out of their Catholicism. Owen supported missionary priests and, in 1576, appears to have planned to join his brothers on the continent.[120] Pugh was probably a member of the community who lived in Rhiwledyn cave, near his estate at Creuddyn, in the early-mid 1580s where the remnants of a printing press, on which

---

116 Peltonen, *Classical humanism*, pp. 74–96.
117 James, 'Concept of order', pp. 281–2.
118 *Wiltshire County Records*, p. 123.
119 F. G. Emmison, *Elizabethan life: disorder* (Essex Record Office; Chelmsford, 1970), pp. 52–3.
120 Owen wrote his will, leaving his property to a younger brother, Foulke. Hugh Owen had been implicated in the Northern Rising (1569) and Ridolfi Plot (1571) and fled to Spain where he served in Philip's army; Robert Owen entered the seminary at Douai. Jones, 'Lleyn recusancy case', pp. 102–4; STAC5/O7/22.

Gruffydd Robert's *Y drych Cristianogawl* may have been printed, were allegedly discovered.[121]

Despite confessionalisation in Ireland between the Gaelic Irish and Anglo-Irish on the one hand, and the New English on the other, it was less religious affiliation than nascent nationalism that appears to have stimulated political participation among the Gaelic Irish. As articulated in bardic poetry, the political agenda was defined by English conquest and governance of Ireland, rather than the imposition of Protestant ideas which, as Ellis has shown, was limited.[122] It was expressed either in terms of denying Ireland had a leader or king – as illustrated by some of Fearghal Óg Mac an Bhaird's contributions to the Maguire poem-book[123] – or by poets laying claims of their patrons to national leadership, as manifested in the poem-books of Hugh MacShane O'Byrne and Feagh MacHugh O'Byrne.[124]

Conversely, the ethnic, political and factional interests of the Palesmen were transcended by economic considerations. Under Elizabeth, the burden of the cess and billeting had increased substantially.[125] It was levied nearly continually, its size increased, its collection was enforced more effectively, prices paid were substantially below market prices while the allowances for carriage were low.[126] The growth in the size of the English garrison also increased, putting greater pressure on billeting. There was no regulation of 'achates' (milk, butter and eggs) that soldiers claimed in addition to billeting, while extortion was rife.[127] Tours by the Viceroy or Lord Deputy only exacerbated the situation: they placed an extra burden on households while powers to levy the cess were claimed by other officials in their absence.[128] At the same time, income from landed estates was in decline. Some areas, notably West Meath, were also subject to substantial levies of coyne and livery (Gaelic customs of purveyance and billeting) by

121 Jones, 'Robert Pugh', pp. 13–15, though the identification of *Y drych Cristianogawl* as the book published by this press has been challenged by Ifano Jones in his *A history of printing and printers in Wales*, pp. 19–22.
122 Caball, *Poets and politics*, pp. 42–5; Stephen G. Ellis, 'Economic problems of the Church: why the Reformation failed in Ireland', *Journal of Ecclesiastical History*, 41 (1990), pp. 239–65.
123 Specifically, the poems 'Cia re bhfuil Éiri ac anmhuin?', 'Brath lendáin ac Leic Lughaidh' and ''Leath re Fódla fuil Uidhir'. Caball, *Poets and politics*, pp. 25–31. See also Mac Erlean (ed.), *Duanaire Dáibid uí bruadair . . . Part III*, pp. 64–73.
124 Bradshaw, 'Native reaction', pp. 73, 75–7. See poem 16, by Tadhg Dall Ó hUiginn, in Hugh MacShane's poem-book and numbers 19, 24, 51 in Feagh MacHugh's.
125 For details of the Palesmen's complaints, see the petitions and responses listed above, n. 37.
126 SP63/5/51, fos. 133r, 134r; Brady, *Chief governors*, pp. 220–4 and Table 6.1 on p. 221.
127 Brady, *Chief governors*, pp. 227–9.
128 Ibid., pp. 222–7.

Irish chieftains and informal exactions or spoilage by soldiers travelling to Connaught.[129] The burden was so high, the Palesmen alleged, that they were forced to give up their farms and either go begging or flee out the Pale, to live 'vnder the savage and rude sorte of Irish men'.[130]

The Palesmen's case may have been extreme – the cess and billeting were specific to the Pale and represented a heavy burden that was not exacted anywhere else in Elizabeth's realms – but it merely throws into sharper relief the importance of economic issues in stimulating participation in public discourse and action. The 'Journall of matters of state' makes clear that issues which affected people's pockets stimulated debate. In the summer of 1561, there were 'Dyversyties of opinions' over whether St Paul's should be restored, after it had burned, prompted by Archbishop Parker's order to the bishops to organise collections of money to pay for the repairs. There was 'Grete murmoring of the people that they should carrie or sell their thinges in such sorte, considering yt was not the Quenes owne worcke . . . many saied the Quene could graunt no such commissions.'[131] The following January, 'there was a grete talcke in London of the fall of money from vs to x grotes the ounces, and the angel to vis viiid', stimulated by news that privy councillors were calling in their creditors or selling plate.[132] Indeed, proclamations against the spreading of false rumours on the debasement of the coinage, first issued in November 1560, had to be reissued in March 1562.[133]

Ideological and economic reasons, as well as ideas about citizenship at a relatively elite level, appear to have greater impact on political awareness and activity than changes to urban society and in officeholding. However, there are examples of public debate for which the motivation is hard to identify. In 1562, for instance, news of Elizabeth's marriage negotiations with Eric XIV of Sweden and his imminent arrival in England were the 'common brute' in Lombard Street and elsewhere.[134] The marriage had an obvious political and religious import: it would define England's political allies and resolve the succession. But it is unclear whether these reasons alone are sufficient to explain the interest which the negotiations excited in London. Was curiosity of Elizabeth and the court significant? Was the 'common brute', as well as the extensive record of court entertainments

129 SP63/5/54, fo. 145r.
130 SP63/5/51, fos. 134r, 136r.
131 Additional 48023, fo. 356v.
132 Additional 48023, fo. 360r.
133 'Machyn's diary', pp. 245, 275.
134 SP70/40, fo. 61v; SP70/40, fos. 77r–80r.

and removes evident in Machyn's diary, more akin to the modern interest in celebrities?

DEFINING THE ELIZABETHAN PUBLIC SPHERE

Evidence from across Elizabeth's dominions, demonstrating that men and women of all social classes discussed major political and religious issues, undermines assertions that a public sphere did not, and could not, have existed at this time. Yet, equally, the public sphere that emerges differs in important ways from that defined by Habermas and some of his critics. First, the Elizabethan public sphere was neither wholly physically located, nor, in Halasz's words, an 'imaginary construct' or unsituated discourse. Rather, it comprised clusters of debate: communities or groups of real people in a physical location who discussed and debated issues. These differ from Calhoun's 'clusters of communication' because physical location was essential to the act of debate: verbal communication remained the central vehicle of debate and so participants had to be in physical proximity to each other to facilitate discussion. Over this body of clusters, lay an arterial network of unsituated discourses – subjects of debate such as religious reform, gender, nationalism – which linked individual communities together so that, in hindsight, we can perceive or trace similarities in concerns and opinions. Yet again, however, this network is not comparable to Calhoun's, which overemphasises continuity. The Elizabethan network was characterised by haphazardness: not all subjects of debate (such as the cess and billeting) were widely shared; discursive themes could break off or end in a discursive cul-de-sac.

Second, and as a consequence, the Elizabethan public sphere actually existed in multiple forms. Third, as some of his later critics have noted, issues such as religion, gender and nationalism played far more significant roles as both subjects of debate and as factors stimulating participation, than Habermas allowed. Fourth, both the social spectrum of participants, and the participation of women (though the sources tend to obscure their involvement), was wider than Habermas perceived for the late seventeenth and early eighteenth centuries. Fifth, the Elizabethan public sphere was geographically extensive: though much of our evidence comes from London and the south-east, there are clear signs of public debate and action in English provinces as well as in Wales and Ireland.

Much work needs to be done to refine this definition further; in particular, to identify the extent of public debate in Wales and to draw out any regional variations in England. As with this survey, there are specific problems with extant sources for both these areas. Assize records, which have proved fruitful for exploring English debate, do not exist for Wales. Quarter session records do remain, but only for Caernarfonshire and they record little in the way of cases of seditious and slanderous words. Equally, assize records for England, as already noted, are only extant for the Home Counties. King's Bench, Chancery and Star Chamber records do throw up interesting cases from across the country, but they are few and far between, especially when the extant records are voluminous and, particularly with Star Chamber, not catalogued well enough to allow relevant cases to be identified quickly. Records for regionally based courts – such as those of the Duchy of Lancaster or the Palatinate of Chester – are no longer extant. Thus, the concerns and actions of those in the south-east are privileged, particularly those of Essex which seems to have a slightly higher incidence of cases than other counties. With research on popular culture increasingly highlighting regional variations, it is imperative that such issues are explored for public debate too. For Wales, records of the Court of Great Session may be useful; for English counties, local archives need to be trawled.

Though the picture painted of Elizabethan public debate is not comprehensive, basic questions remain about what we should actually call the Elizabethan public sphere. It is clear that the variety of participants, subjects of debate and opinions expressed mean we must talk in terms of a multiplicity of 'public spheres'. Yet, it is less clear whether 'sphere' is the correct label for these groups. Not least because of its associations with Habermas's classic definition of the (physically situated) public sphere, 'sphere' does point usefully to the importance of physical location to the 'clusters of debate'. But it does little to highlight the arterial network of unsituated discourses or, indeed, hint at the haphazardly interlinking nature of the 'clusters of debate' themselves. Even the plural, 'spheres', may connote more isolated and unrelated instances of debate, than overlapping and interlinked ones. While 'discourse' may emphasise the 'unsituated' elements of Elizabethan public debate, it seems to encapsulate more effectively the (albeit haphazard) connections, both real and discursive, between individual debates and clusters. Therefore, while we can, I believe, talk in general terms about an 'emergent public sphere' in Elizabeth's reign, 'public discourse' represents more closely the nature of Elizabethan public debate than 'public sphere' or 'public spheres': a haphazardly interlinking network of clusters of debate, comprising real men and women in real places, shaped by social, economic, geographical, ethnic, religious and political factors and exhibiting common themes of debate.

CHAPTER 7

Perceptions of Elizabeth and her queenship in public discourse

On a wooden door, now hanging on the wall of the dining room of Ashridge Manor, Hertfordshire, there is a sixteenth-century painting of an apprehensive looking young woman, approached by nine men armed with pikes (Plate 7.1). It appears to be part of a series. Between the doorway, where the door probably hung originally, and the fireplace, a seated woman is depicted, though the paint is much deteriorated. Above the fireplace itself are the royal arms, flanked by two *trompe l'oeil* twisted pillars and depictions of two gentlemen (on the left) and three women (on the right) in Elizabethan dress. The painting over the fireplace is thought to depict Princess Elizabeth walking in Ashridge Park with her attendants; that on the door and wall appears to be less benign. It is thought to depict Elizabeth's arrest in 1554, with the seated woman probably being an attendant.[1]

If there is consensus about what the paintings depict, it is less clear what they mean. James Sutton's study of the decorative programme at Theobalds has shown that domestic wall-paintings were not solely decorative, but sought to convey didactic messages about political affairs, the family's social standing and their deeds.[2] On the one hand, the paintings at Ashridge may articulate a celebration of Elizabeth as a Protestant champion, by recording one instance of her persecution under Mary. On the other, it could be a more pointed commentary on Elizabeth's failure to reform the church fully by reminding her of her Marian persecution and how, puritans perceived, she was protected by divine

---

1 Reports by P. J. Keevil, 5 Jan. 1982 and 5 Sept. 1977 and an undated note, headed 'Tristram archive' all in the file on Ashridge Manor, Herts (also known as the Manor House, Little Gaddesdon), Wall Paintings Survey, Courtauld Institute, London. See also *Royal Commission on Historical Monuments (England). An inventory of the historical monuments in Hertfordshire* (London, 1910), p. 144; *The Victoria County History of the counties of England: Hertfordshire*, ed. William Page (5 vols., Westminster, 1902–23), II, pp. 209, 212 and plate between pp. 212–13.
2 Sutton, 'Decorative program', passim.

Plate 7.1. Mural thought to depict Princess Elizabeth, Ashridge Manor, Hertfordshire. Crown copyright. NMR.

providence. Thomas Freeman has shown that this was precisely how and why John Foxe utilised iconic moments in Elizabeth's life in the second and subsequent editions of the *Acts and monuments* (commonly known as the 'Book of martyrs').[3] The date of the painting provides no clue as it cannot be identified precisely. Information on its owners only confuses matters further.[4] From the mid-sixteenth century, the house was owned by the Dormer family, including, from 1574, Sir Robert Dormer (1551–1616), who married into the Catholic Montague family and whose sister, Jane, married the count of Feria.[5] May the painting be a *celebration* of Elizabeth's arrest?

The multiple meanings that the paintings at Ashridge suggest should not surprise us. During the first thirty years of her reign, Elizabeth's queenship was debated, defined and challenged in many ways. She was called 'an Arrant hoore', who kept none 'but Raskilles and a forte of whores'.[6] She was reported to have had between two and four children by Leicester, either spiriting them away abroad or throwing them into a fire.[7] Equally, it was reported that she did not menstruate regularly or properly and, because of this or a physical obstruction, was incapable of conceiving.[8] In Ireland, she was called a *cailleach* (old hag) and *phiseogach* (sorceress); her royal style and title were torn out of grammars in the

---

3 Freeman, '"As true a subiect being prisoner"', pp. 104–16; Freeman, 'Providence and prescription', pp. 27–55.

4 There is some confusion over ownership itself. Articles in *Country Life* suggest the house was initially granted to Elizabeth by Edward VI (5 Edward VI) and subsequently to William Gorges, a gentleman pensioner (14 Elizabeth), Henry, Lord Cheney (17 Elizabeth) and Sir Thomas Egerton (2 James I). See 'Ashridge Park, Great Berkhamstead', *Country Life*, 4 (5 Nov.–12 Nov. 1898), p. 560; Arthur T. Bolton, 'Ashridge Park I and II', *Country Life*, 50 (6 Aug. and 13 Aug. 1921), pp. 163–4. However, I have preferred the more recent research of J. T. Smith for the Royal Commission on Historical Monuments who has identified Dormer as the owner instead of Gorges and Cheney, not least because the tablet (marked 'ARD EB [?] 1576') recording rebuilding or enlargement would refer to Dormer and his wife, Elizabeth Browne. Smith points out that the house was of inappropriate size for someone of Dormer's standing and that, therefore, it may have been part of a larger building no longer surviving. See J. T. Smith, *Hertfordshire houses: selective inventory* (London, 1993), pp. 117–18.

5 Smith, *Hertfordshire houses*, pp. 117–18; *The history of parliament. The House of Commons, 1509–1558*, ed. S. T. Bindoff (3 vols., London, 1982), I, pp. 52–3; Hasler, II, p. 49.

6 ASSI 35/27/9, m. 15; ASSI 35/22/3, m. 15.

7 De Silva to Philip II, 8 June 1564 and 4 Feb. 1566, *CSP Spanish*, I, pp. 362, 520–1; letters from Antonio de Guaras, 12, 19, 26 Dec. 1574 and 1 Jan. 1575, ibid., II, p. 491 (Additional 26056 B, fo. 352r); Nicholas Ormanetto, Bishop of Padua, to Ptolemy Galli, Cardinal of Como, 9 Dec. 1575, *Calendar of State papers Rome*, II, p. 238; [Galli] to [Ormanetto], 29 Jan. 1576, *CSP Rome*, II, p. 250; SP12/12/51, fo. 36r; SP12/13/21.I, fos. 56r–57r; ASSI 35/22/10, m. 14; ASSI 35/27/8, m. 31; ASSI 35/28/6, m. 46; Levin, *'Heart and stomach of a king'*, p. 78; Emmison, *Elizabethan life: disorder*, p. 42.

8 De Feria to Philip II, 29 Apr. 1559, *CSP Spanish*, I, p. 63; enclosure in Antonio Maria Salviati, (late) bishop of [S. Papoul], to Cardinal of Como, Jan. 1578, *CSP Rome*, II, p. 363.

diocese of Cork and Ross and there was a widespread refusal to pray for
her, including a boycott in Dublin of thanksgiving ceremonies after the
defeat of the Armada in 1588.[9] She was styled as Deborah, a Protestant
saviour, both by puritans hoping to chivvy her to further church reform
and, from the 1570s, by other subjects who perceived her as a genuine
champion against growing Catholic conspiracy and the machinations of
Spain. From the 1570s, her accession was increasingly celebrated with bell
ringing, bonfires and banquets; some parishes also celebrated her birthday.[10] Laudatory pamphlets, such as *The first anointed Queen I am* (1573)
and *A famous dittie of the ioyful receauing of the Queens most excellent
maiestie* (1584) also circulated.[11]

Despite this variety, little attempt has been made to evaluate contemporary perceptions of Elizabeth and what shaped them, particularly
beyond elite level. Indeed, the recent four-hundredth anniversary of her
death has focused more attention on the manipulation of Elizabeth's
image after 1603 than before.[12] Through the work of Thomas Freeman,
Alexandra Walsham and others, we are increasingly familiar with puritan
perceptions of the queen, defined both by confessional allegiance and
Elizabeth's continued failure to reform the church.[13] Conversely, Anne
McLaren and Carole Levin have argued that perceptions of Elizabeth were
shaped primarily by attitudes towards gender. Elite political discourse
was, according to McLaren, driven by the question of female monarchy,
while Carole Levin has argued that popular criticism of Elizabeth, including cases of sexual slander, were manifestations of contemporaries' concerns over her failure to follow gender expectations by settling the
succession.[14] Similarly, reports that Edward VI was still alive and cases

9 Christopher Highley, 'The royal image in Ireland', in Walker (ed.), *Dissing Elizabeth*, p. 64.
10 For example, GL Guildhall MS 1568/1, part 1, pp. 247, 255, 262, 270, 277, 279, 285, 289, 296,
302, 310, 315, 321, 332 (St Benet, Gracechurch Street, London); Guildhall MS 1046/1, fos. 5v, 7v,
12v, 14r, 16v, 18v, 21r–21v, 24v, 27r, 29v, 32r, 34r, 36v (St Antholin, London); Guildhall MS 1013/
1, fo. 34v (St Mary Woolchurch, London); A. D. Stallard (ed.), *The transcript of the
churchwardens' accounts of the parish of Tilney All Saints, Norfolk, 1443–1589* (London, 1922), pp.
231, 237, 240, 242, 249; Williams (ed.), *Early churchwardens' accounts of Hampshire*, pp. 54–6, 58,
61, 65–6 (Bramley); 105 (Stoke Charity), 129–34, 136–9 (Crondall); Alison Hanham (ed.),
Churchwardens' accounts of Ashburton, 1479–1580 (Devon and Cornwall Record Society, NS, 15;
Torquay, 1970), pp. 167, 169, 172, 174–6, 178, 181, 183, 186, 188; John V. Kitto (ed.), *St Martin's-
in-the-Fields. The accounts of the churchwardens, 1525–1603* (London, 1901), p. 364; Drew (ed.),
Lambeth churchwardens' accounts, pp. 120, 136, 141, 146, 162, 168.
11 *The first anointed Queene I am* (1573); *A famous dittie of the ioyful receauing of the Queen* (1584).
12 Dobson and Watson, *England's Elizabeth*; Doran and Freeman (eds.), *Myth of Elizabeth*.
13 Freeman, '"As true a subiect being prisoner"'; Freeman, 'Providence and prescription';
Alexandra Walsham, '"A very Deborah?"', pp. 143–68.
14 McLaren, *Political culture*, passim; Levin, '*Heart and stomach of a king*', chs. 4 and 5, esp. pp.
66–86, 91–3.

of pretenders have to be attributed to 'the uncertainty of having a woman ruler' rather than to religion, because 'in their protestantism . . . Edward and Elizabeth were very similar'.[15]

Levin's and McLaren's characterisation of Elizabethan public discourse poses problems of methodology and interpretation. McLaren's survey is narrowly focused, not only on elite discourse in print, but within that, on a small number of canonical texts. While Levin's is more wide-ranging, she fails to distinguish between different commentators whose agendas may have been very different. Indeed, neither historian explores participants' social and cultural background, specifically neglecting religious affiliations that may have contributed significantly to their perceptions of Elizabeth. Equally, there is no compelling evidence to demonstrate, as Levin argues, that criticism of Elizabeth escalated in the 1580s when it became less likely that the succession would be resolved dynastically. Connections she makes between anxiety over the succession and interest in monstrous births do not reflect the meanings contemporaries usually derived from the latter. Though Keith Thomas has argued that it may be a mistake to disregard cases where the accused was (or was perceived as) mentally deranged, Levin appears too ready to take the words and actions of such individuals as representative of Elizabethan public debate and ascribes a rationality to them that is simply not there.[16] Finally, the importance of confessional motives cannot be dismissed lightly: as recent research has revealed, Edward's and Elizabeth's religious beliefs were not similar, nor were the confessional directions of their regimes.[17]

Further questions must also be asked. While cases of seditious and slanderous words enable historians to tap into popular public debate, they cannot be assumed to be representative of public debate as a whole. It has long been acknowledged that law and order was imposed more rigorously on those below the governing elite than on the elite itself. Not only may they exaggerate the extent to which those of yeomen status and below were dissatisfied with Elizabeth's queenship but they only reveal negative responses to Elizabeth's queenship. Whilst historians have increasingly questioned Neale's and Strong's depiction of a consistently and genuinely popular queen and highlighted instances of discontent and criticism,

15 Levin, 'Heart and stomach of a king', pp. 100, 119.
16 Keith Thomas, *Religion and the decline of magic: studies in popular beliefs in sixteenth- and seventeenth-century England* (London, 1971), pp. 131–40, 149; Levin, 'Heart and stomach of a king', pp. 106–7.
17 Diarmaid McCulloch, *Tudor church militant: Edward VI and the protestant Reformation* (London, 1999), ch. 4.

more positive aspects should not be ignored and consigned only to post-Armada euphoria. Greater attention must be paid to perceptions of Elizabeth's queenship in Wales and Ireland where the terms of debate, particularly in Ireland, were radically different. Does a 'British' dimension undermine the notion that public discourse focused on gender and the succession?

THE ROLE OF GENDER IN PERCEPTIONS OF ELIZABETH

The debate on female monarchy was not confined to the works of Marian exiles like John Knox and John Aylmer. There were attacks on Elizabeth from Catholic polemicists like William Allen, who, in his *Admonition to the nobility and people of England* (1588), called Elizabeth the 'pretended Queene'.[18] Mary Stuart's claims to the throne (and hence the legitimacy of female monarchy) was defended in John Leslie's *A defence of the right highe, mightye and noble Princesse Marie Quene of Scotlande* (1569) and David Chambers's *Discours de la légitime succession des femmes* (1579).[19] There were also some broader discussions of female monarchy in histories like Arthur Golding's translation, *The abridgement of the Historyes of Trogus Pompeius* (1578).[20] Ordinary Elizabethans also discussed these issues. On 31 January 1586 at Cobham, Joan Lister declared that, 'bycause she [Elizabeth] is but a woman she owghte not to be governor of A Realme'.[21] She dismissed the efficacy of the bridles against misgovernment that Aylmer had identified as characteristic of English governance: 'the Bysshopp of Canterbury & the Counsayle make A foole of the Queenes Majestie', she said.[22] Others focused on Elizabeth's alleged sexual activity. In 1559, a Cambridge student, Clybburne, called Elizabeth a 'rascall'.[23] In 1580, Grant Bedford, a Maidstone mariner, said 'The Quene dothe kepe . . . none other but Raskilles and a forte of whores'.[24] In 1585, Robert Threle, a gentleman of Bexley, alleged Elizabeth was 'an hoore yea and an Arrant hoore'.[25] Accusations that she had had children were made by men

18 William Allen, *An admonition to the nobility and people of England and Ireland* ([Antwerp], 1588; *STC* 368), sig. A3v.
19 Jordan, 'Woman's rule', pp. 437–50.
20 *The abridgement of the Historyes of Trogus Pompeius*, trans. Arthur Golding (London, 1578; *STC* 24292), fos. 1r–1v, 10v–12r (printed as 18), 95–7.
21 ASSI 35/28/5, m. 31.
22 ASSI 35/28/5, m. 31.
23 Depositions of George Withers and George Bond, 28 Mar. 1559, SP12/3/50, I, fo. 160r.
24 ASSI 35/22/3, m. 15.
25 ASSI 35/27/9, m. 15.

and women, labourers, yeomen and clerics, throughout the first thirty years of the reign.[26]

However, it is difficult to sustain Levin's arguments that gender lay at the heart of public debate on Elizabeth's queenship, contributing particularly to allegations of sexual misconduct. Only Aylmer's *An harborowe for faithfull and trewe subiectes* (1559) was written specifically as a defence of female monarchy: it was a response to Knox's *The first blast of the trumpet against the monstrous regiment of women* (1558) which became acutely embarrassing after Elizabeth's accession. John Calvin wrote to Cecil in 1559 to argue that, while female monarchy was generally against divine and natural law, God could (and did) make exceptions.[27] The discussions of female rule in *The historyes of Trogus Pompeius*, though largely negative, comprised a tiny proportion of the text. Moreover, by praising Orithya (daughter of the Amazonian queen, Marthenia) for 'preseruing of her maydenhead while she liued' and condemning the Carthaginians for adopting 'a bloody kinde of Religion' which brought divine retribution in the shape of an invasion by Machaeus, Golding endorsed the positive spin on Elizabeth's failure to marry that developed from the late 1570s. It also emphasised the role of providence and Protestant identity (as the true faith) that had underpinned positive constructions of her queenship since 1558.[28]

Conversely, Knox's treatise was confessionally motivated: he was a Scottish Protestant who wrote *The first blast* as an attack on Mary I, whose regime he saw as punishment for England's 'shamefull reuolting to Satan frome Christ Iesus, and frome his Gospell ones professed' [i.e. under Edward VI].[29] Allen's trenchant criticism of Elizabeth was a postscript to his main attack: that Elizabeth was not the rightful queen because she was a bastard and, most importantly, a heretic who destroyed the true church. Indeed, his allegations about Elizabeth's sexuality – that she 'abused her bodie, against God's lawes' with Leicester and 'divers others' – came not only after an attack on Leicester but were submerged in criticisms that she sought to destroy the nobility and refused to name a successor by decreeing the crown would only pass to her own issue.[30]

---

26 SP12/12/51, fo. 36r; SP12/13/21.I, fos. 56r–57r; ASSI 35/22/10, m. 14; ASSI 35/27/8, m. 31; ASSI 35/28/6, m. 46.
27 Jordan, 'Woman's rule', p. 437.
28 *Trogus Pompeius* (1578), fos. 11r, 96v–97r.
29 Knox, *The first blast*, sig. A2v.
30 Allen, *Admonition*, sigs. B2r, B1v–B2v.

Leslie's and Chambers's treatises sought to assert Mary Stuart's claims to the English crown.

Equally, evidence that gender was an issue for less prominent Elizabethans is limited. The case involving Edward Fogge, a gentleman of Ashford, Kent, and William Padnall (status unknown) in 1570 suggests that not all Elizabethans believed female monarchy was legitimate. Padnall was alleged to have said that he 'care[d] not for quene marye nor for quene Eliza'. His statement does not seem to have been confessionally motivated if Fogge's assessment of Padnall can be believed: Padnall's words were allegedly spoken in response to Fogge's accusation that he was a Catholic.[31] However, others who questioned Elizabeth's political legitimacy did not necessarily do so because of her gender. Mary Cleere questioned Elizabeth's right to the crown because she was 'base borne' and asserted the right of another woman to succeed her: 'an other Ladie is the right inheritor thervnto'.[32] In 1563, Edward Baxter alleged 'that my lord Robert did kepe the Quenes grace' and 'that the Quene was a noughtie woman And cold not Rule her Realme nor Iustice was nott ministred' but it does not appear, as Levin suggests, that Baxter believed Elizabeth was unfit to rule *because* she was Dudley's mistress. The allegation that Dudley 'kept the Quenes grace' was made at Lent; the other allegations were made in July. Moreover, though we can only rely on Baxter's words as reported by Robert Garrerd, the use of 'and' between the later allegations may suggest that Baxter questioned Elizabeth's authority on three separate counts: her sexual inconstancy, her inability to rule, and her failure to maintain law and order. Indeed, the criticisms of Elizabeth were part of a slightly longer list of Baxter's grievances: he continued, 'And that my Lord Keper was a naughtie man & A wreche'.[33]

Reports of Elizabeth's sexual activity need to be examined in the context of their perpetrators. Especially at the beginning of the reign, but extending into the 1570s, foreign ambassadors, based in England and on the continent, circulated reports of Elizabeth's sexual activity and alleged pregnancies and speculated over the outcome of her marriage negotiations. In 1566, the Spanish ambassador, Guzman de Silva, informed Philip II that it was generally thought that Elizabeth would not marry Leicester: she feared that, if the Archduke Charles rejected her,

31 ASSI 35/12/5, m. 22.
32 ASSI 35/19/4, m. 31.
33 The examinacion of Robert Garrerd, 19 Jan. 1563, SP15/11/86, fo. 151r–151v; Levin, *'Heart and stomach of a king'*, p. 76.

a marriage to Dudley would look like 'a matter of necessity rather than of choice'.[34] The same year, he informed Philip of reports that Leicester had slept with the queen on New Year's Night.[35] Earlier, he had reported diverse opinions as to why Elizabeth was planning a progress north, including 'that she is pregnant and is going away to lie in.'[36] The bishop of Padua reported to the cardinal of Como from Madrid in 1575 that Elizabeth had a thirteen-year-old daughter whom she would be willing to give in marriage to 'someone acceptable' to Philip II.[37] These were coupled with reports of both general ill-health – in March 1561, the Venetian ambassador reported to the Doge and Senate that he was 'informed on good authority' that Elizabeth was suffering from dropsy[38] – and that Elizabeth was physically incapable of conceiving. In 1578, the papal nuncio in France reported to the cardinal of Como that he was informed, 'By persons who have some knowledge of the Court of England', that Elizabeth did not have regular periods.[39]

These reports did not seek to question Elizabeth's political legitimacy via her gender or her sexual activity: her legitimacy was already questioned by the circumstances of Henry VIII's divorce and his declaration on the succession. Elizabeth was, in Como's words, the 'pretended Queen'.[40] Primarily, they sought to supply to continental Catholic regimes information that would point to how the Elizabethan succession question would be resolved and hence, the realm's confessional future. The Venetian ambassador's reports that Elizabeth was dropsical were accompanied by intelligence that 'some chief personages of the kingdom . . . are aspiring to that crown, and that some one has already commenced negotiating with this King [Philip II] to favour some designs'.[41] The bishop of Padua's reports that Elizabeth had a thirteen-year-old daughter prompted a reply from the cardinal of Como revealing the pope's hope that the report was true: 'it would enable his Majesty [Philip II] to dispense with war, which of its own nature is so hazardous, and think

34 *CSP Spanish*, I, p. 520.
35 Ibid.
36 *CSP Spanish*, I, p. 362.
37 *CSP Rome*, II, p. 238.
38 Paulo Tiepolo to the Doge and Senate, 6 Mar. 1561, *CSP Venice*, VII, p. 301. See also Il Schifanoya to Octaviano Vivaldino, 27 June 1559, ibid., VII, pp. 105; Giovanni Francesco Morosini to the Signory, 12 July 1576, ibid., VII, p. 551; *CSP Rome*, II, p. 363; de Quadra to Philip II, 13 Sept. 1561, *CSP Spanish*, I, pp. 214; de Silva to same, 18 Dec. 1564, ibid., I, p. 398.
39 *CSP Rome*, II, p. 363. See also *CSP Spanish*, I, p. 63.
40 *CSP Rome*, II, p. 250.
41 *CSP Venice*, VII, p. 301.

of some accord by way of a marriage, which in the end might bring the realm back to the catholic fold.'[42] Reports that seemed dubious were transmitted along with those that appeared to be substantiated because ambassadors felt obliged to convey all information, whether they regarded it was true or not. In July 1576, the Venetian ambassador in France informed the Signory that a report was in circulation that Elizabeth was dead. '[T]he news is not believed,' he stated, 'because it does not come from an authentic source, and moreover the English ambassador is much annoyed at this report and had affirmed to me that the Queen is in excellent health.' He reported it only because he knew 'that news from here reaches Venice'.[43] For all the cardinal of Como's excitement about reports of Elizabeth's daughter, there is a strong thread of scepticism in his, or the pope's, response: 'Were it true that the pretended Queen had that daughter . . .'[44]

Sexual slander was only used to define Elizabeth's queenship at elite level in the 1580s, in polemical Catholic works like Allen's *Admonition*. It was used not because writers identified Elizabeth's gender as 'the most salient aspect of her entity as a ruler' but because it reinforced Catholic depictions of her as a bastard and a heretic.[45] As has already been noted, Allen began his treatise by questioning Elizabeth's dynastic legitimacy: that she was born of an illegitimate and incestuous alliance between Henry and Anne Boleyn and had been declared illegitimate and barred from the succession by act of parliament.[46] It then argued that she was politically illegitimate because she governed without the approval of the papacy which 'by reason of the auncyent Acorde, made between Alexander the III. the yere 1171 and Henry the II then kinge . . . that no man might lawfully take that Crowne nor be accompted as Kinge, till he were confirmed by the soueraigne Pastor of our soules'; an accord renewed, Allen stated, in 1210 by King John.[47] The allegations of her sexual incontinency were used to damn Elizabeth further, painting her and her

---

42 *CSP Rome*, II, p. 250.
43 *CSP Venice*, VII, p. 551.
44 *CSP Rome*, II, p. 250.
45 Levin, '*Heart and stomach of a king*', p. 76.
46 Allen, *Admonition*, sigs. A4v–A5r. Levin states (pp. 80–1) that Allen implies that Anne was Henry's own daughter because 'he did before unnaturally know and kepe both the said Anne's mother and sister'. However, it is more likely that Allen's use of 'incestuous' (e.g. sig. A5r) refers to biblical injunctions against marriage between, or sexual intimacy with, spouses-in-law which, of course, had been the basis for Henry's justification for divorcing Catherine of Aragon, his sister-in-law.
47 Allen, *Admonition*, sigs. A5r–A5v.

court as effeminate and corrupt. Both depictions of Elizabeth as a whore, and the promulgation of such images in the 1580s, were rooted in confessional allegiance and growing polarisation between Protestant and Catholic, England and the continental Catholic powers, over missionary priests, the English crown and the English church. Indeed, the *Admonition* marked a deliberate escalation in the debate, attacking Elizabeth's political legitimacy overtly – something that, according to Peter Lake and Michael Questier, Edmund Campion and Robert Persons had consciously avoided at the beginning of the decade.[48]

Catholic polemic did influence popular negative constructions of Elizabeth's queenship which otherwise appeared to focus on gender. In 1586, for instance, Thomas Lee Ballewe said publicly that 'the papistes in One [i.e. our?] Countrey saye that your Queene . . . is an hore and that she hath had two children'.[49] However, it may be more appropriate to view these constructions within the wider context of verbal abuse of women, in which 'whore' was the most commonly used insult.[50] Laura Gowing's study of early modern London has shown that, though 'whore' was used to accuse women of sexual misdemeanours, it was also used as a general term of abuse that had little to do with adultery or prostitution.[51] It was used by protagonists in cases involving money, goods and land to condemn or discredit female opponents. Indeed, it could be used as much to humiliate men as to expose women's immorality: accusations of whoredom pointed to men's inability to maintain order in their own household and brought shame on the household as a whole.[52]

There are problems with placing accusations against Elizabeth within this context. Our knowledge of sexual slander derives primarily from cases of defamation, rather than of sexual misdemeanour; Gowing's analysis suggests cases were more likely to be brought by women (whereas most slurs on Elizabeth were made by men) and allegations tended to be made between friends and neighbours who, living cheek by jowl, had much opportunity to witness each other's behaviour.[53] Many accusations against Elizabeth were made in the provinces, where court news was, at the very

---

48 Lake and Questier, 'Puritans, papists and the "public sphere"', pp. 600–12.
49 ASSI 35/28/6, m. 46. It is interesting that Lee Ballewe referred to Elizabeth as 'your queen' (raising the possibility that 'one Countrey' is actually 'our Countrey'). Was he French: was 'Lee Ballewe' an Anglicised version, or the clerk's reading, of Le Ballieu or Balleau?
50 Laura Gowing, *Domestic dangers: women, words and sex in early modern London* (Oxford, 1996; 1998 edn), p. 59.
51 Ibid., pp. 79–87.
52 Ibid., pp. 59, 109–10, 94–7, 113–16.
53 Ibid., pp. 60–1, 64, 67–72.

best, second-hand. However, cases of sexual slander and defamation amongst ordinary Elizabethans demonstrate the ultimately limited vocabulary for criticising women. By calling Elizabeth a 'whore', her subjects may not, as Levin has argued, have identified her gender as 'the most salient aspect of her entity as a ruler', but rather have used it to criticise her queenship for other reasons.[54] Elizabeth's gender may only have shaped the (limited) choice of insult and not reflected the cause. Similarly, accusations that she had had children by Leicester could have derived, in part, from conventions of abuse: bastardy was an inherent part of allegations of whoredom. The established definition of a whore – using cosmetics, richly dressed, failing to do womanly tasks – could also have been applied to Elizabeth, whose rich clothes would have been visible during removes and progresses in the south of England as well as in printed woodcuts, and who assumed the traditionally male role of monarch.[55]

That accusations of whoredom against Elizabeth may have been a general insult, rather than a specific comment on female monarchy, makes further sense when the circulation of news and rumour is considered. As was seen in chapter 5, court gossip circulated in London and the provinces.[56] Court gossip provided the grist for the slanderers' mill that observation and direct knowledge did in cases between friends and neighbours. It also provided a context in which the insult 'whore' made sense. Popular perceptions of the court, and hence the gossip that emanated from it, were strongly influenced by historical and chivalric romances, as well as assumptions that the court was a centre of vice.[57] These perceptions provided an established framework in which to characterise

54 Levin, '*Heart and stomach of a king*', p. 76.
55 Gowing, *Domestic dangers*, pp. 79–87.
56 SP70/40, fos. 61r–62r; SP70/40, fos. 77r–80r; Additional 48023, fo. 362r and see above, ch. 5.
57 Fox, 'Rumour and popular political opinion', p. 616. For instance, William Clay, an innholder of Epping, Essex, bequeathed a copy of 'The wanderinge Knight' to his son, Nicholas, in 1583 (F. G. Emmison, *Elizabethan wills of South-West Essex* (Waddesdon, 1983), p. 77). Chivalric figures were also common motifs for painted cloths and domestic wall-paintings, as demonstrated by depictions of the Nine Worthies in two houses in Amersham. See Francis W. Reader, 'Tudor mural paintings in the lesser houses of Buckinghamshire', *Archaeological Journal*, 89 (1932), pp. 129–30 (Old Grammar School, Amersham), 138–45, Plates VIII–XII.B and fig. 4 (61, High Street, Amersham). Other related paintings can be seen in manor houses such as Harvington Hall, Worcestershire (F.W. Reader, 'Tudor domestic wall painting, Part II', *Archaeological Journal*, 93 (1936), pp. 244–5; Edward Croft-Murray, *Decorative paintings in England, 1537–1837* (2 vols., London, 1962), I, p. 187; Elsie Matley Moore, 'Wall-paintings recently discovered in Worcestershire', *Archaeologia*, 88 (1940), plate 88), and Cothay, Somerset (Croft-Murray, *Decorative painting*, I, p. 175. Though note that the image of Reynard the Fox at Cothay is not mentioned in Christopher Hussey, 'Cothay, Somerset, part I', *Country Life*, 62 (1927), pp. 596–604, figs 8, 10, 11, 13–15). For the influence of chivalric language on contemporary political prophecy, see the example of John Tusser of Tolleshunt Darcy, Essex: ASSI 35/25/1, m. 37.

the queen and her courtiers. It enabled the insult of 'whore' to be translated from local situations, when it was used to point to sexual misdemeanours or to discredit opponents in other cases, to a comment on the queen and her regime.

That 'whore' may have been used as a general term of abuse against Elizabeth does not deny that some Elizabethans may genuinely have thought that Elizabeth was sexually active. On the one hand, cases such as that of Anne Dowe – who had said that Elizabeth was pregnant by Leicester – were generated by circulating rumours which, if they cannot be traced back directly to court gossip because of lack of extant evidence, must surely have sometimes derived from there.[58] On the other, perceptions of the court drawn from popular chivalric literature and historical romances encouraged Elizabethans to believe that court life was dominated by illicit affairs. Levin's argument that they reveal deeper concerns about female monarchy, however, is difficult to sustain. Identifying the different perpetrators of such allegations demonstrates that accusations were part of ambassadorial reports which sought to establish the direction of the Elizabethan succession question, confessionally motivated polemical attacks by a Catholic elite, or manifestations of popular discontent. For the latter, it appears that gender may only have been significant in shaping the language of insult, not the motivation behind it. If gender did not lie at the heart of the debate on Elizabeth's queenship, what did?

RELIGIOUS AFFILIATION AND PERCEPTIONS OF ELIZABETH

As the previous chapter indicated, extant evidence suggests that politico-religious issues were key topics of debate in public discourse at both elite and popular level. It also appears that perceptions of Elizabeth, across the social spectrum, were articulated in confessional terms and motivated by religious affiliation. At elite level, conservatives like John Martiall, in his *Treatyse of the crosse* (1564), questioned why the queen ordered crucifixes to be destroyed in parish churches but allowed one to remain on her altar.[59] Later, Allen's *Admonition* questioned Elizabeth's political legitimacy because she was a bastard and her accession had not been sanctioned by the pope and attacked the nature of the English church. Lower down, Peter Hall of Haldon in Kent, said, 'The Quene is not worthie to beare rule or to be supreme hed of the Churche'. The following day, his words

---

58 SP12/13/21.I, fos. 56r–58r.
59 John Martiall, *A treatyse of the crosse* (Antwerp, 1564; STC 17496).

were repeated by John Hall, a husbandman of the same parish (possibly a relative), who added, according to one witness, 'Sayed he noothinge but this? He myghte lawfullye saye theise wordes'.[60] The royal supremacy was also questioned by Alexander Haulle, a Westmorland yeoman,[61] and Stephen Slater, who stated that 'the Quene was not Quene and supreme hedd of Ingland', though he 'praye[d] god she be'.[62] In 1582, William Symecotes, a gentleman from Louth in Lincolnshire, was indicted at Queen's Bench for alleging that, 'Campyon & hys fellowes dyed for theyr conscyenes & not for treason'.[63] In 1587, Anne Burnell claimed that she was the daughter of Philip II and had the arms of England on her back.[64] The following year, a husbandman from Goldhanger in Essex was reported as having said, 'that those mynisters were domme mynisters and dunces that wold praye for the quenes Majestie'.[65]

Conversely, puritans defined Elizabeth's queenship in godly and providential terms. Like many other works, including the prayers, sermons and ballads it spawned, Archbishop Grindal's *A form of prayer with thanksgiving* (1576), the first prayer book issued to be used for the celebration of Accession Day, likened Elizabeth to the reforming Old Testament kings, Jehosaphat, Josiah and Hezekiah.[66] Printed pamphlets and treatises, including Stephen Bateman's *The new arrival of the three Gracis* ([1580?]), Thomas Bentley's *The monvment of matrons* (1582), Thomas Blenerhasset's *A reuelation of the true Minerva* (1582)[67] and Anthony Munday's *Zelauto* (1580) – as well as popular ballads like William Birch's 'A song between the Queen's Majesty and England' and Thomas Deloney's on Catherine, dowager duchess of Suffolk[68] – cast Elizabeth into the same mould. For Bentley, Elizabeth was 'the mightie defender' of the church, who had been 'consecrated' by God 'to be the Queene, the

60 ASSI 35/1/6, m. 12.
61 Attorney General vs. Haulle, 19 Elizabeth I, KB27/1262 (2) (Crown side), m. 13.
62 ASSI 35/27/2, m. 47.
63 Attorney General vs. Symecotes, 26 Elizabeth I, KB27/1289 (Crown side), m. 59.
64 Examinations taken by Mr Dalton touching on Mrs Burnell, 8 Aug. 1587, Lansdowne 53/79, fos. 162r–163r; Mark Eccles, *Christopher Marlowe in London* (Cambridge, Mass., 1934), pp. 147–8, 153–4; Levin, *'Heart and stomach of a king'*, pp. 105–11.
65 ASSI 35/30/1, m. 64.
66 Clay (ed.), *Liturgies*, pp. 548–58; Sandys, *Sermons made by . . . Edwin, Archbishop of Yorke*, see especially pp. 42, 49, 52–77; Edward Hake, *A ioyfull continuance of the commemoration of the most prosperous and peaceable reigne of our gratious and deare soueraigne Lady Elizabeth* (London, [1578], *STC* 12605.5), especially sig. A5v; Walsham, 'A very Deborah?', pp. 143–68.
67 Thomas Blenerhasset, *A reuelation of the true Minerva* (London, 1582; *STC* 3132), sigs ¨r, A2v–B3v, C1r, D1r–D1v.
68 Freeman, 'Providence and prescription', pp. 27–8.

Mother, and the Nursse of my people in Israel.'[69] Provincial civic authorities, like those of Norwich in 1578, likened the queen to Deborah, Judith
and Hester in the entertainments they put on during the queen's progresses.[70] In his speech of welcome during the same entry, the minister of
the Dutch Church in Norwich described Elizabeth as 'the nourse of
Christ his church' who defended 'the miserable and dispersed members
of Christ'.[71]

These perceptions of Elizabeth and her queenship derived primarily
from the religious affiliation of the individuals who expressed them. Peter
Hall, John Hall, Alexander Haulle, Slater, Symecotes and Burnell all
appear to have been Catholics. Symecotes likened Campion to Cranmer,
Latimer and Ridley, three of the most important Marian martyrs: Campion and his fellow martyrs 'were ether honester men or as honest as
cranmer latymer & Rydley'.[72] Burnell was the wife of Edward Burnell, a
prominent Nottinghamshire Catholic gentleman, who was imprisoned in
1577, possibly for Catholicism, and may have been rearrested in 1586 in
the aftermath of the Babington Plot.[73] Conversely, John Hopkyns, vicar
of Nazeing in Essex, who, according to a prisoner in Hertford gaol, had
denied the royal supremacy, must have been a puritan. He had alleged
that, 'There is no supreme head under God but the minister.'[74]

Yet, as the changing nature of puritans' perceptions of Elizabeth
demonstrate, the role of religious affiliation in shaping people's view of
the queen was mediated by events and issues. Growing dissatisfaction at
Elizabeth's failure to reform the church fully caused some Elizabethans to
criticise the queen and her policies and to construct more negative images
of her. In 1560, Robert Taylor, a labourer from Chelmsford, publicly
criticised her religious practice, stating 'that Service that the quene *hadd*
and did vse in her Chappell was but palterye'.[75] Between 1562 and 1567
there were physical attacks on the candlesticks and crucifix on the altar in
the Chapel Royal.[76] Thomas Freeman has shown convincingly how John
Foxe deliberately changed his portrayal in the second edition of the 'Book

69 Thomas Bentley, *The monvment of matrons* (London, 1582; *STC* 1892), passim but especially
　A3r–A3v and p. 307. See also pp. 307–15, 322–4.
70 Bernard Garter, *The ioyfvll receyuing of the Queenes most excellent Maiestie into hir Highnesse Citie
　of Norwich* (London, [1578]; *STC* 11627), sigs. C1v–C2r, C2v.
71 Ibid., sigs. D1r–D1v.
72 KB27/1289 (Crown side), m. 59.
73 *APC*, X, pp. 58–9, 245; XI, pp. 102–3; Eccles, *Christopher Marlowe*, pp. 154.
74 Emmison, *Elizabethan life: disorder*, p. 55.
75 ASSI 35/3/2, m. 10.
76 Aston, *King's bedpost*, pp. 106–7, 97–105.

of martyrs' (1570). The positive picture of her as a providential monarch was replaced by a more critical one, highlighting how she had failed to live up to this standard.[77] It was copied by later preachers and writers, including Edward Dering in his sermon preached before Elizabeth at an unknown Chapel Royal in February 1569 and John Prime's Accession Day sermon in 1588.[78]

It is also possible that some of the first initiatives to mark Elizabeth's accession were conceived as admonitory, rather than celebratory, exercises in response to the failure of church reform.[79] One of the first two parishes to mark Accession Day, in 1564, was St Peter Westcheap, London. There are clear signs that the parish was a godly one, or had a strong godly element within it. Little is known about its rector, Richard Smith (d. 1571), though as a Marian appointment who may have suffered a temporary suspension in 1561, he may have been a conservative.[80] But the curacy was held from at least 1561 (until at least 1569) by William Porrege.[81] A former Marian exile (based in Calais), known to William Bradford, Thomas Cole and John Foxe, he had a long history of nonconformity as well as a minor role in the 'Book of martyrs'.[82] The former culminated in his refusal to wear the surplice in the 1560s, his signing of a petition to the Ecclesiastical Commissioners in March 1565 for exemption from wearing vestments and his temporary suspension, by Parker, the following year at the height of the Vestiarian Controversy.[83] The parish church also

77 Freeman, '"As true a subiect being prisoner"', pp. 104–16; Freeman, 'Providence and prescription', pp. 27–55.
78 McCullough, *Sermons at court*, pp. 36–7; Freeman, 'Providence and prescription', pp. 28, 44–5.
79 This is a summary of arguments laid out in more detail regarding the origins and development of Accession Day celebrations in Natalie Mears, 'Good Queen Bess?: the origins and evolution of the Accession Day celebrations of Elizabeth I' (in preparation).
80 *Novum repertorium ecclesiasticum parochiale Londinense*, compiled G. Hennessy (London, 1898), p. 437 ; GL MS 9537/2, fo. 33v.
81 *Novum repertorium*, compiled Hennessy, p. 438; H. G. Owen, 'The London parish clergy in the reign of Elizabeth I' (Ph.D. thesis, London, 1957), p. 620.
82 Owen, 'London parish clergy', p. 475; Christina Garrett, *The Marian exiles, 1553–1559* (Cambridge, 1938), 258; John Foxe, *Actes and monuments of these later and perilous dayes* (London, 1563; *STC* 11222), pp. 1477–8; John Bradford to Joyce Hales, 8 Aug. [n.y.], Emmanuel College Library, Cambridge (ECL), MS 260, fos. 79r–81v at 79r, 81v; Maidstone PRC 17/40, fo. 225r; John Foxe, *The first (second) volume of the ecclesiastical history containing the actes and monuments* (London, 1570; *STC* 11223), 2286–7. I would like to thank Thomas Freeman for the references to Bradford and Cole.
83 Churchwardens' accounts suggest that he did not wear the surplice throughout his tenure as curate at St Peter Westcheap. They record (irregular) payments for the washing of the church linen (including the surplice) in the late 1550s, but these decline or cease at the start of the 1560s when Porrege was appointed: Owen, 'London parish clergy', pp. 475, 481–2, 481 (fn. 6), 489 (fn. 1); Guildhall MS 645/1, fos. 52v, 57v, 61r, 64v; Usher, 'Deanery of Bocking', pp. 444–5.

exhibited godly inclinations: it was allegedly one of the first to dispose of its organs and, in 1573, got rid of its stone font by the church door, replacing it with a tin basin located close to the pulpit, an increasing hallmark of a Reformed church in the 1570s.[84]

In the context of events in London in the 1560s, and the actions of those in Porrege's circle, the godly inclinations of both Porrege and his parish suggest that the decision to mark Accession Day in 1564 may have been to remind Elizabeth of the hopes for church reform her accession had promised and of her failure to fulfil them. It coincided with the escalation of the Vestiarian Controversy, from Lawrence Humphrey's and Thomas Sampson's first public repudiation of vestments in 1563, with which Porrege was intimately involved. It spoke of Elizabeth in the same 'language' as some of Porrege's friends used at the same time, notably Foxe's recharacterisation of the queen in the second edition of the 'Book of martyrs', prepared in these years. It also invoked well-established traditions of criticising through praise: Alexander Nowell, dean of St Paul's and one of Elizabeth's favourite preachers, said that 'he had no other way to instruct the queen what she should be, but by commending her.'[85] Significantly, apart from an isolated incidence in 1570, which may have been prompted a more positive evaluation of the queen in the aftermath of the Northern Rising, the parish did not mark the accession between 1568 and 1576, when Grindal's appointment as archbishop may have revived hopes of reform.

Moreover, it is difficult to attribute St Peter Westcheap's actions to other factors. The choice of 1564 as the first time to mark the accession suggests that the parish's initiative was neither stimulated by Elizabeth's actual accession in 1558 nor by her recovery from the near-fatal attack of smallpox in 1563. There is no evidence to suggest that initiatives to mark Accession Day, and then its curtailment in 1567, merely reflected changes in record-keeping or in parish organisation. The accounting year at St Peter Westcheap operated consistently from Michaelmas to Michaelmas; there are no gaps in extant accounts or hiatuses in practice. The rotation of churchwardens was also consistent and there is no obvious sign that celebrations were initiated or discontinued by certain wardens in office.

Equally, if puritan calls for further reform shaped their perceptions of Elizabeth, then their campaign angered some conformists and influenced

84 Owen, 'London parish clergy', pp. 475–8, 526–7; G.W.O. Addleshaw and F. Etchells, *The architectural setting of Anglican worship* (London, 1948), pp. 64–5.
85 Ralph Churton, *The life of Alexander Nowell* (Oxford, 1809), p. 92, quoted in McCullough, *Sermons at court*, p. 84.

their own responses to Elizabeth's queenship. In 1574, Thomas Bedell of Writtle, Essex, reacted angrily to attempts to serve a subpoena on Michael Mayshort (or Mayshott), the parish vicar. The precise allegations against Mayshort are unclear but it is possible that he was being prosecuted for riotous assembly on 31 March 1574 (with eight other men) and the destruction of the Jesus Chapel, the Cope Chapel and a pulpit. As the subpoena was delivered, Bedell exclaimed, 'What, is the Queen become a papist now?'[86] Bedell appeared to be angered that Mayshort's actions were deemed to be criminal, suggesting he was a Protestant and had some sympathy for the reformers. Whether he spoke in jest or was genuine, his exclamation implied annoyance at Elizabeth's moderation and apparent toleration of things like the Jesus Chapel. However, subsequently questioned at the assizes for his 'accusation' against the queen, Bedell that revealed his sympathy with the reformers only went so far. His 'accusation' against the queen was taken too seriously, perhaps, by the justices who appear to have accused Bedell himself of being Catholic. He retorted, 'They are not papists who say that the Queen is a papist, but rather divers others who are called Puritans', citing Thomas Cartwright's *Second admonition to parliament* (1572), though he could not find the exact reference he wished.[87] The logic of his answer is contorted: it appears that Bedell was attempting to situate himself between the puritans on the one hand and the conservatives on the other. His perception of Elizabeth was shaped by his own religious views and his response to the puritans' campaign, even if the former appear to have been misconstrued by the justices.

Though religious affiliation was an important factor shaping participation in public discourse, it was not the sole one. It is clear from indictments that some allegations drew on personal and economic hardships that accusers had experienced. Slater's criticisms of Elizabeth were also influenced by the fact that, 'he was pressed to serve as a souldyer in Flanders by comyssyon and had not those thinges which he was promysed'. '[Y]f her majestie were Quene', he concluded, 'she had vylleynes vnder her'.[88] Ralph Watson, a sawyer from Dover, who was indicted in 1584 for alleging that the Scots were going to invade England, had prefaced his comments with the assertion that, 'this is a very evill land to lyve in except yt be for a man that hath a very good Occupacion I wold

86 Emmison, *Elizabethan life: disorder*, pp. 44–5.
87 Ibid., p. 45.
88 ASSI 35/27/2, m. 47.

it were warre, I know a great many Richemen in the land I wold haue some of ther mony yf yt were so come to passe'.[89]

But Elizabethans also measured their queen against long-established notions of good governance. Personal grievances were symptomatic of her failure to live up to standards. In attacking Elizabeth's queenship, Slater made an explicit contrast between the queen and Philip II, 'kinge phillipp was a father to Ingland and did better loue an Inglyshe man then the Quenes majesties did, *for that he wolde gev them mette drynk and clothe*'. His choice of Philip as a foil may partly may have owed something to Philip's Catholicism – shared by Slater – or his gender. But equally, it may have been because, through his leadership at St Quentin and Calais, Philip was Elizabeth's predecessor as England's military leader and thus provided the readiest comparison. Unfortunately, not knowing Slater's age or previous military experience, we cannot ascertain whether this comparison was one born from experience. But, clearly, for Slater it was less that he had been personally hit by a lack of supplies when serving in the Netherlands – though this evidently contributed to his sense of grievance – than that a failure to provide basic supplies suggested a disregard for subjects and the common weal.[90] These concerns were voiced in other contexts too. When Parker ordered the bishops to organise collections in their parishes to pay for the repairs to St Paul's in 1561 there was, 'Grete murmoring of the people that they should carrie or sell their thinges in such sorte, considering yt was not the Quenes owne worcke . . . many saied the Quene could graunt no such commissions.'[91] In 1587, Richard Daye of Wendon alleged that, 'the Queene did Powle [i.e. plunder for tax] the cuntry', implying that Elizabeth disregarded the common wealth and failed either to 'live off her own' or tax her subjects fairly.[92]

PERCEPTIONS OF ELIZABETH IN THE 1580s

Levin has argued that, in the 1580s, there was a significant increase in the numbers of cases of sexual slander, seditious and slanderous words against Elizabeth as well as reports that Edward VI was still alive and instances of pretenders. She has suggested that these reflected growing anxiety and

89 ASSI 35/26/5, m. 17.
90 ASSI 35/27/2, m. 47.
91 Additional 48023, fo. 355r–355v.
92 ASSI 35/29/2, m. 36.

unease at the queen's failure to fulfil gender expectations by marrying and settling the succession.[93] Levin has also pointed to the growing interest in cases of monstrous births at this time, arguing that interest in the physical deformities was either a response to female monarchy (perceived as 'unnatural and frightening') or revealed beliefs that any progeny from a regnant queen would be monstrous in shape.[94] However, there is little evidence to show that there was a significant increase in the types of cases Levin cites in the 1580s, especially as the numbers of cases throughout the reign (particularly of pretenders) are too small for meaningful statistics to be calculated. The majority of printed reports of monstrous births date from the 1560s, not the 1580s. Moreover, there is a scholarly consensus, underpinned by contemporary evidence, that monstrous births were interpreted as divine warnings about general moral or religious behaviour and not as comments on female monarchy.[95]

Though Levin's specific points cannot be sustained, her broader implication that perceptions of Elizabeth in the 1580s were distinctive is worth examination. There does seem to have been a greater sensitivity to comments and actions that could be construed, or more likely, misconstrued, as seditious and treasonable from 1580. For example, in 1580, William Shepherd, rector of Heydon, on the Cambridgeshire/Essex border, was indicted for encouraging his parishioners to become 'true Jesuytts' during his New Year's Day sermon. According to his own testimony, Shepherd had drawn an analogy between 'Christiani a christe' and 'Jesuite a Jesu', exhorting his parishioners to have Christ in their hearts and be true to his teachings: 'to be true christians, true Jesuytts'.[96] It was mistimed, seized upon by a small group of forward Protestants in the parish, led by John Sherif, John Reade and William Dixon, who reported Shepherd to the privy council for commending the Jesuits themselves. Shepherd was found guilty, forced to retract his statement in public and pay the costs not only of the investigation, but for a replacement preacher – the radical, John Ward of Haverhill – and was

---

93 Levin, *'Heart and stomach of a king'*, passim but especially pp. 100, 119.
94 Ibid., p. 85.
95 Katharine Park and Lorraine J. Daston, 'Unnatural conceptions: the study of monsters in France and England', *Past & Present*, 92 (1981), pp. 20–54; David Cressy, *Travesties and transgressions in Tudor and Stuart England* (Oxford, 2000), ch. 2.
96 Mark Byford, 'The price of protestantism: assessing the impact of religious change on Elizabethan Essex: the cases of Heydon and Colchester, 1558–1594' (D.Phil. thesis, Oxford, 1988), pp. 55–8, 440–1. I would like to thank Anthony Milton for this reference. See also, Emmison, *Elizabethan life: disorder*, pp. 48–9.

barred from preaching until he resigned his living a few years later. Events in Heydon were largely the product of personal rivalries – Shepherd called Sherif, Reade and Dixon his 'ill-willers' and there is evidence to suggest that they opposed Shepherd's style of ministry – but they demonstrated how Elizabethans could exploit successfully the regime's sensitivity to comments of political or religious disaffection for their own ends.[97] A more direct instance of the regime misconstruing comments, or acting in a heavy-handed manner, came in 1585 when George Preble, John Newman and Henry Nelson were indicted at the Kent assizes for discussing whether they would serve in the watch for money. Newman had said that he would serve in anyone's stead if he were paid; Preble said he would not serve for the wages. But neither refused to serve and Nelson praised Elizabeth, 'God save the Queenes Majestie we doe now live a peaceable and quiet Lyfe, and sleepe quietlie in our beddes: And if theare shoulde come a change, how shoulde wee then doe?'[98]

Greater sensitivity to the substance of public discourse, particularly over issues of confessional identity and political loyalty, points to fundamental conflicts between the regime and its subjects, at odds with our current understanding of the reign: that the polemical debate between the regime and Catholics in the 1580s was primarily an international one. The case brought against William Symecotes of Lincolnshire in 1582 shows that ordinary Elizabethans participated in their own way in the polemical debate precipitated by Campion's execution and that the regime retaliated. Symecotes was prosecuted at Queen's Bench for alleging that, 'Campyon & hys fellowes dyed for theyr conscyenes & not for treason'.[99] He therefore rejected the regime's claims, laid out in popular texts like *A breefe aunswer*, that Campion was a traitor and instead endorsed the image conveyed by works like Robert Persons's *A brief discours contayning certayne reasons why catholiques refuse to goe to church* (1580) and *A briefe censure upon two bookes written in answere to M. Edmunde Campions offer*

---

97 Byford, 'The price of protestantism', pp. 58–73. Byford argues that Shepherd, a former Augustinian friar and Henrician appointment (he was instituted to Heydon in 1541), was not a religious conservative, though he did seek to emphasise the continuities between pre-reformed and reformed religion. Records demonstrate that Heydon was quick to conform to Edwardian and Elizabethan legislation and that Shepherd himself campaigned against markets and fairs being held on holy days because they distracted people from church. Byford also suggests that Shepherd was able to convert at least a fifth of the parish to Protestantism – if not of the radical kind of Sherif and others. However, he also shows that Shepherd was the target of sustained attack by forward Protestants both before and after 1581. Ibid., pp. 15–55, 67–73.
98 ASSI 35/27/6, m. 27.
99 KB27/1289 (Crown side), m. 59.

of disputation (1581), that the Jesuit missions were pastoral.[100] Indeed, it may support Peter Lake's and Michael Questier's recent arguments that Catholic propaganda was both more sophisticated and more effective than much puritan literature of the same time. Certainly, Symecotes was convinced.[101] Moreover, Symecotes cannot be regarded as an isolated case. Though we have no information about how and why his case reached Queen's Bench, his statements must have been reported to the authorities by a citizen of Gatton, where the words were spoken. This suggests that the regime's actions against Jesuits and seminary priests were matters of debate among Elizabethans, as well as continental Catholics. Though Lincolnshire was religiously conservative, there was sufficient dispute over Campion's execution (or willingness to attack Symecotes) for someone to report him.[102]

However, the decade was also characterised by a strong sense of Catholic conspiracy and rumours of a Spanish invasion, often linked to expressions of support, were a common theme of public debate. As noted in chapter 6, both David Brown in 1581 and William Medcalfe in 1586 were indicted for alleging that the earl of Westmorland was going to invade the realm with Philip II's support.[103] Similarly, Thomas Davye, a Sussex labourer, alleged in 1583, 'A great manye haue gone out of this realme & resisted the Crowne and so would I, yf I could haue free passage for a time'.[104] There was also an isolated rumour of an invasion from Scotland, which was the main entry-point into England by land and was, at the beginning of Elizabeth's reign, commonly feared as the likeliest base from which a Catholic invasion would be launched.[105] In 1584, Ralph Watson was indicted for alleging that there was a town between England and Scotland with a force of 200 horse and 400 foot. '[H]ad the Scottes

100 Robert Persons, *Brief discours . . . why catholiques refuse to goe to church; A briefe censure upon two bookes written in answere to M. Edmunde Campions offer of disputation* (Douai [i.e. Stonor Park], 1581; *STC* 19393), Lake and Questier, 'Puritans, papists, and the "public sphere"', pp. 600–12; William Allen, *A briefe historie of the glorious martyrdom of XII reuerend priests* ([Rheims], 1582; *STC* 369.5).
101 Lake and Questier, 'Puritans, papists, and the "public sphere"', pp. 608–12 and passim; McCoog, SJ, *Society of Jesus*, pp. 146–8; McCoog, SJ, '"Playing the champion"', pp. 119–39.
102 Bishop Aylmer's visitation records for 1565 indicate that parishes were relatively slow to comply with the new settlement and that pockets of genuine Protestant belief, such as at Grantham, were few and far between. See Gerald A. J. Hodgett, *Tudor Lincolnshire* (*History of Lincolnshire*, ed. Joan Thirsk, vol. 6; Lincoln, 1975), pp. 169–85; Eamon Duffy, *The stripping of the altars: traditional religion in England, 1400–1580* (New Haven and London, 1992), pp. 572–7.
103 ASSI 35/23/1, m. 36; ASSI 35/28/1, m. 32.
104 ASSI 35/25/7, m. 29.
105 Dawson, 'William Cecil and the British dimension', pp. 196–216.

gotten the Towne they wold overcome the whole Realme for that is the key from thenc into England', he asserted.[106]

These rumours may have been drawn from those circulating at elite level in the late 1570s and early 1580s.[107] But their significance lay in their characterisation of the invasion as revenge either for the Northern Rising or the execution of the fourth duke of Norfolk.[108] Brown talked of the invasion as a means by which Westmorland could reassert his claims to a lost patrimony; Medcalfe that the earl sought 'to be revenged of the deathe & blud of the late duke of Norfolk'.[109] This link appears to have reflected a number of things. At its simplest, it invoked ideas of male (aristocratic) honour and the language of historical and chivalric romance. Both Brown and Medcalfe talked of the reclaiming of patrimonies and revenge of aristocratic blood. More importantly, it reflected the unpopularity of Norfolk's execution, confessional allegiance and the existence of confessional conflict. There were cases in which people were indicted for criticising the duke's execution: Edward Hardye of Wartling, Sussex, was prosecuted for alleging that the 'Duke of Norfolke was put to deathe onely because he had the good will of the people'.[110] Moreover, Medcalfe's identification of Philip as a supporter of Westmorland may have been confessionally driven. Not only did he state that, as a result of the invasion, 'this world wilbe in better case shortlye', but he appears to have deliberately conceived Westmorland's and Elizabeth's respective allies in confessional terms: 'the kinge of denmarke hath ayded the Quene with tenne thowsand men, which power the kinge of Spaine hathe mett with all, & distroyed & overthrowne'.[111] Denmark was not an obvious ally for Medcalfe to name. It was one of the few Protestant powers in Western Europe but it was neither a leading power nor a prominent English ally,

---

106 ASSI 35/26/5, m. 17.
107 For example, rumours circulated in spring of 1580 of a Catholic league planning a naval invasion. Its destination was variously reported as the Low Countries (Cobham to Elizabeth, 15 June 1580, SP78/4a/90) or Portugal (Cobham to Sussex, 1 Mar.? 1580, SP78/4a/40 (30), fo. 16r–16v), but, by March, there was a consensus that Ireland would be the target, a key entry point to England: [Walsingham?] to Cobham, 2 Feb. 1580, SP78/4a/12; Thomas Cotton to Leicester, 21 Feb. 1580, Cotton Galba C.VII, fo. 25v; same to same, 28 Feb. 1580, Cotton Galba C.VII, fo. 33v; Advertisements from Spain, 2 June 1580, SP94/1/49, fo. 140r; Spanish advertisements, 23 June 1580, SP94/1/51, fo. 145r). There were also reports that the league's destination was England itself (Cobham to [Walsingham], 11 Feb. 1580, SP78/4a/15; R. Lloyd to [Walsingham], 31 May 1580, SP78/4a/76.
108 ASSI 35/28/1, m. 32.
109 Ibid.
110 ASSI 35/25/7, m. 6A.
111 ASSI 35/28/1, m. 32.

though, in the spring of 1585, Elizabeth had sent an agent to encourage Frederick II to assist Henry of Navarre.[112]

The geographical location of these cases is also significant. They all occurred in the Home Counties, neighbouring Howard's heartland of East Anglia but distant from the physical theatre in which the drama of the Northern Rising had been played out. Their sympathies with Westmorland and Norfolk, therefore, were unlikely to have been based on feudal ties, regional identities or, indeed, direct experience of the Rising itself. Yet, what we know of how the history of the Northern Rising was written and circulated during, and in the immediate aftermath of, the rebellion suggests that a confessional dimension to their statements may have been present. As Carol Weiner has shown, the history of the Rising was quickly rewritten to define it as a Catholic conspiracy; a message that was disseminated in popular broadsides and tracts, such as *A discription of Nortons falcehod of York shyre, An answere to the proclamation of the rebels of the North, A ballat intituled Northomberland newes*, as well as ones printed in the 1580s by the likes of Anthony Munday.[113] The proposed marriage between Norfolk and Mary Stuart was presented to a popular audience in similar terms. The propagandist *A discourse touching the pretended match betwene the duke of Norfolke and the Queene of Scottes* (1569) suggested the match was an ambitious plan by Mary to gain the English crown and offered little or no security for Elizabeth or (Protestant) England.[114] Crucially, we know that these kinds of texts circulated in south-east England: we do not have any extant inventories or financial accounts for booksellers in Sussex and Essex, but we know that copies of ballads on the Rising were supplied to Robert Scott in Norwich.[115]

Perceptions of Elizabeth's queenship, and the substance of public debate, in the 1580s were not, therefore, preoccupied with questions of female monarchy and the succession as defined by Levin. Rather, there is much evidence to suggest that polemical debate between Protestants and Catholics, as a result of the regime's harsher policies towards Jesuits, seminary priests, recusants and Catholics, infused domestic debate as well as that on the international stage. However, though this gave the decade a distinctive quality, the recurrence of rumours about an invasion led by Westmorland and sponsored by Spain, rooted the period in the previous

112 MacCaffrey, *Making of policy*, pp. 309–10.
113 Carol Z. Wiener, 'The beleaguered isle: a study of Elizabethan and early Jacobean anti-catholicism', *Past & Present*, 51 (1971), pp. 27–62.
114 Norton, *A discourse touching the pretended match* (1569).
115 Plomer, 'Elizabethan book sales', pp. 321–2.

two decades in which fears of Catholic conspiracy had been rife and had consciously shaped perceptions of key events, like the Northern Rising and the Norfolk marriage plan. Indeed, though we cannot trace precisely the impact of works like *A discourse touching the pretended match* or the many ballads on the Rising, the close parallels between the images of events they presented and the comments made by Brown, Medcalfe and others suggest that the regime's fears during the 1560s had, by the 1580s, become self-fulfilling.

PERCEPTIONS OF ELIZABETH IN WALES AND IRELAND

There was a similarity in the ways in which Elizabeth's queenship was defined and debated in England and Ireland. In England, Elizabeth was called a 'whore'; in Ireland, she was a *cailleach* (old hag) and *phiseogach* (sorceress). The royal supremacy was challenged in England; pages containing references to her royal titles were torn out of grammar books in the diocese of Cork and Ross. Essex ministers may have refused to pray for the queen in 1588; thanksgiving ceremonies after the defeat of the Armada were boycotted in Dublin and counties across Ireland.[116] Yet, there are also signs that this similarity may have been superficial. It appears that both news circulating in Ireland, and some of the inhabitants' concerns, were very different from those in England. Many allegations that Elizabeth was a whore emanating from England arose within specific contexts: ambassadorial reports, Catholic polemic or generalised terms of abuse. Negative markings of Accession Day, like those at St Peter Westcheap in the 1560s, were rare and, by 1588, the festivities in England were both positive and, as will be seen, widespread.[117] To what extent was public debate of Elizabeth's queenship in Wales and Ireland focused on the same issues as in England and driven by the same factors?

It is difficult to ascertain the extent to which Wales shared the concerns that dominated English public discourse. There are extant cases of verbal criticisms of the religious settlement and the disruption of church services: in 1569, the bishop of Bangor was accused of disrupting a service, possibly of ordination, in Dwygevilchi, Caernarfonshire.[118] There were also disputes over clerical livings, including in Llanbederocke and Trevirw, in

---

116 SP12/178/27, fos. 52r–53r; Adam Loftus, archbishop of Dublin, to Burghley, 22 Sept. 1590, SP63/154/37, fo. 130r.
117 See above, pp. 232–3.
118 Indictment against Nicholas Robinson, bishop of Bangor, 13 Nov. 1569, CRO, XQS/1569/37.

Caernarfonshire.[119] But, cases in which the regime was explicitly criticised seem to have been rare. In the mid-1580s, Lewis Gunter of Gilston, Brecnoc, alleged that bishop of St David's, Marmaduke Middleton, had stated publicly that Burghley, Leicester and Walsingham had pocketed £17,000 authorised by warrant to be sent to Ireland. He was also supposed to have called the Lord Chamberlain 'an harebrained foole'.[120]

Similarly, it is difficult to ascertain the motives behind their actions and statements as the evidence is limited and opaque. The allegations against Middleton seem to have been part of a general attack on the bishop by Gunter: he also accused him of unlawful imprisonment, taking bonds for good behaviour in his own name, bribery, collusion in adultery and prostitution and the unlawful sequestration of livings.[121] Gunter also accused Meredith Morgan, archdeacon of Carmarthen, and two of the bishop's officials of abusing their authority and was himself the subject of a counter-claim of slander and lewd behaviour lodged by Middleton.[122] Disputes over clerical livings may have been more to do with the legality of the rivals' claims and the competition for control over tithes than any confessional differences between the ministers. These were certainly the terms in which the bills and answers were conceived and, though some cases, like that at Llanbederocke, resulted in physical scuffles in church in which prayer books were torn from ministers' hands, there is no indication in the court records that it was the prayer book itself that was the point of dispute.[123]

Evidence for Ireland is clearer. There were specific attacks on Elizabeth's queenship. In 1575, Hubert Mac Thomas reported that it was 'common talke' for his master, Kedagh McCormac O'Conor, and his company to refer to Elizabeth as 'the Callioghe of Englande'.[124] In a report of the

---

119 For Llanbederocke see Robynson vs. Roberts, Owen, 27 Elizabeth I, STAC5/R9/26; Roberts vs. Robinson, ap David, 27 Elizabeth I, STAC5/R9/27; Roberts vs. David ap Richard ap Hugh and others, 27 Elizabeth I, STAC5/R24/7; Robinson vs. Roberts, Lloid and others, 27 Elizabeth I, STAC5/R38/14 [membranes 2 and 3 are badly damaged]; Enformacions presented to the queens maiesties Justices of peace . . . by Humffrey Robinsone, 1585, CRO, XQS/1585/unnumbered. For Trevirw, see The Queenes maiesties counsail in the marches of Wales, n.d. [1560], CRO, X/QS/2/4/36–37. See also numbers 38–44b.

120 Gunter vs. St David's, 24 Elizabeth I [but probably at least 27 Elizabeth I], STAC5/G15/23. The uncertainty of the date of this case makes it difficult to identify which Lord Chamberlain Middleton thought was a 'hare-brained fool': Sussex held the post until his death in 1583; he was replaced by Henry Carey, Lord Hunsdon.

121 STAC5/G15/23.

122 Gunter vs. Morgan, 33 Elizabeth I, STAC5/G2/8; St David's vs. Gunter, Heughs, Price, 33 Elizabeth, STAC5/S3/15.

123 For example, STAC5/R9/26, m. 1; STAC5/R9/27, m. 2.

124 The declaration of Hubert Mac Thomas, 6 July 1575, SP63/52/48.XII, fo. 124r.

actions of Sir Richard Bingham, president of Connaught, dating to c.1586, it was alleged that the Burkes 'proceeded against her Maiestie in most odious & vndutifull speeches saying what haue wee to doe with that Caliaghe, howe unwise are we being so mightie a nation, to haue bene so longe subiecte to a woman'.[125] In November or December 1586,[126] Brian O'Rourke was alleged to have obtained a 'pickture of a woman mad of wood with a pin in the belly of it'.[127] He 'wroate upon the breast thearof Queene Elizabeth', called it 'the old Calliath' and 'rayled at it with most spitefull wordes and all his gallowglasse stroake it inall the partes with their weapons' before he 'drewe yt at a garrans [i.e. a horse's] tayll in derision of her maiesties'.[128] John Ball reported a similar incident in O'Rourke's territory dating to the same year: 'beinge . . . at mc glannans towne standinge vpon a grene I sawe the pictar of a woman carved in a blocke standinge vpon whelles of small tymber'. Asking the local inhabit-ants what it was, he was told 'it was made for [a] callyaghe . . . on[e] that denyed a carpenter of mylke.' The under-sheriff later informed him that the 'on[e] that denyed a carpenter myllke' signified the queen.[129] Towards the end of Elizabeth's reign, during raids around Kilgighy and Gortende in Ossory, 'was founde the queens picture behinde the doore, and the kinge of Spayne at the vpper ende of the table'.[130] In 1596, the bishop of Cork and Ross discovered 'her Maiesties stile & title torne out of all the grammars to the number of lxxiiii in one schole' in his diocese. On a search of all other schools, he found the same situation, even in books that 'came new from the merchants shopes'. Questioning two teachers about this, both denied the queen's legitimacy.[131]

As was noted in chapter 6, Elizabeth's claim to the Irish crown was explicitly challenged in bardic poems like Mac an Bhaird's 'Cia re bhfuil

---

125 A letter from a gentleman to his friend, [dated 1585, but probably 1586 or later], LPL, Carew MS 632, p. 15v.

126 The date of this event is unclear: Bingham suggests it was c. November–December 1586, Reasons inducing me to think that I could not acquaint Sir John Perrot, with the treason of the picture, 21 July 1591, SP63/159/18, fo. 24r–24v.

127 The 'pickture' was variously described as either being stolen from Bingham's house or as having been found in a church: George Castell to [your honour], after 30 June 1587, SP63/148/52, fo. 168r; Lord Deputy Fitzwilliam to Burghley, 9 Apr. 1589, PRO, SP63/143/12, fo. 23r.

128 Mr John Bingham's declaration, [1590?], SP63/159/13, fo. 17r; Notes of the charges against O'Rourke, c.Nov. 1591, SP63/161/24, fo. 44r. See also The coppie of William Taffe's declaration, 20 July 1591, SP63/159/17, fo. 23r; John Bingham to Burghley, 8 Aug. 1591, SP63/159/30, fo. 53r–53v; Privy council to Richard Bingham, 13 June 1591, SP63/160/54.I, fo. 119r: Summarie of the defects as Sir Richard Bingham was to be delt within, 13 June 1591, SP63/160/54.II, fos. 119v–120r; Lord Deputy to Burghley, 31 Oct. 1591, SP63/160/56, fo. 122r.

129 Mr John Ball's declaration, [c.1590], SP63/151/96, fo. 259r.

130 The jorney into the Queenes County, 11 Aug. 1600, LPL, Carew MS 601, p. 196v.

131 William Lyon, bishop of Cork and Ross, to Lord Hunsdon, 6 July 1596, SP63/191/8.I, fo. 47r.

Éiri ac anmhuin?', 'Brath lendáin ac Leic Lughaidh' and ''Leath re Fódla fuil Uidhir', and Flann Eoghan Mac Craith's 'Í N-ainm a áirdmic' (c.1590). Mac an Bhaird's apparently deliberate use the archaic 'rí' to denote 'king' may have been to suggest that Ireland lacked a legitimate monarch; in 'Cia re bhfuil Éiri ac anmhuin?' he stated clearly that Ireland had had no king since Donnchadh in 1035.[132] In 'Í N-ainm a áirdmic' (c.1590), Mac Craith did not refer to Elizabeth as queen of Ireland.[133]

As in England, there was a distinct confessional edge to public discourse and actions. O'Rourke's calling Elizabeth a *cailleach* was, at least in part, motivated by religion: he was alleged to have said Elizabeth was 'the mother of all herysie' and, according to Bingham, 'had kept the tyme of Christmas according vnto the popes computacion and to this daie dothe observe all the feasts as they do, withal Idolatryous ceremonie'.[134] The Burkes' antipathy to Elizabeth's queenship derived not from attitudes towards gender and female monarchy but partly to confessionalisation. The author of the account stated the Burkes had argued that, 'The pope and the king of Spayne shal haue the rule of vs, and none other'.[135] The privileging of Philip II's portrait, over that of Elizabeth, in the unidentified house in Ossory, probably articulated similar confessional and political allegiances. Similarly, boycotts of thanksgiving celebrations after the Armada in 1588 suggested antipathy to the English victory and an unwillingness to identify with the confessional message that it promulgated: that England was the divinely chosen nation, Protestantism was the true faith and Elizabeth was its champion. This was certainly how Adam Loftus, the archbishop of Dublin, perceived it. '[V]erie fewe or none almost resorted' to the principal churches in Dublin and other counties, 'notwithstanding the sheriffs of ech county did ther duties with all diligence'. He singled out Dublin lawyers for particular approbation, 'the lawyers in therne time tooke occasion to leaue the towne . . . so bewraying in them selves besides their corruption in religion'.[136]

But there was also a more deep-seated, political antipathy. The Burkes not only articulated confessional hostility to English rule, but nationalistic hostility too. They accounted Ireland to be too 'mightie a nation' to be subject to English rule.[137] For Loftus, the lawyers' actions in 1588 not only

132 Caball, *Poets and politics*, pp. 27–9, 30–1.
133 Mac Erlean (ed.), *Duanaire Dáibid uí bruadair*, pp. 64–73.
134 Sir Richard Bingham to Burghley, 6 Apr. 1589, SP63/143/5, fo. 8r–8v.
135 LPL, Carew MS 632, p. 15v.
136 SP63/154/37, fo. 130r.
137 LPL, Carew MS 632, p. 15v.

revealed 'their corruption in religion', but their 'great want of duty and loyaltie' and was also occasion for the English 'to conceive doubtfull opinion of them.'[138] Mac an Bhaird's and Flann Eoghan Mac Craith's poems challenged Elizabeth's political legitimacy, subtly but clearly. The treatment meted out to the picture or statue of Elizabeth in M'Glannagh's town – comparing the queen to an old hag who denied a workman milk – cannot just be seen as an comment on Elizabeth's failure to govern for the benefit of the common wealth. The events occurred in O'Rourke's country and appear to have been duplicated by O'Rourke himself. O'Rourke was disaffected with the Elizabethan regime; he had assisted survivors of the Armada and, in 1589, broke into revolt against Bingham's and Sir John Perrott's harsh administration. The revolt was only quashed when O'Rourke fled to Scotland; he was immediately captured and was hanged at Tyburn in 1591.[139]

Indeed, by refusing to identify Ireland with the rest of Elizabeth's dominions and rejecting Tudor rule and its legitimacy, these responses to Elizabeth's queenship reinforce, and substantiate, the political readings of bardic poetry by Bradshaw and Caball who have both shown that poetry was a vehicle for contesting English rule.[140] Particularly important is Tadhg Dall Ó hUiginn's poem dedicated to O'Rourke himself, 'D'fhior chogaidh comhailtear síothcháin'. Constructed explicitly as a poem of counsel, it attacked the English and English governance for occupying Ireland, destroying the nobility and bringing war and disorder to the island. It exhorted O'Rourke to become the leader of the *Gaoidhil* (the Gaelic Irish), exploiting the support he could gain from his wider kin (especially the O'Donnells) to mount a strong military defence, including, Tadgh Dall advised, a direct attack on Dublin to undermine English administration.[141] Written c.1588, 'D'fhior chogaidh comhailtear síothcháin' captures the tone of O'Rourke's actions during the Armada and his alleged attack on Elizabeth via the statue. It articulates a rejection of English rule, a denial of Elizabeth's legitimacy and, consequently, a distinct nationalist turn to Irish public discourse.

Thus, though evidence for Wales is limited, public debate in Ireland did demonstrate both similarities and significant differences to that in

---

138 SP63/154/37, fo. 130r.
139 MacCaffrey, *War and politics*, pp. 358–61; Stephen G. Ellis, *Ireland in the age of the Tudors, 1447–1603: English expansion and the end of Gaelic rule* (Harlow, 1998), pp. 334–5.
140 See ch. 6 for a brief discussion on the value of bardic poetry as a source for exploring Gaelic Irish responses to English conquest.
141 Caball, *Poets and politics*, pp. 48–50.

England. Elizabeth's queenship was defined in comparable negative terms: the use of *cailleach* instead of 'whore'. Moreover, there was a strong confessional dimension to the discourse. Equally, though Elizabeth was compared unfavourably to Philip II in England, and there was, in the 1580s, a discourse focused on rumours of a Spanish invasion in revenge for the defeat of the Northern Rising, public debate in Ireland had a much stronger nationalist turn. Marriage and succession were not issues of debate; Elizabeth's political legitimacy, and that of the Tudors as a whole, was. How extensive this turn was is difficult to assess on the available evidence. Certainly, it was characteristic of the Gaelic Irish – men like O'Rourke and the Burkes, the inhabitants of M'Glannagh's town – but, Loftus's comments on Dublin lawyers (many, if not all, of whom would have been educated at the Inns of Court in London) raises the possibility that these concerns began to subsume some of the Palesmen.

POSITIVE PERCEPTIONS OF ELIZABETH

Research over the past ten or so years, and especially around the quatercentenary of Elizabeth's death, into elite and popular perceptions of Elizabeth has tended to emphasise negative constructions. This is particularly the case with popular perceptions because most extant evidence – assize records and other legal documents – naturally focuses on opinions deemed criminal, seditious and slanderous. Yet, it would be a mistake to think that public debate on Elizabeth's queenship was wholly negative; after all, even cases of seditious and slanderous words are relatively few in number, never rising above three per county per year in south-east England. Moreover, they relied on friends and neighbours to report incidents which, whether out of fear or opposition to what had been said, they did. Despite the strong confessional and nationalist feelings expressed by the Gaelic Irish and others, more positive expressions can be found in Ireland and elsewhere. Whatever the roots of the Dublin lawyers of whom Loftus complained, in their petitions to the crown over the cess and billeting, the Palesmen represented themselves as loyal subjects. Kedagh McCormac O'Conor and Brian O'Rourke may have called Elizabeth a *cailleach*, but to men like Domenic Browne, burger of Galway, and George Wyse, mayor of Waterford, she was 'our soferan lady the Queens maiestie'.[142] 'I pray,' he wrote, 'god strengthen our moste

---

142 SP63/36/2.I, fo. 4r.

noble Elizabeth agaynst all her enemyes'.[143] Three small case studies demonstrate that Elizabeth and her queenship were defined in more positive ways: that Elizabethans identified positively with the regime, endorsed Elizabeth's legitimacy and perceived her as a genuine Protestant champion.

In the dining room at Weston Hall, Shipston-on-Stour, Warwickshire, there is a panel frieze, dating to the late sixteenth or early seventeenth centuries, of twenty-two half-length portraits of the kings and queens of England from Henry IV to Elizabeth (excluding Edward V) as well as depictions of Prince Arthur, Charles V, the kings of France from Francis I to Henry IV and leading figures, past and present, in England and the continent, including Cardinal Wolsey, Sir Thomas More, Thomas Cromwell, the second earl of Essex, Catherine de Médici, the dukes of Alva and Guise and the prince of Parma.[144] A similar gallery of contemporary figures – including Elizabeth, William of Orange, Philip II, Ambrogio Spinola (general of the Spanish army in the Netherlands), the explorers, Columbus and Magellan, and the Ottoman sultans, Bajazet and Muhammed II – is at Astley, Lancashire.[145] And Elizabeth, Edward VI, Cromwell and Thomas Cranmer were depicted in Edward Isaac's parlour at Well Court, Kent, in 1574.[146] St Bodfan's (or Bodvan) church, Llanaber, Merionethshire, had a portrait of Elizabeth on the east wall of the chancel, with an inscription 'God bless the Q[ueen]'.[147]

Murals of the royal arms were discovered in Huckster's End, Ashridge, Herts (now in the St Albans Museum), dated to c.1570–80;[148] the north wing of a house on the west side of Bank Street, Braintree, Essex;[149] and in

---

143 SP63/37/13.I, fo. 31r.

144 Croft-Murray, *Decorative painting in England*, I, p. 176; Henry Shaw, *Details of Elizabethan architecture* (London, 1839), plate 3.

145 Nicholas Cooper, *Houses of the gentry, 1480–1680* (New Haven and London, 1999), p. 321.

146 Cooper, *Houses of the gentry*, p. 321.

147 C. E. Keyser, *A list of the buildings in Great Britain and Ireland having mural and other painted decorations of dates prior to the latter part of the sixteenth century* (3rd edn, London, 1883), p. 161; W.E.W.W., 'Llanaber Church, Merionethshire', *Archaeologia Cambrensis*, third series, 5 (1859), pp. 142–3. I would like to thank Patricia Moore, Librarian and Head of Reader Services at *RCAHMW* for her help in identifying the church and for supplying me with information from the commission's files. These record that the painting no longer survives (no trace of it was found on a visit of August 1971).

148 Francis W. Reader, 'Tudor domestic wall paintings, Part I', *Archaeological Journal*, 92 (1935), pp. 267–8.

149 *Royal Commission on Historical Monuments (England). An inventory of the historical monuments in Essex* (4 vols., London, 1916–23), II, p. 32 (Monument 37).

Castell-y-mynach, Pentyrch, Glamorgan, dating to 1602.[150] There are also examples in Tudor Cottage, Chapel Street, Sidmouth, Devon; Newsham Hall Cottage, Woodplumpton, Lancashire, and the Chandos Arms, Little Stanmore, Middlesex, though these may be mid-16th and early 17th century examples respectively.[151] Royal arms also decorated tablecloths and napery, commissioned or purchased by the wealthy. A damask tablecloth, decorated with a portrait of Elizabeth, the inscription 'God save the quene', the falcon badge of Anne Boleyn, the Tudor arms and St George, remains extant; it was possibly owned by Sir Thomas Gresham or another merchant. Further examples are extant in the Victoria and Albert Museum. They would have been used at ceremonial dinners.[152]

As Sutton's study of Theobalds has shown, the depiction of coats of arms and portraits of leading figures in gentry houses and on napery could reflect patrons' genealogical interests, dynastic claims and connections, as well as their deeds. Equally, murals could have educative purposes, teaching heirs moral qualities or identifying to them leading county gentry and their spheres of influence.[153] Depictions of foreign towns or leading continental figures served similar educative purposes on a wider canvas, as well as providing visual lessons in political action and its consequences: the depictions of Don John and the prince of Parma at Theobalds, James Sutton has argued, were used to warn Burghley's political heir, Robert Cecil, of political wiliness and craftiness.[154]

150 *Royal Commission on the Ancient and Historical Monuments of Wales. An inventory of the ancient monuments in Glamorgan* (4 vols., London and Cardiff, 1976–91), IV: 1, p. 353. For details of the owners of Castell-y-mynach see George T. Clark (ed.), *Limbus Patrum Morganiae et Glamorganiae, being the geneaologies of the older families of the lordship of Morgan and Glamorgan* (London, 1886), p. 20.

151 The Devon example has 'ER' with it, but this may refer to Edward VI since the rest of the partition wall (actually a screen) on which the arms is painted is thought to date to the mid-century: Ronald E. Wilson, 'Tudor and Merton Cottages, Sidmouth', *Transactions of the Devonshire Association*, 106 (1974), pp. 155–9 and plates 1–2. The Woodplumpton example is a hybrid of the Tudor and Stuart arms, i.e. supported by the lion and unicorn (Stuart) but surrounded with a circle representing the Garter (Tudor). It may date to 1617, when James passed near Woodplumpton on the way to Scotland. M. E. McClintock and R. C. Watson, 'Domestic wall-painting in the north west', *Vernacular Architecture*, 14 (1983), pp. 55–6. It is now in the Harris Museum, Preston. The example in the Chandos Arms – traces of the royal arms in a first-floor room, over a fireplace – is no longer extant because the building was condemned and destroyed, without the mural being saved. It is therefore impossible to date the painting any more specifically than to the sixteenth or early seventeenth century: *Royal Commission on Historical Monuments (England). An inventory of the historical monuments in Middlesex* (London, 1937), p. 115.

152 David Mitchell, 'Table linen associated with Queen's Elizabeth's visit to Gresham's Exchange', in Saunders (ed.), *The Royal Exchange*, pp. 50–1, 54–6.

153 Sutton, 'Decorative program', pp. 35–7, 38–44. See also, Cooper, *Houses of the gentry*, pp. 320–1.

154 Sutton, 'Decorative program', pp. 46–8.

This may be the purpose of the frieze at Shipston-on-Stour, especially as there is some duplication of figures with those depicted in the great gallery in the west wing of Fountain Court at Theobalds: not only the English monarchs, but, more crucially, Parma and Count Egmont.[155] However, both the inclusion of a longer run of English monarchs, including Elizabeth, and more particularly, the examples from Llanaber, Huckster's End, Braintree and Castell-y-mynach, suggest that churchwardens or patrons commissioned paintings to identify themselves closely with, and hence endorse, the Elizabethan regime. There was no official order for parish churches, like Llanaber, to display the royal arms until 1660.[156] Domestic buildings were not required to display either the royal arms or portraits of the queen. Similarly, the depiction of the royal arms on napery may have enabled owners to manifest their political loyalties to their assembled guests during formal meals. This may have stimulated the purchase of the damask tablecloth with 'God save the quene'. It does not appear to have been commissioned specifically by Gresham – it lacks his own coat of arms – and, therefore, is unlikely to have been used when Elizabeth visited the Exchange: Gresham would have wanted to associate himself more closely and explicitly with the crown by depicting his own arms near those of the queen. Rather, it may have been hastily produced to cash in on the accession of the new queen. David Mitchell has dated it to the beginning of Elizabeth's reign when the foreign weavers, probably based in Kortrijk in the Netherlands, either assumed Elizabeth would adopt her mother's arms or utilised existing patterns.[157]

Though investments in decorated napery and elaborate wall-paintings were characteristic of the aristocracy, gentry and wealthy mercantile class, the articulation of political loyalty through visual and material images cannot be regarded as solely a response by the elite. Not only is the house in Braintree a smaller dwelling for the middling sort, but similar series of pictures of English monarchs and individual woodcuts of the queen printed in Elizabeth's reign could have been pinned on walls in less wealthy homes. In 1560, Gyles Godet printed a series of woodcuts (over twenty-five sheets) depicting the kings and queens of England, with short verses, from Noah to Elizabeth.[158] Three years later, a broadside

---

155 Ibid., pp. 43–4.
156 D. A. L. Maclean, 'The royal arms in English parish churches', *The Armorial*, 1 (1960), pp. 126–7.
157 Ibid., pp. 52–3.
158 [To the reader. Beholde here (gentle reader) a brief abstract of the genealogie of all the kynges of England] ([Imprinted by Gyles Godet, 1560]; *STC* 10022).

comprising a woodcut of Elizabeth in her regalia, and verses beginning 'Loe here the pearle / whom God and man doth loue' was printed, exhorting readers to pray for her good health.[159] Another, more ornate, woodcut entitled 'Elizabetha regina' was printed in c.1590.[160]

If murals, woodcuts and napery depicting Elizabeth or the royal arms demonstrate attempts by Elizabethans to identify themselves with, and hence endorse, the regime, then other actions point to Elizabeth's personal popularity. Though Sir John Neale, Sir Roy Strong and David Cressy may have exaggerated the speed and extent to which celebrations of Elizabeth's Accession Day spread across England, it is clear that, though some parishes like St Peter Westcheap may have used the rituals as a means to admonish Elizabeth for failing to reform the church fully, for many Elizabethans 17 November was an opportunity to celebrate the queen's accession positively.[161] Extant churchwardens' accounts for London parishes show that, after St Peter Westcheap and St Botolph Aldersgate in 1564, Accession Day began to be marked in St Mary Woolchurch in 1566, St Botolph Bishopsgate (from at least 1567), and St Botolph Aldgate, All Hallows London Wall and St Michael le Querne in 1569.[162] A number of other parishes followed in 1570 and 1571.[163] A representative sample of churchwardens' accounts from across England suggests that celebrations outside London began from 1570, shortly after the Northern Rising. One of the earliest instances was at St Michael in Bedwardine, Worcester, in 1569.[164] This was followed by St Thomas, Salisbury in 1569–70,[165] St Edmund, Salisbury[166] and Ashburton, Devon

---

159 'Loe here the pearle' (London, [1563]; *STC* 7588).
160 *Elizabeth. The exhibition at the National Maritime Museum*, ed. Susan Doran (London, 2003), entry no. 209 (p. 202). See also Watt, *Cheap print*, ch. 5.
161 For fuller details, see Natalie Mears, 'Good Queen Bess': the origins and evolution of the Accession Day celebrations of Elizabeth I' (in preparation).
162 Guildhall MS 1013/1, fo. 10r; Guildhall MS 4524/1, fo. 2v; Guildhall MS 1235/1, pt. 1, fo. 94v; Guildhall MS 5090/2, fo. 6r; Guildhall MS 2895/1, fo. 191v.
163 St Mary Aldermanbury (Guildhall MS 3556/1, fo. 17v); St Ethelburg, Bishopsgate (Guildhall MS 4241/1, p. 4); St Michael Cornhill (Waterlow (ed.), *Accounts of the churchwardens of . . . St Michael, Cornhill*, p. 165); All Hallows Staining (Guildhall MS 4956/2, fo. 106v).
164 Amphlett (ed.), *Churchwardens' accounts of St Michael's in Bedwardine*, p. 67. See also pp. 70, 72, 76, 80, 8, 83, 86, 89, 92, 94. Brett Usher has suggested to me that this early instance of Accession Day may have owed much to the former Marian exile, Edwin Sandys, who was bishop of Worcester 1559–70.
165 Swayne, 'Churchwardens' accounts for S. Edmund and S. Thomas, Sarum', p. 284.
166 Ibid., p. 118.

in 1570–1,[167] St Peter, Cheshil, Winchester in 1571 and St Peter, Hertford,[168] St Michael, Bath,[169] Chagford, Devon[170] by 1572.

Some rituals may have been instituted by the regime. Churchwardens' accounts for Ludlow, seat of the Council of the Marches of Wales, record that the first instance of celebrations was 'at the appointment of mr baylieffes'.[171] There is also evidence that some of the more elaborate celebrations were driven by civic authorities and/or the local elite: in 1576, the mayor of Liverpool ordered a bonfire to be built in the market square and for householders to build their own smaller ones across the town. He also organised a banquet for the leading citizens. In York, in 1578, the town's officials were ordered to attend a sermon on 16 November.[172] Equally, most celebrations appear to have been largely spontaneous events, independent of the regime and reflecting Elizabeth's popularity. There was no clear north–south or east–west divide, with southern and eastern parishes establishing traditions of marking Elizabeth's accession earlier than their northern or western counterparts. Accession Day was first marked in St Oswald, Durham in 1580; Pittington, County Durham, in 1588; South Newington, Oxfordshire, in 1589; and Stoke Charity, Hampshire in 1589–90. Conversely, ringing began in Holy Trinity, Chester in 1573.[173] Rather, celebrations were widespread. Moreover, the publication of Grindal's *A forme of prayer* in 1576 appears to have stimulated a whole range of unofficial books, pamphlets and ballads that enabled participants to celebrate the event in more elaborate ways.[174] The churchwardens of St Oswald, Durham, provided 'a tarbarrell at

167 Hanham (ed.), *Churchwardens' accounts of Ashburton*, p. 167. See also, pp. 169, 172, 174, 175–6, 178, 181, 183, 186, 188.

168 Palmer (ed.), *Tudor churchwardens' accounts*, p. 91.

169 C. B. Pearson, 'Churchwardens' accounts of St Michael's, Bath, 1349–1575', *Somersetshire Archaeological & Natural History Society Proceedings*, 26 (1880), p. 131.

170 Osborne (ed.), *Churchwardens' accounts of St Michael's church, Chagford*, p. 224. See also, pp. 225, 231, 235, 244, 251.

171 Wright (ed.), *Churchwardens' accounts of . . . Ludlow*, p. 153.

172 Roy Strong, 'The popular celebration of the Accession Day of Queen Elizabeth I', *Journal of the Warburg and Courtauld Institutes*, 21 (1958), pp. 91–2; David Cressy, *Bonfires and bells*, p. 54.

173 *Churchwardens' accounts of Pittington and other parishes in the diocese of Durham, 1580–1700* (Surtees Society, 84; Durham, 1888), pp. 27, 120; E. R. C. Brinkworth, *South Newington churchwardens' accounts, 1553–1684* (Banbury Historical Society, 6; Headington, 1964), p. 27; Williams (ed.), *Churchwardens' accounts of Hampshire*, p. 106.

174 For example, Guildhall MS 1013/1, fos. 33r, 42r, 43v; Guildhall MS 645/1, fos. 100r, 101r, 103r, 121r; Guildhall MS 1568/1, pp. 270, 279, 285, 302; Guildhall MS 1002/1a, fos. 198r, 204v, 236r; Palmer, *Tudor churchwardens' accounts*, p. 130; Walters (ed.), 'Churchwardens' accounts of . . . Worfield', p. 66.

cronation day' in 1580; those at Tilney All Saints, Norfolk, for 'kylder-kyns' of beer in 1583, 1584 and 1588.[175] All parishioners were encouraged to take part, as the case of Liverpool in 1576 demonstrates.

Importantly, Elizabeth's accession was not the only event to be marked with bell-ringing and celebrations. Some parishes, like St Mary Woolchurch, St Christopher le Stocks, London and St Nicholas, Strood, Kent, marked her birthday.[176] Churchwardens at St Mary Woolchurch, St Peter Westcheap, St Michael's Cornhill, SS Anne and Agnes and other parishes in London and the provinces bought books of homilies 'a gainst the rebelles' in 1569–70.[177] St Mary Woolchurch, St Antholin, St Peter Westcheap, St Christopher le Stocks, St Botolph Aldgate, London, marked the execution of Mary Stuart with bell-ringing.[178] St Peter Westcheap bought 'ii bookes of prayer against the Spaniarde' in 1587–8; the churchwardens of St Peter, Hertfordshire, paid a man for delivering a message for them 'to ringe for our good success against the Spanyard' after the Armada.[179] Parishes like St Christopher le Stocks, St Benet Grace-church Street, London, St Peter, Hertfordshire, Crondall, Hampshire and Prescot, Lancashire, marked the arrest of conspirators, like Parry and Babington, either by bell-ringing or by purchasing pamphlets.[180] Some of the pages of the churchwardens' accounts for St Botolph Aldgate even had elaborate initial letters at the start of the yearly accounts, decorated with the caption 'Vive la royne dengleterre'.[181]

Indeed, there appears to have been a ready market for celebratory pamphlets on Elizabeth. Her entry into provincial towns whilst on progress was marked by broadsides like *The first anointed Queene I am, within this town which euer came* (1573), probably for her visit to Rye in

175 *Churchwardens' accounts of Pittington*, p. 120; Stallard, *Churchwardens' accounts of . . . Tilney All Saints*, pp. 240, 242, 249.

176 Guildhall MS 1013/1, fo. 34v; Freshfield (ed.), *Accomptes of the churchwardens of . . . St Cristofer's*, pp. 8, 9, 10, 17, 18, 21, 22; Guildhall MS 1235/1 (part 1), fo. 150v, 154v; H. R. Plomer (ed.), *The churchwardens' accounts of St Nicholas, Strood* (Kent Archaeological Society Records, 5; n.p., 1927), pp. 50, 53.

177 Guildhall MS 1013/1, fo. 15r; Guildhall MS 645/1, fo. 87v; Waterlow (ed.), *Accounts of the churchwardens of . . . St Michael, Cornhill*, p. 165; William McMurray (ed.), *The records of two city parishes . . . SS Anne and Agnes, Aldergate & St John Zachary, London* (London, 1925), p. 71; Hanham, *Churchwardens' accounts of Ashburton*, p. 168.

178 Guildhall MS 1013/1, fo. 48r; Guildhall MS 1046/1, fo. 31v; Guildhall MS 645/1, fo. 123r; Freshfield, *Accomptes of the churchwardens of . . . St Cristofer's*, p. 17; Guildhall MS 1235/1 (part 2), fo. 11r.

179 Guildhall MS 645/1, fo. 124r; Palmer, *Tudor churchwardens' accounts*, p. 136.

180 Freshfield, *Accomptes of the churchwardens of . . . St Cristofer's*, p. 17; Guildhall MS 1568/1, p. 315; Palmer, *Tudor churchwardens' accounts*, p. 130; Williams (ed.), *Churchwardens' accounts of Hampshire*, p. 138; Bailey, *Churchwardens' accounts of Prescot, Lancashire*, p. 101.

181 For example, Guildhall MS 1235/1 (part 1), fo. 136r.

August 1573, and *A famous dittie of the ioyful receauing of the Queens most excellent maiestie* for London in 1584.[182] Others celebrated the foiling of conspiracies and recounted the execution of plotters, including *The end and confession of Iohn Felton* (1570), *A discouerie of the treasons practised and attempted against the Queenes Maiestie and the realme, by Francis Throckmorton* (1584) and *A proper newe ballad declaring the substance of all the late pretended treasons against the Queenes Maiestie* (1586). Though these may have been produced by a Protestant elite, anxious to impose upon ordinary Elizabethans beliefs of providentialism and conspiracy, extant booksellers' inventories and accounts demonstrate that there was a market in English (and possibly Welsh) counties for these texts. Roger Ward's stock in Shrewsbury included *A reply . . . to a late rayling . . . libel of the papists set vpon postes, and also in Paules church in London* (1579);[183] Thomas Churchyard's *The most true reporte of Iames Fitz Morrice death* (1579);[184] and *A true reporte of a conference had betwixt Doctour Fulke, and the Papists being at Wisbich Castle* (1581).[185] Robert Scott of Norwich stocked at least twenty-five copies of a ballad on the Northern Rising.[186]

These celebrations point to more than just Elizabeth's popularity. In marking her accession, Elizabethans explicitly or tacitly celebrated the restoration of Protestantism which it had brought. Indeed, this purpose appears to have been central to the proliferation of provincial celebrations after the Northern Rising and the Spanish Armada and the latter event seems to have been particularly significant in establishing Accession Day as an integral part of the Protestant calendar, contributing to the continuation of celebrations after 1603.[187] Much of the literature on Accession Day in the 1580s – like John Prime's sermon of 1585, Edmund Bunny's *Certaine prayers and other godly exercises* (1585) and Edward Hake's *A commemoration of the most prosperous and peaceable raigne of our gratious and deere soueraigne lady Elizabeth* (1575) – promulgated a

---

182 *The first anointed Queene I am* (1573). See the notes in Early English Books Online (or on the microfilm reel 1709:08). *A famous dittie of the ioyful receauing of the Queens most excellent maiestie* (London, 1584; *STC* 12798).

183 *A reply . . . to a late rayling . . . libel of the papists* (1579); Rodger, 'Roger Ward', p. 251, no. 63.

184 Churchyard, *True reporte of Iames Fitz Morrice death* (1579) or *A ballat of Fitzmorris* (licensed to Richard Jones, 4 Sept. 1579); Rodger, 'Roger Ward', p. 257, no. 313; Arber (ed.), *Registers of the Company of Stationers*, II, p. 359.

185 *True reporte of a conference had betwixt Doctour Fulke, and the Papists being at Wisbich Castle* (1581); Rodger, 'Roger Ward', p. 256, no. 292; p. 257, no. 340.

186 Plomer, 'Elizabethan book sales', pp. 321–2. There were so many ballads on the Northern Rising, it is impossible to identify which one Scott bought.

187 Cressy, *Bonfires and bells*, 123–9; D.R. Woolf, 'Two Elizabeths? James I and the late Queen's famous memory', *Canadian Journal of History*, 20 (1985), pp. 167–91, especially 184–90.

strongly providential model of Elizabeth's queenship.[188] Moreover, other events that were marked by bell-ringing or pamphlets – Mary's execution, the revelation of plots against Elizabeth – fitted into this picture of England as the chosen nation, under fire from Catholic conspiracy, but emerging triumphant, through divine assistance under their queen, a Protestant champion.

This suggests that if moderate puritans, like John Foxe, Edward Dering, John Prime and William Porrege, increasingly defined Elizabeth's queenship in negative providential terms – emphasising her failure to reform the church fully in 'repayment' for God's protection under Mary – many Elizabethans saw Elizabeth in a positive light. Moreover, this was not just characteristic of the populus, or even the provincial elite. In his *Euphues and his England* (1580), the court dramatist, John Lyly, depicted Elizabeth as both divinely appointed by God to rule and as a Protestant champion. She had been 'called from a prisoner to be a Prince' by God.[189] She was 'Debora, who ruled twentie yeares with Religion' and who had 'established Religion, the maintenaunce where-off, she rather seeketh to confirme by fortitude, than leaue off for fear'.[190] Far from chiding Elizabeth's reforms, or the nature of her church, Lyly praised her passive resistance to conspiracies and plot and emphasised her Protestant commitment, 'being now placed in the seat royal, she first of all stablished religion, banished Poperie, aduanced the word, that before was so much defaced'.[191]

CONCLUSION

Historians have increasingly focused on gender as the key to understanding public discourse on Elizabeth's queenship. For McLaren, elite discourse was dominated by the question of female monarchy and shaped by contemporary attitudes towards women. Levin has argued that ordinary Elizabethans were primarily concerned with the marriage and succession and, specifically, Elizabeth's failure to fulfil gender expectations by having a child who would succeed to the crown. Yet, though evidence of positive perceptions of Elizabeth's queenship, especially as popular level, is more

---

188 John Prime, *A sermon briefly comparing the estate of the king Salomon and his subiectes with queen Elizabeth and her people* (Oxford, 1585; *STC* 20371); Edmund Bunny, *Certaine prayers and other godly exercise, for the seuenteenth of Nouember* (London, 1585; *STC* 4089); Edward Hake, *A commemoration of the most prosperous and peaceable raigne of our gratious and deere soueraigne lady Elizabeth* (London, 1575; *STC* 12605); Strong, 'Popular celebration', pp. 95–7.
189 John Lyly, *Euphues and his England* (London, 1580; *STC* 17068), fos. 118r–119r.
190 Ibid., fos. 112v–113r, 113v–116r, 120v–123v.
191 Ibid., fos. 118r–119r.

limited than negative ones, an assessment of both suggests that female monarchy and issues of gender were less significant than has been thought. At elite and popular level, at home and abroad, there were comments on Elizabeth's political legitimacy, but only some pointed to Elizabeth's gender as a problem. Gendered criticism of the queen was often used in particular ways: by ambassadors who were obliged to report all rumours of Elizabeth's sexual activity in order for their masters to ascertain England's confessional direction, during and after Elizabeth's reign; by Catholic polemicists as a supplementary means to damn a heretical regime. If verbal assaults on Elizabeth at a popular level are placed in the context of verbal abuse, defamation and slander then it is possible that such attacks were general ones on good governance, rather than gendered comments.

Our understanding of public perceptions of Elizabeth's queenship needs to be reshaped in two ways. Close study of extant evidence for England suggests that Elizabeth's own religious practice and the nature of the English church were the real focus of debate and the terms in which Elizabeth's queenship was defined across the religious spectrum. Where it has been possible to ascertain or estimate the background of participants, moreover, confessional allegiance appears to have been crucial in stimulating Elizabethans to participate in public debate. Equally, a 'British' dimension, and particularly the study of Ireland where the material, though limited, is more abundant than for Wales, suggests that religion cannot be identified as the sole subject of debate. There was a strong confessional element to Irish political discourse, though this appears to have operated more as a factor motivating participation than a topic of debate. However, among the Gaelic Irish, and possibly Palesmen in the 1580s, Elizabeth's political legitimacy, English governance and the conquest of Ireland dominated public discourse. Neither was the former primarily a response to female monarchy. Rather, examples such as the statue erected in M'Glannagh's town point to nationalist concerns.

This broad picture needs refinement. Recent research on popular culture has challenged Peter Burke's argument that there was a social and cultural polarisation between 1500 and 1800, resulting in distinct popular and elite cultures. Instead, it has been argued that cultural divisions were vertical, dependent on factors such as 'godliness' which drew together people of diverse social backgrounds into a distinct cultural community.[192] Similar patterns can be seen in the nature of public

---

192 Burke, *Popular culture*; Tim Harris, 'Problematising popular culture'; Amussen, 'Gendering of popular culture'; Underdown, 'Regional cultures?'

discourse where there were common topics of debate and shared opinions, for instance, among socially diverse men and women of puritan leanings. Equally, it has become increasingly apparent that greater attention must be paid to regional and gender differences in popular culture. Such differences also have to be identified in public discourse: as was outlined in chapter 6, public discourse appears to have constituted both distinct, situated spheres (dependent on social, gender and geographical factors) and unsituated discourses which could transcend these boundaries. Thus, the nature of public discourse among, for instance, the Gaelic Irish was significantly different from that of North Welsh recusants, continental Catholic polemicists and English moderate puritans. How far regional and gender differences can be pursued will depend on extant sources: women's perceptions of Elizabeth are underrepresented but a more detailed search of local archives may enable regional difference (or similarities) to be drawn in more detail.

How much closer are we to understanding the meaning, if any, to the depiction of Elizabeth at Ashridge with which this chapter began? The variety inherent in contemporary perceptions of Elizabeth is unhelpful in narrowing the field of possible meanings for this picture: a pointed reminder of Elizabeth's failure to reform the church, a testimony to her as a Protestant champion, a celebration of her imprisonment under Mary? Despite Dormer's Catholic affiliation, that the painting was a celebration of Mary's albeit temporary triumph over her half-sister seems unlikely. Could such a politically dangerous message have been emblazoned on the walls of a public room? After all, mural evidence for recusant chapels suggests that they were usually located in less accessible parts of gentry houses.[193] It may be significant that nearby Huckster's End displayed the royal arms and that this appears to have been a sign of political loyalty and identification with the regime. Was the mural of Elizabeth a celebration of her perceived role as Protestant champion? We may never know the exact purpose of the mural. Perhaps what is more significant is that, whatever the meaning, it focused on what appear to have been the central issues of public discourse in much of Elizabeth's dominions: the confessional identity and direction of the realm.

193 Harvington Hall, Chaddesley-Corbett, Worcs (drops of blood or water, symbolic of the Passion, dating to c.1576–8, found in the attic room: Croft-Murray, *Decorative painting in England*, I, p. 188); Quendon Hall, Essex (saints, inc. St Matthew, in the attic: ibid., I, p. 188); Rushton Hall, Northants (representation in plaster of the crucifixion on a bedroom wall, walled up: Keyser, *List of the buildings*, p. 214).

Conclusion

QUEENSHIP AND POLITICS

On 3 February 1574, Hugh Fitzwilliam informed Bess of Hardwick that 'this day the queen dothe hear all their opinions that hathe bine in Ireland in service and to resolve what is best to be donne there in.'[1] Elizabethan Irish politics appears to have had distinct characteristics: Ciaran Brady's examination of the Viceroys and Lord Deputyships between 1536 and 1588 makes a convincing case that very tense competition, if not outright factionalism, existed over both policy and patronage, though Simon Adams has otherwise shown that factionalism did not mark other areas of Elizabethan politics until the 1590s.[2] However, Fitzwilliam's brief report nevertheless offers a valuable vignette of Elizabethan policy-making, and Elizabeth's queenship, in the first thirty years of the reign. It suggests that Elizabeth took an active role, hearing opinions directly, and that counsel was not offered solely by the privy council: she would hear those who 'hathe bine in Ireland in service', though it is unclear whether this meant just Sussex, Sidney, William Fitzwilliam and other justices or included provincial governors, army captains, English settlers and Palesmen.

In the first thirty years of her reign, Elizabeth exercised her queenship actively. She took charge of most stages of policy-making: she selected trusted individuals to examine sensitive issues separately from the privy council or sought counsel informally from individuals. She was politically astute and reserved decision-making for herself, only taking a back seat in the negotiating of the fine details of policy – such as the substance of projected marriage treaties – and its execution, both of which were left to the privy council. The whole process was dependent on her health,

---

1 Hugh Fitzwilliam to Elizabeth Talbot, 3 Feb. 1574, Folger MS X.d.428 (30).
2 Brady, *Chief governors*, pp. 102–12, 161, 164 and ch. 4; Adams, 'Faction, clientage and politics'; Adams, 'Favourites and factions'; Mears, '*Regnum Cecilianum?*', pp. 46–64.

schedule and willingness to prioritise politics over pleasure: she refused to read important letters from the emperor about a projected marriage with Archduke Charles in 1568 because she was about to go hunting.[3] The only 'flaw' in her queenship was that she was indecisive, but the extent to which blame can be laid at her door has been exaggerated. A major reason why Elizabeth failed to take decisions was because key issues – like the marriage, succession, Mary Stuart – were highly problematic and their remedies equally so.

This depiction of Elizabeth is at odds with current perceptions of the queen, whether they are Christopher Haigh's hysterical, vain and pathologically indecisive hag, McLaren's prisoner of gender, forced to adopt providential models of queenship to legitimate her position, or Stephen Alford's passive queen, who exerted a negative influence on policy by refusing to adopt any of the remedies proposed by her hard-working council. Yet, it is one that chimes most closely with Elizabeth's own perception of herself, articulated in her own words. As Henry VIII's daughter and a legitimate, regnant queen with no superior on earth, she believed England was her realm and its subjects her people; not in the romantic sense that her decisions were shaped by public opinion, but that her subjects should leave her to govern and obey her commands. As she made clear to counsellors on her accession, roles were distinguished, 'I with my Rulinge and yow with your service'.[4] Equally, it is in tune with both the actions and comments of her counsellors, who did not always live up to the ideals of Ciceronian citizenship and concepts of the 'mixed polity' with which they were often imbued. They were not as eager to 'bounce' Elizabeth into policies as has traditionally been thought. As Burghley told Sadler in 1569, 'our partes is to counsell, and after to obay the commandor'.[5] Policy-making was directed by the queen, even if she often refused to come to a decision.

If this appears to revive the earlier depictions, both of near contemporaries, like Robert Naunton, or more recent historians, like Neale, then the similarities are superficial. As Adams has shown, Naunton's account was actually a commentary on Jacobean politics, rather than the Elizabethan court, but it has proved influential through rather unthinking use by subsequent historians, at least until Adams's analysis was published.[6]

---

3   *CSP Spanish*, II, p. 6.
4   SP12/1/6A, fo. 12r.
5   Alford, *Early Elizabethan polity*, p. 33; Additional 33593, fo. 129r.
6   Adams, 'Favourites and factions', passim.

Naunton saw Elizabeth as a master puppeteer, pulling her councillors' strings to divide and rule and maintain her hegemony.[7] Influenced by the 'cult of personality' that dominated European politics in the 1930s, Neale saw Elizabeth as a strong and successful monarch.[8] Barring the odd temper tantrum, relations between Elizabeth and her counsellors were far more harmonious than Naunton implied. More importantly, Elizabeth did not have to defend her position at court: though counsellors were frustrated at her lack of action and criticised the exercise of her queenship at times, they recognised her authority, as Burghley's advice to Sadler demonstrates.[9] Equally, though Elizabeth was politically astute and her refusal to pursue the Protestant cause to the extent of her counsellors' wishes seems judicious considering the political and financial problems it could have excited, she was not Neale's strong and successful monarch. She faced continual pressure, over the succession, Mary Stuart and religious reform; her achievements seem to have owed as much to luck and longevity than to her own abilities and were, in any case, defined by and for an Anglocentric, Protestant minority.

The nature of Elizabeth's policy-making also seems different from orthodox readings. Not only did Elizabeth take charge of most stages, but less bureaucratic, more informal and polymorphic, ways of working were adopted. Counselling was conducted either through groups of specially selected advisers or *ad hoc* and informally. Though some of those that Elizabeth appointed to discuss issues separately from the council and from whom she took counsel informally were privy councillors, like Burghley and Leicester, others, like Heneage and Randolph, were not. Advisers were selected because of their personal relationship with the queen, rather than the official post they held, though their personal relationship was often reflected by appointment to office in the Chamber or privy chamber.

Thus, the centrality given to the privy council by Pulman, Alford and others seems instead to have been assumed by a larger, more amorphous, network of favoured counsellors, agents, ambassadors and officials. It was a network that was based on personal relationships with the queen, intimacy and access; it comprised concentric circles, dependent on degrees

7 Sir Robert Naunton, *Fragmenta regalia; or observations on Queen Elizabeth, her times and favourites*, ed. J. S. Cerovski (Washington, DC, 1985).
8 J. E. Neale, *Queen Elizabeth I* (London, 1934); Neale, 'The Elizabethan political scene', *Proceedings of the British Academy*, 34 (1948), pp. 97–117 and reprinted in Neale, *Essays in Elizabethan history* (London, 1958), pp. 59–84.
9 Additional 33593, fo. 129r.

of trust. Institutional methods were sidelined further. Policy discussions by selected advisers either prefigured those of the privy council (and thus operated in probouleutic fashion) or eclipsed them altogether. Moreover, there is evidence to suggest that both the queen and her advisers sidestepped official channels of communications at times, specifically employing friends, relatives and personal servants as messengers rather than the ordinary messengers at court.

The emphasis that this new paradigm places on informal means of policy-making, access and personal intimacy brings our understanding of Elizabethan politics into closer orbit with those of socially and culturally derived reconstructions of Henrician politics. Differences remain, notably in the absence of factionalism for much of Elizabethan politics prior to 1588 and the prevalence of probouleutic groups, which appear to have played a smaller role under Henry VIII, though further research may revise this. More importantly, Elizabeth's practice suggests close parallels with her continental contemporaries. Probouleutic groups were rooted both in contemporary political thought – notably Elyot's *The gouernour* (1531) and Claude de Seyssel's *La grant monarchie de France* (1515; 1519) – and the practice of the Valois and early Bourborn kings: Francis I, Henry II, Charles IX, Henry III and, with slight modifications, Henry IV. There were also similarities with Philip II. Though his governance was highly conciliar – by 1588 there were fifteen separate councils, not only for constituent parts of his dominions (Castile, Aragon etc.), but for everything from works and forests to crusades – it remained a personal monarchy. Councils never initiated policy, and *juntas* – established to coordinate the councils – were unpopular with the king and shortlived. Philip, meanwhile, attempted to exercise power personally and completely: attending audiences, discussing policy details, reviewing information and considering unsolicited advice from his subjects; he was reluctant to delegate.[10]

These parallels indicate that neither in political practice nor political culture was England isolated from Europe as is often argued, particularly for Elizabethan artistic, material and literary culture. They suggest that as well as assessing the nature of Elizabethan politics in the context of issues that are pertinent to the regime – religion and gender, points to which we shall return – we also need to locate and explore it in a European context. Moreover, this needs to extend beyond the practice of governance to

10 Geoffrey Parker, *The grand strategy of Philip II* (New Haven and London, 1988), ch. 1, esp. pp. 19–31.

individuals' perspectives, particularly Elizabeth's. Historians have usually defined Elizabeth's queenship in terms of her relationship with her subjects: that she was forced into or constrained from implementing policies by 'public opinion' or that she courted such opinion, seeing it as central to her queenship. Yet, one of the main reasons why Elizabeth was reluctant to execute Mary was because she acknowledged Mary as her peer: a divinely appointed monarch who was not subject to the whims and desires of her subjects. Her horizons were shaped by the fact that she was a queen, her peers were fellow monarchs – like Mary, Philip and Henry III – and her subjects were precisely that: subjects. She was aware that a good prince ruled for the benefit of the common weal, but it was not the commonwealth who defined what that benefit was.

THE COURT

If we need to look more at her royal contemporaries to understand Elizabeth's queenship, then we also need to turn away from the monarch to re-evaluate political debate at court. Emphasis on court entertainments, ritual and ceremony has masked the extent to which the court was a dynamic political forum and political debate pervasive. News circulated, through observation, conversation, correspondence and printed pamphlets, around a wide cross-section of courtiers. It was not restricted to those held in Elizabeth's favour or with high office or rank: Philip Gawdy, Hugh Fitzwilliam, Brakinbury, Lady Knyvett and Joan Thynne could be as much in the know as Burghley, Beale or the countess of Shrewsbury. Indeed, Roger Manners was regarded by both Walsingham and Burghley as having enviable access. Neither was it socially stratified: earls and countesses corresponded with household officials and servants, their own and the queen's; sometimes, if some of Brakinbury's comments to the third earl of Rutland are representative, with an unexpected degree of familiarity on the part of the 'inferior'. The accessibility of news was less because the regime was unable to censor and restrict debate than because of the nature of the court itself. Not only did household office give people like Manners, Brakinbury, Dorothy Stafford and Elizabeth Wingfield direct access to galleries of power, but the cheek-by-jowl nature of life at court meant that acquaintances and friendships could develop between those of differing social status, even without familial ties.

Courtiers also participated actively in political debate. Though their opportunities for counselling Elizabeth were limited, even in the context of more informal practices adopted by the queen, they were able to participate by circulating news, debating issues, interpreting for themselves the counsel offered to Elizabeth in plays and sermons and witnessing (and responding to) the discussion of broad political issues in plays like Lyly's *Sapho and Phao*, *Endymion* and *Campaspe*. If my reading of Smith's commissioning of the Hezekiah series of murals at Hill Hall is correct, they were also able to express or fashion a political stance to an external audience through some forms of cultural patronage.

Crucially, though some courtiers did seek to counsel or influence Elizabeth, political debate at court was not unidirectional, constantly focused on the queen. News circulated and issues were debated among courtiers without reference to Elizabeth. Plays and sermons offered advice to courtiers, as well as to the queen. More importantly, courtiers did not interpret plays and sermons that counselled Elizabeth solely in terms of the queen's reactions. The eyewitness account of the first performance of Norton's and Sackville's *Gorboduc*, possibly written by the courtier, John Hales, suggests that audiences interpreted plays and other performances in the light of their own political knowledge and interests. Moreover, even when courtiers articulated a political stance that could be both a criticism of Elizabeth and an attempt to counsel her – such as Smith's Hezekiah murals at Hill Hall – there is not always sufficient evidence to prove that Elizabeth was the intended target. The room in which the Hezekiah murals, for instance, were painted was a small, possibly private, room and there is no evidence to suggest that Elizabeth visited the house.

Emphasising the political vibrancy of the court does more than try to redress the balance of court studies away from the dominance of culture and ritual; it points to the need to re-evaluate the court itself. Elton's rather acerbic statement in his presidential address to the Royal Historical Society in 1975 that studies of the Acatry and Pantry would be more useful than more 'reveries' on tilts and 'pretty pictures of gallants' has been criticised. As Adams says, even if there was sufficient evidence for such studies to be undertaken, they were unlikely to be particularly illuminating.[11] Yet, Elton's comment points in two directions that remain important nearly thirty years later. First, greater awareness of the people who lived and worked in the physical environs of the royal palaces may provide valuable, new ways of understanding the political and the social nature of the court. One of the striking things about political debate at court is the wide social range of participants and the way they interacted with each

---

11 Elton, 'Points of contact: the court', *Studies*, III, p. 53; Simon Adams, 'Politics', *Transactions of the Royal Historical Society*, sixth series, 7 (1997), p. 253.

other across what could otherwise be seen as social barriers. Greater awareness of noble and gentle courtiers and household officials would not only enhance our understanding of political debate at court but also of policy-making: as already noted, Elizabeth's network of trusted counsellors and officials was wide, including a number of privy chamber and household servants.

In this respect, studies like Mark Taviner's on Robert Beale are invaluable, but we need to extend this to less well-known figures also. As Taviner has pointed out, we are limited by extant evidence: one of the reasons why Beale has been such a fruitful example to study is because his extensive archive remains extant.[12] Those of some of his colleagues and contemporaries, like John Somers or Richard Brakenbury, no longer remain — if they ever existed. Consequently, we need to look both at individuals and groups of household officials, using the material qualitatively to paint vignettes that may point to a larger, but unquantifiable, whole. I would not advocate a full-length study of official and extraordinary messengers and of gentlemen ushers, but I have found the declared accounts of the Pipe Office in the Exchequer illuminating about the use of kin, personal servants and other household officials as messengers and about the role of gentlemen ushers, like Brakenbury, who appears to have been a correspondent of both the third earl of Rutland and of the Heneages.

Second, we need to take a more interdisciplinary approach, exploring what Elton denigrated as 'pretty pictures' but in ways that are fully integrated into more conventional, archival research. Greater knowledge of household servants may enable us to identify participants in political debate and chart courtiers' networks, but an understanding of the physical and architectural layout of the palaces in which they worked can bring further nuances. It was only through returning to Simon Thurley's work on Whitehall Palace, and thinking explicitly about the physical layout of the public and private rooms, that I realised why Brakinbury, if he was Richard Brakenbury, was such a good informant for Rutland: as a gentleman usher he helped manage courtiers' access between rooms.[13] He was thus not only able to see who was at court, but with whom they met and talked and who gained access to the queen.

12 Taviner, 'Robert Beale', esp. pp. 1–2.
13 Simon Thurley (with contributions by Alan Cook, David Gaimster, Beverley Nenk and Mark Samuel), *Whitehall Palace: an architectural history of the royal apartments, 1240–1698* (New Haven and London, 1999); Thurley, *The royal palaces of Tudor England: architecture and court life, 1400– 1547* (New Haven and London, 1993).

This interdisciplinarity needs to be genuine. As recent studies of Norton's and Sackville's *Gorboduc* have shown, historians can learn a lot from other disciplines, both in terms of the perspectives they take and the methods they use. But we need to do more than just borrow from each other. As I sought to make sense of political debate at court, I found I had to bridge a gap between the extensive literature on political drama and the considerably less furrowed field of 'conventional' discourse in letters and conversation. It was less the imbalance of material between the two that was problematic, than simply that highly sophisticated studies of the use of drama to counsel Elizabeth were divorced from assessments of both policy-making and political debate at court. We need to integrate different disciplines and the areas they study far more. After all, the court was a cultural, social *and* political forum simultaneously. It is a daunting task: however familiar (though at times, outdated) we may be with different disciplines as young students, years of academic research can make us unintentionally narrow in focus. I certainly do not claim to be a model and whether I have bridged that gap on a permanent basis, or whether my pontoon will collapse under its own flimsiness, is for others to decide. I will just continue to strive.

THE PUBLIC SPHERE

The thirst for news was as pervasive beyond the court's environs as it was within them. News circulated widely – geographically, socially and in terms of gender – across the Elizabethan realms. Though there were no printed newspapers, newsletters or *corantos*,[14] the numbers of small, printed, news pamphlets were more extensive than previous historians have gauged and there is evidence from metropolitan and provincial inventories that they circulated widely in England, if less so in Wales and Ireland. Equally, other forms of communication appear to have been more important than print: news circulated orally, as well as in letters and through acts such as special church services and prayers to mark events or seek divine assistance. Indeed, oral dissemination of news is vital to our understanding of a 'public sphere' across Elizabeth's dominions as it was only this format that was both universal and flexible enough to deal with the linguistic variations across realms and regions.

14 The first *corantos* were imported from Antwerp and the United Provinces; they were not printed in England until 1621. Levy, 'How information spread', p. 22.

Equally, with cases of seditious and slanderous words, reports to the privy council, campaigns by Palesmen against the cess, Irish attacks on statues representing the queen and the commemorations of events like Elizabeth's accession or Mary's execution, the wide circulation of news suggests that a public sphere existed in Elizabeth's realms. Elizabethans actively discussed a whole range of issues including queenship, Elizabeth's marriage and the succession, religious reform, Catholic conspiracy and Irish governance. Moreover, the social, gender and geographical diversity of people involved in public debate was even more pronounced than that in court debate: from gentlemen to labourers, gentlewomen to spinsters, Londoners to those, quite literally, 'beyond the Pale'.

The existence of an Elizabethan public sphere challenges the arguments of historians of Jacobean and Caroline England who have pushed back Habermas's arguments to situate the emergence of the public sphere in the early decades of the seventeenth century. Zaret, for example, has argued that changes in 'communicative practice' (i.e. the increased production of printed pamphlets, the decline of secrecy and privilege in political debate and the deliberate opening-up of information to the public) before and during the Civil War stimulated the emergence of the public sphere by mid-century.[15] Thomas Cogswell has dated it earlier, arguing that, from 1598, ordinary people experienced a 'crude adult education' in politics, as demonstrated by the growth in number and viciousness of manuscript libels of key political figures like Robert Cecil, the duke of Buckingham and Archbishop Laud. With religious tensions and social change, the 'underground' media of manuscript libels made Stuart subjects less biddable than their Tudor predecessors and turned the 'parlour game' of Elizabethan politics into a ferocious public cockpit under the early Stuarts.[16]

Rather, the existence of an Elizabethan public sphere has more in common with the work of Adam Fox, Ethan Shagan and Thomas Betteridge who have, in different ways, highlighted popular access to news, popular participation in politics or appeals to the public in contemporary Protestant historiography from the 1520s.[17] Yet, even here,

---

15 Zaret, *Origins of democratic culture*, passim, but see the introduction.
16 Thomas Cogswell, 'Underground verse and the transformation of early Stuart political culture', in Susan D. Amussen and Mark Kishlansky (eds.), *Political culture and cultural politics in early modern England: essays presented to David Underdown* (Manchester and New York, 1995), pp. 277–300. See also Pauline Croft, 'The reputation of Robert Cecil: libels, political opinion and popular awareness in the early seventeenth century', *Transactions of the Royal Historical Society*, sixth series, 1 (1991), pp. 43–69.
17 Fox, 'Rumour, news and popular political opinion', passim; Fox, *Oral and literate culture*, ch. 7.

there are differences. Shagan's thesis that religious change under the Tudors has to be conceived in terms of popular interaction with authority (and ideas of authority and conformity) does not actually perceive ordinary subjects comprising a 'public sphere', though it seems possible to interpret his use of 'popular politics' in this way.[18] Conversely, though Betteridge situates his exploration of contemporary Protestant historiography within the framework of the 'public sphere', the precise nature of this sphere remains unclear. Though he implies that its members belonged to the political elite and its function was to counsel the monarch (a 'public sphere of counsel'), for the most part, Betteridge's public sphere appears to be either a literary device invoked by historians to legitimate their claims to an authentic and accurate history of the Reformation or a physical or symbolic space ('the public domain').[19]

The 'public sphere' to have emerged from this study of Elizabeth's realms is also very different to that defined either by Habermas or his critics. Though extant evidence of women's participation in public debate in the late sixteenth century is fragmentary, participation in Elizabethan public debate seems to have been far broader than in Habermas's model, socially, geographically and in terms of gender. Print was not the principal vehicle for the dissemination of news. Topics of debate were different: as Zaret had noted for the early and mid-seventeenth century, religion was a key subject of debate, but so too were gender, Elizabeth's marriage and the succession, the legitimacy of English governance of Ireland and the substance of its policy there. Moreover, Elizabethan debate cannot be defined as solely in opposition to the regime. Opposition to the religious settlement of 1559, from both ends of the confessional spectrum, was highly evident throughout the first thirty years of the reign – as were other criticisms – but part of the dominance of hostile responses to the regime in the reconstruction of the Elizabethan public sphere is because most of our evidence of debate (especially for lower social levels) comes from cases of seditious and slanderous words which, by definition, were in opposition to the crown.

---

18 Ethan H. Shagan, *Popular politics and the English Reformation* (Cambridge, 2003). For his more controversial assertions about how the Edwardian regime reaction to popular political activity see Shagan, 'Protector Somerset and the 1549 rebellions: new sources and new perspectives', *English Historical Review*, 115 (1999), pp. 34–63; M. L. Bush, 'Protector Somerset and the 1549 rebellions: a post-revision questioned', *English Historical Review*, 116 (2000), pp. 103–12; G. W. Bernard, 'New perspectives or old complexities?', *English Historical Review*, 116 (2000), pp. 113–20; Shagan, '"Popularity" and the 1549 rebellions revisited', *English Historical Review*, 116 (2000), pp. 121–33.

19 Thomas Betteridge, *Tudor histories of the English Reformations, 1530–83* (Aldershot and Brookfield, VT, 1999), esp. introduction and pp. 44–6, 54, 59, 131.

A further difference is the relationship between the Elizabethan public sphere and the court. One of the striking discoveries for me in this study was how permeable the boundaries were between the two and how difficult it was to draw a line between them. For instance, Philip Gawdy could be regarded as a member of the court, but, as they attended the royal palaces less often in the 1570s and 1580s and their court connections declined, could his parents?

It is also difficult always to identify motives for political participation in the sixteenth century that were similar to those noted by Habermas and later historians. Political enfranchisement, for example, cannot explain participation in many cases, even of gentle status, as Harris found for seventeenth-century London. Ideological factors seem to be crucial – religion and, in Ireland, a nascent nationalism – but more 'bread-and-butter' concerns about the financial cost of policy were also evident, especially amongst Palesmen campaigning against the cess.

These differences mean that the Elizabethan public sphere not only has to be characterised differently from Habermas and more recent commentators, like Calhoun and Halasz, but they also point to new ways in which we need to define the concept of the 'public sphere'. As historians of the seventeenth and eighteenth centuries have also found, the diversity of participants, the variety of topics debated and of opinions expressed in Elizabethan public debate make Habermas's definition of the public sphere as a single, coherent unit difficult to sustain. Equally, however, neither Halasz's definition of the public sphere as an 'unsituated' discourse nor Calhoun's of 'a field of discursive connections' is appropriate. Halasz's model restricts membership of the public sphere to a literate elite and defines participation as the acts of reading pamphlets and publishing one's responses. Whilst this negates the importance of face-to-face verbal discussion, it is also methodologically flawed because Halasz fails to explore the dissemination of pamphlets or to acknowledge that pamphlets could remain unread by their purchasers. Calhoun's model, like Halasz's, does draw attention to the existence of common themes of debates but seems to place too much emphasis on 'unsituated discourses' to the detriment of the physical location in which discussions were conducted. It also potentially imposes too much coherence and connection on what could be vastly different and wholly unconnected discourses.

The Elizabethan material suggests a different model. Elizabethan public debate was characterised by 'unsituated' discourses: certain themes – principally religious reform – were common topics of discussion. They were also discussed by people in different locations and who moved in different circles. Conceptualising the Elizabethan public sphere partly as a set of 'unsituated' discourses enables those themes and connections to be highlighted. Even if groups of participants discussing, for example, further church reform, were unaware of each other they can still be regarded as participating in the same, broad debate and, indeed, the pervasiveness of certain themes is important. Yet, equally, debate has to be seen, as Habermas conceived, as an activity that was usually experienced in a physical location with other participants. The Elizabethan public sphere and the concept of the public sphere itself, therefore, have to be seen as a combination of both. This does not seem to be achieved by Calhoun's definition of individual debates as 'clusters of communication', which appears to emphasise communication (or discourse) over location. Rather, it seems more accurate to define the public sphere as comprising a whole host of small, individual, physically located, public spheres, defined by their topics of debate, their participants, their motives and the physical forum in which debate was held. Over these multiple spheres lay an arterial network of 'unsituated' discourses that connected otherwise distinct and disparate individual spheres principally on the basis on common topics of debate. Crucially, however, this arterial network, unlike Calhoun's 'field of discursive connections', was haphazard: not all spheres were connected to each other. The cess, for instance, was a key issue of debate for Palesmen, but was irrelevant to the inhabitants of Maldon in Essex, who were primarily exercised by religion, queenship and the succession.

In this context, the label 'public sphere' becomes less appropriate, failing to highlight both the diversity of the individual spheres and the existence of overarching discourses. Equally, 'public spheres' may encapsulate both the importance of physical location and the existence of multiple, diverse spheres but fails to indicate the existence of broader discourses that were common to many individual spheres. Without a word existing that combines both the sense of physically located debate and 'unsituated discourses', it seems that we have to think of the 'public sphere' as 'public discourses', recognising that discourses were usually experienced directly, face-to-face with other participants in a physical location.

ELIZABETH'S QUEENSHIP: RELIGION AND GENDER

Elizabeth's gender was an issue of concern for her counsellors, politico-religious polemicists like Knox and Allen and some of her ordinary subjects. Sir Francis Knollys demanded that she 'suppresse and svbiectt hir owne wyll & hir owne affections vnto sownde advice of open cownsayle' or be overthrown.[20] Allen alleged that 'she hathe abused her bodie . . . by vnspeakable and incredible variety of luste, which modesty suffereth not to be remembred.'[21] Joan Lister, an Essex spinster, said that, 'bycause she [Elizabeth] is but a woman she owghte not to be governor of A Realme'.[22] She was called 'an Arrant hoore', 'a noughtie woman' and, in Ireland, a *phiseogach* (sorceress) and a *cailleach* (old hag). But it is difficult to sustain Crane's, Cole's, McLaren's and Levin's arguments that her queenship, in practice and in popular perceptions, was shaped principally by gender.

At both elite and popular level, conventions of sexual slander were utilised to criticise Elizabeth but the criticisms themselves were usually prompted by other factors. Knox's *The first blast* (principally against Mary I) and Allen's *Admonition* both used the monarch's gender to undermine the legitimacy of regimes that they opposed on confessional grounds. Indeed, Allen's attack on Elizabeth's gender and sexuality was a minor skirmish in a larger battle he launched against her as a bastard and a heretic. Much of Levin's evidence of sexual slander comes from continental ambassadorial reports, but here, as some ambassadors made clear, they were only reporting circulating rumours, which their positions obliged them to do. Moreover, their purpose was always to inform their masters of the direction of Elizabethan succession policy, with its important ramifications for the confessional allegiance of the realm, not to define her queenship in certain ways. Finally, popular challenges to Elizabeth's legitimacy were not always grounded in gender theory: Mary Cleere, who questioned Elizabeth's right to the crown, did so because she believed the queen was 'base borne' and 'an other Ladie is the right inheritor thervnto'.[23] Sexual slurs against the queen by her subjects may reflect more the very limited vocabulary for criticising women rather than, as Levin has suggested, concerns about her gender and her failure to fulfil her responsibilities as a queen and woman by having a child to succeed her.

In public discourse, Elizabeth's queenship was defined, both positively and negatively, more by confessionalisation than by her gender. Negative comments from both ends of the confessional spectrum focused on her

---

20 Harleian 6992, fo. 89r.
21 Allen, *Admonition*, sig. B2r.
22 ASSI 35/28/5, m. 31.
23 ASSI 35/19/4, m. 31.

religious beliefs and policies. Puritan-inspired works, from Foxe's 'Book of martyrs' to Grindal's *A form of prayer* (1576) and Thomas Blenerhasset's *A reuelation of the true Minerva* (1582), either fulminated against Elizabeth's failure to reform the church or cast her deliberately into the mould of reforming Old Testament figures, like Hezekiah and Jehosaphat, in order to chivvy her, by example, into reform. Catholics lamented religious change and criticised Elizabeth's policy: Thomas Grene 'hoped to here or see a masse in Burwishe Churche within a twelvemonthes', while William Symecotes argued that, 'Campyon & hys fellowes dyed for theyr conscyenes & not for treason'.[24] Conversely, the growing and spontaneous popularity of marking Elizabeth's accession in England suggests that many English subjects willingly and happily identified themselves with the Protestant affiliation of the realm and the marketing of Elizabeth as a Protestant champion, while boycotts of thanksgiving celebrations after the Armada in Dublin in 1588 suggest that many Irish did not.[25]

In Ireland, confessionalisation was combined with nascent nationalism. Both the Burkes' and O'Rourke's calling Elizabeth a *cailleach* was partly stimulated by confessional differences. The Burkes had apparently alleged that, 'The pope and the king of Spayne shal haue the rule of vs, and none other'; for O'Rourke, Elizabeth was 'the mother of all herysie' and he was accused of having 'kept the tyme of Christmas according vnto the popes computacion'.[26] But the Burkes also believed that Ireland was too 'mightie a nation' to be subject to English rule[27] and O'Rourke opposed the Elizabethan regime, assisting Spanish survivors of the Armada, revolting against Bingham and Perrott, before eventually being hanged at Tyburn in 1591.[28] Poems in the poem-books of Hugh McShane O'Byrne, Feagh McHugh O'Byrne and MacGuire (1566–89), as well as individual ones like 'D'fhior chogaidh comhailtear síothcháin' and 'Cia re bhfuil Éiri ac anmhuin?', all challenged the legitimacy of English governance of Ireland.[29]

Similarly, religious affiliation eclipsed gender in shaping Elizabeth's queenship at court. Both Elizabeth and her counsellors were aware that, because of dominant patriarchal values, her gender appeared to disable

24 ASSI 35/17/3, m. 25; KB27/1289 (Crown side), m. 59.
25 SP63/154/37, fo. 130r.
26 SP63/143/5, fo. 8r–8v; LPL, Carew MS 632, p. 15v.
27 LPL, Carew MS 632, p. 15v.
28 MacCaffrey, *War and politics*, pp. 358–61; Ellis, *Ireland in the age of the Tudors*, pp. 334–5.
29 Bradshaw, 'Native reaction', pp. 72–4, 76; Caball, *Poets and politics*, pp. 27–9, 30–1, 48–50; Mac Erlean (ed.), *Duanaire Dáibid uí bruadair*, pp. 64–73.

her from governance. But the significance of gender was more apparent than real. Elizabeth brushed it aside; counsellors invoked it at moments of frustration but were ultimately unwilling, whatever their Cicero or St German told them, to assume the reins of governance. Conversely, there were very real tensions between Elizabeth and some of her most trusted advisers, principally Burghley, Walsingham and Leicester, over the confessional direction of the realm; tensions that were replicated in the outer reaches of the queen's network and in the court as a whole. These were far more difficult either to resolve or to push behind the tapestry and, indeed, they were only truly settled by the execution of Mary Stuart in 1587 and the accession of James VI in 1603 which, on the one hand, removed the threat of England's reconciliation to Rome and, on the other, provided for a Protestant succession.

Yet, counsellors were ultimately as unwilling to override Elizabeth in religious policy as they were over her gender. The antithesis between gender and religion that has characterised recent debate on Elizabeth's queenship, therefore, does not go far enough. While it identifies contentious issues and the politico-cultural milieu of Elizabethan court politics, it can say little about the power relationships of Elizabeth and her counsellors. For these, we have to return to where we began and look at the practice of policy-making and the attitudes that lay behind it. Elizabeth perceived herself as a divinely appointed monarch, with no superior on earth; her counsellors absorbed theories of counsel and citizenship that augmented their roles. But new concepts of citizenship always had to work with existing notions of deference and social hierarchy. Burghley's words to Sadler were genuine: 'our partes is to counsell, and after to obey the commandor'.

Does this paradigm of Elizabeth's relations with her counsellors alter our perception of her reign having two, coherent periods as Guy has argued? There seems little doubt that the political agendas of the periods either side of Mary's execution were different: marriage, the succession, Catholic conspiracy and the Scottish queen on the one hand, and war, famine, crime and taxation on the other. These produced very different political climates. While, in the early part of the reign, the regime was weak and vulnerable, by the 1590s, it was characterised by acute tensions. Elizabeth's style of queenship also seems different: it is hard to sustain the picture of an active, dynamic, if indecisive, queen far into the final decade. Yet, the political culture of the early period, as defined by Guy, seems more questionable. When I began this book, I believed that the 'first reign' could not be defined as one when ideas of the 'mixed polity' dominated political culture; my research on the late 1570s and early 1580s pointed to a more active, and successful, assertion of 'imperial monarchy' by Elizabeth in the middle years of the reign. As my research progressed, I felt that the mid-Elizabethan period was no odd hiatus but that the pervasiveness of the concept of the 'mixed polity' and the willingness of counsellors to 'bounce' Elizabeth into action had both been exaggerated. Gender and confessionalisation may have stimulated the further development of theories of counsel, particularly that of the 'mixed polity', but they had to operate in the real world. And that was a real world governed by Henry VIII's daughter who could break her maids' fingers and seriously contemplate hanging her secretary without trial. Guy's identification of 1585–7 as a decisive turning point remains valid in terms of the political agenda, but the extent to which it marks changes in the nature of Elizabethan governance, as well as political culture, is more doubtful.

Selected Bibliography

For reasons of space, only material cited in the footnotes is listed. Secondary works that were referenced solely for historiographical reasons are not included.

MANUSCRIPTS

BIBLIOTHÈQUE NATIONALE, PARIS

Fonds français 15973

BRITISH LIBRARY, LONDON

Additional	4149, 4729, 11042, 15891 (Hatton's letter-book), 23240, 33593, 34324, 48023 ('A 'journall' of matters of state'), 48149, 46367
Cotton	Caligula B. 10; Caligula C.1; Caligula C.2; Caligula C.3; Caligula C. 5; Caligula C.6; Caligula C.9 Galba C.5; Galba C.6; Galba C.8; Galba C.9; Galba E.6
Egerton	2713-14, 2804 (Gawdy correspondence)
Harleian	1323, 1582, 6265, 6990-6993, 6999
Lansdowne	19, 29, 34, 59, 94, 102, 104
Royal	17.B.28.3 (Inventory of books in the 'newe librarye', 1581)
RP36	Photocopies of letters from Lord Buckhurst to Sir Thomas Heneage, now in the Beinecke Rare Books and MSS Library, Yale University.

CAERNAR FONSHIRE RECORD OFFICE

XQS and X/QS	Quarter Sessions records, Caernarvon, 1558–88.

273

CAMBRIDGE UNIVERSITY LIBRARY, CAMBRIDGE

Dd. V. 75
Gg. III. 34
Mm.1.29

DR WILLIAMS' LIBRARY, LONDON

Morrice D

EMMANUEL COLLEGE LIBRARY, CAMBRIDGE

ECL 260

FOLGER SHAKESPEARE LIBRARY, WASHINGTON DC.

X.d. 428 (Cavendish-Talbot correspondence)

GUILDHALL LIBRARY, LONDON

Guildhall MS 645/1	Churchwardens' accounts: St Peter Westcheap.
Guildhall MS 1002/1	Churchwardens' accounts: St Mary Woolnoth.
Guildhall MS 1013/1	Churchwardens' accounts: St Mary Woolchurch.
Guildhall MS 1016/1	Churchwardens' accounts: St Matthew Friday Street.
Guildhall MS 1046/1	Churchwardens' accounts: St Antholin.
Guildhall MS 1235/1	Churchwardens' accounts: St Botolph Aldgate.
Guildhall MS 1454/64-	Churchwardens' accounts: St Botolph Aldersgate.
Guildhall MS 1568/1	Churchwardens' accounts: St Benet Gracechurch.
Guildhall MS 2895/1	Churchwardens' accounts: St Michael le Querne.
Guildhall MS 3556/1	Churchwardens' accounts: St Mary Aldermanbury.
Guildhall MS 4241/1	Churchwardens' accounts: St Ethelburga Bishopsgate.
Guildhall MS 4524/1	Churchwardens' accounts: St Botolph Bishopsgate.
Guildhall MS 4956/2	Churchwardens' accounts: All Hallows Staining.
Guildhall MS 5090/2	Churchwardens' accounts: All Hallows London Wall.

HATFIELD HOUSE, HATFIELD, HERTFORDSHIRE

Cecil Papers   7, 9, 10, 11, 140, 148, 155

HUNTINGTON LIBRARY, SAN MARINO, CA.

Egerton MS 1189

LAMBETH PALACE LIBRARY, LONDON

Carew MS 601, 632
LPL MS 3390   Churchwardens' accounts: Holy Trinity Minories.
Talbot MS 3197

MAIDSTONE PUBLIC RECORD OFFICE, KENT

Maidstone PRC 17/40

NATIONAL ARCHIVES, LONDON

ASSI 35	Assizes: Norfolk, Home and South-Eastern Circuits: Indictment Files.
C3/95	Court of Chancery: Six Clerks Office: Pleadings, Series II, Elizabeth I to the Interregnum (Hopton vs. Kettell).
E179/69/93	Exchequer, King's Remembrancer: Particulars of account and other records relating to lay and clerical taxation: Subsidy roll (royal household), assessment, 18 Elizabeth [1575–6].
E190/1129	Exchequer: King's Remembrancer. Port Books, Port of Bristol.
E351/541-2	Exchequer, Pipe Office, Declared Accounts, 1557–96.
KB27/1189–1305	Court of King's Bench, Plea and Crown sides: Coram Rege Rolls, 1559–88.
PRO31/3	Collection of Transcripts: Paris Archives, Baschet's transcripts.
PROB11/68	Prerogative Court of Canterbury and related Probate Jurisdictions: Will registers (49 Brudenell).
PSO5/1	Privy Seal Office: Doquet Books (1571–80).
SP12	State Papers Domestic, Elizabeth.
SP15	State Papers Domestic, Edward VI to James I, Addenda.
SP52	State Papers Scotland, Elizabeth.
SP59	State Papers Scotland, Border Papers.
SP63	State Papers, Ireland, Elizabeth.
SP70	State Papers Foreign, Elizabeth.
SP78	State Papers France.
SP83	State Papers Holland and Flanders.
SP94/1	State Papers Spain.

SP104　　　　　　　　State Papers Entry Books.
STAC4/11　　　　　　　Court of Star Chamber: Proceedings, Philip and Mary
　　　　　　　　　　　　(Mounslowe vs. Kettell).
STAC5　　　　　　　　Court of Star Chamber: Proceedings, Elizabeth I.

NORTHAMPTONSHIRE RECORD OFFICE, NORTHAMPTONSHIRE

Fitzwilliam (Milton) Political 111, 123, 153, 186, 220, 222
DN/Reg 16/Book 22 (3rd series): Consignation Book, 1627 (via the *Clergymen of
the Church of England Database*)

PRINTED PRIMARY SOURCES

24. of August. 1578. A discourse of the present state of the wars in the lowe countryes
　　([London], 1578; *STC* 18438).
The abridgement of the Historyes of Trogus Pompeius, trans. Arthur Golding
　　(London, 1578; *STC* 24292).
Acts of the Privy Council of England, ed. John Roche Dasent *et al.*, new series, (46
　　vols., London, 1890–1964).
An aduise and answer of my lord ye Prince of Orenge (London, 1577; *STC* 25710.5).
Aeschines, 'Against Ctesiphon', ed. and trans. Charles Darwin Adams, *The
　　speeches of Aeschines* (Cambridge, Mass., and London, 1938).
Aggas, Edward, *A declaration set forth by the French king* (London, 1585; *STC*
　　13092).
Allen, William, *A briefe historie of the glorious martyrdom of XII reuerend priests*
　　([Rheims], 1582; *STC* 369.5).
　　An admonition to the nobility and people of England and Ireland ([Antwerp],
　　1588; *STC* 368).
Alumni Cantabrigienses, ed. John Venn and J. A. Venn (10 vols., Cambridge,
　　1922–54).
Amphlett, John, *The churchwardens' accounts of St Michael's in Bedwardine,
　　Worcester, from 1539 to 1603* (Worcestershire Historical Society; Oxford,
　　1896).
Anderson, Anthonie, *A sermon preached at Paules Cross* (London, 1581; *STC* 570).
Antwerpes vnity (London, 1579; *STC* 25711).
The apprehension and confession of three notorious witches (London, 1589; *STC*
　　5114).
Arber, E. A. (ed.), *Transcripts of the registers of the Company of Stationers of
　　London, 1554–1640* (5 vols., London, 1875–94).
Archer, Ian, *et al.* (eds.), *Religion, politics and society, in sixteenth-century England*
　　(*Camden Society*, fifth series, 22; Cambridge and London, 2003).
Ascham, Roger, *The scholemaster: or the plaine and perfite way of teaching children*
　　. . . (London, 1570; *STC* 832).
'Ashridge Park, Great Berkhamstead', *Country Life*, 4 (5 Nov.–12 Nov. 1898), pp.
　　560–3.

Aubrey, John, *The natural history and antiquities of the county of Surrey* (2 vols., Dorking, 1975).

Avale, Lemeke, *A commemoration or dirige of Bastarde Edmonde Boner* (London, 1569; *STC* 977).

Bailey, F. A. (ed.), *The churchwardens' accounts of Prescot, Lancashire, 1523–1607* (Lancashire and Cheshire Record Society, 104; Preston, 1953).

Baker, Thomas H., 'The churchwardens' accounts of Mere', *Wiltshire Archaeological and Natural History Magazine*, 35 (1907–8), pp. 23–92.

A ballat intituled Northomberland newes (London, [1570]; *STC* 7554).

Barnard, John and Maureen Bell, 'The inventory of Henry Bynneman (1583): a preliminary survey', *Publishing History*, 29 (1991), pp. 5–46.

Barron, Caroline, Christopher Coleman and Claire Gobbi (eds.), 'The London journal of Alessandro Magno, 1562', *The London Journal*, 9 (1983), pp. 136–52.

Bell, Gary M., *A handlist of British diplomatic representatives, 1509–1688* (Royal Historical Society, 16; London, 1990).

Bentley, Thomas, *The monvment of matrons* (London, 1582; *STC* 1892).

Best, George, *A true discourse of the late voyages of discouerie for finding of a passage to Cathaya* (London, 1578; *STC* 1972).

Bette, Thomas, *A nevve ballade intitvled, agaynst Rebellious and false Rumours* (London, 1570; *STC* 1979).

Binney, J. Erskine (ed.), *The accounts of the wardens of the parish of Morebath, Devon, 1520–1573* (Devon Notes and Queries Supplement; Exeter, 1904).

Blenerhasset, Thomas, *A reuelation of the true Minerva* (London, 1582; *STC* 3132).

The correspondence of Robert Bowes of Aske, ed. John Stevenson (Surtees Society, 14; London, 1842).

A briefe censure upon two bookes written in answere to M. Edmunde Campions offer of disputation (Douai [i.e. Stonor Park], 1581; *STC* 19393).

Brinkworth, E. R. (ed.), *The archdeacon's court: liber actorum, 1584* (2 vols., Oxfordshire Record Society, 23–24; 1942–6).

South Newington Churchwardens' Accounts, 1553–1684 (Banbury Historical Society, 6; Headington, 1964).

Broke, Thomas, *An epitaphe declaryng the lyfe and ende of D. Edmund Boner &c* (London, 1569; *STC* 3817.4).

Bunny, Edmund, *Certaine prayers and other godly exercise, for the seuenteenth of Nouember* (London, 1585; *STC* 4089).

Byrne, M. St Clair, and Gladys Scott Thomson, '"My lord's books": the library of Francis, second earl of Bedford, in 1584', *Review of English Studies*, 7 (1931), pp. 385–405.

C., H., *A dolefull ditty, or sorowful sonet of the Lord Darly* (London, 1579; *STC* 4270.5).

Calendar of Salusbury correspondence, 1553–c.1700, principally from the Lleweni, Rûg and Bagot collections, ed. W. J. Smith (Board of Celtic Studies, History and Law Series, 14; Cardiff, 1954).

Calendar of State Papers, Foreign. Elizabeth I, ed. J. Stevenson *et al.* (23 vols., London, 1863–1950).

Calendar of State Papers, Ireland: Tudor period, 1571–1575, ed. Mary O'Dowd (Kew and Dublin, 2000).

Calendar of Wynn (of Gwydir) Papers, 1515–1690, in the National Library of Wales and elsewhere (Aberystwyth, Cardiff and London, 1926).

Camden, William, *Annales, or the historie of the most renowned and victorious princesse Elizabeth* (3rd edn, London, 1635).

'William Carnsew of Bokelly and his diary, 1576–7', ed. N. J. G. Pounds, *Journal of the Royal Institution of Cornwall*, new series, 8 (1978), pp. 14–60.

Cartwright, Thomas, *A replye to an ansvvere made of M. Doctor Whitgifte agaynste the admonition to the parliament* ([Hemel Hempstead?], 1573; *STC* 4711).

The second replie of Thomas Cartwright: agaynst Masiter Doctor Whitgiftes second answer ([Heidelberg], 1575; *STC* 4714).

Cecil, William, *The copie of letter sent ovt of England to Don Bernardin Mendoza* (London, 1588; *STC* 15412).

[C]ertayn and tru good nues, from the seyge of the isle Malta (London, 1565; *STC* 17213.5).

Chambers, E. K., *The Elizabethan stage* (4 vols., Oxford, 1923).

Christianson, C. Paul, 'The stationers of Paternoster Row, 1534–1557', *Papers of the Bibliographical Society of America*, 87 (1993), pp. 81–91.

Churchwardens' Accounts of Pittington and other parishes in the diocese of Durham, 1580–1700 (Surtees Society, 84; Durham, 1888).

Churchyard, Thomas, *A discourse of the queens maiesties entertainement in Suffolke and Norfolke* (London, [1578]; *STC* 5226).

A most true reporte of Iames Fitz Morrice Death (London, [1579]; *STC* 5244).

A warning to the wise . . . written of the late earthquake (London, 1580; *STC* 5259).

A scourge for rebels . . . touching the troubles of Ireland (London, 1584; *STC* 5255).

Clark, George T. (ed.), *Limbus Patrum Morganiae et Glamorganiae, being the geneaologies of the older families of the lordship of Morgan and Glamorgan* (London, 1886).

Clay, William Keating (ed.), *Liturgical services: liturgies and occasional forms of prayer set forth in the reign of Queen Elizabeth* (Parker Society; Cambridge, 1847).

A copy of the last aduertisement that came from Malta (London, 1565; *STC* 17214).

Cotton, Charles, 'Churchwardens' accounts of the parish of St Andrew, Canterbury, from AD 1485 to AD 1625. Part IV: 1553–4 – 1596', *Archaeologia Cantiana*, 35 (1921), pp. 41–108.

Curteys, Richard, *A sermon preached at Grenevviche, before the Queenes maiestie . . . the 14. day of Marche 1573* (London, 1574; *STC* 6135).

A sermon preached before the Queenes Maiestie at Richmond the 6. of Marche last past (London, 1575; *STC* 6139).

A declaration and publication of the most worthy Prince of Orange (London, 1568; *STC* 25708).

A declaration of the Queenes Maiesties most gratious dealing with William Marsden and Robert Anderton (London, 1586; *STC* 8157).

A declaration of the recantation of Iohn Nichols (London, 1581; *STC* 18533).

The declarations as well of the French King, as the King of Navarre (London, 1589; *STC* 13098.8).

The private diary of Dr John Dee and the catalogue of his library of manuscripts from the original manuscripts in the Ashmolean Museum at Oxford, and Trinity College, Library, Cambridge, ed. James Orchard Halliwell (Camden Society, 19; London, 1842).

Deloney, Thomas, *A most ioyfull song* (London, 1586; *STC* 6557.6).

The Queens visiting of the campe at Tilsburie (London, 1588; *STC* 6565).

Demosthenes, 'On the Crown', in Demosthenes: *On the Crown (De Corona)*, trans. S. Usher (Warminster, 1993).

The destruction and sacke cruelly committed by the duke of Guyse (London, [1562]; *STC* 11312).

A detection of damnable driftes, practized by three witches (London, 1579; *STC* 5115).

The disclosing of a late counterfeited possession by the deuyl in two maydens within the citie of London (London, 1574; *STC* 3738).

A discourse of the bloody and cruel battaile, of late lost by the great Turke Sultan Selim (London, 1579; *STC* 22180).

Drant, Thomas, *Two sermons preached the one at S. Maries Spittle on Tuesday in Easter weeke 1570 and the other at the court at Windsor the Sonday after twelfth day, being the viij of Ianuary, before in the yeare 1569* (London, 1570; *STC* 7171.5).

Drew, Charles (ed.), *Lambeth churchwardens' accounts, 1504–1645, and vestry book, 1610* (Surrey Record Society, 18; Frome and London, 1941).

Correspondence of Robert Dudley, earl of Leycester, during his government of the Low Countries in the years 1585 and 1586, ed. John Bruce (Camden Society, original series, 27; London, 1844).

Duncan-Jones, Katherine and Jan van Dorsten (eds.), *The miscellaneous prose works of Sir Philip Sidney* (Oxford, 1973).

Eccles, Mark, 'Bynneman's books', *The Library*, fifth series, 12 (1957), pp. 81–92.

Edict du roy sur la reunion de ses subiects, a l'eglise catholique [with an English translation, *The edict, for the reunitying of his subiectes in the Catholique, Apostolique and Romishe Churche* by Hector Rowland] (London, 1585; *STC* 13092.5).

The edict or proclamation set forthe by the French Kinge vpon the pacifying of the troubles in Fraunce (London, 1576; *STC* 13091).

Edwards, Richard, *The excellent comedie of two the most faithfullest freendes, Damon and Pithias* (London, 1571; *STC* 7514).

Elderton, William, *A new Yorkshyre song* (London, 1584; *STC* 7559).

Elizabeth I: collected works, ed. Leah Marcus, Janel Mueller and Mary Beth Rose (Chicago and London, 2000).

Elizabeth. The exhibition at the National Maritime Museum, ed. Susan Doran (London, 2003).

Elyot, Thomas, *The boke named the gouernour* (London, 1531; *STC* 7635).

Emmison, F. G., *Elizabethan wills of South-West Essex* (Waddesdon, 1983).

Essex domestic wall-paintings, 14th–18th century (University of Essex Exhibition Catalogue, 1989).

A famous dittie of the ioyfull receauyng of the Queens most excellent maiestie, by the worthy citizens of London the xij day of Nouember 1584 (London, 1584; *STC* 12798).

Fenner, Dudley, *The ansuuere copies vnto the confutation of Iohn Nichols his recantation* (London, 1583; *STC* 10764.3).

Field, John, *An admonition to the parliament* ([Hemel Hempstead?], 1572; *STC* 10847).

The first anointed Queene I am, within this town which euer came (London?, 1573; *STC* 7582.5).

A fourme of common prayer to be vsed . . . and necessarie for the present tyme and state (London, 1572; *STC* 16511).

A fourme to be vsed in common prayer . . . for the deliuery of those christians that are nowe invaded by the Turke (London, [1565]; *STC* 16508).

A fourme to be vsed in common prayer . . . for the preseruation of those christians and their countries that are nowe invaded by the Turke (London, [1566]; *STC* 16510).

Foxe, John, *Actes and monuments of these later and perilous dayes* (London, 1563; *STC* 11222).

The first (second) volume of the ecclesiastical history containing the Actes and Monuments (London, 1570; *STC* 11223).

The French kinges declaration vpon the riot, felonie, and rebelleion of the duke of Mayenne (London, 1589; *STC* 13098.5).

Freshfield, Edwin (ed.), *Accomptes of the churchwardens of the paryshe of St Cristofer's in London, 1575 to 1662* (London, 1885).

G., F., *The end and confession of Iohn Felton* (London, 1570; *STC* 11493).

Garter, Bernard, *The ioyfull receyuing of the Queenes most excellent Maiestie into hir Highnesse Citie of Norwich* (London, [1578]; *STC* 11627).

Gibson, Strickland (ed.), *Abstracts from the wills and testamentary documents of binders, printers and stationers of Oxford, from 1493 to 1638* (London, 1907).

Gibson, William, *A discription of Nortons falcehod of York shyre* (London, [1570]; *STC* 11843).

Golding, Arthur, *A briefe discourse of the late murther of master G Saunders* (London, 1577; *STC* 11986).

Gray, George J. and W. M. Palmer (eds.), *Abstracts from the wills and testamentary documents of binders, printers and stationers of Cambridge, from 1504 to 1699* (London, 1915).

Gregory, Ivon L., 'Kilkhampton churchwardens' accounts, 1560–1605', *Devon and Cornwall Notes and Queries*, 24 (1950–1), pp. 33–40.

The remains of Edmund Grindal, ed. William Nicholson (Parker Society; Cambridge, 1843).

Hake, Edward, *A commemoration of the most prosperous and peaceable raigne of our gratious and deere soueraigne lady Elizabeth* (London, 1575; *STC* 12605).

A ioyfull continuance of the commemoration of the most prosperous and peaceable reigne of our gratious and deare soueraigne Lady Elizabeth (London, [1578], *STC* 12605.5).

Hall, H. R. Wilton (ed.), *Records of the old Archdeaconry of St Albans: a calendar of papers, AD 1575 to AD 1637* (St Albans and Hertfordshire Architectural and Archaeological Society; St Albans, 1908).

Hall, Joseph, *Virgidemiarum* (London, 1597; *STC* 12716).

Hanham, Alison (ed.), *Churchwardens' accounts of Ashburton, 1479–1580* (Devon and Cornwall Record Society, new series, 15; Torquay, 1970).

Hind, Arthur M., *Engraving in England in the sixteenth and seventeenth centuries* (3 vols., Cambridge, 1952–64).

Historical Manuscripts Commission. Report on the manuscripts of the Lord De L'Isle and Dudley (6 vols., London, 1925–66).

Historical Manuscripts Commission. Report on the manuscripts of Allan George Finch, of Burley-on-the-Hill, Rutland (4 vols., London, 1913–65).

Historical Manuscripts Commission. Report on the manuscripts of the family of Gawdy, formerly of Norfolk (1509–1675) (London, 1885).

Historical Manuscripts Commission. The manuscripts of his grace the duke of Rutland, GCB, preserved at Belvoir Castle (4 vols., London, 1888–1905).

Historical Manuscripts Commission. Calendar of the manuscripts of the most honourable the marquis of Salisbury, K. G. etc. . . (24 vols., London, 1883–1976).

Historical Manuscripts Commission. Report on manuscripts in the Welsh language (6 vols. in 2, London, 1898–1910).

The history of parliament. The House of Commons, 1509–1558, ed. S. T. Bindoff (3 vols., London, 1982).

The history of parliament. The House of Commons, 1558–1603, ed. P. W. Hasler (3 vols., London, 1981).

Holinshed, Raphael, *The firste volume of the chronicles of England, Scotlande, and Irelande* (London, 1577; *STC* 13568a).

Hulbert, Anna, 'Report on Bratoft, Lincolnshire, allegory of the Spanish Armada, August 1977', Wall Paintings Survey, Courtauld Institute, London.

Inventaire des arrêts du conseil d'état (règne de Henri IV), ed. Noël Valois (4 vols., Paris, 1886).

Isocrates, 'To Nicocles', in *Isocrates,* trans. George Norlin (3 vols., Cambridge, Mass., 1954).

A iustification of the Prince of Orendge agaynst the false sclaunders (London, 1575; *STC* 25712).

Jahn, Robert, 'Letters and booklists of Thomas Chard (or Chare) of London, 1583–4', *The Library,* fourth series, 4 (1924), pp. 219–37.

Jones, Ifano, *A history of printing and printing in Wales to 1810* (Cardiff, 1925).

'Journal of Sir Francis Walsingham from December 1570 to April 1583', ed. T. C. Martin, *Camden Miscellany VI* (Camden Society, original series, 106; London, 1871), pp. 1–49.

Keevil, P. J., Reports dated 5 Jan. 1982 and 5 Sept. 1977 and an undated note ('Tristram archive'); File on the Manor House, Little Gaddesdon, Herts, Wall Paintings Survey, Courtauld Institute, London.

Keyser, C. E., *A list of the buildings in Great Britain and Ireland having mural and other painted decorations of dates prior to the latter part of the sixteenth century* (3rd edn, London, 1883).

Kitto, John V. (ed.), *St Martin's-in-the-Fields. The accounts of the churchwardens, 1525–1603* (London, 1901).

Knox, John, *The first blast of the trumpet against the monstrvovs regiment of women* (Geneva, 1558; *STC* 15070).

The lamentable and true tragedie of M. arden of Feuersham (London, 1592; *STC* 733).

Le relazioni degli ambasciatori Veneti al Senato durante il secolo decismoseto, ed. Eugenio Albèri (series 1, vol. IV, Florence, 1860).

A letter sent by I. B. Gentleman vnto his very frende Maystet R. C. Esquire (London, 1572; *STC* 1048).

A letter written by a French gentleman to a friend of his at Rome (London, 1587; *STC* 19078.6).

Letters and Papers, Foreign and Domestic, Henry VIII, ed. J. S. Brewer *et al.* (22 vols., London, 1864–1932).

Letters and State Papers relating to English affairs, preserved principally in the Archives of Simancas, ed. M. A. S. Hune (4 vols., London, 1892–99).

Letters of Queen Elizabeth and King James VI of Scotland, ed. John Bruce (Camden Society, original series, 44; London, 1849).

Lewis, E. A. (ed.), *The Welsh port books, 1550–1603* (Cymmrodorion Record Society, 12, London, 1927).

The life off the 70. archbishopp off Canterbury Presentlye Sittinge Englished [trans. John Stubbs?] ([Zurich], 1574; *STC* 19292a).

Lincolnshire pedigrees: volume II, ed. A. R. Maddison (Harleian Society Publications, 52; London; 1903).

Lodge, Edmund, *Illustrations of British history, biography and manners* (3 vols., London, 1791).

'Loe here the pearle' (London, [1563]; *STC* 7588).

Lyly, John, *Euphues and his England* (London, 1580; *STC* 17068).

    'Campaspe' and 'Sapho and Phao', ed. G. K. Hunter and David Bevington (Manchester and New York, 1991).

    Endymion, ed. David Bevington (Manchester and New York, 1996).

M., W., *A true discourse of the late battaile fought betweene our Englishmen, and the Prince of Parma* (London, 1585; *STC* 17156).

Mac Erlean, John C. (ed.), *Duanaire Dáibid uí bruadair (The poems of David Ó Bruadair), Part III: containing poems from the year 1682 till the poet's death in 1698* (Irish Text Society, 18; London, 1917).

The diary of Henry Machyn, citizen and merchant of London, from AD *1550 to* AD *1563*, ed. J. G. Nichols (Camden Society, original series, 42; London, 1848).

Maillard, André, *An advertisement to the King of Navarre . . . Truly translated according to the copy printed in French* (London, 1585; *STC* 13127).

The complete works of Christopher Marlowe, ed. Fredson Bowes (2 vols., Cambridge, 1973).

Marprelate, Martin, *O read ouer d. John Bridges* ([East Moseley, Surrey], 1588; *STC* 17453).

Martiall, John, *A treatyse of the crosse* (Antwerp, 1564; *STC* 17496).

Masters, Betty R. and Elizabeth Ralph (eds.), *The church book of St Ewen's, Bristol, 1454–1584* (Publications of the Bristol and Gloucestershire Archaeological Society Records Section, 6; London and Ashford, 1967).

McMurray, William (ed.), *The records of two city parishes . . . SS Anne and Agnes, Aldergate & St John Zachary, London* (London, 1925).

Melancthon, Philip, *Of two woonderful popish monsters* (London, 1579; *STC* 17797).

Mellys, John, *The true description of two monsterous children* (London, 1566; *STC* 17803).

Merbury, Charles, *A briefe discourse of royall monarchie, as of the best common weale* (London, 1581; *STC* 17823).

The misfortunes of Arthur: a critical, old-spelling edition, ed. Brian Jay Corrigan (New York and London, 1992).

Montanus, Reginaldus Gonsalvius, *A discovery and playne declaration of sundry subtill practises of the holye inquisition of Spayne. Set forth in Latine, and newly translated* [by V. Skinner] (London, 1568; *STC* 11996).

A discovery and playne declaration of sundry subtill practises of the holye inquisition of Spayne (London, 1569; *STC* 11997).

Mornay, Philippe de, *A necessary discourse concerning the right which the house of Guyze pretendeth to the crown of France* (London, 1586; *STC* 12508).

A moste true and maruelous straunge wonder . . . of xviii monstrous fishes taken in Suffolke at Downam bridge (London, 1568; *STC* 12186).

Munday, Anthony, *A breefe aunswer made vnto two seditious pamphlets . . . Contayning a defence of Edmund Campion* (London, 1582; *STC* 18262).

A breefe and true reporte of the execution of certayne traytours at Tiborne (London, 1582; *STC* 18261).

The Englyshe Romayne life. Discoueringe: the liues of the English men at Roome (London, 1582; *STC* 18272).

Munter, Robert, *A dictionary of the print trade in Ireland, 1550–1775* (New York, 1988).

Murdin, William (ed.), *Collection of state papers, relating to affairs in the reign of Queen Elizabeth from the year 1571 to 1596 . . .* (London, 1759).

A myraculous, and monstrous, but yet most true, and certayne discourse, of a woman (now to be seene in London) of the age of threescore yeares . . . (London, 1588; *STC* 6910.7).

Naunton, Sir Robert, *Fragmenta regalia; or observations on Queen Elizabeth, her times and favourites*, ed. J. S. Cerovski (Washington, DC, 1985).

Nelson, Thomas, *A proper newe ballad declaring the substance of all the late pretended treasons against the Queenes Maiestie* (London, 1586; *STC* 18426.5).

le Neve, John, *Monumenta Anglicana* (5 vols. in 4, London, 1717–19).

Newes from Vienna (London, 1566; *STC* 24716).

Norton, Thomas, *A discourse touching the pretended match betwene the Duke of Norfolk and the Quene of Scottes* (London, 1569; *STC* 13869).

A declaration of the fauourable dealing . . . for the examination of certaine Traitours (London, 1583; *STC* 4901).

Novum repertorium ecclesiasticum parochiale Londinense, compiled by G. Hennessy (London, 1898).

Nowell, Alexander, *A true report of the disputation or rather priuate conference had in the Tower of London, with Ed. Campion Iesuite* (London, 1581; *STC* 18744).

The offer and order giuen forthe by Sir Thomas Smyth Knighte (London, s.n.; *STC* 22868.5).

Oliver, Leslie Martin, 'A bookseller's account book, 1545', *Harvard Library Bulletin*, 16 (1968), pp. 139–55.

Omont, M., 'Inventory of books at the palace of Richmond, 1535', *Études Romanes dédiées à Gaston Paris* (Paris, 1891), pp. 1–13.

An order of praier and thankes-giuing for the preseruation of the quene maiesties life and salfetie (London, 1585; *STC* 16516).

The order of prayer . . . to auert Gods wrath from vs, threatned by the late terrible earthquake (London, 1580; *STC* 16512).

An order of prayer and thankesgiuing, for the preseruation of her maiestie and the realme, from the bloodie practises of the pope (London, 1586; *STC* 16517).

Osborne, Francis Mardon (ed.), *The churchwardens' accounts of St Michael's church, Chagford, 1480–1600* (Chagford, 1979).

Owen, George, Lord of Kemeys, *The Taylor's cussion*, ed. Emily Pritchard (Olwen Powys) (London, 1906).

P., I., *A meruaylous straunge deformed swine* (London, 1570; *STC* 19071).

Paige, Donald, 'An additional letter and booklist of Thomas Chard, stationer of London', *The Library*, fourth series, 21 (1940), pp. 26–43.

Palmer, Anthony (ed.), *Tudor churchwardens' accounts* (Hertfordshire Record Society Publication, 1; Cambridge, 1985).

Park, Thomas (ed.), *Nugae Antiquae: being a miscellaneous collection of original papers . . . by Sir John Harington . . . Selected . . . by the late Henry Harington* (2 vols., London, 1804).

Parker, Matthew, *De antiquitate Britannicae ecclesiae & priuilegiis ecclesiae Cantuariensis, cum archiepiscopis eiusdem 70* (London, 1572–4; *STC* 19292).

Correspondence of Matthew Parker, DD, Archbishop of Canterbury, ed. John Bruce and Thomas Thomason Perowne (Parker Society; Cambridge, 1853).

A particular declaration or testimony, of the vndutifull and traitorous affection borne against her Maiestie by Edmund Campion (London, 1582; *STC* 4536).

Pearson C. B., 'Churchwardens' accounts of St Michael's, Bath, 1349–1575', *Somersetshire Archaeological & Natural History Society Proceedings*, 26 (1880), pp. 101–38.

Pemberton, Caroline (ed.), *Queen Elizabeth's Englishings* (Early English Text Society, original series, 113; London, 1899).

Penry, John, *A viewe of some part of such publike wants & disorders* ([Coventry], 1589; *STC* 19613).

Perry, Maria, *The word of a prince: a life from contemporary documents* (Folio Society; London, 1990).

Persons, Robert, *A brief discours contayning certayne reasons why Catholiques refuse to goe to church* (Douai [i.e. East Ham], 1580; *STC* 19394).
   A briefe censure vppon two bookes written in answere to M. Edmunde Campions offer of disputation (Douai [i.e. Stonor Park, Pyrton], 1581; *STC* 19393).

Pet, Cornelius, *An example of Gods iudgement shew[n] vpon two children* (London, 1582; *STC* 10608.5).

Philips, John, *The examination and confession of certaine wytches at Chensforde in the countie of Essex* (London, 1566; *STC* 19869.5).

Pilkington, James, *The true report of the burnyng of the steple and church of Poules* (London, 1561; *STC* 19930).
   The burnynge of Paules Church (London, 1563; *STC* 19931).
   The plagues of Northomberland (London, 1570; *STC* 1421).

Plomer, H. R. (ed.), *The churchwardens' accounts of St Nicholas, Strood* (Kent Archaeological Society Records, 5; n.p., 1927).

Plutarch, *Moralia*, trans. Frank Cole Babbitt (14 vols., London and New York, 1927–).

Prime, John, *A sermon briefly comparing the estate of the king Salomon and his subiectes with queen Elizabeth and her people* (Oxford, 1585; *STC* 20371).

Proceedings and ordinances of the privy council of England, 10 Richard II–33 Henry VIII, ed. H. Nicolas (7 vols., London, 1834–7).

A proclamacyon set fourth by the Erle of Sussex (Dublin, 1561; *STC* 14138).

A proclamacyon. Sett furthe by the Lorde Justice (Dublin, 1564; *STC* 14139).

The proclamation and edict of the Archbyshop, and Prince Elector of Cvlleyn (London, 1583; *STC* 11694).

A proclamation for waightes (London, 1587; STC 8167).

The Queenes maiesties proclamation against the Earle of Tirone (Dublin, 1595; *STC* 14145 (English) and 14146 (Gaelic)).

R., C., *A true discription of this marueilous straunge fishes* (London, 1569; *STC* 20570).

A rehearsall both straunge and true, of hainous horrible actes commited by . . . four notorious witches (London, 1579; *STC* 23267).

Relations des ambassadeurs Vénitiens sur les affaires de France au xvie siècle, ed. M. N. Tommaseo (2 vols., Paris, 1838).

A reply . . . to a late rayling . . . libel of the papists set vpon postes, and also in Paules church in London (London, 1579; *STC* 19179).

Rodger, Alexander, 'Roger Ward's Shrewsbury stock: an inventory of 1585', *The Library*, fifth series, 13 (1958), pp. 247–68.

Rokeby, Rafe (the younger), 'Oeconomia Rokebiorum', in *A history of Richmondshire*, ed. T. D. Whitaker (2 vols., London, 1823), I, pp. 158–79.

Royal Commission on Historical Monuments (England). An inventory of the historical monuments in Essex (4 vols., London, 1916–23).

Royal Commission on Historical Monuments (England). An inventory of the historical monuments in Hertfordshire (London, 1910).

Royal Commission on Historical Monuments (England). An inventory of the historical monuments in Middlesex (London, 1937).

Royal Commission on the Ancient and Historical Monuments of Wales. An inventory of the ancient monuments in Glamorgan (4 vols., London and Cardiff, 1976–91).

Russia at the close of the sixteenth century, comprising the treatise 'Of the Russe Common Wealth' by Dr Giles Fletcher, and the travels of Sir Jerome Horsey, knt, ed. Edward A. Bond (Hakluyt Society; London, 1856).

S[erres], W[illiam], *An answere to the proclamation of the rebels of the North* (London, 1569; *STC* 22234).

Sandys, Edwin, *Sermons made by the Most Reuerende Father in God, Edwin, Archbishop of Yorke* (London, 1585; *STC* 21713).

Schmidt, Albert J., 'A treatise on England's perils', *Archiv für Reformations Geschichte*, 46 (1955), pp. 243–9.

Seyssel, Claude de, *La grant monarchie de France composee par missure Claude de Seyssel lors euersque de Marseille et a present Archeuesque de Thurin adressant au roy tres crestien francoys premier de ce nom* (Paris, 1519).

The monarchy of France, trans. by J. H. Hexter, ed., annotated and introduced by Donald R. Kelley with additional translations by Michael Sherman (New Haven and London, 1981).

The shape of ii monsters (London, 1562; *STC* 11485).

A shorte forme of thankesgeuing for the delyuerie of the isle of Malta from the Turkes (London, 1565; *STC* 16509).

A short-title catalogue of books printed in England, Scotland, and Ireland and of English books printed abroad, 1475–1640, compiled by A. W. Pollard and G. R. Redgrave, revised and enlarged by W. A. Jackson, F. S. Ferguson and K. F. Pantzer (3 vols., London, 1986–1991).

Smith, J. T., *Hertfordshire houses: selective inventory* (London, 1993).

Spenser, Edmund, *The shepheardes calendar* (London, 1579; *STC* 23089).

Stallard, A. D. (ed.), *The transcript of the churchwardens' accounts of the parish of Tilney All Saints, Norfolk, 1443–1589* (London, 1922).

The state of the church in the reigns of Elizabeth and James I, ed. C. W. Foster (Lincoln Record Society, 23; Lincoln, 1926).

The state papers and letters of Sir Ralph Sadler, ed. Arthur Collins (2 vols., Edinburgh, 1809).

State papers and manuscripts relating to English affairs, existing in the archives and collections of Venice, and in other libraries of Northern Italy, ed. R. Brown et al. (37 vols., London, 1864–1947).

State papers, relating to English affairs, in the Vatican Archives and Library, ed. J. M. Rigg (2 vols., London, 1916–26).

Sterrie, D., *A briefe sonet declaring the lamentation of Beckles* (London, 1586; *STC* 23259).

A straunge and terrible wunder wrought very late in the parish church of Bongay (London, 1577; *STC* 11050).

Strype, John, *The life of the learned Sir Thomas Smith, kt. DCL* (new edn., Oxford, 1820).

Stubbe, John, *The discouerie of a gaping gvlf whereinto England is like to be swallowed by an other French marriage* (London, 1579; *STC* 23400).

John Stubbs's 'Gaping Gulf' with letters and other relevant documents, ed. Lloyd E. Berry (Charlottesville, VA, 1968).

A summe of the Guisian ambassage to the bishop of Rome (London, 1579; *STC* 6319).

Swayne, H. J. Fowle (ed.), *Churchwardens' accounts for S. Edmund and S. Thomas, Sarum, 1443–1702* (Wiltshire Record Society; Salisbury, 1896).

Tedder, William, and Anthony Tyrrell, *The recantation as they were seueralie pronounced by William Tedder and Anthony Tyrrell* (London, 1588; *STC* 23859.3).

Tighe, W. J., 'The counsel of Thomas Radcliffe, earl of Sussex, to Queen Elizabeth I concerning the revolt of the Netherlands, September 1578', *Sixteenth Century Journal*, 18 (1987), pp. 323–31.

[To the reader. Beholde here (gentle reader) a brief abstract of the genealogie of all the kynges of England] ([Imprinted by Gyles Godet, 1560]; *STC* 10022).

A true and perfect discourse of three great accidents that chaunced in Italie within twentie and six dayes (London, 1588; *STC* 14285).

The true copie of a letter from the Queenes Maiestie . . . vpon the apprehension of diuers persons, detected of a most wicked conspiracie (London, 1586; *STC* 7577).

The true coppie of a letter written from the leager by Arnham (London, [1591]; *STC* 781).

A true discourse of the assault committed vpon the person of the most noble prince, William, Prince of Orange (London, 1582; *STC* 25713).

A true discourse of the late battaile fought betweene our Englishmen, and the Prince of Parma (London, 1585; *STC* 17156).

A true report of the inditement, arraignement, conuiction, condemmation, and execution of Iohn Weldon, William Hartley, and Robert Sutton (London, 1588; *STC* 25229.3).

A true report of the taking of Marseilles by the fauourers of the league (London, 1585; *STC* 17468).

A true reporte of a conference had betwixt Doctour Fulke, and the Papists being at Wisbich Castle (London, 1581; *STC* 11457).

A true reporte of the taking of the the great towne and castell of Polotzko (London, 1579; *STC* 20092.5).

The Victoria County History of the counties of England: Hertfordshire, ed. William Page (5 vols., Westminster, 1902–23).

Wall, Alison (ed.), *Two Elizabethan women: correspondence of Joan and Maria Thynne, 1575–1611* (Wiltshire Record Society, 38; Devizes, 1983).

Walsall, John, *A sermon preached at Paul's Crosse by Iohn Walsall, one of the preachers of Christ his Church in Canterburie 5 October 1578* (London, [1578?]; *STC* 24995).

Walters H. B., 'The churchwardens' accounts of the parish of Worfield. Part VI, 1572–1603', *Transactions of the Shropshire Archaeological and Natural History Society*, third series, 10 (1910), pp. 59–86.

Waterlow, Alford James (ed.), *The accounts of the churchwardens of the parish of St Michael, Cornhill in the city of London, from 1456 to 1608* (n.p., 1883).

Watson, Foster, *Vives: On education. A translation of the 'De tradensis disciplinis' of Juan Luis Vives* (Cambridge, 1913).

Williams, J. F. (ed.), *The early churchwardens' accounts of Hampshire* (Winchester and London, 1913).

Wiltshire County Records: minutes of proceedings in sessions, 1563 and 1574 to 1592, ed. H. C. Johnson (Devizes, 1949).

Wright, Thomas (ed.), *Churchwardens' accounts of the town of Ludlow in Shropshire from 1540 to the end of the reign of Queen Elizabeth* (Camden Society, 102; London, 1869).

Z., Q., *A discouerie of the treasons practised and attempted against the Queenes Maiestie and the realme, by Francis Throckmorton* (London, 1584; *STC* 24050.5).

SECONDARY WORKS

Adams, Simon, 'Faction, clientage and party: English politics, 1550–1603', *History Today*, 32 (1982), pp. 33–9.

'Eliza enthroned?: the court and its politics', in Christopher Haigh (ed.), *The reign of Elizabeth I* (Basingstoke and London, 1984), pp. 55–77.

'The Dudley clientele, 1553–1563', in G. W. Bernard (ed.), *The Tudor nobility* (Manchester and New York, 1992), pp. 241–65.

'Favourites and factions at the Elizabethan court', reprinted, with postscript, in Guy (ed.), *Tudor monarchy*, pp. 253–74.

'Politics', *Transactions of the Royal Historical Society*, sixth series, 7 (1997), pp. 247–65.

Adamson, John, 'The making of the *ancien-régime* court, 1500–1700', in Adamson (ed.), *The princely courts of Europe: ritual, politics and culture under the Ancien-Régime, 1500–1700* (London, 1999), pp. 7–41.

Adamson, John, (ed.), *The princely courts of Europe: ritual, politics and culture under the Ancien-Régime, 1500–1700* (London, 1999).

Addleshaw, G. W. O. and F. Etchells, *The architectural setting of anglican worship* (London, 1948).

Alford, Stephen, *The early Elizabethan polity: William Cecil and the British succession crisis, 1558–1569* (Cambridge, 1998).

Altman, Joel, B., '*Quaestiones copiosae*: pastoral and courtly in John Lyly', in Altman (ed.), *The Tudor play of mind: rhetorical inquiry and the development of Elizabethan drama* (Berkeley, CA and London, 1978), pp. 196–228.

Altman, Joel, B., (ed.), *The Tudor play of mind: rhetorical inquiry and the development of Elizabethan drama* (Berkeley, CA and London, 1978).

Amussen, Susan Dwyer, 'The gendering of popular culture in early modern England', in Harris (ed.), *Popular culture in England*, pp. 48–68.

Amussen, Susan Dwyer and Mark Kishlansky (eds.), *Political culture and cultural politics in early modern England: essays presented to David Underdown* (Manchester and New York, 1995).

Andrews, K. R., N. P. Canny and P. E. H. Hair (eds.), *The Westward enterprise: English activities in Ireland, the Atlantic, and America, 1480–1650* (Liverpool, 1978).

Archer, Ian, 'Popular politics in the sixteenth and early seventeenth centuries', in P. Griffiths and M. Jenner (eds.), *Londinopolis* (Manchester, 2000), pp. 26–46.

Armesto, Felipe Fernández, *The Spanish Armada: the experience of war in 1588* (Oxford, 1988).

Astington, John, *English court theatre, 1558–1640* (Cambridge, 1999).

Aston, Margaret, *The king's bedpost: Reformation and iconography in a Tudor group portrait* (Cambridge, 1993).

Atherton, Ian, 'The itch grown a disease: manuscript transmission of news in the seventeenth century', in Joad Raymond (ed.), *News, newspapers and society in early modern Britain* (London, 1999), pp. 39–65.

Axton, Marie, 'Robert Dudley and the Inner Temple revels', *Historical Journal*, 13 (1970), pp. 365–78.

Baker, Keith Michael, 'Defining the public sphere in eighteenth-century France: variations on a theme by Habermas', in Calhoun (ed.), *Habermas and the public sphere*, pp. 181–211.

Barnett, R. C., *Place, profit, and power: a study of the servants of William Cecil, Elizabethan statesmen* (Chapel Hill, NC, 1969).

Bernard, G. W., 'New perspectives or old complexities?', *English Historical Review*, 116 (2000), pp. 113–20.

Betteridge, Thomas, *Tudor histories of the English Reformations, 1530–83* (Aldershot and Brookfield, VT, 1999).

Bevington, David and Peter Holbrook, 'Introduction', in Bevington and Holbrook, (eds.), *The politics of the Stuart court masque* (Cambridge, 1998), pp. 1–19.

Bevington, David and Peter Holbrook, (eds.), *The politics of the Stuart court masque* (Cambridge, 1998).

Bindoff, S. T., Joel Hurstfield and C. H. Williams (eds.), *Elizabethan government and society: essays presented to Sir John Neale* (London, 1961).

Blanchard, Ian, 'Sir Thomas Gresham, c.1518–1579', in Ann Saunders (ed.), *The Royal Exchange* (London, 1997), pp. 11–19.

Bland, D. S., 'Arthur Broke's *Masque of beauty and desire*: a reconstruction', *Research Opportunities in Renaissance Drama*, 19 (1976), pp. 49–55.

Bliss, Alan, 'The English language in early modern Ireland', in Moody, Martin and Byrne (eds.), *A new history of Ireland III: Early modern Ireland*, pp. 546–60.

Blomefield, Francis (and Charles Parkin), *An essay towards a topographical history of the county of Norfolk* (11 vols., London, 1805–10).

Bolton, Arthur T., 'Ashridge Park I and II', *Country Life*, 50 (6 Aug. and 13 Aug. 1921).

Bradshaw, Brendan, 'The Elizabethans and the Irish', *Studies*, 66 (1977), pp. 38–50.

'Native reaction to the Westward enterprise: a case-study in Gaelic ideology', in Andrews, Canny and Hair (eds.), *The Westward enterprise*, pp. 65–80.

'Manus "the Magnificent": O'Donnell as Renaissance prince', in Cosgrove and McCartney (eds.), *Studies in Irish History*, pp. 15–36.

'The Elizabethans and the Irish: a muddled model', *Studies*, 70 (1981), pp. 233–44.

'Transalpine humanism', in J. H. Burns and Mark Goldie (eds.), *The Cambridge history of political thought, 1450–1700* (Cambridge, 1991; 1996 edn), pp. 95–131.

'The bardic response to conquest and colonisation', *Bullán: an Irish Studies Journal*, 1 (1994), pp. 119–22.

Brady, Ciaran, 'Political women and reform in Tudor Ireland', in Margaret MacCurtain and Mary O'Dowd (eds.), *Women in early modern Ireland* (Edinburgh, 1991), pp. 69–90.

The chief governors: the rise and fall of reform government in Tudor Ireland, 1536–1588 (Cambridge, 1994).

Brady, Ciaran, and Raymond Gillespie (eds.), *Natives and newcomers: essays on the making of Irish colonial society, 1534–1641* (Bungay, Suffolk, 1986).

Brayshay, Mark, 'Royal post-horse routes in England and Wales: the evolution of the network in the later-sixteenth and early-seventeenth century', *Journal of Historical Geography*, 17 (1991), pp. 373–89.

Brayshay, Mark, Philip Harrison and Brain Chalkley, 'Knowledge, nationhood and governance: the speed of the royal post in early modern England', *Journal of Historical Geography*, 24 (1998), pp. 265–88.

Brewer, John and Roy Porter (eds.), *Consumption and the world of goods* (London and New York, 1993).

Brown, Keith M., 'The price of friendship: the "well-affected" and English economic clientage in Scotland before 1603', in Mason (ed.), *Scotland and England*, pp. 139–62.

Burgon, J. W., *The life and times of Sir Thomas Gresham* (2 vols., London, 1839).

Burns, J. H. and Mark Goldie (eds.), *The Cambridge history of political thought, 1450–1700* (Cambridge, 1991; 1996 edn).

Bush M. L., 'Protector Somerset and the 1549 rebellions: a post-revision questioned', *English Historical Review*, 116 (2000), pp. 103–12.

Byrom H. J., 'Edmund Spenser's first printer, Hugh Singleton', *The Library*, fourth series, 14 (1933), pp. 121–56.

Caball, Marc, '*The Gaelic mind and the collapse of the Gaelic world*: an appraisal', *Cambridge Medieval Celtic Studies*, 25 (1993), pp. 87–96.

Poets and politics: reaction and continuity in Irish poetry, 1558–1625 (Cork, 1998).

Calhoun, Craig (ed.), *Habermas and the public sphere* (Cambridge, Mass., 1992).

Canny, Nicholas, *The Elizabethan conquest of Ireland: a pattern established, 1565–1576* (Hassocks, 1976).

'The formation of the Irish mind: religion, politics and Gaelic Irish literature, 1580–1750', *Past & Present*, 95 (1982), pp. 91–116.

Cautley, H. M., *Royal arms and commandments in our churches* (Ipswich, 1934).

Cavanagh, Sheila T., '"The fatal destiny of that land": Elizabethan views of Ireland' in Hadfield (ed.), *Representing Ireland*, pp. 116–31.

Chilton, Arthur, 'Queen Elizabeth at Tilbury', *Essex Review*, 53 (1944), p. 68.

Christian, Margaret, 'Elizabeth's preachers and the government of women: defining and correcting a queen', *Sixteenth Century Journal*, 24 (1993), pp. 561–76.

Clark, Peter, *The English alehouse: a social history, 1200–1830* (London and New York, 1983).

Clark, Peter, A. G. R. Smith and Nicholas Tyacke (eds.), *The English Commonwealth, 1547–1640* (Leicester, 1979).

Clarke, Desmond, and P. J. Madden, 'Printing in Ireland', *An Leabharlann*, 12 (1954), pp. 113–30.

Cockburn, J. S., 'Early modern assize records as historical evidence', *Journal of the Society of Archivists*, 5 (1974–7), pp. 215–31.

Cogswell, Thomas, *The blessed revolution: English politics and the coming of war, 1621–1624* (Cambridge, 1989).

'Underground verse and the transformation of early Stuart political culture', in Amussen and Kishlansky (eds.), *Political culture and cultural politics in early modern England*, pp. 277–300.

Cole, Mary Hill, *The portable queen: Elizabeth I and the politics of ceremony* (Amherst, 1999).

Coleman, C. and David Starkey (eds.), *Revolution reassessed: revisions in the history of Tudor government and administration* (Oxford, 1986).

Coleman, Janet, *English literature in history, 1350–1400: medieval readers and writers* (London, 1981).

Collinson, Patrick, *The Elizabethan puritan movement* (Oxford, 1967).

'The downfall of Archbishop Grindal and its place in Elizabethan political and ecclesiastical history', in Clark, Smith and Tyacke (eds.), *The English Commonwealth, 1547–1640*, pp. 39–57.

'The monarchical republic of Queen Elizabeth I', *Bulletin of the John Rylands University Library of Manchester*, 69 (1987), pp. 394–424.

'Puritans, men of business and Elizabethan parliaments', *Parliamentary History*, 7 (1988), pp. 187–211 and reprinted in Collinson, *Elizabethan Essays*, pp. 59–86.

'The Elizabethan exclusion crisis and the Elizabethan polity', *Proceedings of the British Academy*, 84 (1993), pp. 51–92.

'*De republica Anglorum*: or, history with the politics put back', in Collinson (ed.), *Elizabethan essays* (London, 1994), pp. 1–29.

'Ecclesiastical vitriol: religious satire in the 1590s and the invention of puritanism', in Guy (ed.), *Reign of Elizabeth I*, pp. 150–70.

Collinson, Patrick (ed.), *Elizabethan essays* (London, 1994).

Conrad, F. W., 'The problem of counsel reconsidered: the case of Sir Thomas Elyot', in Fideler and Mayer (eds.), *Political thought and the Tudor commonwealth*, pp. 75–107.

Cooper, Helen, 'Location and meaning in masque, morality and royal entertainment', in Lindley (ed.), *The court masque*, pp. 135–48.

Cooper, Nicholas, *Houses of the gentry, 1480–1680* (New Haven and London, 1999).

Cornelius, David B., *Devon and Cornwall: a postal history, 1500–1791* (Postal History Society, 31; Reigate, 1973).

Cosgrove, Art and Donal McCartney (eds.), *Studies in Irish History* (Dublin, 1979).

Council, Norman, 'O Dea certe: the allegory of *The fortress of perfect beauty*', *Huntington Library Quarterly*, 39 (1976), pp. 329–42.

Cowan, Brian, 'What was masculine about the public sphere? Gender and the coffeehouse milieu in post-Restoration England', *History Workshop Journal*, 51 (2001), pp. 127–57.

'The rise of the coffeehouse reconsidered', *Historical Journal*, 47 (2004), pp. 21–46.

Crane, Mary Thomas, 'Video and taceo: Elizabeth I and the rhetoric of counsel', *Studies in English Literature 1500–1900*, 28 (1988), pp. 1–15.

Cressy, David, *Bonfires and bells: national memory and the Protestant calendar in Elizabethan and Stuart England* (London, 1989).

'Literacy in context: meaning and measurement in early modern England', in Brewer and Porter (eds.), *Consumption and the world of goods*, pp. 305–19.

Travesties and transgressions in Tudor and Stuart England (Oxford, 2000).

Croft, Pauline, 'The reputation of Robert Cecil: libels, political opinion and popular awareness in the early seventeenth century', *Transactions of the Royal Historical Society*, sixth series, 1 (1991), pp. 43–69.

Croft-Murray, Edward, *Decorative paintings in England, 1537–1837* (2 vols., London, 1962).

Crofts, J., *Packhorse, wagon and post: land carriage and communications under the Tudors and Stuarts* (London and Toronto, 1967).

Cross, Claire, *The puritan earl: the life of Henry Hastings, third earl of Huntingdon, 1536–1595* (London, Toronto and New York, 1966).

Cunningham, Bernadette, 'Native culture and political change in Ireland, 1580–1640', in Brady and Gillespie (eds.), *Natives and newcomers*, pp. 148–70.

Curteis, Tobit, 'The Elizabethan wall-paintings of Hill Hall: influences and techniques', in Roy and Smith (eds.), *Painting techniques: history, materials and studio practice*, pp. 131–4.

Cust, Richard, 'News and politics in early seventeenth-century England', *Past & Present*, 112 (1986), pp. 60–90.

Dawson, Jane E., 'William Cecil and the British dimension of early Elizabethan foreign policy', *History*, 74 (1989), pp. 196–216.

Daybell, James, '"Suche newes as on the Quenes hye wayes we have mett": the news and intelligence networks of Elizabeth Talbot, countess of Shrewsbury (c.1527–1608)', in Daybell (ed.), *Women and politics*, pp. 114–31.

Daybell, James (ed.), *Women and politics in early modern England, 1450–1700* (Basingstoke, 2004).

Dewar, Mary, *Sir Thomas Smith: a Tudor intellectual in office* (London, 1964).

Dickerman, Edmund M., *Bellièvre and Villeroy: power in France under Henry III and Henry IV* (Providence, RI, 1971).

Dix, E. R. McClintock, 'Humphrey Powell, the first Dublin printer', *Proceedings of the Royal Irish Academy*, 27 (1907), section C, pp. 213–16.

'William Kearney, the second earliest known printer in Dublin', *Proceedings of the Royal Irish Academy*, 28 (1908), section C, pp. 157–61.

'Initial letters used by John Francton, printer at Dublin', *Irish Book Lover*, 3 (1911), pp. 58–9.

'Humphrey Powell, Dublin's first printer: some new information', *Bibliographic Society of Ireland Publications*, 4 (1928), pp. 77–80.

Dobranski, Stephen B., '"Where men of differing judgements croud": Milton and the culture of coffee houses', *The Seventeenth Century*, 9 (1994), pp. 35–56.

Dobson, Michael and Nicola J. Watson, *England's Elizabeth* (Oxford, 2002).

Doran, Susan, *Monarchy and matrimony: the courtships of Elizabeth I* (London, 1996).

Doran, Susan and Thomas S. Freeman (eds.), *The myth of Elizabeth* (Basingstoke, 2003).

Dorsten, J. A. van, *Poets, patrons and professors: Sir Philip Sidney, Daniel Rogers, and the Leiden humanists* (Leiden and Oxford, 1962).

Drury P. J., '"A fayre house, buylt by Sir Thomas Smith": the development of Hill Hall, Essex, 1557–81', *Journal of the British Archaeological Association*, 136 (1983), pp. 98–123.

Duffy, Eamon, *The stripping of the altars: traditional religion in England, 1400–1580* (New Haven and London, 1992).

Duindam, Jereon, *Myths of power: Norbert Elias and the early modern court*, trans. Lorri S. Granger and Gerard T. Moran (Amsterdam, [1994?]).

Dunne, T. J., 'The Gaelic response to conquest and colonisation: the evidence of the poetry', *Studia Hibernica*, 20 (1980), pp. 7–30.

Dunne, T. J. (ed.), *The writer as witness: literature as historical evidence* (*Historical Studies*, 16; Cork, 1987).

Durant, David N., *Bess of Hardwick: portrait of an Elizabethan dynast* (London, 1977).

Eccles, Mark, *Christopher Marlowe in London* (Cambridge, Mass., 1934).

Edwards, R. D., 'Ireland, Elizabeth I and the Counter-Reformation', in Bindoff, Hurstfield and Williams (eds.), *Elizabethan government and society*, pp. 315–39.

Eley, Geoff, 'Nations, publics, and political cultures: placing Habermas in the nineteenth century', in Calhoun (ed.), *Habermas and the public sphere*, pp. 289–339.

Elias, Norbert, *The civilizing process*, trans. Edmund Jephcott (2 vols., Oxford, 1978, 1982).

The court society, trans. Edmund Jephcott (Oxford, 1983).

Ellis, Stephen G., 'Economic problems of the Church: why the Reformation failed in Ireland', *Journal of Ecclesiastical History*, 41 (1990), pp. 239–65.

Ireland in the age of the Tudors, 1447–1603: English expansion and the end of Gaelic rule (Harlow, 1998).

Elton, G. R., *Studies in Tudor and Stuart politics and government* (4 vols., Cambridge, 1974–92).

'Tudor government: the points of contact. I. Parliament', *Transactions of the Royal Historical Society*, fifth series, 24 (1974), pp. 183–200.

'Tudor government: the points of contact. II. The council', *Transactions of the Royal Historical Society*, fifth series, 25 (1975), pp. 195–211.

'Tudor government: the points of contact. III. The court', *Transactions of the Royal Historical Society*, fifth series, 26 (1976), pp. 211–28.

The parliaments of England, 1559–1581 (Cambridge, 1986).

'Tudor government', *Historical Journal*, 31 (1988), pp. 425–34.

'Queen Elizabeth', in Elton, *Studies*, I, pp. 238–46.

'Arthur Hall, Lord Burghley and the antiquity of parliament', in Elton, *Studies*, III, pp. 254–73.

'Piscatorial politics in the early parliaments of Elizabeth I', in Elton, *Studies*, IV, pp. 109–30.

Elton, W. R. and John M. Mucciolo (eds.), *The Shakespearean international yearbook 2: where are we now in Shakespearean studies?* (Aldershot, 2002).

Emmison, F. G., *Elizabethan life: disorder* (Essex Record Office; Chelmsford, 1970).

Fideler, Paul A. and T. F. Mayer (eds.), *Political thought and the Tudor commonwealth: deep structure, discourse and disguise* (London, 1992).

Fisher, R. M., 'Privy council coercion and religious conformity at the Inns of Court, 1569–84', *Recusant History*, 15 (1979–81), pp. 33–61.

Fox, Adam, 'Rumour, news and popular political opinion in Elizabethan and early Stuart England', *Historical Journal*, 40 (1993), pp. 597–620.

Oral and literate culture in England, 1500–1700 (Oxford, 2000).

Fraser, Nancy, 'Rethinking the public sphere: a contribution to the critique of actually existing democracy', in Calhoun (ed.), *Habermas and the public sphere*, pp. 109–42.

Freeman, Thomas S., '"The reformation of the church in this parliament": Thomas Norton, John Foxe and the parliament of 1571', *Parliamentary History*, 16 (1997), pp. 131–47.

'"As true a subiect being prisoner": John Foxe's notes on the imprisonment of Princess Elizabeth, 1554–5', *English Historical Review*, 117 (2002), pp. 104–16.

'Providence and prescription: the account of Elizabeth in Foxe's "Book of martyrs"', in Doran and Freeman (eds.), *Myth of Elizabeth*, pp. 27–54.

Garnham, Nicholas, 'The media and the public sphere', in Calhoun (ed.), *Habermas and the public sphere*, pp. 359–76.

Garrett, Christina, *The Marian exiles, 1553–1559* (Cambridge, 1938).

Gee, Stacey, 'The printers, stationers and bookbinders of York before 1557', *Transactions of the Cambridge Bibliographical Society*, 12 (2000), pp. 27–54.

Goldberg, Jonathan, *James I and the politics of literature: Jonson, Shakespeare, Donne, and their contemporaries* (Stanford, CA, 1989).

Gowing, Laura, *Domestic dangers: women, words and sex in early modern London* (Oxford, 1996; 1998 edn).

Graves, M. A. R., 'Thomas Norton, the parliament man: an Elizabethan MP, 1559–1581', *Historical Journal*, 23 (1980), pp. 17–35.

'The management of the Elizabethan House of Commons: the council's "men-of-business"', *Parliamentary History*, 2 (1983), pp. 11–38.

'The common lawyers and the privy council's parliamentary men-of-business, 1584–1601', *Parliamentary History*, 8 (1989), pp. 189–215.

Thomas Norton: the parliament man (Oxford, 1994).

'Elizabethan men of business reconsidered', *Parergon*, 14 (1996), pp. 111–27.

Griffiths, P. and M. Jenner (eds.), *Londinopolis* (Manchester, 2000).

Griffiths, Ralph A. and James Sherborne (eds.), *Kings and nobles in the later Middle Ages: a tribute to Charles Ross* (Gloucester and New York, 1986).

Gruffydd, R. Geraint, 'The Renaissance and Welsh literature', in Williams and Jones (eds.), *The Celts and the Renaissance*, pp. 17–39.

Gurr, Andrew, *Play-going in Shakespeare's London* (Cambridge, 1987).

Guy, John, 'The French king's council, 1483–1526', in Griffiths and Sherborne (eds.), *Kings and nobles in the later Middle Ages*, pp. 274–94.

'The king's council and political participation', in Guy and Fox, (eds.), *The Henrician age*, pp. 121–47.

'Privy council: revolution or evolution?', in Coleman and Starkey, (eds.), *Revolution reassessed*, pp. 59–85.

'The 1590s: the second reign of Elizabeth I?', in Guy (ed.), *Reign of Elizabeth I*, pp. 1–19.

'The Elizabethan establishment of the ecclesiastical polity', in Guy (ed.), *Reign of Elizabeth I*, pp. 126–49.

'The rhetoric of counsel in early modern England', in Hoak (ed.), *Tudor political culture*, pp. 292–310.

'General introduction', in Guy (ed.), *Tudor monarchy*, pp. 1–10.

'Tudor monarchy and its critiques', in Guy (ed.), *Tudor monarchy*, pp. 78–109.

'The Marian court and Tudor policy-making', Early modern seminar, University of Cambridge, May 1998.

'Elizabeth I: the queen and politics', in Elton and Mucciolo (eds.), *The Shakespearean international yearbook 2*, pp. 183–202.

Guy, John, (ed.), *The reign of Elizabeth I: court and culture in the last decade* (Cambridge, 1995).

The Tudor monarchy (London and New York, 1997).

Guy, John and Alistair Fox (eds.), *The Henrician age: humanism, politics and reform, 1500–1550* (Oxford, 1986).

Habermas, Jürgen, *The structural transformation of the public sphere: an inquiry into a category of bourgeois society*, trans. Thomas Burger with Patrick Lawrence (Cambridge, Mass., 1989).

Hadfield, A. (ed.), *Representing Ireland: literature and the origins of conflict, 1534–1660* (Cambridge, 1993).

Haigh, Christopher, *Elizabeth I* (Harlow and London, 1988; revised edn, 2001).

'Catholicism in early modern England: Bossy and beyond', *Historical Journal*, 45 (2002), pp. 481–94.

Halasz, Alexandra, *The marketplace of print: pamphlets and the public sphere in early modern England* (Cambridge, 1997).

Hammer, Paul E. J., 'Patronage at court, faction and the earl of Essex', in Guy (ed.), *Reign of Elizabeth I*, pp. 65–86.

The polarisation of Elizabethan politics: the political career of Robert Devereux, second earl of Essex, 1585–1597 (Cambridge, 1999).

Hammerstein, Helga, 'Aspects of the continental education of Irish students in the reign of Queen Elizabeth I', in Williams (ed.), *Historical Studies*, pp. 137–53.

Harlow C. G., 'Robert Ryece of Preston, 1555–1638', *Proceedings of the Suffolk Institute of Archaeology*, 32 (1971–3), pp. 43–70.

Harris, Frances, *A passion for government: the life of Sarah, duchess of Marlborough* (Oxford, 1991).

Harris, Tim, 'The problem of "poular political culture" in seventeenth-century London', *History of European Ideas*, 10 (1989), pp. 43–58.

'Problematising popular culture', in Harris (ed.), *Popular culture in England*, pp. 1–27.

Harris, Tim (ed.), *Popular culture in England, c.1500–1800* (Basingstoke and London, 1995).

Harrison, Thomas P., Archibald H. Hill, Ernest C. Mossner and James Sledd (eds.), *Studies in honor of DeWitt T. Staines* (Austin, TX, 1967).

Hassell Smith, A., *Country and court: government and politics in Norfolk, 1558–1603* (Oxford, 1974).

Heisch, Allison, 'Queen Elizabeth I and the persistence of patriarchy', *Feminist Review*, 4 (1980), pp. 45–56.

Highley, Christopher, 'The royal image in Ireland', in Walker (ed.), *Dissing Elizabeth*, pp. 60–76.

Hindle, Steve, 'Hierarchy and community in the Elizabethan parish: the Swallowfield articles of 1596', *Historical Journal*, 42 (1999), pp. 835–51.

Hoak, Dale (ed.), *Tudor political culture* (Cambridge, 1995).

Hodgett, Gerald A. J., *Tudor Lincolnshire* (*History of Lincolnshire*, ed. Joan Thirsk, vol. VI; Lincoln, 1975).

Holmes, Clive, *Seventeenth-century Lincolnshire* (*History of Lincolnshire*, ed. Joan Thirsk, vol. VII; Lincoln, 1980).

Howell, Ben, *Law and disorder in Tudor Monmouthshire* (Cardiff, 1995).

Hudson, Winthrop S., *The Cambridge connection and the Elizabethan settlement of 1559* (Durham, NC, 1980).

Hussey, Christopher, 'Cothay, Somerset, part I', *Country Life*, 62 (1927), pp. 596–604.

Imray, Jean, 'The origins of the Royal Exchange', in Saunders (ed.), *The Royal Exchange*, pp. 20–35.

James, Mervyn, 'The concept of order and the Northern Rising, 1569', in James (ed.), *Society, politics and culture*, pp. 270–307.

James, Mervyn, (ed.), *Society, politics and culture: studies in early modern England* (Cambridge, 1986).

Jardine Lisa and Antony Grafton, '"Studied for action": how Gabriel Harvey read his Livy', *Past & Present*, 128 (1990), pp. 30–78.

John, Lisle Cecil, 'Roger Manners, Elizabethan courtier', *Huntington Library Quarterly*, 12 (1948–49), pp. 57–84.

Jones, E. Gwynne, 'The Lleyn recusancy case, 1578–1581', *Transactions of the Honourable Society of Cymmrodorion* (1936), pp. 97–123.

'Robert Pugh of Penrhyn Creuddyn', *Transactions of the Caernarvonshire Historical Society*, 4 (1942–3), pp. 10–19.

'The duality of Robert ap Hugh of Penrhyn Creudynn', *Transactions of the Caernarvonshire Historical Society*, 17 (1956), pp. 54–63.

Jones J. G., 'The Welsh poets and their patrons, c.1550–1640', *Welsh History Review*, 14 (1979), pp. 245–77.

Jones, Norman and Paul Whitfield White, '*Gorboduc* and royal marriage politics: an Elizabethan playgoer's report of the premiere performance', *English Literary Renaissance*, 26 (1996), pp. 3–16.

Jordan, Constance, 'Woman's rule in sixteenth-century British political thought', *Renaissance Quarterly*, 40 (1987), pp. 421–51.

King, John N., 'Queen Elizabeth I: representations of the Virgin Queen', *Renaissance Quarterly*, 43 (1990), pp. 30–74.

Kocher, Paul H., 'François Hotman and Marlowe's *Massacre at Paris*', *Publications of the Modern Language Association*, 56 (1941), pp, 349–68.

'Contemporary pamphlet backgrounds for Marlowe's *Massacre at Paris*', *Modern Language Quarterly*, 8 (1947), pp. 151–73.

Lake, Peter, *Moderate puritans in the Elizabethan Church* (Cambridge, 1982).

Lake, Peter and Michael Questier, 'Puritans, papists, and the "public sphere" in early modern England: the Edmund Campion affair in context', *Journal of Modern History*, 72 (2000), pp. 589–627.

Lake, Peter with Michael Questier, *The anti-christ's lewd hat: protestants, papists and players in post-Reformation England* (New Haven and London, 2002).

Lee, Patricia-Ann, 'A bodye politique to governe: Aylmer, Knox and the debate on queenship', *The Historian* (USA), 52 (1990), pp. 242–61.

Lehmberg, Stanford E., *Sir Walter Mildmay and Tudor government* (Austin, TX, 1964).

Levin, Carole, *'The heart and stomach of a king': Elizabeth I and the politics of sex and power* (Philadelphia, PA, 1993).

Levy, F. J., 'How information spread among the gentry, 1550–1640', *Journal of British Studies*, 112 (1982), pp. 11–34.

'The decorum of news', *Prose Studies*, 21 (1998), pp. 12–38.

Lewis, I. (ed.), *Symbols and sentiments: cross cultural studies in symbolism* (London, 1977).

Lindley, David (ed.), *The court masque* (Manchester, 1984).

Litzenberger, Caroline, *The English Reformation and the laity: Gloucestershire, 1540–1580* (Cambridge, 1997).

'Defining the Church of England: religious change in the 1570s', in Wabuda and Litzenberger (eds.), *Belief and practice in Reformation England*, pp. 137–53.

MacCaffrey, Wallace T., *The shaping of the Elizabethan regime: Elizabethan politics, 1558–1572* (Princeton, NJ, 1968).

Queen Elizabeth and the making of policy, 1572–1588 (Princeton, NJ, 1981).

'The Newhaven expedition, 1562–1563', *Historical Journal*, 40 (1997), pp. 1–21.

MacCulloch, Diarmaid, *Suffolk under the Tudors: politics and religion in an English county, 1500–1600* (Oxford, 1986).

Tudor church militant: Edward VI and the Protestant Reformation (London, 1999).

MacCurtain, Margaret and Mary O'Dowd (eds.), *Women in early modern Ireland* (Edinburgh, 1991).

Maclean, D. A. L., 'The royal arms in English parish churches', *The Armorial*, 1 (1960), pp. 126–30.

McClintock, M. E. and R. C. Watson, 'Domestic wall-painting in the north west', *Vernacular Architecture*, 14 (1983), pp. 55–8.

McCoog, Thomas M., SJ, '"Playing the champion": the role of disputation in the Jesuit mission', in McCoog (ed.), *The reckoned expense*, pp. 119–39.

The Society of Jesus in Ireland, Scotland and England, 1541–1588: 'our way of proceeding' (Leiden, 1996).

McCoog, Thomas M., SJ., (ed.), *The reckoned expense: Edmund Campion and the early English Jesuits* (Woodbridge, 1996).

McCullough, P. E., *Sermons at court: politics and religion in Elizabethan and Jacobean preaching* (Cambridge, 1998).

'Out of Egypt: Richard Fletcher's sermon before Elizabeth I after the execution of Mary Queen of Scots', in Walker (ed.), *Dissing Elizabeth*, pp. 118–49.

McGrath, Patrick, 'Elizabethan Catholicism: a reconsideration', *Journal of Ecclesiastical History*, 35 (1984), pp. 414–28.

McLaren, A. N., *Political culture in the reign of Elizabeth I: queen and commonwealth, 1558–1585* (Cambridge, 1999).

Magnusson, Lynne, 'Widowhood and the politics of reception: Anne Bacon's epistolary advice', paper at 'Rethinking women and politics in early modern England', University of Reading, 16 July 2001.

Mason, Roger A., 'Scotching the Brut: politics, history and national myth in sixteenth century Britain', in Mason (ed.), *Scotland and England*, pp. 60–84.

'The Scottish Reformation and the origins of Anglo-British imperialism', in Mason, (ed.), *Scots and Britons*, pp. 161–86.

Mason, Roger A., (ed.), *Scotland and England, 1286–1815* (Edinburgh, 1987).

Scots and Britons: Scottish political thought and the union of 1603 (Cambridge, 1994).

Mears, Natalie, '*Regnum Cecilianum?*: a Cecilian perspective of the court', in Guy (ed.), *Reign of Elizabeth*, pp. 46–64.

'Counsel, public debate, and queenship: John Stubbs's *The discoverie of gaping gulf*, 1579', *Historical Journal*, 44 (2001), pp. 629–50.

'Politics in the Elizabethan privy chamber: Lady Mary Sidney and Kat Ashley', in Daybell (ed.), *Women and politics in early modern England*, pp. 67–82.

Miller, Amos C., *Sir Henry Killigrew: Elizabethan soldier and diplomat* (Leicester, 1963).

Mitchell, David, 'Table linen associated with Queen's Elizabeth's visit to Gresham's Exchange', in Saunders (ed.), *The Royal Exchange*, pp. 50–6.

Moody, T. W., F. X. Martin and F. J. Byrne (eds.), *A new history of Ireland III: Early modern Ireland, 1534–1691* (Oxford, 1976, 1991 edn).

Moore, Elsie Matley, 'Wall-paintings recently discovered in Worcestershire', *Archaeologia*, 88 (1940), pp. 281–8.

Morgan, D. A. L., 'The house of policy: the political role of the late Plantagenet household, 1422–1485', in Starkey (ed.), *English Court*, pp. 25–70.

Mortimer, Ian, 'Tudor chronicler or sixteenth-century diarist? Henry Machyn and the nature of his manuscript', *Sixteenth Century Journal*, 23 (2002), pp. 981–98.

Neale, J. E., *Queen Elizabeth I* (London, 1934).

'The Elizabethan political scene', *Proceedings of the British Academy*, 34 (1948), pp. 97–117 and reprinted in Neale, *Essays in Elizabethan history*, pp. 59–84.

'November 17th', in Neale, *Essays in Elizabethan history*, pp. 9–20.

Essays in Elizabethan history (London, 1958).

O'Buachalla, Breandán, 'Poetry and politics in early modern Ireland', *Eighteenth Century Ireland*, 7 (1992), pp. 149–75.

Ó Cuív, Brian, 'The Irish language in the early modern period', in Moody, Martin and Byrne (eds.), *A new history of Ireland III: early modern Ireland*, pp. 509–45.

O Riordan, Michelle, *The Gaelic mind and the collapse of the Gaelic world* (Cork, 1990).

Orgel, Stephen, *The illusion of power: political theatre in the English Renaissance* (Berkeley, CA, and London, 1975).

Ovenden, Richard, 'Jaspar Gryffyth and his books', *British Library Journal*, 20 (1994), pp. 107–39.

Park, Katherine and Lorraine J. Daston, 'Unnatural conceptions: the study of monsters in France and England', *Past & Present*, 92 (1981), pp. 20–54.

Parker, Geoffrey, *The grand strategy of Philip II* (New Haven and London, 1988).

Parmelee, Lisa Ferraro, 'Printers, patrons, readers and spies: importation of French propaganda in late Elizabethan England', *Sixteenth Century Journal*, 25 (1994), pp. 853–72.

Good newes from Fraunce: French anti-league propaganda in late Elizabethan England (Rochester, NY and Woodbridge, Suffolk, 1996).

Peck, Linda Levy (ed.), *The mental world of the Jacobean court* (Cambridge, 1991).

Peltonen, Markku, *Classical humanism and republicanism in English political thought, 1570–1640* (Cambridge, 1995).

Pincus, Steve, '"Coffee politicians does create": coffeehouses and Restoration political culture', *Journal of Modern History*, 67 (1995), pp. 807–34.

Plomer H. R., 'John Francton and his successors', *Irish Book Lover*, 3 (1911), pp. 109–10.

'Some Elizabethan book sales', *The Library*, third series, 7 (1916), pp. 318–29.

Pollard, Mary, 'James Dartas, an early Dublin stationer', *Irish Book Lover*, 2 (1976), pp. 227–9.

Dublin's trade in books, 1550–1800 (Oxford, 1989).

Prest, Wilfred R., *The Inns of Court under Elizabeth I and the early Stuarts, 1590–1640* (London, 1972).

Pulman, Michael Barraclough, *The Elizabethan privy council in the fifteen-seventies* (Berkeley and Los Angeles, CA, 1971).

Quinn, David B., 'Information about Dublin printers, 1556–1573, in English financial records', *Irish Book Lover*, 27 (1942), pp. 112–14.

Raymond, Joad (ed.), *News, newspapers and society in early modern Britain* (London, 1999).

Pamphlets and pamphleteering in early modern Britain (Cambridge, 2003).

Read, Conyers, *Mr Secretary Walsingham and the policy of Queen Elizabeth* (3 vols., Oxford, 1925).

Lord Burghley and Queen Elizabeth (London, 1960).

Mr Secretary Cecil and Queen Elizabeth (London, 1962 edn).

Reader, Francis W., 'Tudor mural paintings in the lesser houses of Buckinghamshire', *Archaeological Journal*, 89 (1932), pp. 116–73.

'Tudor domestic wall paintings, Part I', *Archaeological Journal*, 92 (1935), pp. 243–86.

'Tudor domestic wall painting, Part II', *Archaeological Journal*, 93 (1936), pp. 220–62.

Roberts, J. F. A., 'English wall-paintings after Italian engravings', *Burlington Magazine*, 28 (1941), pp. 86–92.

Roberts, Peter R., 'Elizabethan "overseers" in Merioneth', *Journal of the Merioneth Historical and Record Society*. 4 (1961–4), pp. 7–13.

Roy, Ashok and Penry Smith (eds.), *Painting techniques: history, materials and studio practice. Contributions to the Dublin congress, 7–11 September 1998* (London, 1998).

Ryan, Laurence V., *Roger Ascham* (Stanford, CA, 1963).

Saunders, Ann (ed.), *The Royal Exchange* (London, 1997).

Scalingi, Paula L., 'The scepter or the distaff: the question of female monarchy', *The Historian* (USA), 41 (1978–79), pp. 59–75.

Scott-Warren, James, 'News, sociability, and book-buying in early modern England: the letters of Sir Thomas Cornwallis', *The Library*, 7th series, 1 (2000), pp. 381–402.

Shaaber, Matthias A., *Some forerunners of the newspaper in England, 1476–1622* (Philadelphia and London, 1929).

Shagan, Ethan H., 'Protector Somerset and the 1549 rebellions: new sources and new perspectives', *English Historical Review*, 115 (1999), pp. 34–63.

'"Popularity" and the 1549 rebellions revisited', *English Historical Review*, 116 (2000), pp. 121–33.

Popular politics and the English Reformation (Cambridge, 2003).

Shaw, Henry, *Details of Elizabethan architecture* (London, 1839).

Shephard, Amanda, *Gender and authority in sixteenth-century England: the Knox debate* (Keele, 1994).

Silke, John J., 'Irish scholarship and the Renaissance', *Studies in the Renaissance*, 20 (1973), pp. 169–206.

Simms, Katherine, *From kings to warlords: the changing political structure of Gaelic Ireland in the later Middle Ages* (Woodbridge, Suffolk, 1987).

'Bardic poetry as a historical source', in Dunne (ed.), *The writer as witness*, pp. 58–75.

Simpson, Richard, 'Sir Thomas Smith and the wall-paintings at Hill Hall, Essex: scholarly theory and design in the sixteenth century', *Journal of the British Archaeological Association*, 130 (1977), pp. 1–20.

Skinner, Quentin, 'Meaning and understanding in the history of ideas', *History and Theory*, 8 (1969), pp. 3–53 and reprinted in Tully (ed.), *Meaning and context*, pp. 29–67.

'Some problems in the analysis of political thought and action', in Tully, *Meaning and context*, pp. 97–118.

Reason and rhetoric in the philosophy of Hobbes (Cambridge, 1996).

Smuts, Malcolm, 'Cultural diversity and cultural change at the court of James I', in Peck (ed.), *The mental world of the Jacobean court*, pp. 99–112.

Starkey, David, 'Representation through intimacy: a study in the symbolism of
    monarchy and court office in early-modern England', in Lewis (ed.),
    Symbols and sentiments, pp. 187–224.
  'Court and government', in Coleman and Starkey (eds.), *Revolution reassessed*,
    pp. 29–58 (reprinted in Guy (ed.), *Tudor monarchy*, pp. 189–213).
  'Intimacy and innovation: the rise of the privy chamber, 1485–1547', in Starkey
    et al. (eds.), *The English court*, pp. 71–118.
  'A reply: Tudor government: the facts?', *Historical Journal*, 31 (1988), pp.
    921–31.
  Elizabeth: apprenticeship (London, 2000).
Starkey, David *et al.* (eds.), *The English court: from the Wars of the Roses to the
    Civil War* (London and New York, 1987).
Steer, Francis W., 'Painting in a Norfolk church of Queen Elizabeth at Tilbury',
    Essex Review, 53 (1944), pp. 1–4.
Stephens W. B., 'Literacy in England, Scotland and Wales, 1500–1900', *History of
    Education Quarterly*, 30 (1990), pp. 545–71.
Stone, Lawrence, *Family and fortune: studies in aristocratic finance in the sixteenth
    and seventeenth centuries* (Oxford, 1973).
Strong, Roy, 'The popular celebration of the Accession Day of Queen Elizabeth
    I,' *Journal of the Warburg and Courtauld Institutes*, 21 (1958), pp. 86–103.
Sutherland, N. M., *The French secretaries of state in the age of Catherine de Médici*
    (London, 1962).
Sutton, James, 'The decorative program at Elizabethan Theobalds: educating
    an heir and promoting a dynasty', *Studies in the Decorative Arts*, 7
    (1999–2000), pp. 33–64.
Talbert, Ernest William, 'The political import and the first two audiences of
    Gorboduc', in Harrison, Hill, Mossner and Sledd (eds.), *Studies in honor of
    DeWitt T. Staines*, pp. 89–115.
Taylor, John, *English historical literature in the fourteenth century* (Oxford, 1987).
Thomas, Graham C. G., 'The Stradling library at St Donats, Glamorgan',
    National Library of Wales, 24 (1986), pp. 402–19.
Thomas, Keith, *Religion and the decline of magic: studies in popular beliefs in
    sixteenth- and seventeenth-century England* (London, 1971).
Thurley, Simon, *The royal palaces of Tudor England: architecture and court life,
    1400–1547* (New Haven and London, 1993).
Thurley, Simon (with contributions by Alan Cook, David Gaimster, Beverley
    Nenk and Mark Samuel), *Whitehall Palace: an architectural history of the
    royal apartments, 1240–1698* (New Haven and London, 1999).
Tittler, Robert, *Nicholas Bacon: the making of a Tudor statesman* (Athens, OH,
    1976).
Tout, T. F., 'Literature and learning in the English civil service in the fourteenth
    century', *Speculum*, 4 (1929), pp. 365–89.
Tully, James (ed.), *Meaning and context: Quentin Skinner and his critics*
    (Cambridge and Oxford, 1988).

Underdown, David, 'Regional cultures? Local variations in popular culture during the early modern period', in Harris (ed.), *Popular culture in England*, pp. 28–47.

Usher, Brett, 'The deanery of Bocking and the demise of the Vestiarian Controversy', *Journal of Ecclesiastical History*, 52 (2001), pp. 434–55.

W., W. E. W., 'Llanaber Church, Merionethshire', *Archaeologia Cambrensis*, third series, 5 (1859), pp, 142–3.

Wabuda, Susan, and Caroline Litzenberger (eds.), *Belief and practice in Reformation England: a tribute to Patrick Collinson from his students* (Aldershot, 1998).

Walker, Greg, *The politics of performance in early Renaissance drama* (Cambridge, 1998).

Walker, Judith M. (ed.), *Dissing Elizabeth: negative representations of Gloriana* (Durham, NC and London, 1998).

Wall, Alison, 'For love, money, or politics? A clandestine marriage and the Elizabethan Court of Arches', *Historical Journal*, 38 (1995), pp. 511–33.

Walsham, Alexandra, '"A very Deborah"? The myth of Elizabeth I as a providential monarch', in Doran and Freeman (eds.), *Myth of Elizabeth*, pp. 143–68.

Warner, Michael, 'The mass public and the mass subject', in Calhoun (ed.), *Habermas and the public sphere*, pp. 377–401.

Watt, Tessa, *Cheap print and popular piety, 1550–1640* (Cambridge, 1991).

White, N. B., 'Elizabethan Dublin printing', *Irish Book Lover*, 21 (1933), p. 113.

Whitfield White, Paul, 'Politics, topical meaning, and English theatre audiences, 1485–1575', *Research Opportunities in Renaissance Drama*, 34 (1995), pp. 41–54.

Wiener, Carol Z., 'The beleaguered isle: a study of Elizabethan and early Jacobean anti-catholicism', *Past & Present*, 51 (1971), pp. 27–62.

Wiesener, Louis, *The youth of Queen Elizabeth, 1533–1558*, ed. from the French by Charlotte M. Yonge (2 vols., London, 1879).

Williams, Glanmor, *Recovery, reorientation and Reformation: Wales, c.1415–1625* (Oxford, 1987).

Williams, Glanmor and Robert Owen Jones (eds.), *The Celts and the Renaissance: tradition and innovation* (Cardiff, 1990).

Williams, T. D. (ed.), *Historical studies: papers read before the Irish conference of historians*, 8 (1971).

Williams, W. Ogwen, 'The survival of the Welsh language after the Union of England and Wales: the first phase, 1536–1642', *Welsh History Review*, 2 (1964), pp. 67–93.

Wilson, Ronald E., 'Tudor and Merton Cottages, Sidmouth', *Transactions of the Devonshire Association*, 106 (1974), pp. 155–9.

Winston, Jessica Lynn, 'Expanding the political nation: *Gorboduc* at the Inns of Court and succession revisited', *Early Theatre*, 8 (forthcoming: 2005).

Woolf, D. R., 'Two Elizabeths? James I and the late Queen's famous memory', *Canadian Journal of History*, 20 (1985), pp. 167–91.

Worden, Blair, *The sound of virtue: Philip Sidney's* Arcadia *and Elizabethan politics* (New Haven and London, 1996).

Wright, Pam, 'A change in direction: the ramifications of a female household, 1558–1603', in Starkey *et al.* (eds.), *The English court*, pp. 147–72.

Zagorin, Perez, *The court and the country* (New York, 1969).

Zaret, David, 'Religion, science, and printing in the public spheres in seventeenth-century England', in Calhoun (ed.), *Habermas and the public sphere*, pp. 212–35.

The origins of democratic culture: printing, petitions and the public sphere in early-modern England (Princeton, NJ, 2000).

UNPUBLISHED THESES

Byford, Mark, 'The price of Protestantism: assessing the impact of religious change on Elizabethan Essex: the cases of Heydon and Colchester, 1558–1594' (D.Phil. thesis, Oxford, 1988).

Frescoln, Katherine Pitman, 'Thomas Randolph: an Elizabethan in Scotland' (Ph.D. thesis, West Virginia, 1971).

Goldsmith, J. B. Greenbaum, 'All the queen's women: the changing place and perception of aristocratic women in Elizabethan England, 1558–1620' (Ph.D. thesis, Northwestern, 1987).

Leimon, M. M., 'Sir Francis Walsingham and the Anjou marriage plan, 1574–81' (Ph.D. thesis, Cambridge, 1989).

Mears, Natalie, 'The "personal rule" of Elizabeth I: marriage, succession and catholic conspiracy, c.1578–1582' (Ph.D. thesis, St Andrews, 1999).

Merton, C., 'The women who served Queen Mary and Queen Elizabeth: ladies, gentlewomen and maids to the Privy Chamber, 1553–1603' (Ph.D. thesis, Cambridge, 1993).

Owen, H. G., 'The London parish clergy in the reign of Elizabeth I' (Ph.D. thesis, London, 1957).

Taviner, Mark, 'Robert Beale and the Elizabethan polity' (Ph.D. thesis, St Andrews, 2000).

Walsh, Sebastian, '"Most trusty and beloved": friendship, trust and experience in the exercise of informal power within the early Elizabethan polity – the case of Sir Nicholas Throckmorton' (BA dissertation, Durham, 2004).

Winston, Jessica Lynn, 'Literature and politics at the early Elizabethan Inns of Court' (Ph.D. thesis, University of California, Santa Barbara, 2002).

Woudhuysen, H. R., 'Leicester's literary patronage: a study of the English court, 1578–82' (D.Phil. thesis, Oxford, 1980).

Index

TITLES IN THE SERIES

The Common Peace: Participation and the Criminal Law in Seventeenth-Century England*
CYNTHIA B. HERRUP

Politics, Society and Civil War in Warwickshire, 1620–1660*
ANN HUGHES

London Crowds in the Reign of Charles II: Propaganda and Politics from the Restoration to the Exclusion Crisis*
TIM HARRIS

Criticism and Compliment: The Politics of Literature in the England of Charles I*
KEVIN SHARPE

Central Government and the Localities: Hampshire, 1649–1689*
ANDREW COLEBY

John Skelton and the Politics of the 1520s*
GREG WALKER

Algernon Sidney and the English Republic, 1623–1677*
JONATHAN SCOTT

Thomas Starkey and the Commonweal: Humanist Politics and Religion in the Reign of Henry VIII*
THOMAS F. MAYER

The Blind Devotion of the People: Popular Religion and the English Reformation*
ROBERT WHITING

The Cavalier Parliament and the Reconstruction of the Old Regime, 1661–1667*
PAUL SEAWARD

The Blessed Revolution: England Politics and the Coming of War, 1621–1624
THOMAS COGSWELL

Charles I and the Road to Personal Rule*
L. J. REEVE

George Lawson's 'Politica' and the English Revolution*
CONAL CONDREN

Puritans and Roundheads: The Harleys of Brampton Bryan and the Outbreak of the Civil War
JACQUELINE EALES

An Uncounselled King: Charles I and the Scottish Troubles, 1637–1641*
PETER DONALD

*Also published as a paperback

Printed in the United Kingdom
by Lightning Source UK Ltd.
133910UK00001B/201/P